Bealine Charlie Oscar

Other books by Simon Hepworth

Late Shift (a paranormal crime novel)
The Dark Part of the Sky (an anthology of Bomber Command ghost stories)
Striking Through Clouds (with Andrew Porrelli)
Nothing Can Stop Us (with Andrew Porrelli and Harry Dison)
514 Squadron Profile (with Chris Ward)
The Beach Boys (with Andrew Porrelli and Roger Guernon)

All are published by Mention the War Ltd.
Visit www.bombercommand books.com for full details.

Bealine Charlie Oscar

The Mystery of Flight CY284

Simon Hepworth

MENTION
THE WAR
PUBLICATIONS

First Published in the UK 2018 by Mention the War Limited, 12 Newcastle Street, Merthyr Tydfil, Wales, CF47 0BH.

Second edition published in the UK 2019 by Mention the War Limited.

The publisher and author acknowledge the role of the National Archives in Kew, London, in preserving and making available documents relating to the investigation into the loss of flight CY284. Access to the material, and reproduction thereof in this book, is under the National Archives Open Licence V2.0. All documentation and images reproduced in this book are accessed under Open Licence V2.0 unless otherwise stated.

The author and publisher have used their best endeavours to present information passed to them in the correct context, and in good faith. Wherever possible, all such information is directly attributed, except where the original source cannot be ascertained, or wishes to remain anonymous. In the latter case, it is presented as such where it is believed to be directly relevant to the account. Any person objecting to such information being attributed to them is invited to contact the publisher at *mtwpublications@gmail.com.*

A copy of this work is available through the British Library.

Cover design: Topics – The Creative Partnership Ltd.

ISBN: 978-1911255451

*This book is dedicated to the 66 passengers and crew
of Cyprus Airways flight CY284,
lost when Comet 4B G-ARCO crashed in the Mediterranean
at about 0325hrs GMT on 12th October 1967,
and to their families and friends,
who have never forgotten them.*

Contents

Forewords

It was a great pleasure to meet Simon Hepworth and his son William nearly two years ago at the National Archives of the United Kingdom at Kew Gardens in Surrey. It was also a privilege to join forces with Simon with the difficult aim of digging deeper in pursuit of a 'daunting task': trying to find some equitable answers to the unanswered questions which, for more than 50 years, have confronted the relatives of the deceased victims of the bombing resulting in the crash of Bealine Charlie Oscar, otherwise known Cyprus Airways Flight CY 284, on 12 October 1967.

What exactly happened to Flight CY284 on 12 October 1967? Why was it bombed? And who was responsible?

My research into this immense tragedy had originally been prompted by Michael Thomaides whose father was one of the 66 persons killed by the bombing. As a result, and having studied all the files available at the time at the National Archives of the United Kingdom in Kew Gardens in Surrey, we published our findings in a joint article in 2011 in London-based Greek community weekly *Eleftheria*, i.e. *Freedom*, at www.eleftheria.co.uk.

As events were to unfold, Simon joined our efforts. He did so quite by chance having contacted Michael Thomaides following a posting on the *Pprune* forum (The Professional Pilots Rumour Network). Michael put me in touch with Simon and, thus, our cooperation over this matter began in the Reading Rooms of the National Archives in Kew, this unique 'store of knowledge and official documentation' as I call this magnificent institution which I first visited back in the mid-1980s and have never stopped visiting ever since.

I take this opportunity to thank the staff at the National Archives for their role in helping to facilitate the research behind this book.

Simon Hepworth's experience in policing and aviation was heaven sent for me, as well as for Michael and for the other relatives of the victims of this tragedy. The involvement of Simon enhanced our search to uncover the truth behind the bombing of Bealine Charline Oscar, who was responsible and why. Simon knew more than I did about aircraft accident investigations, methodology and procedures. He also has ties to the police and experience of police investigations and criminal intelligence. Simon's background not only proved to be an important tool for us. It also became the key to explaining complex methods which Michael and I were not familiar with.

Vivid proof of Simon's experience and knowledge is to be found in his composition – in a relatively short time – of this remarkable book *Bealine Charlie Oscar – The Mystery of Flight CY284*. His book draws upon almost all of the official documents in the released files at Kew plus many more from other sources.

In a sensitive and serious way, the book addresses the questions identified above. It comes close to providing proper answers and, in so doing, is richly illustrated in ways which brings to life the turbulent period of history when the bombing took place. The book ends with a fair set of conclusions based on the information available in the public domain at the time of writing.

I pray that the book prompts anybody 'in the know' to come forward and fill the remaining gaps. I also hope that the book spurs those in power to disclose the outstanding official documentation which remains classified. By such means, justice may be served, even if belatedly.

The book is humbly dedicated to the 66 passengers and crew who perished on Cyprus Airways Flight CY284 and to their families and friends who have never forgotten them. The book is also dedicated to Cyprus Airways, the much-loved airline of my native country which I had the most memorable pleasure to serve for almost six years from 1965 until 1971, the year in which I settled permanently in London.

Simon Hepworth, thank you.

Fanoulla Argyrou
Researcher/journalist/author, London 22 September 2018

***

At the age of 36 my father, Michalakis Thomaides, was a successful businessman in Cyprus when he so unfairly lost his life along with other 65 passengers and crew on Cyprus Airways flight CY 284 on 12th October 1967 at Kastellorizo, Greece.

May they always Rest in Peace!

We, the wives, husbands, children and grandchildren, will remember them with love and we will never stop to fight for justice for the killing of 66 innocent people by someone we believe must have been a cowardly fanatic.

Thanks to Simon Hepworth and Fanoulla Argyrou for the whole research and investigation they have done through the British National Archives and for publishing this book!

Maria-Niki M Thomaides
Daughter of deceased passenger Michalakis Thomaides

On a Personal Note

I remember the day of the crash very clearly. Eight years old at the time, I had been at school where teacher had focussed on what we were told was the discovery of America by Christopher Columbus on that day, in 1492. When my sisters and I got home, Gordon Blackwood's car, a steel blue Singer saloon, was parked in the lane at the end of our drive.

My mother was sitting by the kitchen window waiting for us. Walking into the house, I asked her what was wrong, and she told us that Gordon had been killed. He had been a close friend and a near neighbour of our family, as well as a colleague of my father, at that time a First Officer with BEA on the Trident fleet.

My mother, under questioning from us as to what had happened, told us simply that his aircraft had crashed, and it would be on the television news. It all seemed so unfair, as it did to the many other people affected by the tragedy.

Over the next few months, the disaster was mentioned sporadically, then infrequently, eventually fading from the news and, for the most part, from public awareness. My parents spoke warmly of Gordon for the rest of their lives and kept in contact with Joyce Blackwood for the rest of hers.

In 1981, by then working for British Aerospace, I found a copy of the Accidents Investigation Branch report in the technical library. At least it told me what had happened, though not why.

The advent of the internet, and my growing interest in writing aviation books, led me to start looking into the *Charlie Oscar* incident in greater depth. I had used the resources of the National Archives in London when researching the disappearance of my great uncle and his crew in their Lancaster in 1944. In the intervening half century, access to documents and other information had made it possible to lift the veil of secrecy which seemed, to my mind, to have settled over the whole affair.

I therefore admit to a wholly personal motive in writing this book. There was never any true closure for the family and friends of the 66 people who lost their lives in the Mediterranean just before dawn on 12th October 1967. As a child, the loss of someone close to our family circle made a very significant impact. My sense of loss, though, is nothing compared to that of the spouses, children and siblings of the victims. The half-century of silence has made this all the harder to bear. I dedicate this book to the 66 and their families.

Simon Hepworth
Leeds, England, October 2018

Part One: Flight

Comet 4B G-ARCO as she appeared in the world's press after her loss (TNA).

RUDDER CONTROL ROD
ELEVATOR DE-ICING SUPPLY
STABILIZER DE-ICING SUPPLY
DOME FREIGHT COMPARTMENT
REAR PRESSURE BULKHEAD
PASSENGER WARDROBE
LITERACK SEAT AND LIFEJACKETS
JET PIPE SUPPORT RAILS
THRUST REVERSER OUTLET
AIR BRAKE (UPPER SURFACE ONLY)
LANDING GEAR DOOR SERVODYNE
FLAP LINKAGE
AIR BRAKES (UPPER AND LOWER SURFACES)
AIR BRAKE JACK
FUEL PUMP
AILERON OPERATING MECHANISM
INTEGRAL FUEL TANK
REAR TOILETS
PASSENGER ENTRY DOOR
AFT PANTRY (FIXED UNIT)
AFT PANTRY (REMOVABLE UNITS)
REAR PASSENGER COMPARTMENT
REAR FREIGHT HOLD
FLAPS SERVODYNE
INTEGRAL FUEL TANK
FIRE EXTINGUISHER BOTTLES
ROLLS-ROYCE AVON 525 B
RECTIFIERS
COLD AIR UNIT
HEAT EXCHANGER
AIR CONDITIONING EQUIPMENT
FORWARD PRESSURIZATION PACK
INTER-COMPARTMENTAL BULKHEAD CONTAINING SUPPLY AND RE-CIRCULATING AIR DUCTS
CENTRE SECTION FLEXIBLE FUEL TANK
HYDRAULIC EQUIPMENT BAY
CONDITIONED AIR SUPPLY GRILLES
FRONT PASSENGER COMPARTMENT
FRONT FREIGHT HOLD
FORWARD TOILET
ELECTRICAL EQUIPMENT BAY
FORWARD PANTRY
RADIO STATION
RADIO EQUIPMENT
STEERABLE NOSEWHEEL
CREW DOOR
AIRCRAFT SYSTEMS STATION (3rd PILOT)
2ND PILOTS STATION
1ST PILOT'S STATION
PRESSURE BULKHEAD
SEARCH RADAR

Comet 4B layout (Comet 4B Technical Manual, BEA October 1967)

'An Uneventful Flight'

BEA Comet 4B G-ARCO, christened 'RMA John Hind', photographed at London Heathrow airport in 1962 (John Hamlin)

"Good morning Nicky, Bealine Golf Alpha Romeo Charlie Osc…[1]"

Senior First Officer Mike Thomas, co-pilot of a British European Airways Comet 4B airliner, did not get the chance to finish his opening message to Nicosia Air Traffic Control. Exactly why he was cut off in mid-sentence will never be known, but between two and seven minutes later his life was to be tragically ended.

The weather had been the usual autumnal low cloud and drizzle as Captain Blackwood and his fellow flight deck crew, along with their 38 passengers, plus one cat resting in splendid solitude in its pet carrier in the rear hold, had started their journey from London's Heathrow airport at 10.45pm UK time the previous evening. The first leg of the flight, operating as British European Airways flight BE284, was to Ellinikon airport, Athens. The aircraft would then fly on to

---

[1] 'Bealine' was the airline callsign used by British European Airways. 'Golf Alpha Rome Charlie Oscar' was the phonetic form of the registration letters of the aircraft, G-ARCO. This registration was in sequence on the British Civil Aircraft Register rather than having any special significance. The crew having introduced themselves to each Air Traffic Control service en route with the full call-sign and ensuring that there was no other aircraft with a similar callsign that might cause confusion, subsequent transmissions were abbreviated, variously, to 'Golf Charlie Oscar', 'Bealine Charlie Oscar' or simply 'Charlie Oscar'.

Nicosia, Cyprus, on behalf of Cyprus Airways, operating as CY284[2]. BE/CY284 was a routine scheduled service, flying the route four times a week. As well as the passengers, their luggage and the cat, small, high-value items of freight were conveyed in the hold. On this flight, as a national carrier, BEA was also entrusted with the Royal Mail.

The aircraft, crew and food on board weighed 36,264 kilos and the fuel load for the first sector was 24,878 kilos. Together with the passengers, their luggage, the freight and the aforementioned cat, this gave a take-off weight of 70,320 kilos, 1,058 kilos short of the maximum take-off weight for the prevailing conditions.

As the Comet climbed through the cloud to clearer air above, the passengers settled back to relax during the flight to Athens, whilst the cabin staff prepared to offer coffee, tea and refreshments. The flight was scheduled to take just under three and a half hours. BEA ran the service as a Night Tourist flight, the prestige first class cabin remaining unoccupied. The service was aimed at people for whom the inconvenience of flying in the middle of the night was compensated for by the reduced fares.[3]

Charlie Oscar completed the first leg of the trip and landed at Athens at 0111hrs, GMT, 0311hrs local time and four minutes ahead of schedule. While Charlie Oscar was prepared for her flight to Nicosia, a further 31 passengers had joined the flight at Athens.

On this second sector, SFO Thomas acted as co-pilot, handling the throttles, radio communications and navigation whilst Capt. Blackwood flew the aircraft. SFO Palmer sat behind the two other pilots, his role on this flight being to manage the aircraft's complex systems and monitor the two pilots flying the aircraft. In the Sixties, jet airliners did not benefit from computerisation and a flight deck complement of three was the norm for European routes. BEA's philosophy was that all three pilots should work as a team, rather than focussing on one specific aspect of aircraft operation. Each of the three pilots would fly the aircraft on one sector or another; SFOs Thomas and Palmer swapping duties and seats between the second and third pilot roles.

---

[2] Cyprus Airways, the Cypriot flag carrier, was a fledgling airline as indeed Cyprus was a newly-independent nation. As a legacy of Britain's long association with the Mediterranean island, BEA owned a 22.7% shareholding in Cyprus Airways and was supporting it by operating jets on a number of major routes on its behalf, including the that between Nicosia and Athens. This route was politically the most significant for the majority of Cypriots, who were of Greek ethnicity. Enosis, union with the Hellenic motherland, was still the ultimate goal of many Cypriot politicians, though there were others on the island, especially amongst the second largest ethnic group, of Turkish heritage, who most certainly did not share that dream.

[3] The Tourist Excursion return fare on flight 284 was £76 8s to Athens and £85 to Nicosia. The single fares were £56 4s and £65 respectively, so for passengers intending to travel two ways, the night flight represented something of a bargain. £85 in 1967 prices equates to an impressive £1,500 in 2018. The average UK wage at the time was £891 p.a. or £74 5s (£74.25) a month so flying was not yet an affordable means of travel for most people. Source: BEA.

The 75-minute turnround gave the passengers and crew chance to stretch their legs in the terminal. With the exception of three passengers and the captain, all those traveling onwards to Nicosia took advantage of the opportunity. For security and safety reasons, the passengers could not be left alone on the aircraft. So that he could monitor the activity of the cleaners and caterers, as well as deal with the paperwork for the next sector, Capt. Blackwood sat in the first-class cabin during the turnround.

During the first sector, which was later to be described in the press simply as 'an uneventful flight', the only technical issue to bother Capt. Blackwood was a fault with his beam compass. This was part of the Comet's instrument landing system but was duplicated so had not presented any serious problems. He had made an entry in the aircraft technical log and reported it to the duty engineer, Mr. N. Karaindros, at Athens. In turn, Mr. Karaindros, who was employed by Olympic Airways and was in charge of the servicing crew, directed Mr. A. Kalesidis, an instrument specialist, to deal with the defective instrument.

Mr. Kalesidis carried out a functional check of both systems and changed over the amplifiers. They appeared to work fine, and so he swapped them back, and they continued to perform satisfactorily. Mr. Kalesidis made an appropriate entry in the tech log and explained to Capt. Blackwood that the instrument now appeared to be serviceable.

Meanwhile, the rest of the ground staff continued with the routine tasks involved in preparing Charlie Oscar for the onward flight to Nicosia. Mr. D Argymou oversaw pre-departure checks, including the refuelling. He was assisted in the checks by Mr. A. Anagousto, an aircraft mechanic; both men were satisfied that there were no outstanding defects. Refuelling the aircraft took twenty minutes, in which time BP of Greece supplied 2,385 imperial gallons of kerosene. Added to the unused fuel brought from London, this gave the aircraft a total fuel load of 4,808 gallons, a weight of 17,309 kilos. This was sufficient for 3½ hours flying. If Charlie Oscar could not land in Nicosia, the diversion airport would be Lod, in Israel (now Ben Gurion Airport, Tel Aviv).

Mr. George Diamandaras, BEA's Traffic and Administration officer, was responsible for looking after passenger handling.

Several other BEA staff were involved in turning Charlie Oscar round at Athens. Mr. Sabellarion serviced the toilets and loaded suitcases into the no. 2 hold; Mr. Pagonis, a Traffic Clerk, ensured that cargo, including newspapers, mail and a consignment of shoes, was correctly loaded, the weight amounting to 328kg. This was loaded into Hold 1 and comprised thirteen packages of newspapers, one package of Caterpillar spares, one cinema film and four packages of handbags, merchandise believed to belong to a Cyprus Airways Senior Steward, Frixos Michael. The cinema film was being sent from the British Embassy in Addis Ababa to the RAF Cinema Corporation in Nicosia. The film itself is not named. In Hold 2 were 24 pieces of baggage and twenty bags of mail.

17

The mail loaded at Athens had originated at various locations across Europe, as well as New York. Part of the mail consignment was for the United Nations mission in Cyprus. Hold 3 contained eight pieces of baggage, uplifted at Heathrow and belonging to last minute passengers, including three BEA staff traveling off duty. A further eighteen or nineteen bags, belonging to London-originating passengers were in Hold 4. Finally, in Hold 5, were the remainder of the London bags, totalling sixteen or seventeen, along with some 500 kilogrammes of freight. This comprised two packages of clothing, one unspecified container, the cat in its carrier, film mounts, tender documents, print material, films, spares, fuel injection equipment, propellers (small, presumably), hair products, turbine parts and ten packages of radio parts.

Mr. Morsetakis, Traffic Officer, prepared the ship's papers (see Appendix 1). He did not speak to the crew, though he did hand the papers to Capt. Blackwood, then left the aircraft once the loadsheet was signed. Michael Zographos, Operations Officer, obtained the weather folder and put in a flight plan, which had been prepared by Olympic Airways. He had a conversation with Capt. Blackwood, who was sitting near the galley entrance to the cabin, who signed the flight plan and fuel load. For the next sector, the maximum take-off weight would be 61,400 kilos; at a total weight of 58,939 kilos, Charlie Oscar was some two and a half tonnes short of this, a comfortable margin.

Capt. Blackwood checked the details of the en-route weather, which gave generally fine and clear conditions, some scattered cumulus and altocumulus cloud between 3,000 and 10,000 feet, with a small probability of cumulonimbus clouds from 3,000 to 30,000 feet. At their cruising altitude of 29,000 feet, the wind would be from 350 degrees at 45 knots, and the temperature would be approximately minus 40 degrees Centigrade. They would be above the icing level, and conditions would not give rise to turbulence. At Nicosia, there would be scattered cloud at about 5,000 feet with visibility up to 40 kilometres. The wind would be from the north at 12 knots. There was a ten percent probability of scattered showers, which would reduce visibility in their vicinity to six kilometres. Unless they were unlucky enough to encounter a thunderstorm, the weather did not look like it was causing any problems.

Mr. Televantos was the loader and tractor driver. From Customs, he took the bags belonging to the Athens-Nicosia passengers to the aircraft, though he did not carry out any loading himself.

Mr. Kalaitzis, Catering Loader, brought trays from the Catering Section and collected from the airport restaurant flasks containing the breakfasts that would be served on the Nicosia sector. Assisted by Mr. Chiladakis, he loaded the trays and flasks on to Charlie Oscar.

Cleaning the aircraft cabin was carried out by Mr. Lemneon, who noted that some passengers remained on board, almost certainly the three referred to by other staff.

Checking the cabin staff and loading the passengers was the responsibility of Mr. Carnemidas, Tarmac Controller. He was aware that the three passengers and Captain Blackwood were still onboard, therefore a guard was left on the aircraft during refuelling in case of a safety incident requiring their evacuation.

BEA's Duty Officer, Mr. C. Coliandris, did not meet Capt. Blackwood. In his report he noted he had overheard Mr. Karaindros, the Olympic Airways engineer, comment something to the effect that "…some sheets were missing from the Technical Log." He had taken this up with Mr. Karaindros, who clarified the matter, explaining that there had been a minor error in adding up the flying hours on the paperwork, which he had corrected.

Mr. Coliandris went on to note that the Charlie Oscar departed for Nicosia at 0425hrs local time, five minutes earlier than scheduled.

66 Souls on Board

Captain Gordon Blackwood, 45, from Bracknell, Berkshire, was in command of the aircraft, with SFO Mike Thomas, from Farnborough, Hampshire as co-pilot. Also on the flight deck was a third fully-qualified pilot, SFO Dennis Palmer.

All three men were highly experienced, and all had served in the Royal Air Force prior to joining BEA. Capt. Blackwood had joined the RAF in 1942, at the age of twenty. Sent to Canada to train as a pilot, his grades were sufficiently high that he was kept on as an instructor, rather than being posted straight back to Britain. This would almost certainly have saved his life; at that time most new RAF pilots were moved straight into Bomber Command, where the level of fatalities was very high. When he eventually left his training role, it was to be posted to the Mediterranean theatre of operations. 33-year-old Mike Thomas, who had joined BEA ten years earlier, was married with a son and daughter. Dennis Palmer, 35, had been a member of the Royal Auxiliary Air Force before joining BEA in 1957 and had been an industrial chemist with a firm of paper manufacturers in Aberdeen. He now lived with his wife, their son and daughter, in Goring-on-Thames, near Reading.

The three crew knew each other well, the Comet 4B fleet in BEA comprising only thirteen aircraft at that time. Over the preceding seven days, Dennis Palmer and Mike Thomas had flown together twice; to Gothenburg and Oslo the previous Friday and to Edinburgh and back the day before the London to Athens and Nicosia flight. Mike Thomas had not originally been rostered for BE/CY284. A colleague, John Weldon, had just found out that his wife had been diagnosed with cancer, so Mike volunteered to swap duties with him.

The cabin staff for the first sector, Senior Steward Tony Talaska, Stewards Clive Hummerstone and Alan Heard, and Stewardess Wendy Gibbs, were also British. They would leave the flight at Athens and operate a return flight to London on another BEA Comet service, arriving back at Heathrow the following day. After reaching Nicosia, Charlie Oscar would spend just over four hours on the tarmac before starting the return trip to Athens and London Heathrow as CY/BE265. The three pilots would operate CY/BE265 the following day. As long as there were no delays, Gordon Blackwood would be back at his home, a historic Tudor house, in Bracknell, Berkshire, by the time his daughter, fifteen-year-old Elizabeth, returned from school on Friday afternoon.

Gordon's wife, Joyce, was away that week visiting the couple's elder daughter, 21-year-old Jill, at the home in Lincolnshire she now shared with her husband Robert. Whilst her father was flying, Elizabeth was left to her studies, and to care for the three dogs, two horses and two cats who also shared the family home. She had little time to get bored and had friends to call on just down the road if required. A mature and confident young lady, Elizabeth was the babysitter of choice for the family of another BEA pilot with four young children and knew the family well. Whilst she enjoyed her child-minding duties, not least for the pocket money it earned her, occasionally there were other demands on her time and the previous weekend she had managed to persuade her father to stand in for her. His friend's children liked the tall man with the bushy moustache and were happy to spend the evening in his company.

The layout of the de Havilland DH106 Comet 4B was slightly different from most airliners, at the time and today. The forward entrance and exit was to the starboard[4] side of the aircraft, rather than the port. However, as modern airbridge gantries were far from commonplace, most people had to enter and leave by portable steps wheeled to the aircraft door, so this was not an impediment to the boarding and disembarkation process. Equally unfamiliar would be the seat numbering on the Comet; row 1, which usually is the first row of passenger seats, was at the back, with subsequent rows of seats numbering to the front. In BEA's configuration, the Tourist (Economy) Class cabin contained 79 seats, in fifteen rows of five and one of four. Three seats, lettered A, B and C, were in a single unit on the port side of the cabin, with a unit of two seats, D and E, on the starboard.

In seat 1A, businessman Michael Costa Thomaides was a regular traveller on the London to Nicosia service. The son of an orange grove owner, in late 1950s he had started off as a sales commission agent, studying at nights to get his Pitman college diploma. He then set up a fruit and vegetable packing business, specialising in potatoes, carrots, grapes and citrus fruit. The venture soon proved to be successful, growing in to one of the largest agricultural produce traders in Cyprus. By 1967 the company was exporting to the UK, with offices in Long Acre Street, Covent Garden in London, as well as in Rotterdam. Amongst his customers, Michael's company exported potatoes to the Smith family, famed for the "Smith's Crisps" line of snacks, with whom he became close friends.

Because of the volume of work, which expanded to Egypt, Greece and even Turkey, before the 1963 troubles, Michael decided to move into shipping instead of chartering vessels. By 1965, along with his brother and his UK partners, Anthony and Robert Beeson, he was one of the first Cypriot ship-owners, with a refrigerated vessel, the *Cyprian Trader* and a bulk carrier, the *Cyprian Producer*. He found he still had to charter additional capacity to cope with the volume of work.

Michael had signed a sales agreement with Smith's Potato Crisps, covering 25 countries in the Middle East and Eastern Mediterranean. This included Michael's company building the most advanced snack food factory in Europe.

---

[4] The author has used conventional aviation terminology throughout this book, to be consistent with the language used in the investigation reports. Port refers to the left-hand side of the aircraft looking forward, starboard to the right. The terms 'forward' and 'aft' refer to the front and back of the aircraft respectively.

He purchased the land, near Famagusta in Cyprus, in the summer of 1967[5]. Michael had good reason to look forward to his return home from another few weeks away on a successful business trip; his wife was expecting their third child within the next month.

Immediately in front of Michael Thomaides, in seats 2A and B, sat a Welsh couple, Hugh Seymour Griffiths and his wife, Lily, who were from the village of Cosheston, a couple of miles from Pembroke Dock. Hugh was a pharmacist, running a local shop. They were taking their first flight to Cyprus, where they would be visiting Hugh's brother, a civil servant, who was due to leave the island. This would be their only opportunity to undertake the visit, so Lily was prepared to overcome her reluctance to fly in order that they could enjoy the holiday.

Mrs. Margaret Joyce sat across the aisle from the Griffiths, in seat 2D. Despite being some ten years younger than the couple opposite, she would have found them amenable company on the trip. The wife of the Rev. Henry Joyce, vicar of Hathersage in Derbyshire, Margaret was originally from much further north, having been born in Cumberland. She was on the way to visit her daughter who was in hospital in Cyprus at the time.

A 23-year-old American passenger of Cypriot heritage, Sotiris Georgiou, had the port side window seat, 4A. He had arrived in London from New York, where two cars of friends and family had accompanied him to Kennedy airport to see him off. He has stayed overnight in London with the family of his sister-in-law before transferring to BE284 for his onward journey to Cyprus. He was returning to Neokhorio Kythrea, a town just north east of Nicosia, to visit the family had left four years earlier when he moved to the USA. Sotiris worked as a car mechanic, specialising in Mercedes vehicles. . Also in row 4, across the aisle in 4D, was 54-year-old widow, Mrs. Lily Marlborough, from Stockton-on-Tees. The diminutive lady, only 5 feet 1 inch tall, with auburn and grey hair, was on her way to visit her 20-year-old daughter, Christine, who had moved to Cyprus with her 18-month-old son, Graham, and husband, Bob, who was serving with the Royal Signals on a three-year posting. On 11th October, Christine was surprised though delighted to receive a letter from Lily, saying that she would be arriving at 6 am the following day. Lily was another first-time flier with, according to her son in press reports, a terrible fear of flying which she overcame in order to visit her daughter. Her son's wife and child had planned to accompany Lily but cancelled their plans due to the four-year-old son being unwell.

---

[5] Michael's wife and brother continued with the project after his death, finishing the factory in 1969. Later, students would visit from Reading University for training purposes. The factory was lost in 1974 to the Turkish invading forces but continued to be used under the enforced new ownership. The Thomaides Group continues to thrive in Cyprus, under the leadership of Michael's first son, Artemis, his daughter Maria and Michael, born in November 1967, who bears the name of the father he never had the opportunity to meet.

68-year-old Anna Stewart was accompanying her long-time friend, Miss Jean Falconer, who was a retired schoolteacher. The two ladies, sitting in seats 7D and E, were from Edinburgh, where Anna's husband practised as an advocate. Jean had moved to Balloch, Inverness-shire, but still kept in touch with her friend. They were on their way to a holiday in Cyprus.

The McComb family, occupying seats 8A, B and C, were returning to Cyprus after an extended five-week holiday. 24-year-old Roy was serving with the RAF in Cyprus and was flying with his wife Elaine and their eighteen-month-old son, Roydon George. They had been staying with Elaine's family in Mexborough, near Doncaster. Roy's family were originally from Osmotherly, North Yorkshire, where they had lived at The Lady Chapel. Roy went to school in Northallerton and, at the age of 16, joined the RAF as an Aircraft Apprentice. In 1965, he married Elaine and their son, Roydon George, was born the following year.

Across the aisle from the McCombs, in seat 8E, was Costas Efstathiou, described as a stocky man, 5 feet 7 inches tall. Aged 34, he was a hairdresser living in Alkrington, Middleton, on the northern edge of what is now the Manchester conurbation, and had lived in England for many years.

Doctor George Ioannides, 48, in seat 9A, was the son of the Head Master of the prestigious Pancyprian Gymnasium in Nicosia Cyprus, and Athena Ioannidou, a very well-known and respected woman in Cyprus, who directed the Nicosia Pancyprian Academy for Girls. George attended elementary school in the 1920s in Germany, where his father was studying at Leipzig University for his Doctorate degree. George's younger brother Christos became a lawyer and later on a judge in Cyprus, whilst George gained his medical degree from Athens University and, in the 1950s, practised in the Victoria Hospital, Accrington, Lancashire. Going on to practice medicine for several years in London, he was appointed as a consultant in charge for the North Paddington area hospitals. He was also in charge of the Pathology Department at the National Temperance Hospital in London. When he returned permanently to Cyprus, he married Ioanna Callimachou. Dr. Ioannides was therefore familiar with the medical system in London, having many contacts. On this trip he had escorted to London a seriously injured child of a close friend who had a road accident in Nicosia. He was returning in time for the annual memorial service for his father, who had died on October 13th, and for his daughter's second birthday on October 14th.

In seat 9D sat Police Sergeant Rodosthenis Christou, who had been born in the village of Arminou in Paphos, Cyprus on 17th of September 1927, the son of Athena Saloumi and Christos Mesariti. After his birth, his parents moved to another village, Mantria in Limassol, where he studied at the school of Mitsi Lemithou. He was one of four children.

After finishing school Rodosthenis went to the Police Academy, where he graduated and was later described as a model police officer. Some years later he was transferred to the police force in Famagusta. On one occasion, due to sickness, he was admitted to Famagusta hospital where he was particularly taken with one of the nurses caring for him, Eleni Kakouri Petrou. He asked her for a date, they fell in love and got married. They had four children, Sotos, Athina, Petros and Vasso.

As a prosecutor for the police force, he wanted to further his studies and become a solicitor. He was well-educated and could speak four languages. With this intention in mind, he decided to travel to England to find ways to further his education through long-distance learning.

Rodosthenis booked a direct flight to London where he was greeted by family and stayed for a month. On his return home he also wanted to book a direct flight but had to settle for BE/CY284 which, despite the stop in Athens where additional passengers boarded, was a through flight so he could at least complete the journey on the same aircraft. From Athens, Rodosthenis would be joined by his goddaughter, 24-year-old Niki Rodosthenous, a beautician. Back home in Cyprus, his family were eagerly awaiting his arrival and had planned a family celebration to celebrate his return. Another American passenger, Mr. Michael O'Brien, was travelling with his 22-year-old British wife, Maureen. Mr. O'Brien, described as 5 feet 4 inches tall with an American-style crew cut, was the son of a US Air Force major, who was stationed at McGuire Air Force Base in Maryland. His 22-year-old wife, with her short auburn hair and blue eyes, was from Warrington, Cheshire. The couple occupied seats 10D and E.

In seats 12A and B sat Mr. Loizos Nicolaides, 30, and his 23-year-old wife Irinoula, from the village of Pera Pedio. Their son Andreas, whose age was not recorded but whom a press photograph suggests was about four years old, was in the row in front of them. Mr. Nicolaides worked for the General Insurance Company of Cyprus, part of the Bank of Cyprus. The family was returning from London, where they had taken Andreas for a medical examination.

Another family with military connections were the Taskers, in seats 14A and B. Mrs. Janet Tasker was returning with her 3-year-old son Guy to Cyprus, where her husband was an NCO in the British armed services.

In seats 15A and B, 25-year-old Anne Harbstreet, and her father Nicolas Peters, were travelling together from Elizabeth, New Jersey, USA. Anne's husband had recently been posted to Vietnam, where the war was raging, and Nicolas thought it would help his daughter cope if they went to visit relatives in Cyprus.

Sitting in seats 10A and B were Mrs. Katerina Liassides, 52, who lived in Muswell Hill, London, and 74-year-old Mrs. Melanie Papaioannou, whose son lived in Kingston Hill, Surrey. 53-year-old Mrs. Liassides had received a telegram earlier that day urging her to travel to Cyprus as soon as possible, as her brother was critically ill[6]. Notwithstanding the advice of her family to wait for the weekend, she insisted on booking her ticket for the next available flight.

---

[6] Ironically, her brother lived for a further six months.

The flight deck crew of Charlie Oscar. Left to right: Captain Gordon Blackwood, Senior First Officer Mike Thomas and Senior First Officer Dennis Palmer. All three men were married, with children, had previously served in the RAF and lived in the Home Counties near their base at Heathrow.

Formal portrait photographs of the cabin staff were provided to the media by Cyprus Airways. From left to right: Popi Fottou, Thelma Efremi, Nicos Hasapopolous, John Loizou.

Above: Captain Gordon Blackwood (third from left) with the crew of a BEA Comet 4B, after the aircraft's inaugural service to Malta (Capt. Maurice Hepworth). Below left: Gordon and Joyce Blackwood on their wedding day on October 14th 1944 at St. Peter's Church, Harold Wood, Essex. Right: Gordon, a very keen sailor, at the helm of a sailing boat. (both photos: Jill Harper)

Above left: Michael Thomaides disembarking from a BEA Comet 4B on a previous flight to Nicosia. The 35-year-old businessman was a frequent traveller (Michael Thomaides). Right: Sotiris Georgiou, 23, was returning to visit his family and hoped to find a bride. The photograph, signed by Sotiris, is from his US citizenship certificate (Georgiou family)..

One of Michael Thomaides' two ships, the Cyprian Producer. He was successfully developing his company into a significant enterprise at the time of the crash (Michael Thomaides).

Police Sergeant Rodosthenis Christou, left, early in his career with Cyprus Police and right, with Eleni, the wife he met when she was nursing him in hospital (Helen Kyriakou).

Left: 48-year-old Doctor George Ioannides (Ioannides family). Right: Costas Efstathiou, a hairdresser from Middleton, Manchester.

Above: Roy and Elaine McComb at their wedding in 1965. Roy was serving with the RAF in Cyprus in 1967; he and Elaine were returning form a five-week holiday in England with their son, eighteen-month-old Roydon George (below left). Roydon and his father now lie together in Dekelia, Cyprus (below, right). Elaine was never found (McComb family).

Top: Loizos and Irinoula Nicolaides and their son, Andreas (right). Above left: Mary Dalton (courtesy of Sheila Bond.). Right: Retired forestry worker Ioannis Tsiakouris.

Above: The cabin crew from BE284 on their arrival at Heathrow the day after the crash. The policy of changing from BEA to Cyprus Airways cabin staff saved their lives (TNA).

Below left: Mike and Sally Thomas on their wedding day. Right: Mike Thomas in a relaxed pose (Thomas family).

Lily Marlborough was on her way to visit her daughter's family in Cyprus (Christine Marlborough).

Mrs. Liassides was initially told that the flight was full, so made to leave the travel agent. However, they called her back to the desk and told her that there was, in fact, a spare seat on the flight. Melanie Papaioannou lived in the village of Pareklishia, thirteen miles east of Limassol, where her husband was the priest. The couple had six sons and a daughter. Melanie Papaioannou was described to the author as a very dynamic person with a strong personality. Once or twice a year, she would travel to London to visit her two sons, who were in the restaurant business. She was quite happy travelling alone, on one occasion visiting New York to see her eldest son. On this occasion, Melanie had been in Surrey for a month, and decided to return home without notifying her family there, in order to surprise them. Melanie's daughter and family received the news a few days later, without realising that Melanie had been on the flight.

22-yr-old Mary Dalton was travelling to visit her father, serving with the Royal Signals on the island. She had not seen him for over a year so was understandably excited by the prospect of the reunion. She intended to stay in Cyprus for six weeks.

Hilary Smith, 32, and Joyce White, 29, were colleagues and great friends who frequently socialised together and made the most of BEA's staff travel concessions to travel abroad. They would often plan holidays together, and this was the third time the duo had visited Cyprus. Both women worked for BEA as cashiers at the West London Air Terminal. Hilary's father was a Baptist minister at a church in Richmond, Surrey. Joyce lived in Twickenham, not too far from her friend and equally convenient for their mutual workplace. They had completed their shifts that day before heading to Heathrow airport to catch their flight. In accordance with the staff travel scheme, they could only fly at the 90% discount rate if there were empty seats on the flight. They had considered themselves fortunate that neither sector was full, so both were accepted for the flight. Their good fortune increased even further when they were offered seats in the otherwise-empty first-class compartment by their cabin staff colleagues.

Also travelling from London were a retired forestry worker from Strovoles, Mr. Ioannis Tsiakouris, who had taken his son to school in London; Mr. David Powell, 27, who lived in Eltham Park Gardens, south east London, and Mrs.

Rosalie Stone, aged 72, who had booked her flight in London and was visiting her son who lived in Nicosia.

As well as the BEA cabin crew, six passengers from London left the flight at Athens. Miss P. Downie, who lived in Battersea, was another BEA staff passenger, working in Ground Communication at West London Air Terminal. Mr. P.C. Bulgarides, who worked for Greek Line, was travelling on from Athens to Rome and Genoa before returning to London while a Greek seaman, Mr. Tsolakakis, having bought his ticket in Londonderry, Northern Ireland, was finishing his journey in Athens. Miss Petroboulou, who worked at Pembridge Gardens Hotel in the West End, had bought a return ticket from London to Athens earlier that day. Two tickets had been issued by Olympic Airways, the Greek national carrier. Mr. Papadopoulos had started his journey in Athens, flying to Zurich, Geneva, Paris and London. This was the final leg of his trip. Mr. Tsopourides, from Saloniki in Greece, had flown to Athens and thence to Frankfurt, Dusseldorf and London. From Athens he would take another flight home to Saloniki. All six collected their belongings when Charlie Oscar came to a stop on the apron at Ellinikon airport and went their separate ways to get on with the rest of their lives.

Twenty of the 31 passengers boarding at Athens comprised a group of Jehovah's' Witnesses, who were travelling to an international convention in Cyprus of members of their faith. They had made a block booking; the names of those travelling had been amended but the overall number in the group remained unaltered. The eventual members of the group on the flight were: Mr. Archillea Afatitis, 28, a painting contractor from Neon Iraklion and his new wife, Reveka, 20, who had originally booked under her maiden name, Sifneou. They had decided to combine their honeymoon with a trip to the Jehovahs Witnesses convention. The group also comprised Miss Areti Exarcheas, 21 from Egalso; Mrs. Constantinas Hristaki from Polikatikia; Mrs. Iphigenia Kalogeropoulou from Old Psychicon; Miss Despina Karakosta, 60 from Ionia; Mr. Charalabos Kontominas and his wife Stavoulas, from Piraeus; Mr. Georgios Koutroubinis and his 54-year-old wife, Eleni, aged 31 from Ionia; Mr. Gerasimo Thiakou, 48 and his wife Polixeni, 22, from Athens, Mr. Vasilios Markidou and his 22-year-old daughter Eleni, also from Athens; Mrs. Eirini Papanicolaou, 61, and Mr. Ioannis Rigou, 60, were both from Heraklion; Miss Maria Parzopolou, also aged in her sixties came from Ahia Paraskavi. Miss Arini Voliotou, 25 was from Athens; 31-year-old Mrs. Paraskevis Vougioukas, was also from Ionia. The final member of the group is believed to have been Mr. Elias Evgeros, 28, from Petras. The other Athens passengers were a mixture of individuals and couples. As expected, Niki Rodosthenou had joined Rodosthenis Christou. William Sheris, an American, was travelling from Fairfax, Virginia. 64-year-old Mrs. Dorothea Rachovidou was returning to Limassol from a visit to her daughter, who lived in the Greek capital. Mr. Nicos Papapetrou was a shoe salesman from Larnaca. He was returning from his fifth trip to Greece in the past twelve months. He supplemented his income of £80 a month with the money he gained as a professional gambler, whilst he developed a side-line in importing leather goods and watches. Mr. Konstantinos Paleologous and his wife Theognosia, from Piraeus, were visiting their daughter in Cyprus.

One passenger wanting to join the flight at the last minute found that he had to work very hard to make it happen. Avraam Solomou worked directly for the Cypriot Foreign Minister, Spyros Kyprianou. His duties were officially those of chauffeur and personal assistant. However, Mr. Solomou had been an active member of the EOKA[7] organisation, which had undertaken paramilitary activity in the 1950s during the Cypriot struggle for independence from the UK. He had permanent scars from bullet wounds to verify his credentials as a freedom fighter[8].

Mr. Solomou needed to return to Nicosia for an important appointment the following day but he had been issued with an incorrect ticket and could not get on to the flight. He had become quite assertive, according to check-in staff, insisting that it was essential that he was on CY284, and refusing to wait for the flight later that morning. Eventually, the matter was resolved and Mr. Solomou was allowed to take one of the empty seats, believed to be 16C.

Senior Steward Ioannis Loizou managed the cabin crew and in-flight service from the forward galley. He was assisted in this by Stewardess Calliopi Fottou. Ioannis was known by the anglicised version of his forename, John, whilst Calliopi was known to her friends and colleagues as Popi. Working from the aft galley were Steward Nicos Hasapopoulos and Stewardess Thelma Efremi.

Cyprus Airways was an even closer-knit community than BEA. John Loizou and Nicos Hasapopoulos had been in the same school class for twelve years before joining the airline. John's brother, Louis, also a steward with Cyprus Airways, was a class mate of Nicos' brother. Louis frequently worked on the Comet services and was due to operate the Athens to Nicosia flight, CY264, later that day. As the Loizou brothers were both staying in Athens before their flights, they had shared a meal with colleagues and friends in the evening before John reported for duty at Athens airport. This included Nicos Hasapopoulos as well as two stewardesses from Louis' flight. As they enjoyed their evening out, John told Louis that he was expecting a VIP passenger, General Georgios Grivas, to travel on the flight. The brothers discussed this at some length as they had previously had what Louis later described as raucous encounters with members of the General's entourage. Grivas had led the EOKA organisation during the country's struggle for independence from Britain and was now the leader of the Cypriot National Guard. Cyprus was still going through a period of upheaval, in which Grivas was a prominent figure.

---

[7] EOKA [Ethniki Organosis Kyprion Agoniston - National Organization of Cypriot Fighters]
[8] Spyros Kyprianou was a prominent Cypriot politician and went on to serve as President of Cyprus from 1977 to 1988.

Senior Steward Frixos Michael had offered to swap flights with John Loizou, as he was shipping an expensive consignment of handbags to Nicosia. Whilst he would usually have obliged, on this occasion John had declined, for a very special reason. He had been in a long-distance relationship with a BEA stewardess who lived in London. According to Louis, his brother was very much in love with Josephine Coldicott, who was based in London. John and Josephine had limited opportunities to spend time together, and when she wrote saying that she had ten days leave to spend with him in Cyprus, he could not have been more delighted. Louis remembers his brother confiding in him that he wanted to propose to Josephine, as she was, for him, 'the one'. Josephine, who was entitled to use BEA's concessionary travel scheme, had written to John a few days earlier, to tell him that she planned to be on the London to Nicosia flight on the night of 11th October, the service that would depart Athens as CY284:

7/10/67

Dear John,,

Just a very quick note to say thank you for your wonderful letter. It was so good to hear from you as always. Unless I hear from you otherwise, I shall arrive at Nicosia at 0550 on CY284. As it is very early in the morning, you may also be working etc. I shall understand if you are not at the airport John and perhaps you could leave a message for me with Cyprus Airways at the airport, letting me know the exact place where to go and I can get a taxi.

˙ I'm so looking forward to seeing you again and as I haven't been too well and been working hard, I really need a holiday. The only thing I must say is that I'm feeling nervous at meeting you again after so long. I've been looking in the shops to buy you a present, but I couldn't make up my mind so will wait and ask you and I can send it on to you when I come back here.

I will bring the cigs and drink off for you though as I did before.

Take care of yourself John and I hope to see you some time next Thursday.

God Bless.

Lots of love from

Josephine xxxxx

John had every intention of being on that flight, though he hadn't mentioned the fact to her, and was determined to surprise Josephine when he took over at Athens as senior steward for the flight to Nicosia.

The passengers, both joining and transit, were welcomed on board. Josephine Coldicott was absolutely delighted to be greeted by John Loizou so much earlier than she had anticipated. There was no sign of General Grivas, so the BEA staff passengers, now including Josephine, were ushered into the otherwise-unused first-class cabin, a regular perk for those who were flying among friends. John and Josephine, especially, wanted this to be a trip to remember.

Avraam Solomou, left, had a particularly pressing reason to be on board CY284. Right: Avraam Solomou with his two children and those of his boss, Foreign Minister Spyros Kyprianou.

Four of the passengers who joined the flight at Athens. Above from left: Irini Papanicolaou, Ioannis Rigos, Rebecca and Achillea Afatitis. All four were part of the group travelling to an international convention of Jehovah's Witnesses in Cyprus.

Joyce White (left) and Hilary Smith (right) were colleagues at BEA's West London Air Terminal (BEA).

Left: Katerina Liassides was returning to Cyprus in response to a family emergency. She just managed to secure a ticket on the afternoon of the flight (Andria Soteriou / George Demetriou.) Right: Melanie Papaioannou decided to surprise her family by returning home without telling them she was on the flight (Melanie Doritou.)

Left: General Georgios Grivas was expected by the cabin crew to be a passenger on the flight but travelled from Athens to Nicosia the following day. Right: Josephine Coldicott, who was travelling to spend a holiday with her boyfriend, Senior Steward John Loizou (BEA).

The letter from Josephine Coldicott to her boyfriend, John Loizou. The letter sealed the fate of both of them as John turned down an request from another steward to swap flights with him. (Louis Loizou).

Above: The Loizou brothers with colleagues and friends at the Vasilis Tsitsanis nightclub in Athens. The photo was taken at 0220hrs on 12th October 1967, shortly before John left for work (there is no suggestion he had anything other than soft drinks before flying). From left: Louis Loizou, Adrin Cherchian, two unidentified friends, John Loizou, Nicos Hasapopolous, Vera Sophocleous. Adrin, Vera and Louis were operating CY264, scheduled to fly from Athens to Cyprus some twelve hours afterwards. Nicos was on CY284 with John. Below: John Loizou's identity card (all photos and information courtesy of Louis Loizou).

Into the Night

Doors closed, and the aircraft secured by the cabin staff, the three pilots methodically went through the procedures that brought Charlie Oscar back into life. Ground power was used to feed the electrical systems, until the four Rolls-Royce Avon turbo jets were running. The Ground Power Unit, a massive towable generator, was moved out of the way, no longer required. The checklists confirmed that everything was in order and Charlie Oscar was ready to depart for Nicosia. As soon as Capt. Blackwood was satisfied, SFO Thomas spoke to the Athens tower on 121.7 MHz.

0219hrs[9]

CO: *Athinai*[10], *Bealine Golf Alpha Romeo Charlie Oscar, start-up clearance.*

CO: *Athinai, Bealine Charlie Oscar.*

Grd: *Time 19, stand by for start-up.*

CO: *Standing by.*

0220hrs

Grd: *Bealine Charlie Oscar, clear to start up.*

CO: *Charlie Oscar.*

All four Avon engines running smoothly, the crew completed their pre-taxi checks, and then asked for permission to leave their parking bay on the apron.

0227hrs

CO: *Athinai, Bealine Charlie Oscar, taxi clearance please.*

Grd: *Bealine Charlie Oscar, wind 360, ten knots. Clear to runway 33.*

CO: *Roger, taxi to 33.*

SFO Thomas eased the throttles forward sufficiently to allow the aircraft to start moving, manoeuvring Charlie Oscar carefully across the apron, and onto the taxiway. Away from the floodlit stands, the pilots were guided by the lights either side of the tarmac path which led to Runway 33. SFO Thomas then contacted the tower, obtaining permission to transit the airways that would be their route to Nicosia.

CO: *Athinai, Golf Charlie Oscar, do you have the clearance?*

Grd: *Affirmative, Athinai Control clears Golf Charlie Oscar to Nicosia airport via R19. Maintain flight level 290. Turn left after take-off, 180, 4000 feet, then Sounion direct.*

Taking off to the north north west, due to the northerly wind blowing at ten knots, the aircraft would climb straight ahead whilst the undercarriage retracted, flap settings were adjusted, and the airspeed increased to the point where a steady

---

[9] All times taken from the ATC transcript are GMT, local time in Athens being two hours ahead.

[10] The ATC transcript was provided by Athens Air Traffic Control Centre, from hand-written notes. It is not known whether the crew would have called ATC as Athinai, or the anglicised form Athens. However, as a courtesy, many pilots would address their ATC counterparts using the local name for the city.

climb could be initiated. As soon as he could do so safely, and usually before reaching 500 feet, Capt. Blackwood would commence a turn to the left. This would take the aircraft away from the built-up areas in Athens and the port of Piraeus, in order to reduce the disturbance to the local population generated by a Comet at climbing power. As Charlie Oscar reversed her course she would head to the south of the airport till reaching four thousand feet, when she would head straight for another air navigation beacon, at Cape Sounion.

CO: Roger, Golf Alpha Romeo Charlie Oscar is clear to Nicosia, R19, flight level 290, turn left after take-off, clear to 180 to 4000 feet then to Sounion direct.

Grd: Affirmative. 180 radial of Athinai VOR, 4000 feet, then turn left Sounion beacon direct.

0228hrs

CO: Roger, 180 radial from Athinai VOR to 4000, Sounion direct.

Grd: Clearance correct. Clear for back track.

The taxiway, at that time, did not extend to the southern end of Runway 33, so the Comet had to use the runway itself to reach the turning area at its extremity. Despite being well sort of the maximum take-off weight, common sense and best practice meant starting the take-off roll with as much of the runway ahead of the aircraft as possible.

0229hrs

CO: Charlie Oscar lining up, ready to go.

Grd: Charlie Oscar, clear for take-off. Turn left as soon as practicable.

CO: Roger, clear for take-off.

Charlie Oscar had reached the end of Runway 33 and had turned to line up with the runway centreline. The cabin crew had conducted their safety checks and taken their own seats. The final pre-take-off checks were correct. At Mike Thomas' request, Athens ATC gave the go-ahead for him to advance the throttles to take-off power, release the brakes and accelerate until they lifted off the ground. The instruction to turn to the left was emphasised once more. Somewhere between thirty-five and forty seconds later, Charlie Oscar was airborne.

0231hrs

Grd: Bealine Charlie Oscar, airborne at 31. Contact 119.1.

CO: Roger, good day.

Grd: Good day.

ATC confirmed the time of departure as 0231hrs. Safely established in the climb, Mike Thomas retuned the aircraft's VHF radio to 119.1 MHz, the frequency for Athens Approach, responsible for coordinating aircraft movements in the vicinity of Athens airport.

The cockpit of the Comet 4B. The instruments and controls are a world away from today's electronic equipment but were very advanced at the time. To the right is the flight engineer (P3) station; the captain (P1) and co-pilot (P2) stations are shown very clearly in this photograph (HSA).

0232hrs

CO: *Athinai, Bealine Golf Alpha Romeo Charlie Oscar.*

App: *Charlie Oscar, Athinai Approach. Report passing Sounion, climbing as cleared.*

CO: *Charlie Oscar, roger. Passing 4000 feet. I'll call you passing Sounion.*

App: *Thank you.*

The Comet climbed quickly; there was not a full load, either of passengers or fuel, so there was plenty of power to spare. Charlie Oscar had reached 4,000 feet as previously cleared.

0235hrs

CO: *Athinai, Golf Charlie Oscar, Sounion 36, passing 105, climbing to 290, 19B at 46, over.*

0236hrs

App: *Roger, Charlie Oscar. Contact Athinai Control 124.4.*

CO: *124.4, goodnight.*

App: *Goodnight.*

Three minutes later, Mike Thomas gave Athens Approach a further update, with Charlie Oscar having reached the Sounion beacon at an altitude of 10,500 feet.

As previously cleared, Capt. Blackwood was continuing their climb to the assigned en-route altitude of 29,000 feet. He expected to join the high-altitude airway, R19, and pass the next reporting point, R19B, at 0246hrs. As they were now leaving the vicinity of Athens airport, they were passed over to the Athens Control Centre (ACC), who coordinated high-altitude flights in the region. SFO Thomas duly obliged, changing frequency once more, to 124.4MHz.

0236hrs

CO: Athinai Control, Bealine Golf Alpha Romeo Charlie Oscar, good morning.
ACC: Golf Charlie Oscar, good morning, go ahead.
CO: Sun 36[11], passing IIS, climbing to 290 R19B 46, over.
ACC: Roger, continue to FL290, over.
CO: Golf Charlie Oscar.

SFO Thomas confirmed that they had passed Sounion beacon at 0236hrs, and was passing overhead Ioulis, about ten miles to the south east of Cape Sounion. The crew confirmed that they expected to reach R19B at 0246hrs.

In the cabin, John Loizou and his cabin team were heating the meal boxes which contained the hot breakfasts for the passengers. On such a short flight, preparing and serving the meals had to be accomplished without delay. Tea and coffee would also be offered, along with bar sales. With the seatbelt signs off and the aircraft climbing through calm air, passengers were now free to stand up and move around the cabin, which complicated the meal service, but the crew coped admirably.

0240hrs

ACC: Charlie Oscar, Athinai.
CO: Bealine Mike Foxtrot, this is Bealine Charlie Oscar, go ahead.
CO: Bealine Mike Foxtrot, Bealine Mike Foxtrot, this is Charlie Oscar, go ahead.
CO: Athinai, Bealine Charlie Oscar, not receiving Bealine Mike Foxtrot now.

Charlie Oscar had received a transmission from the BEA Comet[12] flying the reciprocal service from Nicosia to Athens. However, at this point, it is apparent that they were not able to make themselves heard in return and brought this to the attention of Athens Control Centre.

0242hrs

ACC: Charlie Oscar, Athinai. Present flight level?
CO: Charlie Oscar, 215.
ACC: Expedite your climbing to pass R19B 280 or above.

---

[11] It is possible that there was a slight discrepancy between the time shown on the aircraft clock and that recorded on the transcript. It is likely that this was less than one minute; however, the Comet could travel eight or nine miles in that time.

[12] The return service, operating as CY285 to Athens, then BE285 onwards to London Heathrow, was being operated on this night by Captain L. Emmerson, in Comet 4B G-APMF, phonetically Golf Alpha Papa Mike Foxtrot. The flight had been delayed at Nicosia due to technical problems.

CO: Charlie Oscar.

Charlie Oscar was now at 21,500 feet, and still climbing. Aware of the approach of Bealine Mike Foxtrot, Athens instructed Charlie Oscar to climb as quickly as possible, to get above the other aircraft before their paths crossed.

0245hrs

CO: Athinai, Charlie Oscar passing 280.

ACC: Roger, roger.

0246hrs

CO: Athinai, Golf Charlie Oscar, past 19B 46, flight level 290, Rhodes 03, over.

0247hrs

ACC: Rhodes 03, Maintain 290, report Rhodes, over.

CO: Charlie Oscar.

It was less than fifteen minutes since they had taken off from Athens. They had climbed to 28,000 feet as quickly as possible, which was acknowledged by the controller. One minute later, Charlie Oscar passed the reporting point at Red 19B, and advised Athens of this, as was required. Thomas added that they were at their cruising altitude of 29,000 feet and expected to pass Rhodes at 0303hrs. Athens ATC acknowledged the message, instructing the crew to maintain that altitude and report overhead Rhodes.

0258hrs

CO: Good morning.

MF: Good morning.

Apart from the stars a few minutes of total darkness, remained before the eastern sky would begin to brighten[13]. Capt. Emmerson, in Bealine Mike Foxtrot, saw the landing lights of Charlie Oscar approaching from the west, a thousand feet above him, which was the minimum legal separation by height. The greeting, 'Good morning,' came over the VHF radio, to which he responded in kind, flashing his own aircraft's landing lights. The exchange was picked up at Athens Control Centre. Such courtesies were not unusual in the small hours at an otherwise deserted location.

0304hrs

CO: Athinai, Bealine Golf Charlie Oscar, Rhodes at 04, 290, 19C 16, over.

ACC: Bealine Charlie Oscar, Athinai Control, roger.

SFO Thomas advised Athens that Charlie Oscar was passing Rhodes at 0304hrs, still at 29,000 feet, and that they estimated the reporting point at R19C at 0316hrs. There was no mention of anything untoward onboard the aircraft. In the cabin, John Loizou and his team had cleared away the remnants of the passengers' hot breakfasts and were in the rear galley, preparing to count and

---

[13] Sunrise in Antalya on 12th October is 0705LT / 0505Z. Sun rises six minutes earlier at 29,000 feet; therefore sunrise would have been 0659LT/ 0459Z. Twilight (astronomical) was 0635LT on the ground and 0529LT/0229Z at 29,000 feet.

Journey's End. Flight CY284 was supposed to terminate on the apron at Nicosia but it was not to be. This photograph, taken around the time of the disaster, shows, from left to right, a Cyprus Airways Vickers Viscount, and two Comet 4Bs, of Olympic Airways and BEA respectively (www.militaryhistories.com).

seal the bars. Louis Loizou recalls that, at this point in the relatively short flight, the aisle would be occupied by many passengers standing up to stretch their legs for a few minutes before the aircraft began its descent into Nicosia.

0316hrs

MF: Athinai, Mike Foxtrot. Charlie Oscar calling you. Do you read?

ACC: Athinai, relay please.

MF: Roger. Break. Charlie Oscar, go ahead.

MF: Mike Foxtrot, Charlie Oscar, thank you very much. Romeo 19 Charlie 16, 290, abeam Myrtou 40.

ACC: Mike Foxtrot received. Advise to contact Nicosia 126.3.

MF: Charlie Oscar, you are cleared to Niki, 126.3. Goodnight.

0317hrs

CO: Charlie Oscar, roger. Thank you, goodnight

MF: Roger, Goodnight.

At 0316hrs, twelve minutes after his last call to Athens, SFO Thomas had tried to contact the controller to confirm that Charlie Oscar was passing the second en route reporting point, R19C. They were now out of range of the radio, so Capt. Emmerson in Mike Foxtrot, hearing the message, relayed it to Athens. Once again, this was routine practice at the time.

0318hrs

CO: Good morning Nicky, Bealine Golf Alpha Romeo Charlie Osc…

As SFO Thomas keyed his microphone and started his initial contact call to Nicosia ATC, in the passenger cabin, all hell broke loose…

Part Two: Recovery and Investigation

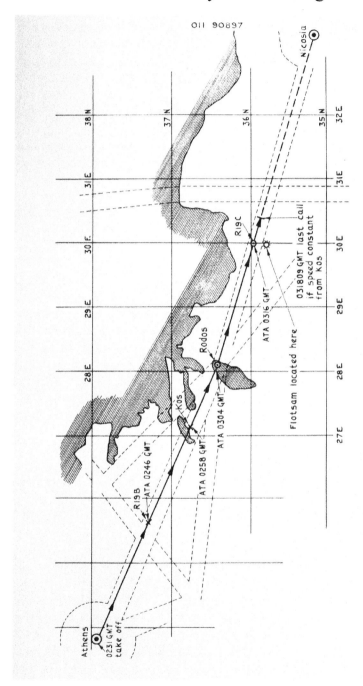

Times and locations of CY284 on 12th October 1967 (RAE Report).

'The Most Amazing Type of Accident'

On hearing the transmission at 0318Z from SFO Thomas in Charlie Oscar, Nicosia Air Traffic Control Centre acknowledged the call and asked him to go ahead. There was only silence. Despite repeated attempts to contact Charlie Oscar, nothing further was heard. The ATC supervisor instigated a special watch for any sign of the aircraft, whether by radio or on radar. This included the RAF air traffic monitoring facilities at the Near East Operations Centre (NEOC), Episkopi, as well as civil ATC. The RAF controllers commenced their own watch log at 0335Z, 17 minutes after the last call.

SFO Thomas had previously told Athens that Charlie Oscar was estimated abeam the Myrtou beacon at 0340Z. The standard approach procedure would have given an arrival time at Nicosia airport ten minutes afterwards.

0350Z came and went with neither sight nor sound of Charlie Oscar. At 0404Z Wing Commander Furth, the Operations Officer at NEOC, asked a Hastings flight from Akrotiri to Luqa, Malta, to divert to UR 19 C, the last reported position of CY284, and commence a search. At 0405Z, Mr. C. Coliandris, the Duty Officer at Athens airport, received a telephone call from the Flight Information Centre, Ellinikon, that Nicosia had had no contact with Charlie Oscar. Nicosia asked that Capt. Emmerson, in Mike Foxtrot, who had arrived in Athens at 0335Z, be contacted in respect of any information he might have about Charlie Oscar. The duty operations clerk, Mr. Troianos, got in touch with Capt. Emmerson straight away, asking about the exact conversation he had with Charlie Oscar and if he had noticed anything wrong. Capt. Emmerson replied that everything had seemed to be OK, confirmed that he had passed on the instruction to switch to the Nicosia frequency, and added that the last words from Charlie Oscar were "OK, thank you." Mr. Troianos returned to the duty office and passed the information to FIC Ellinikon.

At 0420Z, Michael Zographos, the Operations Officer who had spoken to Capt. Blackwood on board Charlie Oscar during the turnround at Athens, called FIC Ellinikon for a further update but there was nothing to report. Two minutes later the operations team tried to phone Nicosia, but the line was now unserviceable; they asked to be given top priority as soon as contact could be restored. The FIC, however, were managing to maintain communications with Nicosia, and told the operations team that there was still no word.

Michael Zographos contacted the Met office at 0440Z and obtained the actual weather between Athens and Nicosia for the period 0300 to 0400Z, recognising that this data would be crucial in the early stages of any investigation. At 0443Z, Nicosia formally notified Athens that Charlie Oscar was overdue, on receipt of which Mr. Coliandris invoked the Area Air Accident Procedure. He advised the Acting Station Superintendent, Mr. Zarbis, and all other officials on duty at Ellinikon airport. The airport ATC called back to for details of the radio frequencies in use, and the survival equipment carried on board Charlie Oscar.

They were informed that this consisted of lifejackets only. The Deputy Commanding Officer of the airport ensured that the ship's papers were preserved and retained, along with details of all the ground staff who had been involved in the turnround, just two and a half hours earlier.

Flight Lieutenant Dennis King was stationed with 70 Squadron at RAF Akrotiri. On the morning of 12th October, he was in charge of the duty Search and Rescue (SAR) crew. Their aircraft, callsign Playmate 36, was a Handley-Page Hastings, serial number TG524. At 0420Z, F/L King had received instructions to take off and search for the missing Comet. Airborne from Akrotiri at 0440Z, the crew flew along the line of airway R19 to the R19C reporting point. With the dedicated SAR aircraft on its way, the Hastings that had originally been deployed was stood down and allowed to continue its journey to Luqa. En route, at an altitude of only one thousand feet, nothing unusual was seen by Playmate 36. Establishing by radio bearings and visual reference to landmarks on the Turkish coast, the crew commenced a creeping line-ahead search, which involved flying a set pattern at right angles to R19. This would gradually progress eastwards, back towards the Cypriot coast. On the second leg, which was northbound, at 0615Z, the crew sighted small white paper-like objects floating on the surface of the sea, and then larger pieces of wreckage coloured white and orange. They then spotted empty lifejackets, followed by bodies. Three miles east and slightly to the south of R19C, they had found what remained of Charlie Oscar.

Playmate 36 reported the find[14] and spent the next half hour making low passes over the crash site, which was marked with smoke flares. There was no sign of life. A ship, the Hungarian SS *Balaton,* was identified, steaming to the south east of the wreckage field, so Playmate 36 diverted to attract its attention. After two or three low passes, in accordance with SAR procedures, the captain's attention was caught, and the *Balaton* altered course to the direction indicated by Playmate 36.

At about 0715Z, with the *Balaton* making her way to the scene, Playmate 36 returned to the crash site, flying repeatedly over it at 50 feet, examining the wreckage and directing in a second SAR Hastings, Playmate 37. Having noted all there was to see at that stage, Playmate 36 carried out a more general search, and continued to shepherd the *Balaton* to the location. F/L King's report went on to give more specific details:

> There were two main areas of wreckage, the southerly being more dense than the northerly.

---

[14] When the message was received from Playmate 36 that the wreckage had been sighted, Mr. Papapetros, the Commander of Nicosia Airport, made a private call to Mr. Colliandris at Ellinikon airport, asking if the 'Mr. Papapetros' named on the passenger list was his brother. He then confirmed to Mr. Colliandris that aircraft wreckage had been found 70 miles south of the island of Kastellorizo.

There was a general area of light wreckage surrounded by a kerosene slick – disposition as shown on Sketch sheet. Most bodies were seen floating face downward, naked or partially naked, on the whole mainly intact. Clothing when seen attached was either around the head or the feet, or items of tight clothing – i.e. corsets or brassieres.

The general impression was gained that some bodies in the southerly area were wearing life jackets – about ten in all. Several life jackets and one baby life cot were seen floating around inflated. The main debris floating on the surface was fabric and broken pieces of plywood and drifting to the south were boxes and containers.

To the north of the slick was a circular silver object, approximately 6-10 feet in diameter, floating beneath the surface. We did not see any baggage – suitcases etc, or any major airframe components, or recognisable aircraft structure.

Playmate 37, Hastings WD475 flown by Squadron Leader Edwin Waddingham, left Akrotiri at 0556Z to carry out a search over Cyprus. When Playmate 36 found the remnants of CY284, the second Hastings made its way to assist, arriving in the crash area at 0730Z. The main wreckage field was pinpointed at 35° 55' N, 30° 01' E. Most bodies now appeared to be in the northern area and, as had been noted by Playmate 36, the crew of 37 had a strong impression that some were wearing life jackets.

At 0820Z, the SS *Balaton* arrived on scene and started picking up bodies from the southern area. The captain of the *Balaton* submitted a single-page report to the investigation, via the British vice-consulate in Piraeus. In total, 24 were recovered directly by the *Balaton*'s crew, these being nine males and fifteen females, all of whom were adults. None of these were wearing lifejackets. Five were noted as fully clothed, five totally naked and fourteen partially clothed. The exact nature of individual injuries varied but overall, they were described as '...*generally frightful.*' As with other factors, the differences in appearance between bodies were considered to be significant as the investigation progressed. The captain noted that '*On the backs of female bodies could be seen slight burnings, around a redder centre were whitened skins.*' The sea surface was covered with a film of oil and some of the bodies smelled of '*petroleum*[15]'. Two wrist watches were recovered, the captain noting that these had stopped 5.27 and 5.30. There was also general wreckage; seats and cushions, lifejackets, clothing, newspapers and medicines, none of which the *Balaton* collected. Having completed her grim task, the *Balaton* delivered the 24 bodies to the *Navarinon*.

---

[15] The captain probably meant aviation fuel; his report concluded, 'I beg pardon about my English, I know not a perfect one.'

Playmate 36 left to guide in a Turkish patrol vessel, P127 *Bozcaada[16]*, which commenced recovering bodies in the northern area. The Hastings then departed to bring in more units of the Turkish Navy and, whilst doing so, noted the appearance of a slick of heavy oil or 'brown powder' in the vicinity of the *Balaton*. A third Hastings, TG533, Playmate 38, also attended the scene, carrying a paramedic team. However, as there was no actual requirement for paramedics under the circumstances, Flight Lieutenant Mercer and his crew occupied their time with making a wider area patrol. They noted a group of some fifteen to twenty bodies along with wreckage, some four miles from the *Balaton*.

Playmate 36 was finally stood down from the scene at about 1100Z; on leaving, F/L King noted that the oil slick had thickened and, in an area previously considered clear of bodies, were some five bodies without life jackets; the crew's impression was that they had just 'popped up'. This was corroborated by the crew of 37, who also noted that more wreckage was also appearing on the surface. The bodies were noted as being close together in groups, including two together, still strapped into their seats. The wreckage consisted as sound-proofing, flooring, seat cushions and clothing, along with a black 5-gallon drum, seemingly empty as it was floating high in the water. There was also a four-foot-long yellow drum, a white horseshoe-shaped object, thought to be a window frame or toilet seat, and two light blue objects which the crew thought might be child's flotation cots, inverted. As more wreckage continued to appear into the afternoon, it was considered likely that the fuselage was disintegrating under the water, which was some 9,000 feet deep at this point. To the south / south west of the oil slick in the main wreckage area, Flight Sgt. J. Budgen, the flight engineer on Playmate 37, reported seeing a whole single seat, empty, half-submerged, and between six and ten seat cushions.

At 1130Z, a large German merchant vessel, the MV *Astrid*, belonging to Transmarin of Hamburg and commanded by Capt. H. Rohde, arrived to assist. She took up station to the south east of the main wreckage area. The crew of the *Astrid* started to recover bodies from the sea. Capt. Rohde submitted his report when he returned to Hamburg on 7th November. The *Astrid* had been en route from Beirut to Constanza when she was asked to divert to the crash site. On arrival, the crew noted parts of the wreckage but no bodies. The wreckage comprised interior doors, many lifejackets, seat stuffing, carpets, overcoats, parts of suits, travel bags, children's shoes and two pilots' caps along with two

---

[16] Bozcaada was originally built in Canada in 1941, as a Bangor-class minesweeper of 672 tons. Commissioned into the Royal Canadian Navy on 11th November 1941 as HMCS Swift Current, she was active for the rest of the war. Sold to the Turkish Navy in 1958, she remained in service until 1971.

uniform jackets, with gold buttons but no stripes on the sleeves[17]. The ship's lifeboat was lowered with a recovery crew; unfortunately, its diesel engine broke down, so the crew had to row, making their task more arduous. After searching the area for two hours, the crew of the *Astrid* learnt by radio that the *Balaton* had already found 24 bodies so, presuming that the other ship was at the main crash site, some three-and-a-half to four miles distant, the Astrid went to join her. En route to the second location, many pieces of wreckage were noted, but could not be recovered as the ship's boat was now hoisted. When the *Astrid* reached the vicinity of the *Balaton*, she redeployed the lifeboat and recovered a female body along with lifejackets, ladies' handbags and passports. The *Astrid* remained on station until about 1710Z, when the body, wreckage and other recovered items were passed to the Greek warship, *Navarinon*. At the end of his report, Capt. Rohde observed,

> 'Out of this direction and the distance and the concentration of wreckage material on two positions might be concluded, that the Comet broke into two pieces in a certain height, so that one part with higher aerodynamic resistance came down in the second position and the other part with less resistance came down 3.75 sea-miles further on in the first position as mentioned above. And also, it might be concluded that the last course of the Comet was nearly southeast[18].'

Playmate 37 loitered in the area after the departure of 36, and noted the arrival of more surface vessels, with units of the Turkish Navy to the north, where a US Navy Albatross aircraft was conducting an airborne sweep. Amongst the vessels arriving were two RAF Air Sea Rescue launches, Sapphire 54 and *55*. Sapphire 54 had deployed from Limassol on a routine voyage to Cape Arnauti but, whilst en route, the captain, Flight Lieutenant Guy Hubbard, was told to proceed to the crash area. Sapphire 54 reached the location at 1140Z, approaching from the southeast. The wreckage observed was as reported by the *Astrid*. F/L Hubbard then received directions from the search aircraft to investigate a number of other areas of debris and, at about 1330Z, started to recover bodies, which eventually totalled six. The datum point for Sapphire 54's search was 35° 55' N, 30° 01' E. Hubbard noted that the bodies were totally or almost totally naked, and that none were wearing lifejackets. Remaining clothing appeared mostly to be displaced around the neck or ankles. F/L Hubbard went on to describe the severity of the injuries, summed up as '...*whole but very knocked about*'. One male body, he noted, '...*had very noticeable markings on his back, red and white mottling up the spine fanning out across the shoulders.*' F/L Hubbard's crew also recovered several inflated lifejackets along with at least one still packed in its holder, along

---

[17] The uniform jackets probably belonged to the cabin staff as the pilots' jackets had gold braid stripes on the sleeves. It is possible that the caps, similar in design to those worn by pilots, also belonged to the stewards (see photo of BEA crew on p. 28).
[18] The phraseology is exactly as used by Capt. Rohde.

Above: Handley Page Hastings TG524 of 70 Squadron, RAF, despatched to search the area underneath R19C. The wreckage of Charlie Oscar was located by her crew.

Above left: This photograph of an RAF search and rescue crew based at RAF Akrotiri appeared in the Cypriot newspaper Filelefteros. It is thought it shows the crew of Flight Lieutenant Dennis King (Chrystanthos Chrystanthou). Above right: Turkish Navy patrol vessel P127 Bozcaada pictured in her wartime years when she was a Bangor-class minesweeper, HMCS Swift Current. (Mark Nelson, www.ReadyayeReady.com)

MV Astrid, a German freighter, was diverted to the scene and assisted in recovering bodies and wreckage (Micke Asklander).

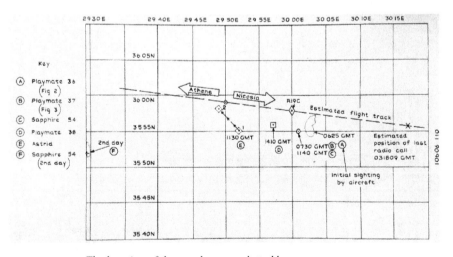

The location of the wreckage, as plotted by recovery crews.

54

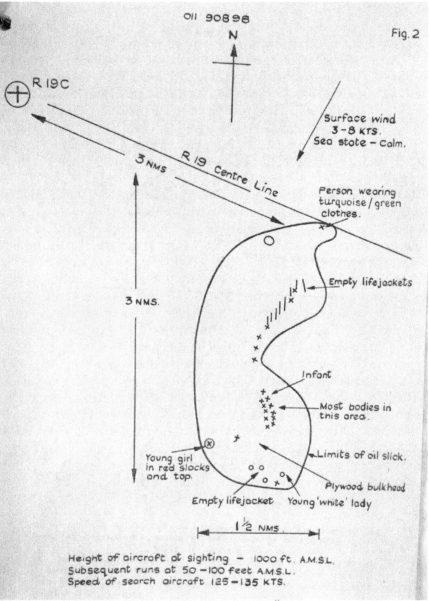

OII 90898

N

Fig. 2

R 19C

Surface wind
3-8 KTS.
Sea state - Calm.

R 19 Centre Line

3 NMS

3 NMS.

Person wearing
turquoise/green
clothes.

Empty lifejackets

Infant

Most bodies in
this area.

Young girl
in red slacks
and top.

Limits of oil slick.

Plywood bulkhead

Empty lifejacket   Young 'white' lady

1½ NMS.

Height of aircraft at sighting — 1000 ft. A.M.S.L.
Subsequent runs at 50 –100 feet A.M.S.L.
Speed of search aircraft 125 –135 KTS.

Flotsam located by aircraft 'Playmate 36' at 0625hrs GMT (RAE Report).

with various other personal effects and a Marconi radio or electrical instrument in a box. They also saw the cat, which was still in its carrier but clearly having exhausted all of its nine lives. The cat was not recovered. The sea was covered by a light slick of kerosene. *Sapphire 54* handed over all bodies and wreckage recovered to the *Navarinon* and left the scene, returning to Limassol.

RHMS Navarinon, of the Royal Hellenic Navy, was commanded by Captain D.P. Alexandrou. Travelling east, the ship arrived on scene at 1315hrs local time, 1115Z. On sighting the wreckage, Capt. Alexandrou altered course to the south to establish the southern end of the area. The RAF had continued to mark the site which Capt. Alexandrou estimated to be three to five miles long by two to three miles wide. The *Navarinon* zig-zagged carefully northwards, Capt. Alexandrou directing his ship's boats towards bodies and wreckage. As a Greek warship, however, it was imperative that the *Navarinon* did not trespass into Turkish territorial waters, which imposed a northern boundary for the ship's effective search area.

The first body received by the *Navarinon* was from the Kastellorizo Harbour boat, skippered by the Harbour Master himself. The actual recovery location was not noted. Capt. Alexandrou had a conversation with the Harbour Master, who was accompanied by the Customs Officer of the island. The Harbour Master related that he had been out fishing north-west of the island of Kastellorizo and had seen an aircraft descend at a steep angle (indicated as 45 degrees), leaving a trail of smoke or flames. The Harbour Master did not see the aircraft hit the water as it had disappeared behind the island's mountain[19]. One of the fishermen from Kastellorizo was Nikos Misomikes who, understandably, recalled the events of the day half a century later. In particular, he remembers that the bodies he and his colleagues recovered were definitely not wearing life jackets[20].

This truly international recovery effort was made possible by ships and aircraft from Hungary, Greece, Turkey, West Germany, the United Kingdom and USA. Israel also offered assistance. Turkey's not inconsiderable contribution included five warships and two helicopters. However, the records held on file in the National Archives in London, whilst comprehensive in all other regards, do not appear to contain any reports from Turkish recovery crews.

The day was spent scouring the area for bodies which, it was established, lay mainly in two clusters, one north and one south. Those found in the northern wreckage had been gathered by Turkish ships and were taken initially to the port of Finike. The bodies recovered in Greek waters, to the south, were transferred to the *Navarinon* and, when the work was done, the Greek warship conveyed them to Rhodes. After being unloaded at Finike, the bodies in what became

---

[19] Attempts were made by the investigation team to interview the Harbour Master; however, he retracted his eyewitness account of the crash itself. Capt. Alexandrou commented that the Harbour Master may have been trying to impress him with his story.

[20] Told to Roger Aves who was researching the incident in Kastellorizo, on behalf of the author, July 2018.

known as 'the Turkish group' were flown to Rhodes for the complex and demanding, but absolutely crucial, process of post-mortem examination.

On his return to Heathrow that morning, Captain Emmerson submitted a full report in relation to his encounter with Charlie Oscar shortly before the latter went missing.

'I was in command of this flight (CY/BE285) which departed late from Nicosia due to hydraulics snag. After leaving the island we were climbing through FL250 when we saw another aircraft approaching above us. This was F-LTAC, an Air France Caravelle, I think. The night was very dark, no visible horizon, sky clear, stars visible. There was no cloud, no icing, no turbulence. Met had forecast thunderstorms in the Nicosia area, but we never saw any at all after take-off. After passing Rhodes I noticed an aircraft coming towards us and above me with landing lights on and a voice called out "Good morning." I replied, "Good morning" and flashed my landing lights on and off. Later I heard CO give his position over Rhodes and Athens control acknowledged and requested him to report UR 19C. Later on, I heard CO calling Athens control, but Athens did not hear him, so I asked Athens if he could read CO. Athens replied he could not, so I relayed CO's position (UR 19C) and ETA Nicosia to Athens. Athens said, "Thank you" and would I tell CO to change to Nicosia control. This I did, CO said "Goodnight" and I replied "Goodnight". After which I heard no more. I cannot think of any reason either weather-wise or control wise which would have any bearing on this tragic business.

Captain L. Emmerson.

BEA's Ops Control Centre, under the supervision of the Duty Operations Superintendent (DOS) was the communications, command and control centre of the airline. There, on a 24/7 basis, the operations staff and those responsible for maintenance control (Maintrol) worked together to deliver the daily flying programme across the network. They also had to recover the operation after any disruption to service, in this era which was just on the very edge of the introduction of automatic landing. Weather, particularly fog, which was a much bigger problem then, owing to greater atmospheric pollution, snow and ice caused major problems. In those days strikes, and political events affected parts of the network on most days. Because of these factors, both crew and aircraft would frequently be out of position.

This daily challenge was directed by Fleet Controllers who, with their assistants, worked with Maintrol to cover the flying programme of a fleet while ensuring that each aircraft was in the right place overnight for maintenance checks, or back at LHR for base maintenance, or overnighting at an outstation to be in position to operate the first inbound service the next day. News of aircraft movements (arrivals, departures, delays and load messages) poured in by Telex message to the Printer Room alongside the OCC. These would be sorted and distributed by a Filter Clerk who would provide the message to the relevant Fleet Assistant. At the same time, it was necessary to update the flight information boards used to inform the Flight Enquiry Clerks whom the public called to request expected arrival times of inbound flights.

While these activities still tend to happen today, in an airline's OCC, it should be remembered that in the 1960s everything was done by means of hand-written data and the manual maintaining of flight movement information on a fleet of around 300 aircraft across Europe. There were no computers in those days.

David Nicholas was an Operations Officer in the BEA OCC on the night of 11th / 12th October 1967. He recalls;

'It was a normal night in every respect, to the best of my recollection. The outbound flight to Athens and Nicosia, BE/CY284 had departed before we started work and the reciprocal flight (CY/BE285, operated by G-APMF) was preparing to leave Nicosia.

'The first message that we received was by telephone to the DOS, probably, though I cannot confirm it, from Cyprus Airways in Nicosia, who as well as being partially owned by BEA were our Ground Handling Agents. The message was that G-ARCO had lost contact with Nicosia Area Control Centre (ACC) immediately following its first call after crossing the boundary into Cypriot airspace. From recollection the aircraft had transmitted on the Nicosia ATC VHF frequency "*Nicky, Bealine Golf Alpha Romeo Charlie Osc...*" and had not made any further transmission when Nicosia replied, "*Go ahead....*"

'Although the ATC controller had not detected the truncation of "*Oscar*", this became apparent when the tape recording was replayed and was assumed to be the moment when disaster overtook the aircraft. Nicosia ATC advised that the aircraft had not entered radar cover and that they had initiated the Alert Phase (ALERFA). They then rang off with the promise to keep us advised.

'A further call after the ETA of the flight had elapsed indicated that no radar or radio contact had been made since the initial message, and the DOS announced to the OCC staff that he was initiating the company's Accident Procedure as the aircraft had now passed its fuel endurance without contact.

'Subdued, we all worked on, mechanically continuing the normal procedures required to prepare the company's operations for the new day, while a sense of numbness remained below the surface. Although the shift staff were of men and women of varying ages, from close-to-retirement to teenagers like me, nobody wept, nobody lost their composure and the normal procedure of cancelling the inbound flight[21] and publishing across the company the reason as 'Operational' was put in motion. The Comet Fleet assistant rearranged the fleet operating pattern for the day to ensure that subsequent services assigned to Charlie Oscar were covered by other aircraft, and Crew Control were advised that the aircraft crew was, pending confirmation, to be assumed to be lost. The human tragedy aside, the loss of staff also had future ramifications for the crew rosters for the Comet fleet.

'Behind the scenes, though it didn't cross my mind at that moment, someone – probably the Comet Fleet Manager – was preparing to advise the next of kin of the crew that their loved ones were missing, while a similar process took place in the Cabin Crew Centre. The ripples were starting to spread even before the fate of the aircraft was known for certain.

'I ended my duty at 0730, and as the early shift arrived most of the staff were unaware of the night's events and received the news with grim acceptance. The discovery by search aircraft of a fuel slick, floating wreckage and bodies in the sea in the early hours of daylight confirmed the worst fears and raised uncomfortable recollections of the earlier Comet 1 disasters (to which it was later found to have no relevance once the evidence of an explosion was found). In contrast to recent years, the 1960s were a period when fatal accidents were much more frequent than now. Many of the staff had experienced the Vanguard (G-APEE) crash at LHR in 1964, and the earlier BEA Comet accident (G-ARJM) at Ankara in 1961. Other British aircraft had crashed in that decade, often flying into high ground in the years before terrain avoidance systems were introduced. Older staff had experienced the war only 20-odd years previously and had in many cases directly experienced the loss of friends and colleagues in action. The entire culture was considerably different; nobody was offered any counselling and certainly would not be sent home in the aftermath of an accident. The important thing was to protect the integrity of the company's operation regardless of the challenges that occurred. A considerable esprit de corps had evolved over those years.'

Joyce Blackwood had driven up to Lincolnshire the previous day to spend a few days with their elder daughter Jill at the farm she and her husband Robert ran. At about 9.30 am two women were sitting in a bedroom chatting when the telephone rang. Robert answered it in his office and called Joyce downstairs, saying that it was the BEA duty officer asking for her. She took the call and, after a pause while she listened to the message he was passing, Jill heard her

---

[21] The return flight in this case was CY/BE265, scheduled to be operated by G-ARCO, departing Nicosia at 0755Z.

mother say, "*Is there no hope at all, then?*" After another pause for the answer, Joyce put the phone down in silence.

Gordon had spoken on the phone the previous day to his father, mentioning that he had a night flight to Athens and Nicosia. His father, habitually an early riser, was at home with his wife when he heard the initial announcement on the radio that a BEA Comet had crashed whilst on a flight between the two airports. He turned to his wife and said, simply, "*I'm afraid we've lost Gordon.*"

Bill Brindley, another close friend of the Blackwoods, had reported for duty at BEA's Operations Centre in the Queen's Building at Heathrow. Inevitably the crash was subject of much discussion amongst the crews and staff there. Bill spoke to the duty officer who told him that Joyce was in Lincolnshire. Bill immediately asked to be stood down from his flight to help provide immediate support to the Blackwood family and was excused.

Mike Thomas' wife Sally was on her way to drop off their daughter Alison at nursery when she heard on the radio that Charlie Oscar was missing. When she got home, she found various officials from BEA on her doorstep.

In Cyprus the family of Rodosthenis Christou were eagerly awaiting his return but, instead of celebrating his arrival, they were informed of the terrible tragedy with the plane exploding in mid-air. The authorities informed the family that there was a bomb on the aircraft and there were no survivors. The welcoming party became a solemn event. His children later recalled the day they heard the dreadful news[22]. His elder son Sotos, fifteen years old at the time, remembered, '*I found out about my dad's death when I went home and saw my mum crying and saying, "Your dad is dead, he is not coming back."*'

Athina, Rodosthenis' elder daughter, was twelve at the time: '

> When I finished school and I was on my way to get the bus, a man who was acquainted with our family who also owned the kiosk near the bus stop, told me the plane in which my dad was travelling in, crashed and my dad was dead. I was feeling so alone and scared. When I got off the bus, I took my shoes and my socks off and I started to run to get home quickly so that I could be told all was a lie and my dad would be waiting there for me. When I finally got home to my dismay it was all true.'

As well as Sotos and Athina, Rodosthenis left two younger children, Petros, seven years old and Vasso, who was aged sixteen months at the time. The body of Rodosthenis Christou was found in the main group and picked up by a Greek ship. Due to the extremely severe injuries he had received, his family were not allowed to view him. His death affected all the family socially, physically and emotionally. His grand-daughter, Helen Kyriakou, told the author,

---

[22] In a letter to the author via Helen Kyriakou.

'His youngest daughter Vasso was never given the opportunity to know her father or even to say the word "Dad". All was stolen from her. His widow Eleni was forced to become the father and mother of his children. In his memory all his children along with his wife changed their surname from Christou to Rodosthenous. Since his death, his wife was continuously asking "Why?" and she took that to her grave after 50 years of being apart. Rodosthenis was a loved person, outgoing, philanthropist, family oriented and he loved helping people without expecting anything in return. People who had the privilege to know him spoke very highly of him with passion and great affection. He was a very special and unique man.'

Nick Georgiou , a brother of Sotiris, was awaiting the arrival of CY284 at Nicosia airport. When the dreadful news was broken to the friends and relatives that Charlie Oscar was overdue, Nick telephoned another brother, Renos, who also lived in New York. Sotiris had four brothers living in the US, Renos, Constantinos, Polyvios and Andrew. They immediately made arrangements to cross the Atlantic to Athens together. Andrew and Renos continued to Cyprus to support their family whilst Constantinos and Polyvios made their way to Rhodes in the hope of recovering Sotiris' body. After John Loizou and Nicos Hasapopoulos had left the group to go to work, Louis had returned to his hotel in the expectation that they would meet up soon afterwards in Cyprus. John would, they hoped, have Josephine in tow. Louis told the author:

'I went to bed and woke up around dawn, with a feeling I had never experienced before or since. It was a definite feeling of the presence of someone close. My head was, for some reason, filled with thoughts of what I would do if I knew that a flight I was due to work on was going to crash. I knew I would refuse to fly on it even if I lost my job as a result. I went back to sleep for a bit, then got up quite early and went to a local market. When I returned to the hotel to get ready for work, the news was on the radio and everybody was talking about it. Even though I was very shocked and upset at losing John, I still had to work the flight. What made it really difficult was that some of our passengers were regular travellers and knew John and me. They asked me if John was on the flight, and I was not able to bring myself to answer them. It all affected my family and I greatly. He is still my brother and not for one moment has been out of my thoughts.'

The official notification of the loss of Charlie Oscar, her passengers and crew, was issued by the Air Registration Board on a pro-forma Preliminary Report. After confirming the aircraft type, registration and owner, the report gave the place, time and date as, '*Approx. 0317Z 12th October 1967,*' going on to give the details of the occurrence as known at that time:

61

Flight LONDON/NICOSIA via ATHENS. Ten miles east of R19C Airway inside Cyprus Flight Information Region (approx. position 100 miles East of Rhodes), aircraft crashed, and wreckage and bodies sighted in sea by RAF. Captain Blackwood, two First Officers, three cabin staff and fifty-nine passengers believed killed.

Details not yet available from Athens regarding final pre-departure inspection.

On 5th October 1967, at BEA Heathrow, an inspection on the flap hinge bracket assembly, as called for in HSA Signal AS.1243 22411 of 29.9.67, was completed. The starboard bracket was found cracked and repaired as detailed in signal.

During major check completed 22.12.66, certain parts of BEA Modification A-1-1703/HAS were carried out (Bulletin 4/3516 refers).

Attached for information is (a) copy of the BEA Modification Sheet but at present BEA Inspection are checking to see which parts were completed.

Note: Dep LAP   2145Z 11.10.67
*   AR ATH   0115Z 12.10.67*
*   Dep ATH   0230Z 12.10.67*
*   ETA NIC   0355Z 12.10.67. A/c crashed 0317Z (approx.)*

Date of Manufacture:	*6.4.61*
Date of C of A Expiry:	*11.4.68*
Date of last Check 1:	*14.9.67*
Date of last Major Check (M2):	*22.12.66*

Next due for Major on 28th October 1967.

Total Hrs. flown since new at C of A Renewal at last Check 1:	*15543*
Total Landings since new at C of A Renewal at last Check 1:	*8758 approx.*
Hrs. flown since C of A Renewal at last Check 1:	*1361.39*
Hrs. flown since Last Check 1 10.10.67:	*222.23*
Hrs. flown since last Major Check:	*2038.14*

Signed: EFH Bryant for Surveyor i/c.

Highlighting these issues did not point towards them as a 'probable cause' as it was far too soon. Such airframe wreckage as had been recovered was just now being taken to Rhodes; however, the notification acted as a prompt to other Comet 4 operators to consider their own fleets in this context.

Adding its own notification was Hawker Siddeley Aviation (HSA), a company that included de Havilland, the original manufacturer of the Comet type, amongst its constituent firms.

Mr. T. Burrell, from HSA's head office at Hatfield, sent the following cable to all operators of the DH106 Comet and their respective airworthiness authorities at 1515hrs the following day:

Comet 4B G-ARCO was lost on a flight from Athens to Nicosia on 12th October 1967 with 66 persons on board.

It has been reported that some wreckage was signed on surface of sea. There are no known survivors.

Investigation is proceeding.

To date there are no indications of the cause of the accident.

Operators and Airworthiness Authorities will be kept informed.

As a British-registered aircraft had crashed in international waters, responsibility for leading the investigation fell to the Air Accident Branch (AIB) of the Board of Trade. The Chief Investigator of Accidents was Group Captain John Veal, CBE, AFC and he took personal control of the matter. Working with him were Eric Newton, Chief Investigating Officer, and Norman Head, Principal Inspector. These three men would spearhead what was expected to be a complex and difficult operation to establish why Charlie Oscar crashed. Norman Head was immediately despatched to Athens to get the investigation underway.

BEA's own internal investigation was led by Captain William Baillie, the airline's General Manager, who travelled to Rhodes to await the landing of bodies and wreckage from the *Navarinon*. Capt. Baillie was joined there by Mr. Head. Before leaving Heathrow, Capt. Baillie told the press, "It is the most amazing type of accident in this day and age because it happened from a cruising altitude of 29,000 feet."

Having made personal contact with the families of the flight crew and put in place the necessary measures to notify the relatives of the passengers, by whatever practical means, BEA and Cyprus Airways were able to release details of those on board CY284.

With so little wreckage recovered, and almost nothing from the airframe itself, hopes were pinned on a pathological examination of the bodies. This appallingly unpleasant task fell to Group Captain Ken Mason, MD, DMJ, a Consultant Pathologist with the RAF Institute of Pathology and Tropical Medicine.

After the post-mortem examinations, the bodies of the victims were released for burial. On Monday 16th October, a BEA Argosy cargo aircraft conveyed to Nicosia the coffins containing the bodies of fifteen of the Cypriot passengers, including cabin attendants Thelma Efremi and John Loizou, Dr. George Ioannides, Loizos and Irinoula Nicolaides, Michael Thomaides, Rodosthenis Christou and Niki Rodosthenous, Costas Efstathiou, Avraam Solomou, Nicolas Peters and Anne Harbstreet.

Popi Fottou's body was taken to Athens, where her fiancé lived. The British passengers were mostly returned to their homeland. Twelve of the Greek passengers were buried together on Rhodes. Still unaccounted for, and now presumed dead, were the three flight crew, Captain Gordon Blackwood, SFO Mike Thomas and SFO Dennis Palmer, along with steward Nicos Hasapopoulos, Andreas, the young son of Loizos and Irinoula Nicolaides, Vasilios Markidis, Konstantinos and Theognosia Paleologos, Nicos Papatreou, William Sheris, Mary Dalton, Sotiris Georgiou, Mrs Katerina Liassides, Elaine McComb, and Michael O'Brien. Their bodies have never been recovered.

For Joyce Blackwood this was to be something of a comfort; Gordon had long held the view that he hated the thought of being buried or cremated and had an enduring love of the sea. In a press interview some months after the tragedy, Joyce said she believed that a resting place in the sea was something of which he would have approved.

The funerals of most of the Cypriot victims were noted in *Cyprus Mail*. Th newspaper reported that Cyprus Airways staff had acted as pallbearers for John Loizou and Thelma Efremi. The service was held at Ayii Omoloyitades church, the same location as the funerals in 1961 for a further three Cyprus Airways cabin crew, killed when their Comet 4B had crashed on take-off from Ankara. The funeral was attended, noted the paper, by the Minister of Communications and Works, Mr. Titos Phanos, Cyprus Airways manager, Mr. Evdokios Savvas, Civil Aviation Director, Mr. L. Xenopoulos and BEA's Eastern Mediterranean Traffic Superintendent, Mr. Woodruffe. As a mark of respect to all victims, Cyprus radio had played quiet classical music all morning.

Dr. George Ioannides was accorded the honour of the Cypriot President, Archbishop Makarios, conducting his funeral service at the Phaneromeni Church. John Jakouris' funeral was held at Strovoli whilst that of Avraam Solomou was held at Tymbou, attended by Mrs. Kyprianou, wife of the Foreign Minister. Several funerals took place in Limassol, including the Nicolaides couple, whose pallbearers were drawn from their colleagues at the Bank of Cyprus, the others were for beautician Niki Rodosthenous and Dorothea Rachovidou.

Businessman Michael Thomaides was honoured in Famagusta in the presence of the mayor and leading citizens. His coffin was borne by staff and colleagues from his company. The funeral of Sergeant Rodosthenis Christou was attended by a police guard of honour.

The formalities completed, the families were now left to grieve, and to ask how and why their loved ones were killed. For the investigators, the hard work to provide the answers was only just beginning.

ΛΙΓΟ ΠΡΟΤΟΥ ΤΟ ΧΩΜΑ ΤΗΣ ΚΥΠΡΟΥ ΣΚΕΠΑΣΗ ΕΚΕΙΝΟΥΣ ΠΟΥ ΕΦΥΓΑΝ ΓΙΑ ΠΑΝΤΑ ΑΠΟ ΤΗ ΖΩΗ

Filelefteros newspaper published a montage of photographs from the funerals in Cyprus. Cyprus Airways staff bearing the coffins of Thelma Efremi and John Loizou (second from left). Avraam Solomou's funeral at Tymbou (right) was attended by the wife of his boss, Foreign Minister Spyros Kyprianou (Chrystanthos Chrystanthou). Below: Crew of the Greek destroyer Navarino unload the body of a victim at Rhodes (Cyprus Mail).

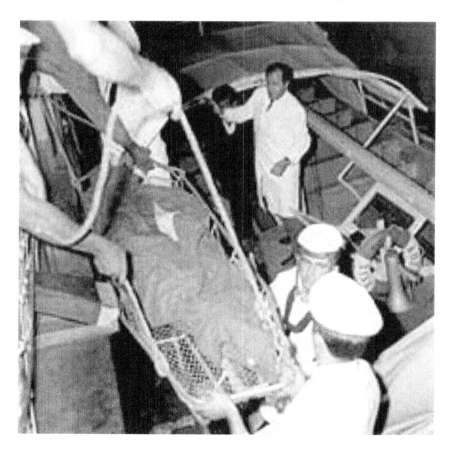

65

Press photos summing up the human emotions involved in the tragedy. Above left: Anguish on the face of Avraam Solomou's brother, having just identified the victim at Rhodes Hospital. Above right: Two colleagues of Steward Nicos Hasapopoulos, whose body was never recovered. Left: Sailors on the Navarinon carefully move a victim's body (all Chrystanthos Chrystanthou). Right: The stress and torment of dealing with the loss of one of his aircraft with all on board is evident on the face of BEA's General Manager, Capt. William Baillie (TNA).

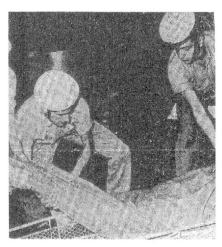

Nicosia Air Traffic Control Centre around the time of the crash. The controllers were responsible for aircraft movements in the Nicosia Flight Information Region and received the last call from Charlie Oscar. By the time they replied, it was too late to stop the chain of events unfolding (www.militaryhistories.co.uk). Below: Amongst the few pieces of wreckage recovered were seat cushions and covers. This cover, in a red fabric, was almost new at the time of the incident (Michael Thomaides).

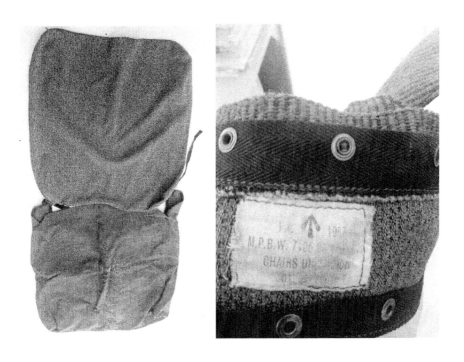

A Heated Discussion

Whilst the scientists, engineers and technicians had been diligently searching for the cause, in the wider world there was an information vacuum, which was inevitably then filled with speculation, within the press and from interested parties and groups. Amongst these were a number of BEA Comet pilots, who naturally had a vested interest in the reason being determined, not least because it was their necks on the line should the aircraft still be fundamentally flawed. Based at Heathrow Airport, many of the pilots lived in the wealthier areas skirting south and west London, and a number of Conservative MPs were quite happy to take up their cause, particularly as it was an opportunity to hold the Labour government to account.

At the time, BEA was not a particularly settled or, indeed, a happy organisation. Its rapid expansion had resulted in a sustained shortage of trained and experienced aircrew. In the Sixties, of course, most of the senior pilots had, like Gordon Blackwood, cut their teeth in the cauldron of the Second World War. Indeed, that conflict had ended only 22 years earlier and had churned out countless young men who had grown up very quickly in a hostile environment, and who knew how to do little other than fly aeroplanes. The reduction to peace time levels of the RAF had reduced the supply of trained pilots, so BEA and BOAC, the two British state airlines, had established a training college for pilots at Hamble, just outside Southampton, where they trained their own crews. The result was that older hands often resented having to fly with, and indeed mentor, co-pilots who were had very few flying hours. However, other pilots considered that the early Hamble graduates were of very high quality as instrument pilots. They might have had only 200 hours, but their progress was swift, and many were to rise to high positions within the airline. Comet co-pilots were the experienced ones from the RAF and Navy and were usually Senior First Officers. It is not thought that there were many ex-Hamble co-pilots in the Comet fleet at that time[23].

On 22nd October, Capt. HM Bailey wrote to the General Manager, his near-namesake Capt. William Baillie, about possible causes of the accident, in particular problems with the Comet's flying controls. This followed a meeting of BEA's Comet pilots.

> While admitting the impossibility of freeing the controls in the event of a physically-jammed servodyne (my colleagues) clearly felt that malfunctioning could be ruled out – except, of course, unless hampered by external objects like baggage.
>
> Since this meeting, however, evidence has come to hand of complete seizure of the flying controls of one of our Comets – twice in one flight.

---

[23] Source: Bill Innes

Capt. K. Blevins, Comet Flight, describing the events states: "The date was 5-3-65, the aircraft G-APMC, sector Nicosia to Ankara. P2 was flying – during climb out from Nicosia he commented the controls were stiff, and had I noticed it on the last sector from Beirut?

I took over the controls, and between us we found as the speed was increased from about 220 kts on, the controls became progressively stiffer, until at about 280 kts, they were immoveable and 'graunching' the trim wheel only compressed the trim strut.

With reduction of power, and same attitude, speed was decreased, and controls became (progressively) free again. This exercise could be (and was) repeated with same results.

A slow gentle return to Nicosia – a complete control run check and an air test revealed nothing. On the air test, need I say, all was quite normal, and symptoms could not be reproduced. Air Safety Report completed, and the cause was never found but 'grease freezing' was suspected."

I do not share the suspicion of the grease freezing in April in Nicosia. Clearly, also, fouling of the control runs can be ruled out since the seizures were a product of, and synchronised with, the airspeed.

Returning to the two crashes in the light of the above and recalling the Ankara[24] one reminds one that nearly everything, as opposed to the Rhodes accident, is known.

It is known:

No explosive decompression.

No bomb.

No engines failure.

No electrics failure.

No collision.

No lightning strike.

No unserviceability.

No structural failure.

It is also known that to initiate the steep nose up to the stall the control column must have been back and there can only be one of two reasons for it not going forward to the recovery – wilful retarding[25] by the pilot or malfunctioning.

---

[24] See Appendix 8.

[25] Bill Innes: The Ankara accident was blamed on the co-pilot's artificial horizon sticking. Comet flight trainers of the time insisted rotation should be to 15 degrees up and the thinking was that the co-pilot carried on pulling back on the stick. The fuel in the tanks was quite low so he could well have caused one or more flame-outs. He was an Ex-RO so perhaps lacked the feel of a more experienced pilot.

Since indications of malfunctioning are now to hand the evidence may perhaps encourage a re-assessment of it to be a possible cause of both losses. Such malfunctioning may take the form of seizure, partial seizure or erratic or unstable oscillation.

A staff passenger last night out of Malaga, Capt. Webster, one of our Comet ex First Officers, said he recalls that when on Comets he remembers that a Comet on a night flight to Athens had stiffening of the controls to the extent that its captain was preparing an emergency landing into Araxes, but the controls freed themselves and he carried on.

Capt. Webster cannot remember the crew names involved.

Verification might be obtained by circular-inviting Comet pilots to report to you any past malfunctioning of controls.

The General Manager evidently took these points seriously, as he forwarded the letter, under Confidential cover, to a Mr. Brinjes of the Air Safety Branch, copying it to Capt. Charlie Owens, the Flight Manager, Comet Flight. He asked that it be brought to the attention of Norman Head and also asking, as Capt. Bailey had suggested, that Capt. Owens

'…write confidentially to his Captains. I should be grateful if you would carefully frame this particular note so that the right questions are asked, otherwise we won't get the right answers.

Even if it is subsequently discounted as a possible cause of the Charlie Oscar accident, I would like to do everything we can to satisfy our pilots that it will not cause an accident in the future.'

Another Comet pilot, Brian Weaver, was at a meeting of Comet pilots and BEA management on 30th October. The following day, he wrote to his local MP, Cranley Onslow:

No firm conclusions were reached after 4 hours discussion and after heated argument however:

It was considered that the accident could have been caused by turbine blades leaving the engine as per the Mexicana accident[26] 12 months ago.

It became apparent during the evening that there have been flying control 'snags' on Comet aircraft which have never been satisfactorily explained or cleared and which are still present.

There still lingers in many pilots' mind the possibility of a small bomb or explosion in the front freight hold.

It is not beyond the bounds of possibility that a mid-air collision could have occurred in an area where there is a large amount of 'unscheduled' military flying and ferrying of aircraft.

---

[26] See Appendix 8.

Irrespective of any suppositions there remains the firm and only positive evidence to the cause of the accident and which is at the bottom of the Mediterranean Sea. Equipment is available to locate and recover the wreckage and it is now only up to the Board of Trade to authorise the search…. I would be grateful if you would use your influence with the Board of Trade to ensure that every effort is made to recover the wreckage. They must not be put off by cost or difficulties involved. For unless it is found the cause of this tragedy will not be positively identified.

Chris Allenby, writing to Cranley Onslow the same day, included in his comments:

After the Mexicana Comet crash a year ago, modification action was commenced by Hawker-Siddeley on reinforcing the studs holding the engine casing in the area of the centre bearing to obtain maximum possible containment of turbine blades should the bearing fail. After a year, only 4 out of 48 engines now flying in BEA Comets are now 'modded'.

At last night's meeting, a lot of further information emerged on pilots' experiences with jamming, jumping, stiffening or locking of flying controls, both in flight and during pre-flight testing – this information our management are digesting. Much but not all the information has been entered in aircraft tech logs over the years but being random in occurrence and very difficult or impossible to reproduce on test – has produced no conclusive answers. This weight of evidence on control problems, plus several autopilot runaways and undetected disengagements, in our view warrant an immediate investigation and many of us feel the aircraft should be grounded until every possible aspect has been fully cleared. There are also certain disturbing connections with the '61 crash at Ankara, the findings of which many pilots felt were inconclusive.

Present medical / forensic evidence is still only of a negative sort, i.e. no definite signs of fire, explosive decompression or of engine break up – although the origin of metal found in two bodies has not been fully determined.

Perhaps the most important point from your angle was the stated views on possible recovery of any wreckage. We all go at very strong impression that hope had been virtually abandoned in this direction – that the decision was out of BEA's hands and with the BoT… Now we feel that the Americans have offered and would welcome a chance to try this recovery operation, both for valuable experience at this depth and also possible future AID action on any Concorde or 2707 problems – remembering that most if not all supersonic flight will be over water. We therefore were dismayed to hear that after only three weeks and sundry committee meetings, only a week remained in order to secure the use of the main US recovery craft – NO DECISION HAS YET BEEN MADE!

Now although the control problems have raised very serious doubts – I am not convinced that a mid-air collision can be ruled out. It was with tremendous reluctance and only after indisputable evidence had been produced that the Turks admitted a mid-air collision a few years ago. It is very suspicious that the Turkish radar was u/s on the night of the Comet accident (!) which incidentally occurred at an airways junction at a time of heavy USSR involvement with air reinforcements to Egypt. This junction of airways is very close to a straight line joining these two countries!

In view of the foregoing we would ask you to use your utmost endeavours to bring pressure and enquiries to diplomatic and intelligence sources plus the BoT to at least make determined attempts at visual underwater inspection and/or recovery of vital wreckage if humanly possible.

Senior First Officer John Weldin, of Camberley, was rather more outspoken when he wrote to Bill Mallalieu on 2nd November 1967:

…I would like to draw your attention to the very unsatisfactory state of affairs regarding the accident investigation.

A meeting was held last Monday by the Management to tell the Comet Pilots what had been achieved so far. I have nothing but praise for the way in which the Engineering Branch have chased every minor detail in the absence of any real facts but am very disturbed by the attitude shown by the Flight Branch Management. The impression given to all the Pilots present was that it was a hopeless task to try to raise the fuselage or flight recorder – and our Operations Director "assumed" that the Board of Trade were looking into the matter. His right-hand man, the General Manager Flight, who is in charge of the BEA investigation team, then said the task was impossible as the aircraft was lying in 9 to 15 thousand feet of water and the currents at that depth were of the order of 40 knots. This statement was disproved by some information supplied by a pilot obtained from, I think, the Oceanic Department of the Admiralty that currents at that sort of depth should never exceed 4 knots.

The general feeling amongst the Pilots is one of disgust at such a weak management not demanding an attempt at raising the aircraft, as this is the only way the name of the Comet can be cleared. The future name of the British Aircraft Industry could also be at stake.

A further statement was made by the Management at the same meeting assuring us that they all had faith in the safety of the Comet, but as a precaution the Queen would not be flying to Malta in one! My attitude must I suppose be coloured by the fact that I knew all three pilots in 'CO' and am daily involved in flying the remaining 12 aircraft, but I would question the decision that the aircraft are safe for fare paying passengers but not the Royal Family. I would point out that we were told that this decision was taken as a prudent measure; there was no question that the fleet could not supply an aircraft due to shortage. All the pilots present at the meeting will verify these facts.

I should be very grateful for any steps you could take to ensure that the Board of Trade are not going to shelve the issue as a matter of finance or impracticability. The Comet pilots feel very strongly in this matter and believe that with the modern devices available on loan from the USA there is a reasonable chance of salvaging the aircraft and then perhaps finding the cause of the accident.

By 16th November, Bill Mallalieu, having received these letters amongst others, had a draft reply prepared for Onslow, in which he said;

…Their anxiety that everything possible should be done, including salvage of the wreckage, to discover the cause of the accident is very understandable. The salvage question was examined with Ministry of Defence and United States salvage experts almost immediately after the accident…I should make it clear that I can see no grounds to be optimistic regarding the possibility of a successful operation.

The pilots had also sought the involvement of their trade union, the British Air Line Pilots' Association (BALPA), whose General Secretary, Air Commodore Philip Warcup, wrote to the Rt. Hon Anthony Crosland MP, President of the Board of Trade on 31st October:

…The Association has studied what little evidence is available, but it must take cognisance of the fact that the Comet pilots are extremely disturbed about this accident, not least because the causes of it at the moment are a matter of conjecture. This last accident must be seen against the background of the accidents to a BEA Comet in Ankara on 21st December 1961 and to the one belonging to King ibn Saud. Both of these were investigated but the reasons given for the accidents were unconvincing to the professional pilot body and this doubt has been reinforced by the accident which occurred on 12th October.

This letter will be followed up within the next few days by a more detailed technical appreciation of the possible cause of the accident. However, the Association does not consider that the aircraft suffered from explosive decompression and bases this view on the pathological evidence from the bodies recovered. There have been, in the past, some isolated occurrences of controls jamming at altitude and at normal cruising speed, the causes of which have not been satisfactorily explained. Whilst this cause cannot be ruled out completely, it would appear from the time of the last broadcast by Captain Blackwood and the time taken from victims' watches of the probable impact with the sea that the aircraft's descent path was to all extents and purposes vertical and therefore it is our view that jamming of the controls was is unlikely. Similarly, for the same reasons, possible causes such as smoke, fire or bursting of the turbine blades also became unlikely. Corrosion has been considered but in view of the maintenance work carried out on the aircraft and the weather prevailing it is not thought that this was a possible cause.

As far as is known by this Association, any technical investigations carried out by the Board of Trade and BEA have not revealed any possible reasons for the accident. We are therefore left in an area of conjecture which is not only dispiriting from the pilots' point of view but could have a very adverse effect on BEA's traffic. It is for these reasons that the Association considers it absolutely vital that the real cause of the accident is established beyond doubt.

This can only be done if the wreckage and, if possible, the flight recorder is recovered. We are aware that the crash occurred where the depth of the water can be up to 1134 fathoms. At first sight this may rule out the possibility of salvage, however, the Association has been making enquiries of American sources and those reveal that the United States Navy has equipment available which is capable of carrying out salvage operations at this depth. Moreover, it is understood that part of this equipment is based with the Sixth Fleet in the Mediterranean and therefore, providing a decision is made quickly, could be made available for this operation.

It has been made clear to us that the Americans consider the salvage operation would be quite feasible with their equipment and the depth of water does not present any insoluble problem. We understand that the cost of this operation will be comparatively high, but it is suggested that cost cannot be measured in pounds, shillings and pence alone. What is at stake is the continued use of a well-known British aircraft and the traffic which it engenders in British European Airways and Dan-Air Services and, not least, the reputation of the British aircraft manufacturing industry.

The pilots' concerns were such that, according to correspondent James Wilkinson the *Daily Express* on 1st November, he had asked to be taken off the Comet fleet because, according to an unnamed colleague, of a '...*dislike of certain technical equipment used in the airline.*' Officially, the paper noted, Capt. Bailey was on the Sick List. The article continued:

'The British Airline Pilots' Association has sent a telegram to the Board of Trade urging it to call in the American Navy to recover the wreckage lying under 6,000 ft of water. Unless the cause of the crash is definitely determined the operators cannot go on flying Comets in fairness to their flying crews and the passengers. The wreckage has got to be brought up to settle the question – but our Government is quibbling over the cost.'

When the newspaper article came to the attention of Jan Riddoch, he was compelled to address the issues it raised, for the benefit of the President of the Board of Trade:

I have spoken to Air Commodore Warcup…He told me that although the pilots are somewhat edgy about the Comets because the cause of the recent accident is unknown, BALPA has not recommended the grounding of the Comets and no BALPA spokesman made the statement quoted in the Daily Express article. It was known that BEA had a long meeting with the Comet pilots the day before yesterday and BALPA were under strong pressure from the Press yesterday. In order to forestall possible irresponsible reporting in the Press, BALPA sent a telegram yesterday to the President yesterday to warn him that a letter was on the way. I understand that the letter has now been received and that the main burden of it is that every effort should be made to salvage the wreckage and find out the cause of the accident. I told Air Commodore Warcup that it was untrue to say that the Government were "quibbling over the cost". There were very serious practical problems of detecting and salvaging the wreckage because of the depth, which was now known to be greater than was previously reported. However, the practicability of salvage was still being studied. Air Commodore Warcup agreed to tackle the Daily Express with a view to having the misrepresentation corrected.

The article mentions a Captain Bailie (sic), who had asked to be taken off Comets. Captain Bailie should not be confused with the Captain Baillie who is the Master of the Guild of Air Pilots[27]. Long before the Comet accident, Captain Bailie had criticised the control system of the Comet because of a tendency to locking. His views, however, were not shared by the bulk of Comet pilots…

…I have spoken again to the Air Registration Board this morning. They have no evidence which would justify a recommendation to the Board of Trade to suspend the certificates of airworthiness of the Comets. Attention has been concentrated on the pressure cabin and on the engines. The reduction in cabin pressure has, in the view of the ARB, adequately taken care of any risk that may exist in regard to the cabin; the inspection of the engine casing adequately takes care of any

---

[27] Presumably this is Captain William Baillie, General Manager of BEA.

doubt that has been cast on the engines. If the certificate of airworthiness were suspended now, it would result from a political decision. The ARB will certainly recommend to the President the grounding of the Comets if and when such grounding is in their view justified.

Riddoch's report outlined, in detail, the power of the Board of Trade in respect of any certificate of airworthiness, concluding, '...*such a decision would have to be a well-considered and deliberate one if it were taken against, or in the absence of advice from the Air Registration Board.*' A handwritten addendum then noted:

'The President wishes to send a 'long and reasoned' personal reply to Air Commodore Warcup. On the 'Aluminaut', the President feels that if there is any reasonable chance of success, the money to hire it should be spent.'

The 'long and reasoned' personal reply from Tony Crosland to Philip Warcup focussed entirely on the matter of salvaging Charlie Oscar:

'Thank you for your letter of 31st October about the Comet accident. May I first say that we see no reason, in spite of what you say, to doubt the conclusions reached as to the causes of the Ankara and the Alps accidents.

…The possibility of clues as to the cause of the accidents (sic) being provided by the wreckage available is, I am told, by no means yet exhausted, and although there must clearly be a possibility that the cause of the accident will not be determined without evidence from the wreckage itself it would be premature to assume this is so. This does not of course mean as a corollary that recovery of the wreckage will ensure discovery of the cause....The sea in the area in which the wreckage is believed to lie extends to a depth of about 1585 fathoms, which is considerably greater than the depth you mentioned, and the distance from the shore increases the salvage problem.

You say that the Americans have indicated to you that the consider the salvage operation would be quite feasible with their equipment, and that the depth of water does not present any insoluble problems. I understand that this view differs considerably from the advice we have had in discussion with the United States Navy, including their Supervisor of Salvage. Nor does your understanding of the availability of equipment with the Sixth Fleet appear to be supported by the information they have given us. It may be that the advice of your American informants was given against the report that the tail of the aircraft, intact, was at one stage floating on the water and that life jackets were worn by some of the victims, which would have some significance. As you may know by now, neither of these reports can be substantiated.

Our discussions with the United States experts reveal that, of the present vessels, only the Aluminaut has any potential salvage capability at the depth in which the wreckage lies, and that this is small being a few hundred pounds. The Aluminaut is of course basically a search vessel, and although it has so far not dived below 6,250 feet it is, I understand, insured for depths down to 8,000 feet while its owners seem satisfied that it can operate down to 10,000 feet.

We have, in fact, just received proposals on the use of the Aluminaut for search for, and salvage of, the flight recorder. They will unfortunately have to be recast as they were submitted against incorrect assumptions regarding the sea depth and wreckage position. We shall then, I hope, be in a position to decide the practicability of the operation. It seems clear, however, that there is very little likelihood indeed of mounting any successful operation to retrieve a large part of the wreckage as distinct from the flight recorder alone. The Aluminaut, I am told, is incapable of salvaging any pieces of wreckage of any appreciable size while the salvage of innumerable small pieces would prove an insuperable task. I am assured by the salvage experts that the introduction of cable lifting devices for the heavier pieces would be quite impracticable.

As soon as I have received the amended proposals...I shall immediately consider them with expert advisers from the United States Navy, and the Ministry of Defence, as well as our accident investigators. I shall then, I hope, be in a position straight away to decide on the practicability or otherwise of any salvage operation.

I should like to take this opportunity of expressing my sympathy with the families and friends of those of your members who lost their lives in this tragic accident.

Given the evident strength of feeling of at least some of the pilots, it is perhaps not surprising that an article appeared in *The Sunday Telegraph* of 5th November. The normally staid newspaper, in its 'Close Up' feature headed *Why the Comet pilots are so angry'*, described the 30th October meeting as *'...a highly emotional confrontation between BEA's Comet pilots and their bosses.'* The article continued:

'The disaster is even more mysterious than the metal fatigue catastrophe which twice felled the Comet 1 in 1954. When an off-the-cuff estimate of 3 million dollars was put to the pilots as the cost of recovering possibly useless wreckage, it evinced this furious reaction from one of them: "The Queen was about to fly to Malta by Comet, but this has been changed on the grounds that because of the accident BEA will have no spare aircraft. This is bloody flannel: if it isn't safe enough for the Queen, it isn't safe for anyone."

Captain Roy Merrifield, a senior Comet captain and BALPA's chairman later told Close Up: "The pilots were unhappy because they felt that a negative view was being taken of the chances of recovery. It is our necks which are involved and on the available evidence there is no clue to the cause. That is why BALPA feels that an effort should be made regardless of cost…unless there is another accident which reveals how this one happened."

Cost apart, senior BEA officials and others had privately presented an armada of problems to prove the impossibility of finding the wreck. According to one expert, the Comet's carcass might have been swept away at a depth of 7,000 feet by 40-knot currents. As it happens, a Comet pilot who knows something about diving techniques had approached the National Institute of Oceanography (as did Close Up) where it was gently explained that currents of such force were exceedingly rare events caused by "rather large earthquakes."

As the week progressed, BEA's estimate of the depth at which the Comet lies increased from between 6,000 and 7,000 feet to 9,000 feet.

Where, in fact, is the aircraft now lying? Weighing all that is known so far, the chances are that it is very near 35 degrees 55 minutes North, 30 degrees 01 minutes East, in the centre of the area where the RAF found oil, debris and corpses just 3 hours, 7 minutes and 51 seconds after the aircraft's routine call to Nicosia. Disaster almost certainly struck the Comet during that brief message.

The distance between the RAF's central 'datum point' and the spot from which the message was transmitted is no more than two nautical miles. How deep is the water there? The standard Admiralty chart's nearest sounding, about 4.5 nautical miles off, records 7,260 feet. The existence of a more detailed chart might account for the latest estimated depth of 9,000 feet and the description circulating in some quarters of "a steeply sloping shelf."

Having, it appears, having talked itself round to concluding that BEA's estimates were not demonstrably unreasonable, the article concluded by quoting a Mr. Markel, described as *in charge of the Aluminaut'* as stating, *'Given that we have a reasonably accurate bearing on where the Comet went in, we should be able to find it in a couple of days or so.'*

It is understandable that the Comet pilots were concerned about the progress of the investigation and, in particular, any perceived reluctance on the part of BEA's management to back their calls for the wreckage to be raised. The Comet 4B fleet remained in service with BEA, and Olympic Airways, and they were still expected to fly their aircraft. With their own necks on the line, a parsimonious approach by the powers-that-be was simply not acceptable.

BALPA itself had been carrying out its own assessment of the information and evidence, necessarily relying on the information that was coming in to the AIB and BEA. This was published as a Technical Appreciation by Capt. E Pritchard, on 2nd November 1967[28]. A small annotation in the top right-hand corner reads 'One of Two'. There is no second such document in the National Archive files, however. Whilst there was much detail in common with the reports of the two other organisations, BALPA's report is commendably concise and clear. It did note that, whilst the lighter wreckage had drifted somewhat between the time it was first spotted at 0625Z, and a summary of disposition two hours twenty minutes later, bodies that had not yet been recovered had not drifted to any noticeable extent. This led the author of the report to conclude that the bodies had, therefore, probably not moved since the time of impact. Capt. Pritchard moved on to construct a 'Theoretical Analysis from Wreckage Recovered'. His conclusions were:

- The disaster was almost instantaneous, the evidence being the truncated radio call and the discovery of the wreckage very close to reporting point R19C.
- The aircraft split into two parts, thus accounting for the fact that some bodies were unclothed and other partially or fully clad. His rationale was based on research involving the dropping of dummies into water from high altitude, following the earlier Comet crashes.
- The fuselage aft the wing trailing edge might have come down as a separate part, this being suggested by the recovery of the dead cat in its intact container[29], along with a relatively-undamaged barograph and electrical instruments. All of these had been listed as being loaded into Hold 5 at the rear of the fuselage. This indicated that the impact at the tail had been much less severe than elsewhere.
- The reason for the fuselage breaking up was questioned. There was, said Capt. Pritchard, no evidence of an explosion, whether by explosive vapours, decompression or an 'infernal machine'. He considered that the most likely cause of any break-up was the aircraft exceeding the designed structural load.
- The aircraft still had electrical power, even if only from the batteries. This was proven by the state of the Graviner fire extinguisher, which was discharging at the moment of disintegration.
- The nose section broke off immediately after impact, evidenced by the recovery of the pilots' hats and the cushion from the flight deck jump seat.

---

[28] The BALPA Technical Appreciation is shown in full, as Appendix 6.
[29] Capt. Pritchard shows the cat as having been recovered; a handwritten comment states 'Not recovered, only seen.'

- Capt. Pritchard was unable to draw any conclusions from the partially-reconstructed seating plan, together with details of severity of injuries and state of clothing of the recovered bodies.
- Weather was discounted as a factor.
- Capt. Pritchard took cognisance of the reports from various colleagues of controls stiffening on the Comet. He noted:

There have, in the past, been quite a few cases of jammed control on various types of aircraft throughout the world, but in all cases the aircraft have flown for a considerable period of time, as indeed the two Comet cases quoted. It is recognised that if the controls jammed in the full deflection or part deflection this would cause an accident, but in the case of the Comet control system, there is no evidence since the Comet has entered BEA service of servodyne failure. Assuming that controls did jam on 'CO', there was no mention of this by Captain Blackwood to Athens on his FIR boundary report. His initial call to Nicosia has all the marks of a routine transmission. The aircraft was known to be flying at 0318 GMT, the watches recovered are stopped between 0320 and 0325Z giving a time span of as little as two minutes or as long as seven minutes. The span of two minutes indicates an almost vertical descent at close on 15,000 f.p.m., the span of seven minutes indicates that the aircraft flew for that time at least some 50 miles along its track. The wreckage was, for all practical purposes, found at the position of UR 19C. Jamming of the controls in the normal cruise configuration therefore does not appear likely. However, it does not rule out the possibility that full deflection was applied for some reason, the answer must by necessity lie in the wreck.

- The failure of a cabin or freight hold door would have caused a rapid decompression, which was not supported by the pathological evidence. For the same reason, it was equally unlikely that the pressure hull had failed due to either the disintegration of the turbine engine or because of corrosion, and indeed there was no untoward issue with corrosion across the Comet 4B fleet.
- Cracks in the compressor casing, although having been found in other Comet 4 aircraft, including two BEA 4Bs, would not have caused a catastrophic disintegration.

Capt. Pritchard ended with the comment:

Whilst many theories can be advanced and a number of them rejected on the grounds of what little concrete information is available, the probable real solution lies within the wreck. If it is practical and possible to retrieve this wreckage, then every effort should be made; because I feel that in the absence of concrete evidence any explanation offered may be supposition based on theory and not fact.

In fact, out of sight of the pilots and the wider public, the question of salvaging the remains of Charlie Oscar and, in particular, her flight recorder, were being considered in detail.

From the outset, it was recognised that the paucity of wreckage, especially parts of the airframe and engines, and the absence of the flight data recorder, was likely to hinder or prevent the investigation determining the cause of the crash. The depth of water was, of course, likely to be a massive problem, if not insurmountable. The uneven sea bed made it very difficult to assess how deep the wreckage of Charlie Oscar might lie, On 16th October, Mr. Riddoch and Eric Newton, along with John Veal, attended a meeting with Mr. Peter Flett, Marine Salvage Officer with the Ministry of Defence. Also attending was Commander Sims-Ross, of the United States Navy.   Mr. Flett explained that the Royal Navy's equipment was inadequate for the task, especially considering the depth of water in which Charlie Oscar now lay. The MoD considered that the US Navy was much better equipped, and indeed the latter had useful experience in very deep-water salvage [30]. Commander Sims-Ross told the meeting, following enquiries he had made with Washington over the weekend, that two vessels, the *Aluminaut* and the *Alvin*, might be considered if the decision was taken to try to locate and recover the wreckage.

Aluminaut, an aluminium submersible vessel, had been designed to operate at depths of 12-15,000 feet, though at the time was only cleared to 6,000 feet. The vessel was capable of searching half a square mile per day; with the poor visibility at that depth meant that the chances of success were put at 10%. In its favour, *Aluminaut* had been used to search for the errant H-bomb off Palomares. Commander Sims-Ross said that the vessel was, he believed, presently in Miami but could be shipped over in a specific craft. The Reynolds Aluminium Company, who had constructed and operated *Aluminaut*, were keen to get involved. A cost estimate had been provided, the monthly sum of US $200,000 per month including the crew. Sims-Ross pointed out that *Aluminaut* was an observation rather than recovery vessel, and it would not be able to salvage any wreckage from Charlie Oscar.

Alvin, in contrast, was equipped for salvage operations, and could also operate down to 6,000 feet of water. In essence, the two vessels would work in tandem, *Aluminaut* searching and the *Alvin* retrieving. There was a challenge in terms of plotting position to the degree of accuracy required.

The transfer of the two vessels to and from the United States would take an estimated one month in each direction, and the time on station for the search was

---

[30] In January 1966, a B-52 bomber, carrying three hydrogen bombs, had collided with a KC-135 aerial tanker during an attempted mid-air refuelling operation over Palomares, Spain. Two of the bombs fell onto land but the third dropped into the Mediterranean Sea. The US Navy had managed to locate the two sites and recover the missing H-bomb, to the relief of the local populace at least.

81

estimated to be a further month, taking the estimated cost, if all went well, to around US $2,000,000. This would cover a search area of some 15 square miles, assuming that operations were possible every day. It was noted that the crash position was, at that time, believed to be no more accurate than plus or minus five miles, meaning that the potential search area would therefore be of the order of one hundred square miles. Given the time of year, plus the time for the equipment to reach the scene, the Eastern Mediterranean would almost certainly experience spells of bad weather, increasing the overall cost even further, but still with what was considered to be no more than a 10% chance of success.

The meeting also considered the possibility of using television cameras to explore the seabed. Suitable equipment in the US was rigged to operate at depths of up to 4,700 feet, though it could be extended to 6,000 with additional cable. Such equipment was offered at no cost other than incurred expenses.

John Veal further noted in his minutes that a Dr. Fleming, of the National Institute of Oceanography, had spoken to him on 24th October about methods which might be put to use in searching for Charlie Oscar. The Institute was independent but operated under a grant from the US Department of Education and undertook expeditions and seabed searches in many parts of the world. Dr. Fleming offered his view that side-scan sonar would be a much less expensive means of locating the wreckage than the employment of the submersibles. The equipment, he pointed out, was very much cheaper to acquire and operate, and a much greater area could be covered in a given time. Veal told Dr. Fleming that no decision had yet been made about searching or attempting to salvage wreckage, but that, should the decision be made to do so, he would certainly be interested in talking further.

In fact, the meeting was held on 30th October; Drs Fleming and Lawton joining Veal, Head, Newton and Flett. Dr. Lawton had focussed on the use of sonar search tools; the technique entailed towing a narrow beam search sonar at approximately one knot. The effective side scan range was between 200 yards and a quarter of a mile. The doctors had also considered the possibility of using magnetometers but had decided against this due to the lack of ferrous materials in aircraft structures, this being because of their effect on the compass. Position fixing, they continued, could be accurate to perhaps fifteen feet. This would be accomplished using acoustic beacons on the sea bed, arranged in a triangle, which would act as reference points. Their precise position did not need to be accurately pinpointed as they would be used, quite literally, for triangulation. The beacons had a range of five miles. The sonar would then be towed by cable from a parent ship, the slow rate of progress through the water allowing the equipment to follow at a steep angle; at this speed the scientists calculated that the length of quarter-inch steel cable required should not exceed 2,600 fathoms (15,600 feet) to put the sonar at the presumed search depth of 1,585 fathoms (9,510 feet). The Institute had a ship, *Discovery* which was equipped with winches capable of handling that amount of cable. Dr. Lawton also suggested that cameras could be used to take photographs of the sea bed, the Institute having three suitable cameras, two stereo and one mono, which would be suitable. Notwithstanding the problems of light transmission at the search depth the cameras would, he believed, have a range of 15 to 20 feet. He produced some detailed sea bed photos taken at a depth of 2,000 metres (6,500 feet).

Television was an alternative to the use of still cameras; however, there were a number of technical difficulties including the fact that the maximum depth at that time for television cable was 4,700 feet, although this might be extended to 6,000 feet. In addition, there were anticipated problems with the high frequency signals used and the need for repeaters in the cable.

Dr. Lawton was not able to offer any suggestions on the problems of salvaging wreckage as, he said, that was not something the Institute considered. However, they had used a dredge to obtain samples of rocks and other materials from the sea bed at great depths. This task was very delicate, and they had been able to use an aperture on the dredge of four feet. The meeting considered that attempting to pick up specific items of use to the investigation was quite distinct from general dredging for seabed materials, and it was concluded that dredging was not a practicable option.

In terms of costs, Dr. Lawton estimated that use of *Discovery* and the equipment he had mentioned might run to between £50,000 and £100,000 per month; whilst the anticipated search area of some sixteen square miles might take one month in fairly calm conditions, this might be extended considerably during the autumn and winter months. Dr. Lawton could also not actually confirm at that time that *Discovery* and the associated equipment would definitely be made available, that being a matter for the Institute's Director to decide as a matter of policy.

The discussion then considered the other alternatives, including the aforementioned *Aluminaut* and *Alvin*, together with two other deep-sea submersibles, *Trieste* and *Archimedes*. Whilst Trieste should be capable of operating at the depths anticipated, the vessel was presently undergoing extensive alteration. *Archimede* was similarly capable and was based in the Mediterranean port of Toulon. Mr. Flett was opposed to the idea of using the submersibles, pointing out that none of them had the requisite capability to salvage the wreckage, if they found it, though he conceded they might be able to secure lifting wires to any pieces the team might want to lift.

Drs Fleming and Lawton were thanked for their proposals, Veal telling them that these would be examined, and he would get in touch once a decision had been reached on whether or not it was practicable to undertake a search or salvage operation.

The Aluminaut was a deep-sea salvage vessel and considered by many to be essential in determining the cause of Charlie Oscar's loss. Sadly, the operation was determined to be too impracticable to make the significant cost worthwhile (TNA).

On 9th November, John Veal met with Bill Mallalieu, the Minister of State at the Board of Trade. They were joined by Mr. Riddoch, Mr. Flett, Commander Sims-Ross and Captain Searle, Supervisor of Salvage for the US Navy. Mr. Mallalieu explained to the Americans that he was grateful for their cooperation over recent weeks and that he was most anxious that the wreckage of G-ARCO should be recovered with a view to discovering the cause of the tragedy. However, he pointed out, the Government needed some idea of the chances of success should it go down the vastly expensive road of hiring the *Aluminaut*.

Captain Searle explained that the *Aluminaut* could work for fairly long periods at considerable depths. It was not, however, insured to work at depths greater than 8,000 feet and greater depths would be even more risky. Capt. Searle described the search for the flight data recorder as looking for a needle in a haystack. The chances would be greater if the recorder had remained attached to the tailplane, and if the tailplane was still intact; however, under the likely circumstances of the aircraft hitting the water at high speed it was likely that neither of these would be the case. The *Aluminaut*'s sonar could detect objects down to the size of an oil barrel but it would be unable to distinguish the recorder from other objects. He reiterated the problems of accurate navigation, telling Mallalieu that the *Aluminaut* might inadvertently cover the same ground repeatedly without knowing it. Capt. Searle considered that the prospect of salvage was even poorer.

John Veal said that recovery of the flight data recorder would be useful, but if the search concentrated on locating wreckage, they would need most of the aircraft to be recovered to gain anything of value. Whilst the location of the crash was known to within two miles, the wreckage would have been scattered over a wider area due to the hydrofoil affect as it sank to the seabed.

Capt. Searle added that whilst photographing the wreckage might be a cheaper operation, it was only of benefit as a preliminary to recovering it. John Veal considered that siting the wreckage and obtaining photographs would be useless for the purpose of determining what had caused Charlie Oscar's loss, and that only recovery of the wreckage would reveal the true picture.

In conclusion, Mallalieu asked Searle if his considered opinion was that attempts to salvage the aircraft were impracticable. Searle told him that it depended upon the value placed by the Government on recovering the wreckage. He thought that recovery would be much more difficult than in the case of the H-bomb off Palomares, and it would certainly be costlier. He cautioned against accepting the earlier estimates provided by Reynolds which, he said, had not considered ancillary administrative costs which might alter the figures beyond recognition.

An alternative hypothesis had been suggested by Mr. W.L.G. Stanley. Chief Experimental Engineer in the Rocket Department of Rolls-Royce; this entailed an electrolytic method, and involved dragging an array of light chains, probably of steel, along the sea bed. As Mr. Stanley explained in a letter to Mr. K.G. Wilkinson, Chief Engineer of BEA, contact with aluminium alloy would cause a small current to flow around a circuit, which would include a small cathode of the same material as the chain. Mr. Stanley said that he had confirmed the principle on a small-scale experiment using copper chain, though he did accept that there would be problems to be considered at the sort of depths envisaged.

In the end, Mallalieu decided that it was time to draw a line under the consideration of salvage. Taking heed of the advice from various quarters, he appeared before the House of Commons on 22nd November to say:

> The possibility of salvage has been carefully examined with Ministry of Defence and United States Navy experts and I have personally discussed the matter with the United States Navy Supervisor of Salvage. It is clear that salvage of the wreckage would be impracticable and that an attempt at recovery of the flight recorder alone would be an extremely difficult, lengthy and perhaps hazardous operation with little prospect of success. In view of this, and evidence which indicates detonation of a high explosive in the aircraft cabin, my Rt. Hon. Friend has decided that the question of salvage should not be pursued.

Bodies of Evidence

The task of conducting post-mortems on the recovered victims fell to Group Captain Ken Mason, of the RAF Aviation and Forensic Pathology Department. Born in 1920, Mason was to spend thirty years working as an RAF pathologist, having been described by his colleagues in his later career at the University of Edinburgh[31] as '...*very much a pioneer of aviation pathology.*'

The work of Mason and his colleague, Squadron Leader Stan Tarlton, was to be arduous in the extreme. The department having been informed of the crash on the morning of 12th October, the duo travelled to Greece, leaving Heathrow at 2245hrs that evening and arriving in Athens at 0215hrs on 13th October, precisely 24 hours after Charlie Oscar had undertaken the same trip. They were informed when they got to Athens that the majority of bodies were being transported to Rhodes, where they were expected early that same morning. They therefore travelled on to Rhodes, arriving at 0930hrs.

Mason and Tarlton held a meeting at 1130hrs with Capt. Baillie and Dr. Preston, Chief Medical Officer of BEA, along with two Greek representatives, Mr. P. Apostolides of the Foreign Office and K. Christopoulos, Health Council of Civil Aviation. Also present were unnamed representatives of Cyprus Airways and Mr. Canyon, from the British Association of Embalmers. Mr. Christopoulos outlined the official position regarding health aspects of identification, embalming and burial of the bodies. Mason and Tarlton were opposed to the idea of inviting relatives of the victims to identify the bodies as this would, they felt, interfere with their work. Mr. Christopoulos over-ruled their protestations, explaining that the presence of relatives was essential to the identification process.

Mason and Tarlton then made their way to Rhodes Hospital to organise the post-mortem examinations. Whilst attempting to do so, they were constantly interrupted by supposedly-urgent telephone calls, most of which turned out to be from the press. As a result, they did not manage to start the post-mortems until 1500 hrs, by which time they had gone thirty hours without sleep.

Mason considered that conditions were not ideal. The mortuary actually consisted of a single table with no drain. There was a wash basin which quickly

---

[31] John Kenyon ('Ken') French Mason CBE served for three decades as a forensic pathologist in the Royal Air Force. Focusing on aviation medicine, he rose through the ranks to become group captain and director of the RAF's Aviation and Forensic Pathology Department and was regularly summoned to investigate aviation accidents. In recognition of his contributions to the forensic pathology of aircraft accidents, in 1973 he was awarded a Commander of the Order of the British Empire (Military Division). He subsequently held the post of Professor of Forensic Medicine at the University of Edinburgh. Afterwards he developed a third career in medical law. His career eventually spanned 74 years. He passed away on 26th January 2017 at the age of 97. Stan Tarlton passed away in 2014.

Above left: Photographed after conducting forensic examinations of victims of the Stockport air crash in April 1967, Group Captain Ken Mason (left) and Squadron Leader Stan Tarlton (right) were considered the foremost aviation pathologists of their time. Their expertise was to prove invaluable to the investigation. (Stephen Morrin). Above right: The limited facilities at the hospital on Rhodes are clear in this photograph from the Illustrated London News. The result was that the post-mortem examinations were not as thorough as the pathologists would have liked (ILN).

became clogged up. The location of the mortuary also meant that it was impossible to work without children and adults looking through the window. By now, of course, Mason and Tarlton were extremely fatigued and managed to complete on six examinations before having to call a halt at 1900hrs in order to attend a conference with Capt. Baillie.

The Greek authorities were unhappy, according to Mason in his later report[32] and the team felt itself under great pressure which affected their work. The following day the pressure grew further when the local Health Officer expressed his concerns about the general risk to health engendered by the investigation. Mason felt a degree of sympathy with that view; there was no facility for refrigerating the bodies which had been in the sea and then in transit for some 24 hours before they even reached Rhodes. However, the Health Officer understood the pathologists' plight and agreed to let them carry on. However, the arrival of the nineteen bodies from Turkey, delivered to the mortuary on the afternoon of 13th October, resulted in the Public Prosecutor directing that all

[32] Aviation Pathology Report No. 15 1967, RAF Institute of Pathology and Tropical Medicine; AVIA101/225 The National Archives, London.

bodies were to be sealed in coffins by the end of the following day, Saturday 14th October.

In the course of the 13th, Mason and Tarlton performed heroically and completed a total of 21 further autopsies; their work was further interrupted by the visit of a plane-load of relatives who were legally entitled to inspect each body. Christopoulos later reported that *'Identification of the bodies was rendered easier by the reliable evidence and declarations of the relatives who had arrived and in one difficult case by other elements of medical jurisprudence (operation scars, personal effects, etc.)*[33] To Mason's considerable chagrin, the visitors also included, at the insistence of the Public Prosecutor, a number of Italian press photographers[34]. To add to the team's problems, the only deep freeze available to preserve blood samples and similar specimens was in a hotel, and Mason considered that it was unreasonable to press on the management more than one day's batch.

On the 14th, a service was held in the mortuary area. On this occasion, Cypriot relatives and press were admitted. The locally available porters, enlisted from the docks, went on strike for higher wages on several occasions. Despite all these immense frustrations, Mason and Tarlton completed the remainder of the autopsies, bar four, in what they considered to be somewhat unsatisfactorily. The other four bodies were removed by their families before post-mortem examinations could take place.

The Public Prosecutor was keeping up the pressure for a swift completion of the autopsies before dusk, with any remaining unidentified bodies being sealed in coffins and buried locally. However, he took a reasonable approach when it became apparent at the appointed hour that only six bodies were yet to be named.

There was more work for the pair the following day, 15th October, as they met up with Norman Head of the AIB to examine lifejackets and the small amount of wreckage that had been recovered. After this, Mason and Tarlton finished the identification procedure for the remaining six bodies[35], before holding a press conference with Norman Head that evening. The two RAF men returned from home Rhodes on the morning of the 17th October.

In his report, Mason acknowledged the assistance given to them by BEA, Cyprus Airways and the local authorities. They were particularly grateful for the presence of a photographer and interpreter.

In the immediate absence of a conclusive cause of loss, the possibility of a bomb could still not be definitely ruled out. On 13th October, the day he travelled

---

[33] Christopoulos' report (as translated), AVIA101 210 Chief Investigating Officer's Report – TNA.

[34] Photographs of a number of the dead, including a young child, appeared in the international press. The British press was, and remains, restrained in this regard. These photographs, although made available to the author, do not appear in this book.

[35] Christopoulos noted, 'Of the 51 bodies undergoing necrotomy, on two of them complete identification was not established, except nationality. These were taken to London for further collection of medico-jurisprudence elements of identification.'

to Greece, Norman Head had issued an urgent request to Ken Mason that all pieces of metal recovered from bodies be returned to the AIB by the quickest means and also suggested that all the bodies be X-rayed. There had been previous cases[36], mostly in North and South America, in which airliners had been brought down by the detonation of explosives in the passenger cabin or cargo hold. Investigation of the wreckage had revealed noticeable fragments of metal. In the case of suicide, the predominant characteristic had been the use of hand grenades, which dispersed large pieces of metal, and it was considered highly likely that a similar occurrence in Charlie Oscar would have left such evidence in the remains of the victims.

Mason and Tarlton having completed as best they could their incomprehensively difficult task over the weekend, went home to prepare their interim report[37]. By the time this was eventually released the salient points had already been communicated directly to Eric Newton and his team. There had initially been statements, by the RAF crew and others, that some of the bodies had been wearing lifejackets. It was only after the post mortems that the team was able to clarify that no one had been so protected. Mason and Tarlton noted that, by the time of the interim report, the seating positions of 28 passengers boarding in London were known, this information coming from the London – Athens cabin crew. They also recognised a potential significance in the distribution of the bodies, in terms of their recovery in either the 'Greek' (southern) or the 'Turkish' (northern) group.

The cause of death and pattern of the injuries was summarised as:

> Death was ascribed to multiple injuries in 35 cases, to cardiac rupture in 5 and to aortic rupture in 5. In 2 instances, the cause of death was somewhat obscure:- in one adult, death appeared to be due to multiple injuries, but histology suggested a small amount of sea water having been inhaled terminally; in 1 child (Case 39) death was ascribed to 'shock' but again, on histology, there seemed evidence of inhalation of seawater and, although there were no gross signs such as frothing at the mouth or water in the stomach, there is a suspicion that drowning played some part in the death. One adult woman showed frothing at the nose and was stated by the Turkish authorities to have drowned; there was no internal evidence of this, however, and, despite the absence of pulmonary rib markings, histological appearances in the lungs raise the possibility of blast injury playing a part in the death. One case (No.6) was sufficiently distinctive to merit isolation and is discussed individually below.

---

[36] See Appendix 11.
[37] AVIA13 1383 Accident Investigation – National Archives.

The most obvious feature in the post mortem room was the isolation of a relatively small group (12 bodies) which showed very little external evidence of violence. At the other end of the scale, 21 bodies were described as having extreme injury; a somewhat subjective group of moderate injury (14 bodies) was also classified[38].

The uniformity of injury among those showing extreme injury was striking. Basically, the picture was one of massive head injury combined with severe injury to the thoracic spine (usually amounting to transection) and full fracture of the sternum; atrioventricular rupture was common and abdominal laceration invariable.

Most of the 'slightly injured[39]' group had died from single injuries in the cardio-vascular system, but that the frequency of abdominal laceration even in this group was noteworthy. Mason and Tarlton also commented on the differences in the ratio of extreme to slight external injuries between the northern and southern groups; the latter had a significant number of 'extreme injury' cases and fewer with slight visible injuries. Whilst not in itself conclusive, the difference was marked.

The clothing retained on the bodies, if any, was also recorded, though the pathologists noted that some might have been displaced while the bodies were in the sea, or when they were recovered and taken on board the various ships in the recovery flotilla.

The interim report considered similarities between the victims recovered from Charlie Oscar, and those from the Elba and Naples Comet crashes thirteen years earlier. Whilst there was no suggestion that the various injuries and clothing retention or loss were specific to accidents involving that particular aircraft type, they had all occurred in the Mediterranean and involved British aircraft. The results of the previous investigations were, therefore, readily available for comparison. Mason and Tarlton noted the common high frequency of head injuries, severe thoracic injuries and internal injury with an absence of severe external damage to many of the bodies. This suggested that there had been a degree of similarity in the process of descent following a catastrophic failure, and the destruction of the various aircraft when hitting the sea.

Where the accident to Charlie Oscar diverged from the earlier disasters was in the notable delineation of the group of relatively (externally) uninjured bodies. The report noted that the group comprised:

a. Members of the three families with children (although one child and one adult were missing).

b. Two stewardesses were included.

---

[38] The report helpfully linked the injuries by severity to the seating plan provided by the British cabin crew.

[39] Whilst it might appear anomalous to refer to victims who had suffered fatal injuries as 'slightly injured', this was the wording adopted by Mason and Tarlton so is used in that context.

c. With one exception, the remaining members of the group were young females, one married, from a noticeably aged passenger complement.

According to the rudimentary seating plan[40] reconstructed with the help of the London-Athens cabin crew and passengers, all the 'slightly injured' passengers, whose seating could be placed, were located between rows 6 and 12, on the port side of the aircraft. The report considered that the twenty-strong group of Jehovah's Witnesses, mostly elderly, would probably have been sitting together in the rear portion of the cabin.

The pathologists concluded that it was:

'...difficult to conceive of any mechanism for the production of the severe head and thoracic injuries other than the casualties being projected onto the roof of the passenger cabin, and there is some further proof of this in the frequent occurrence of extension fractures of the ankles. Undoubtedly this was the primary injury in most cases, the pelvic and limb injuries being subsequent to rupture of the cardiovascular system.

Mason and Tarlton stressed that any explanation of the mechanism by which the injuries were sustained must at the same time explain the presence of the 'slightly injured' group. They felt it was inevitable that the findings could only be satisfied on the basis of the 'slightly injured' group being thrown clear of the aircraft either before, or at the same time as, the other victims had been thrown around inside the fuselage. They went on to consider a number of possible scenarios based on the assumption that all the passengers gad been seated according to the seating plan provided to them after the interviews of the passengers and crew who disembarked at Athens.

Following the earlier Comet Mk1 tragedies, the first cause of loss considered by Mason and Tarlton was cabin pressurisation failure. It was also apparent to them that the head injuries in the earlier crashes were similar to those found in Charlie Oscar. However, they noted that no similar string of mishaps had occurred in any other major aircraft type, so cautioned against conclusions being drawn too hastily. They also pointed out that the Comet 4B was vastly different to the earlier model, and that it had probably been tested more thoroughly than any other aircraft in service. Had a cabin failure similar in scale to the earlier Comets occurred, it was seemingly impossible to explain why many passengers in the centre of the cabin had been spared the effects of turbulence. If it was on a markedly smaller scale it might still have been sufficient to destroy the side of the aircraft, allowing the ejection of the 'slightly injured' group. The second possibility, however, implied that the occupants might have fallen from different

---

[40] The assumptions made about the final seating pattern rely on no one having changed seats after the turnround at Athens. With the Tourist Class cabins being one-third empty, there is no guarantee that this was actually the case. However, it is unlikely that a significant number of passengers would have changed seats unless there was some reason to do so.

heights, with the 'slightly injured' group have fallen the greatest distance[41]. The evidence from the body recovery, with two distinct groups about half a mile apart, suggested that any ejection of the victims had occurred at a height significantly lower than Charlie Oscar's cruising altitude of 29,000 feet. In particular, a number of the 'slightly injured' group retained some of their clothing, which was at variance with the experiments conducted after the Comet Mk 1 disasters.

The second possibility was loss of control of the aircraft, which might have been caused by one or more of a number of factors. These could have included, the pathologists suggested, pilot incapacitation, engine disintegration, sabotage, collision or lightning strike. As all three pilots were amongst the missing victims, there was no evidence to show or disprove incapacitation. A collision in the area of the passenger cabin would have produced a less uniform pattern of injuries, although they accepted that the point of impact might have been in the vicinity of the flight deck or outside the pressure cabin itself. Lightning strike could not be wholly excluded, but the pathologists noted that no steel possessions of the passengers, such as had been recovered, were found to be magnetised. Consideration of engine break up or sabotage, they stated, should be discussed in relation to Case No. 6, 28-year-old Mr. Achillea Afatitis, who was traveling with his new wife as part of the group of twenty, mostly older, Jehovah's Witnesses.

Mr. Afatitis' body was distinctive for several reasons:
a. He had arm injuries, sustained before death, suggestive of flailing.
b. His upper body was peppered with minute dark specks.
c. His trachea strongly appeared to be affected by heat.
d. His shirt also had minute holes similar to those in his chest.

The skin lesions appeared to be very superficial puncture wounds which showed marked heat coagulation. The minor lesions, along with the heat coagulation in the throat, showed vascular reaction, inflammation caused by minute blood vessels, suggesting that Mr. Afatitis had still been alive at the time the damage was caused. This was to prove a very significant development. Whilst nothing was found in the lesion examined, Mason and Tarlton noted that any such foreign body would have disappeared if it was liquid and would have been lost during the recovery and examination process, if it was a minute metallic object.

Mason and Tarlton returned to the original, though ultimately erroneous, reports that some passengers were wearing life jackets, and therefore considered the possibility of a ditching which had proved non-survivable. They considered

---

[41] Previous work had concluded that occupants falling from height were spared the 'cement mixer' effect of being flung around the cabin, and that impact with the sea would have caused fatal internal injuries, but without the external trauma of those inside the tumbling fuselage. Similarly, experiments after the Comet Mk 1 crashes suggested that a fall into the sea from a height greater than a few hundred feet would have so torn the clothing that it would be dislodged either on contact with the sea, or by the action of waves before the body was recovered.

the possibility that Mr. Afatitis' skin lesions had been caused by spraying with hot fuel, though they noted that there was no contamination with carbon monoxide, which might have been expected in such circumstances.

In their consideration of sabotage as the cause of the disaster, Mason and Tarlton considered reported American experience that large metallic fragments would be present, and none of these were found, either physically or by X-ray, in Mr. Afatitis' body, or any other victim.

If the cause had been a bomb or similar event, the pathologists reported, the medical evidence suggested three subsequent sequences in the destruction of Charlie Oscar:

1. That a massive defect was produced in the aircraft at 29,000 feet.
2. That the aircraft was put out of control and broke up under increasing stress at a much lower height.
3. That, being out of control, the aircraft struck the water, possibly port wing first, and disintegrated as it sped over the water, spilling victims as it went.

They considered it was probable that the engineering evidence would strongly support a massive defect having occurred at altitude, and that the available medical difference would provide little to help distinguishing between possibilities 2 and 3. Whilst the lung appearances in the 'slightly injured' group were comparable to those ascribed to free-fall water impact in the earlier Comet crashes, there was no reason they could not equally have been sustained by victims being thrown clear when Charlie Oscar hit the surface of the sea. Similarly, the more severe external injuries sustained by other victims were sufficiently uniform for them to have been caused in a non-survivable ditching, which was, to all intents and purposes, a crash into the sea rather than a controlled landing on water. In a pre-meditated water landing, however unsuccessful, it would have been expected that passengers would be wearing life jackets. Mason and Tarlton were able to examine a few life jackets but could find no evidence that any had been fastened to passengers, corroborating the observation of Nikos Misomikes. They did express some surprise that so many life jackets appeared to have come free from their stowage under the seats without some effort by the passengers, but the AIB investigators convinced them that no particular conclusions should be drawn from that.

Amongst the relatives in Rhodes was Polyvios Georgiou, who now faced the further distress of finding out that his brother Sotiris was amongst the eleven passengers and four crew whose bodies had not been recovered. Amongst the more bizarre incidents in what was an unremittingly horrendous experience was what Polyvios later described to the author as '...a relentless attempt by some of the Jehovah Witnesses to convert my brother and I from being Greek Orthodox to becoming Jehovahs Witness disciples.'

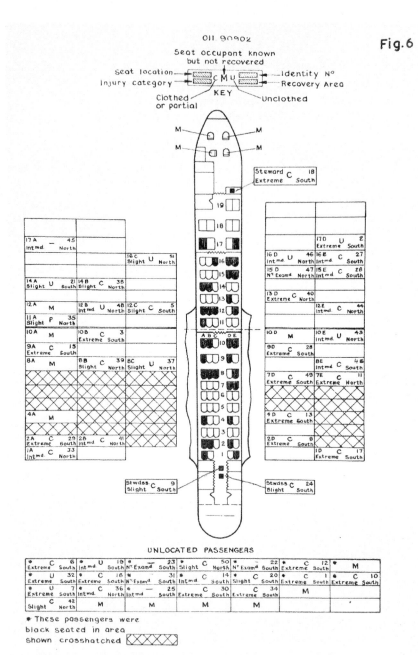

The seating plan of Charlie Oscar with relevant details considered by Mason and Tarlton in their pathology report (RAE Report via TNA)

'The Answer Lies Somewhere Amongst This List'

Chief Investigator Eric Newton (left) with colleague J. Letts, at the scene of the Stockport air disaster on 4th June 1967. Newton was a highly respected investigator and authority on air disasters (Manchester Evening News).

At the beginning of the investigation, determining the cause beyond any reasonable doubt appeared to be a very tall order. Almost no substantial wreckage had been recovered, and there was no sign of the 'black box' flight data recorder. Charlie Oscar had crashed into the Mediterranean at precisely the point where there was an abyss, the water being an estimated 9,000 feet deep.

Speculation on the cause of the loss of Charlie Oscar was rife from the outset. By the standards of the time, in an age before social media and instant communication, the news-gathering operation was stunningly effective. The press lost no time in supplementing the scant facts of the crash and the names of the victims with personal details, interpretation and speculation. British newspapers carried the story from 13th October, initial reports such as that in the Daily Telegraph setting the tone. *'The cause of the crash remains a complete mystery,'* its readers were informed, though barely 24 hours had elapsed since Charlie Oscar was lost. In spite of the absence thus far of any evidence whatsoever, a number of causes were being mooted.

Eric Newton had compiled a generic list of possible causes, the document bearing a handwritten comment[42], 'The answer lies somewhere amongst this list!' The items on his list were:

1. **Pressure fuselage failure.**
   a. Corrosion
   b. Fatigue
   c. Overstressing (over-pressurisation)
   d. Faulty repairs
   e. Door, hatch, window blow out
2. **Sabotage.**
   a. Explosive
   b. Incendiary
   c. Acid or mercury in stressed areas
   d. Jamming or damage to vital controls
3. **Basic structural failure of airframe.**
   a. Fatigue
   b. Overstressing
   c. Corrosion
4. **Atmospheric Upset.**
   a. Turbulence
   b. Lightning
5. **Collision.**
   a. With another aircraft
   b. Radio sonde (Long duration type)
   c. Meteorites
   d. UFO
   e. Satellite rocket booster fall out
6. **Loss of Control.**
   a. Violent evasive action
   b. Pilot incapacity, including food poisoning
   c. Servodyne or hydraulic failure
   d. Auto pilot
   e. Instruments
   f. Passenger running amok, gunman, madman, etc.
7. **Engines.**
   a. Major structural failure of compressor or turbine causing –
   b. Cutting of flying controls
   c. Disruption of pressure fuselage
   d. Fire

---

[42] AVIA101 208 - TNA

8. Fire.
a. At engine following 7 above causing fuel tank explosion
b. Internal in cabin or freight hold
c. Deliberate by passenger (suicide)
9. Lightning Strike.
a. Strike damage to wing structure, pressure fuselage or fuel tanks
b. Shock pressure wave causing structural damage to airframe

The investigators had very little to go on at the outset. Apart from the 51 recovered bodies, the evidence consisted of debris, almost all of which was identified as being fragments of the cabin fixtures. There was, of course, the data gathered right at the outset; the ATC recordings and weather records had been promptly and correctly seized and preserved for detailed scrutiny.

The weather forecast issued by the Athens meteorological office had been fair with scattered thunderstorms. However, Capt. Emmerson, in Mike Foxtrot, had reported that flight conditions had been clear and smooth. The thunderstorm activity was mainly to the east of Cyprus.

The wind direction and speed at altitude had been:

FL300[43] 350 deg / 45 knots
FL240   360 deg / 40 knots
FL180   360 deg / 35 knots

At 0320hrs, around the time of the crash, an observation at Rhodes noted the surface wind as calm, visibility 25 km and the sky clear. Analysis by the UK Met Office at Bracknell, which sat by coincidence a mile or so from Capt. Blackwood's home, analysed the conditions and noted that conditions were not favourable for clear air turbulence, mountain waves or wind shear. The report noted, *'The only other remote possibility is an encounter with a thunderstorm top but even this would be unlikely to produce more than…severe (turbulence) between 8,000 and 25,000 feet.'*

Weather was, it appeared, not a causal factor in the loss of Charlie Oscar. If no cause could be positively identified, the investigators would have to laboriously consider and disprove as many of Newton's list of possibilities as they could. In the words of Sherlock Holmes, *"When you have eliminated the impossible, whatever remains, however improbable, must be the truth[44]."*

The investigation was necessarily complex, and there were several strands being explored simultaneously   . Memories of the earlier Comet disasters had

---

[43] Flight Level (FL) is the height, in hundreds of feet, above the pressure setting 1013.2 millibars. Whilst it is a nominal figure, it ensures that all aircraft at a specific location will be using the same reference point, which ensures safe separation. FL 300 is, therefore, nominally, 30,000 feet, whilst FL 240 and FL180 are 24,000 and 18,000 feet respectively.
[44] The Sign of the Four, by Sir Arthur Conan Doyle.

Above: Minute fragments of metal were recovered from the bodies and wreckage. This shows Specimen MX246, which was embedded in a passenger seat. Below: A slide from the electron microscope examination of fragments of metal. (RAE Report).

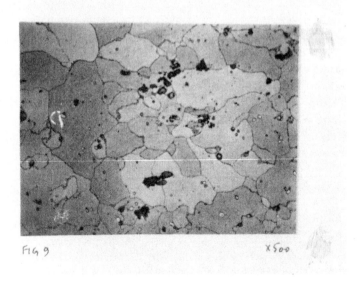

FIG 9   X500

surfaced almost immediately, and there was a growing concern, in the absence of any clues to the cause of the tragedy, that a similar weakness in the structure of the aircraft had returned to claim more victims. As a precaution, therefore, HSA, after consultation with the AIB, contacted all Comet operators stating:

In view of the present uncertainty of the cause of the recent Comet accident it has been decided that as a precautionary interim measure, operators are advised to reduce the maximum cabin operating pressure differential to 6 psi.

This would have the effect of restricting the worldwide Comet fleet to flights at a maximum altitude of 27,000 feet, compared with its normal ceiling of 35,000 feet. This, in turn, would lead to higher fuel consumption. Whilst this was, as stated, 'advisory', it was unlikely to be disregarded and would at least allow the Comets to keep flying.

A number of specific lines of investigation were now started, working in parallel, in order to confirm or eliminate various possible causes of the disaster.

Metal Fragments

Hugh Gordon-Burge, BEA's Air Safety Advisor[45], returned to the UK with several small pieces of metal given to him by Ken Mason following the post-mortems. On the same day, boxes of material recovered from the crash scene were also returned to the UK and transferred to the Royal Aircraft Establishment at Farnborough for detailed examination. The recovered wreckage included seat cushions, a fire extinguisher, personal effects, 23 adult and three baby lifebelts.

The three fragments of metal had been found embedded in separate bodies and it was important that these could be identified, to determine whether they were from the aircraft structure, an innocent object or were shrapnel from an explosive device. They were preserved as evidence and, on 27th October, Mr. Goulding of the AIB delivered them to Mr. Forsyth at the Metallurgy Department of the Royal Aircraft Establishment, Farnborough for examination. The delivery coincided with the visit of a BEA delegation to the RAE, to inspect the flotsam.

The metal fragments were very small but, given that they had been recovered from bodies, it was crucial that they be identified. Three such specimens were examined. A covering letter from John Veal to Mr. Yallop at the Royal Armaments Research and Development Establishment (RARDE) added some supplementary information:

Specimen R.42 (in bottle) a small piece of aluminium (approximately .6-inch x .4 inch) with a wax-like deposit, some apparent human tissue and what appears nylon or glass fibre cloth weave adhering to it. This specimen was removed from one of the

---

[45] Hugh Gordon-Burge was a pilot with RAF Coastal Command during the Second World War, then flew with Aer Lingus from 1946 to 1955. After that, he worked for the AIB until joining BEA in 1965 (Flight International 22nd April 1965).

bodies. Also, in the bottle is a small piece of semi-circular steel with what appears to be a thread cut on the inside, and also a separate flake of green paint.

Specimen R.41 (in plastic bag) a small piece of light alloy (possibly magnesium alloy) and measuring about ½ inch long and .2 inch wide.

A separate piece of aluminium alloy, heavy gauge sheet, about 1½ inches by 1¼ inches with two rivets (purple identification). This appears typical of aircraft structure.

We require an examination of these samples to determine, in particular, whether there is any evidence of explosives or whether the material is consistent in any way with part of a known type of detonator or timing device. Specimen R.42 is of interest in this respect as the gauge of the metal appears to be too thin for any part of the aircraft structure, and it appears to be of soft pure aluminium and not aluminium alloy normally employed in aircraft structure. We would like a spectrographic check on this material and a chemical analysis of the wax-like deposit adhering to it.

The results of the swabs came through on October 24th but were negative. This was not surprising to Newton, as the wreckage had been in the sea and had then apparently been washed prior to despatch to RARDE.

Analysis showed that Specimen R.42 consisted of two pieces of crumpled foil with an adhesive layer between, forming a sandwich, along with several small pieces of red plastic material and a small steel fragment. Each piece of foil was only 0.006 inches thick and was commercial purity aluminium. Comparisons with samples provided by HSA showed that these were fragments of acoustic sheet, the sandwich filling being self-adhesive damping tape and Aquaplas 100, a soundproofing compound. The red plastic was probably glue used in the construction of aircraft partitions and the metal fragment was identified as the split end of a locking nut.

Specimen R.41 was a piece of metal 0.45 x 0.2 x 0.1 inches. The material was identified as a magnesium alloy casting, and possibly part of a broken weld.

The third item mentioned in the covering letter was, presumably, Specimen MX246, which was badly corroded, though with signs of the original paint scheme still visible. This had been found embedded in a passenger cabin seat frame. 0.116 inches thick, it was probably a high strength extrusion alloy. With the item were two pop rivet fragments, but these were not examined in any detail.

In addition, one of the very few structural parts recovered proved to be a piece of aluminium alloy sheet with a rolled edge, with the remains of two rivets and indications of two other rivet holes, with a pitch of approximately 5/8ths of an inch. The edge of a spot weld could be distinguished as well as a flake of aluminium paint. It was identified as part of a capping strip from the frame of an engine door.

All the specimens examined were identified as aircraft materials.[46]

Graviner Fire Extinguisher

Amongst the debris recovered from the crash site was a triple-headed Graviner type 71A automatic fire extinguisher, part of the aircraft's installed equipment. It was identified as having come from the starboard side of the centre section of Charlie Oscar. After recovery and return to England, the bottle had been sent to the manufacturer for examination. It was concluded that the fire extinguisher had been fired electrically by an inertia (crash) switch, and that all parts of the operating mechanism appeared to have functioned correctly. Further examination at Farnborough confirmed that all three charges had been correctly fired, showing that the crash switch had been working as designed, and that the electrical supply was also functioning at the point of firing. As a matter of detail, it was noted that all three outlet indicators on the bottle were in the out position, showing that all three had been activated. However, three plungers would ordinarily retract after discharge, but two of these were still in the out position. The three indicators and two plungers were all damaged, distorted and broken so that they were trapped in the out position. The damage picture was consistent to all of these. However, the third plunger had retracted within the head, though the indicator showed that it had actually been out during discharge, so had gone through its expected cycle. The plunger is moved out from the head by fluid pressure during discharge and is then retracted by a spring, once the fluid has been discharged and the pressure reduced accordingly. The minimum time required for the bottle to discharge is two seconds, and therefore bottle discharge must have taken place for at least two seconds before the indicators were damaged, in order for the third plunger to have time to return to its housing undamaged. Testing showed that the two damaged plungers probably extended due to inertial loading and were damaged as a result, whereas the third had remained retracted so had avoided damage. The damage to the head was consistent with that expected when the aircraft struck the sea, but as the discharge had to last at least two seconds in order for the third head to have time to retract again, there must have been two inertial loads, the first sufficient to trip the crash switch and the second to cause the damage observed. This could have occurred if the aircraft had hit the sea and bounced at least once, or if the first discharge had occurred sometime before impact with the sea.

The inertia switch was mounted in the nose of the aircraft with the recovered bottle being, as mentioned, in the centre section. The electrical wiring passes from the nose along the bottom of the forward fuselage to the aircraft centre section. Discharge of the bottle can only be activated by positive electrical

---

[46] There is no assessment in the records of how the fragments came to be in the bodies; the most obvious conclusion would be that the victim was struck by, or impacted, the part of the aircraft from which the materials originated.

energising, a short circuit not being sufficient. This led to the conclusion that the electrical circuit was complete at the time of discharge.

Significantly, the bottle had been recovered from the northern area, away from other flotsam and the bodies associated with the centre section of Charlie Oscar. It was considered highly unlikely that it would have separated on impact with the sea, and the examiners concluded that it probably detached due to the aircraft breaking up in the air. HSA calculated that, if the forward fuselage became detached suddenly, for example due to downward inertial loading on it, the load would be sufficient to trigger the crash switch, causing the bottle to discharge. A downward rotation of the forward fuselage, effectively causing it to 'snap off', would preserve the electrical wiring long enough for the bottle to discharge fully. The single fire extinguisher recovered had therefore provided very strong evidence that Charlie Oscar had broken up in mid-air.

Passengers' Watches

A total of ten wrist watches had been recovered from the bodies of the victims during the post mortem examinations. A prominent watch business, Watches of Switzerland, of New Bond Street, London, examined all the watches and established that most had stopped suddenly although three had, despite the catastrophic impact, stopped only when they wound down. It was noted with interest that these tended to be the cheaper watches. Seven of the watches had stopped at between twenty and twenty-five past either four or five o'clock [47]. Overall, the balance of evidence was that the watches had stopped at about 0325hrs GMT. Eight watches were contaminated by kerosene; where these could be linked to individual passengers, it was noted that they came from the southern group of bodies. The investigators were able to conclude that the earliest time of impact indicated by the watches was, therefore, at most two minutes after the last radio transmission, with the majority suggesting that the impact occurred some seven minutes after the final words of SFO Thomas.

Freight Hold Door Failure

One possible cause of the disintegration of Charlie Oscar was the failure of the door to one of the three freight holds, these being pressurised. The team was mindful of explosive decompression having been the cause of the loss of at least two Comets previously. However, Mason and Tarlton had not found any evidence that the victims had injuries through that particular cause. This suggested that the passenger cabin itself had not been instantaneously ripped

---

[47] The hour's difference could be explained by the difference in local time between London and both Athens and Nicosia.

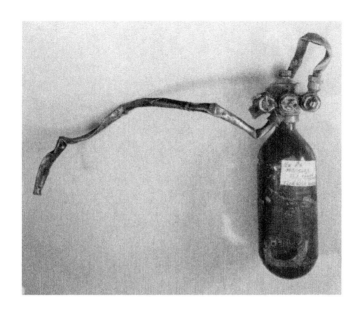

Above: The damaged Graviner fire extinguisher from Charlie Oscar which provided evidence that the aircraft had broken up in mid-air (TNA). Below: The layout of fixed fire extinguishers in the centre section of the Comet 4B and 4C. The bottle recovered from Charlie Oscar was that fitted next to No. 3 engine zone at position 6. (Comet 4B Technical Manual, BEA October 1967).)

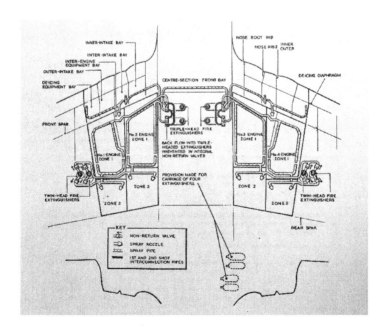

General view of portion of test fuselage used in the test with luggage bay door in position (TNA).

apart through a catastrophic failure of the fuselage skin, as previously, or the failure of a cabin door. It fell to HSA to investigate this possibility.

The aircraft manufacturer needed to establish whether a luggage hold door might, therefore, have failed in flight and, if so, whether that failure would have led to the disintegration of the airframe. This might be a consequence either of the fuselage being unable to withstand the decompression or of a loss of control due to the disruption to the airflow. At the time, HSA had a test fuselage, which had originally been built as a Comet 3 but was substantially the same structure as a Comet 4B for the purpose of the test. Given that failures of intact and undamaged freight doors did not routinely fail in flight, as they were designed not to do so, the assumption was that there would need to be a failure to the hold door itself or to the housing.

The testing team obtained a section of the Comet 3 fuselage which incorporated a luggage bay door and surrounding structure. A sealed wooden box was placed around the freight hold entrance, attached to the outside skin of the fuselage to enable suction loads to be applied, replicating the pressure differential experienced in normal flight. The load used was 9 psi[48]. All doors installed in the pressure cabin opened inwards, so a positive pressure differential would seal them in place.

---

[48] psi= pounds per square inch. The Comet was normally allowed to operate up to a maximum pressure differential of 8.75 psi.

The luggage bay door used had previously been subjected to 120,000 cycles of pressure, least ten times the number that Charlie Oscar herself had been through in her service life. To simulate the worst case envisaged, cracks had been artificially created and extended to increase the likelihood of a failure.

Initially the locking pins were correctly engaged, as would be the usual practice, and the door was subjected to 25 cycles. The door was then removed and examined, with no further damage being found. The process was continued up to 250 cycles, with period removal and checking. The testers then fitted the door without its locking pins engaged and subjected it to a further 150 cycles. At no point did the door fail; it had simply wedged itself further and further into its housing, to the extent that there were noticeable marks on the side of the door pan. The testers concluded that the door was not going to be the point of failure, as it had satisfactorily demonstrated its fail-safe qualities.

Fuel Tank Explosion

The task of assessing the probability of an explosion having occurred in the centre fuel tanks of Charlie Oscar fell to one H.E. Livermore, Senior System Engineer of the Engine Installation Section of Hawker Siddeley's Design Office. Mr. Livermore's report into this aspect, was succinct; after a short calculation of time airborne, remaining fuel in the centre tanks, altitude, outside air temperature and airspeed, he concluded:

'The estimated air temperature in the centre tank at the time of the accident is +3 degrees C which is 18 degrees C below the lower limit of inflammability for kerosene in the vapour phase. It is known, however, that the lower limit of inflammability is extended downwards in temperature very considerably when fuel mist is present, but before this can be of significance to this accident, a means whereby fuel mist can be generated in the centre tank must be discovered[49]'

---

[49] The UK Government Health and Safety Executive offers the following information as to how this might occur. In the context of industrial hazard scenarios, there are four principal ways in which mists are usually formed:
1. Spray discharge from a pressurised liquid reservoir.
2. Condensation of a saturated vapour.
3. Agitation and splashing.
4. Air stripping.
In normal flight, with an unpressurised fuel tank, vapour at the temperature calculated, agitation and splashing being well within levels of safe containment and the fuel tank not being exposed to fast moving air, none of these were at all likely to be present. The reader, if interested, can learn more in 'Generation of flammable mists from high flashpoint liquids – Literature Review' by Simon Gant (HSE 2013).

Mid Air Collision

Meanwhile, the direction of the investigation took a sudden turn on 5th November when the investigation team became aware that a metal object, apparently from an aircraft, had been recovered from the sea near the island of Symi, ten to fifteen miles west of Rhodes, a few days previously. A report on 2nd November in the Greek newspaper Ethnos, linked the finding with Charlie Oscar, despite the not inconsiderable distance from the crash site, by pointing out that a police identity card belonging to a 'Miss Exeshea[50]' had also been found on a beach on Rhodes, having drifted some 100 miles from the crash site. The tank bore a tag with the following information written on it:

a. Capacity 335 gallons
b. Model 1F.100D/F
c. Part No. 180-48502-401
d. Date 7.28.65
e. Spec. No. MIL.T 7378
f. Serial No. OLO.976

This indicated that the drop-tank had been intended for use with a North American F100D/F Super Sabre fighter-bomber, an aircraft used by the USAF and the air forces of a number of other nations. Significantly, the drop-tank bore a small trace of red paint. The drop-tank had been forwarded to the Greek authorities where it was examined by the Greek Civil Aviation Administration, Royal Hellenic Air Force and Olympic Airways. Whilst it was quickly identified as being military in origin, and not part of Charlie Oscar, the trace of red suggested that it might have been in collision with an aircraft bearing paint of that colour. BEA's aircraft had red-painted wings and the airline's logo was, in fact, a red square. The intriguing possibility arose: had Charlie Oscar collided with another aircraft?

A mid-air collision could certainly have accounted for the sudden interruption to SFO Thomas's last radio message. It was also a solution that would have removed any suspicion that there had been security flaws at Ellinikon Airport; for that reason, the Greek authorities were quite keen that the possibility of a collision should be explored to the greatest extent possible.

Whilst there were no commercial aircraft movements unaccounted for, there had been some speculation that a collision with a military aircraft had occurred, although no nation was admitting to the loss of such an aircraft in the area at the time. The investigation records contain a handwritten page, author unknown but quite possibly Norman Head, noting that enquiries had been made in Athens to establish whether any other aircraft were missing. It transpired that a T33 training aircraft of the Royal Hellenic Air Force had crashed the day before Charlie Oscar, to the south of Crete. The crew had been rescued by an RAF

---

[50] Probably 21-year-old Miss Areti Exarcheas who was part of the group of Jehovah's Witnesses on board Charlie Oscar.

Search and Rescue vessel. On an unspecified date, but probably around the same time as the T33, a Royal Hellenic Air Force helicopter flying from Crete to Athens had landed at Sparta because of high winds. Due to communications issues, the aircraft and crew had been considered missing for some time before their whereabouts became known. At the same time, Air Commodore Johnson in Athens had contacted the British Air Attaché in Ankara to conduct similar enquiries with Turkish authorities. No reports had been received to date, but the author commented that 'Greeks have no knowledge of Turkish or other aircraft reported missing or damaged.' Additional enquiries were made with the Near East Operations Centre (NEOC) asking whether there was any explanation for Charlie Oscar not having been picked up on radar when she was passing the reporting point at R19C. The answer given was that it was possible to detect aircraft at R19C if the operator had specific cause to monitor that area, but it was not being watched in this case, the area being deemed friendly territory. The NEOC also confirmed that the only other aircraft in the area was BEA Comet Mike Foxtrot. A further note by the same author as previously recorded:

> 'Note of text of cable received by Carden (Olympic Rep. LAP). Telephoned here at 1415hrs. "Information received from Olympic Committee of Investigation: -
>
> The drop tank is held under guard at Athens Airport under supervision of Deputy Tech Director, Olympic Airways. It is a 355[51]* gal tank from an F100 aircraft. It appears to have been forcibly detached from aircraft as the attachment lugs are sheared off. Seems to have been in contact with something solid as the whole front end is concertinaed in such a way that experts exclude water impact damage. Distinct signs of red paint from the thing it hit. Date of manufacture of tank 28.7.65. In same area where tank was picked up an identity card was recovered, it believed to one (sic) of the Comet passengers.

The investigation team had, understandably, asked for the drop tank to be brought to England for examination, by BEA Argosy freighter. This was done, and the drop tank duly arrived on 20th November. The smear of red paint was considered to be the clue most likely to prove or negate physical contact with Charlie Oscar, so Government's Chemical Inspectorate at the Royal Arsenal, Woolwich, was tasked with carrying out a detailed examination. Whilst the results were awaited, Sir John Veal telexed the Civil Air Attaché in the British Embassy, Washington, with the details of the item, asking for information 'required with extreme urgency', of the country to which it had been supplied and, if possible, the aircraft identification. An answer was received the same day from Sir Patrick Dean, the British Ambassador to the US, stating:

---

[51] The drop-tank's tag showed the capacity as 335 gallons.

Above: A USAF North American F100 Super Sabre, carrying drop tanks, similar to that found in the vicinity of the crash site (US Air Force). Below: Diagram showing details of the fuel drop-tank (TNA).

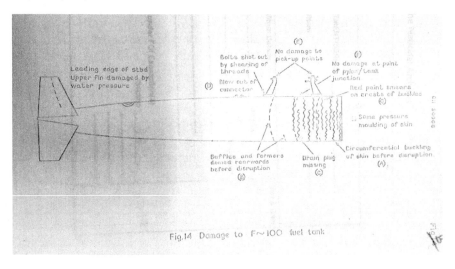

Fig.14 Damage to F~100 fuel tank

Enquiries so far have not been able to establish to which country auxiliary fuel tank serial no OLO-976 supplied and likelihood of doing so considered remote. Tanks are supplied to USAF, Turkey and France.

They are used as loose equipment in the USAF and transferable between units and aircraft. There are no means of identifying user unit or aircraft except where additional details are painted on tank.

USAF F100s known to fly in the general area of the Mediterranean in which wreckage found. This and first enquiries continuing.

Sir P Dean.

Sir Patrick was able to send additional information on 22nd November:

Further to my Allot 199 [52] still having difficulty in obtaining information on supply history of auxiliary fuel tank and enquiries continuing. From the information on identification plate however can be stated that it is not a tank delivered to the Turkish Air Force. The reported position of the Comet wreckage not on the regular routes flown by USAF F.100s in that part of the Mediterranean but possible for them to overfly on diversion or emergency. Suggested that enquiries made with HQ USAFE Wiesbaden, Colonel Patillo, Flight Safety Officer or with Technical Control.

The Ambassador sent a further message to Veal later that day:

According to North American Aviation Company's records if serial number OLO-976 correct part number should read 180-48501-502. Consignment of a number of these tanks shipped from plant on 3 August 1965 under packing sheet number 65-7892 to Aviano Air Base Italy, freight bill number 5682. Bill of lading number C-5098304. Shipped by air from Los Angeles under air bill number 015-LAX-737292.

2. Aviano is USAF Base housing 40th consolidated aircraft maintenance squadron, 40th tactical group, 17th air force, Ramstein, Germany, USAFE.

3. DOD requested to trace tank movement, but this will inevitably take time. Suggest direct enquiries made through accredited channels with HQ USAFE.

Sir P. Dean.

On 29th November, the eagerly-awaited results of the paint examination were fed back to Eric Newton, in a report by Mr. H Wells. Once again, the details provided show the extremely thorough and methodical way in which the examination was carried out. Mr. Wells noted that the paint smear on the drop tank had been examined and compared with some BEA Comet red paint applied

---

[52] Allot was a reference number for telexes.

to a test panel. The drop tank specimen consisted of a half-round section of light alloy 2¼ inches long, painted with a thin coat of yellow primer followed by a coat of aluminium paint and carrying a smear of red paint approximately 1½ inches by ¼ inch. The BEA Comet red paint was applied to an aluminium panel over a pale-yellow primer. The results were:

1. The general appearance of the smear did not suggest that it was the result of an impact.

2. The smear's appearance under microscopic examination suggested that it had been applied as wet paint, and that its presence on the drop tank was a result of contact with a freshly-painted object. A number of fibres were partially embedded in the smear and it was considered unlikely that these would have been present if the smear had resulted from a collision with Charlie Oscar.

3. The two red samples were each a fairly close match to a different British Standard colour of red.

4. Examination under ultra-violet light showed them fluoresce differently, suggesting a difference in composition.

5. When the spectrophotometric reflection characteristics of the two samples were examined, the BEA Comet sample showed a strong infra-red scattering, suggestive of a white pigment, which was to be expected in BEA's shade of red. The drop tank specimen had no such pigment.

6. The composition of inorganic constituents differed greatly, the drop tank sample consisting mainly of barium, calcium and silicon whilst the BEA sample was based on titanium. The drop tank sample contained no titanium; the BEA sample was devoid of barium.

7. Both paint samples contained phthalic acid, indicative of the presence of alkyd resin. However, this resin was widely used, and it was felt that this was not significant.

8. Tests with sulphuric acid indicated the use of quite different red pigment dyestuffs in the two paint samples.

9. Careful removal of the red paint smear on the drop tank with solvent revealed that there was no damage or disturbance to the underlying aluminium paint. That would have been inconsistent with the transfer of paint in a violent impact.

Mr. Wells was quite clear in his conclusion:

'The above observations, measurements of physical characteristics and chemical analysis show clearly that the smear of red paint on the piece of drop-tank differs significantly in composition from the BEA Comet paint, and that the smear is not the result of violent impact with a red painted object.'

Two days after Mr. Well's report, word was received from a Mr. van Cott of the US Embassy. He had been informed that the drop tank was one of a pair dropped by a USAF F100, tail number 50-3970, on 14th July 1967 in clear conditions at a position 15 miles south of Incirlik Airbase, Turkey, from where the tanks had been obtained. The aircraft had been towing a target drogue sleeve and the tanks had been jettisoned to ensure that when the drogue was released the cable would not foul one of the tanks. The pilot had watched the tanks until they hit the water. Jettisoning had been in accordance with international procedure.

Charlie Oscar had definitely not had a mid-air collision with the aircraft carrying the drop-tank, and no aircraft was missing or had damage to suggest contact with the Comet.

Engine Disintegration
The particles in the seat cushions had passed into them at very high velocity. One possibility considered for their presence was the disintegration of an engine, the number 2 engine (port inner) sitting just a few feet from the seat from which the cushion originated. The manufacturer of the Avon engine, Rolls-Royce, was consulted and Mr. Peter Marks, Technical Services Director of the company's Aero Engine Division wrote to Eric Newton:

> Further to our conversation on the subject of impact velocities of particles in seat cushions, our stress people have now come up with some results on the maximum speed at which rotating parts could be ejected from an Avon engine.
>
> At maximum take-off speed, the peripheral velocity of the three stages of turbine blading is 800 ft. per sec. From the IP turbine shroud alone – i.e., assuming detachment from the rest of the IP blade at take-off conditions – this would rise to 1120 ft. per sec.
>
> These figures, of course, make no allowance for the considerable influence of the casing in reducing the effective speed.
>
> As we suspected, therefore, impact velocities of the order RARDE have quoted for the particles in the seat cushion (3,000 to 20,000 ft. per sec.) could not possibly be produced by debris originating from the engine.

Whatever had been the source of the microscopic metal fragments, they had been travelling far too fast to have originated in a disintegrating engine. It was also clear that none of the bodies recovered, and subsequently examined by Mason and Tarlton, had shown any indications of smoke inhalation, extreme heat or other evidence of there having been a fire on board Charlie Oscar. Nor did their condition, and the circumstances of their recovery suggest that the airframe had suffered a catastrophic structural failure whilst cruising at 29,000 feet. As a result of the various workstreams, Newton was able to eliminate the possible causes on his original list. Only two significant possibilities remained; sabotage, and loss of control.

A Logical Man

The AIB now engaged with the Structures Department of the Royal Aircraft Establishment (RAE) at Farnborough, in the hope that they could put the explosion of a device into the context of a Comet 4B fuselage in flight at 29,000 feet. The work was supervised by Fred Jones, a 47-year-old structural expert, who had established a reputation as an air safety expert not least because of his involvement in the examination of the wreckage from the earlier BOAC Comet crashes. Fred Jones ultimately received an OBE[53].

Jones was a thorough man, with an excellent track record of deducing the cause of aircraft losses from the scantest of available evidence. His autobiography, *Air Crash – The Clues in the Wreckage*, gives plenty of evidence to suggest that he was indeed an expert in his field, with numerous examples of how he established the cause and the sequence of events from minute examination of countless pieces of wrecked aircraft. In the case of Charlie Oscar, however, he had to fill in the gaps due to the absence of any significant airframe wreckage, and work on the recollection of ground staff and disembarked passengers and crew as to who was probably sitting where. He was not helped by the fact that fifteen passengers were missing and four had not been subjected to post-mortem examination. Jones certainly had his work cut out with Charlie Oscar.

Jones' report[54] started with an overview of the flight, the material recovered from the crash scene and what was known of the passengers. He noted:

> Surface craft, engaged on recovery, were deployed in the two areas 'Northern' and 'Southern', and all bodies and flotsam were identified in the first instance, by these areas. It became apparent to the pathologists examining the bodies, that these could be divided into two general groups – extremely injured, and others. Furthermore, with a few exceptions, those in the extreme injury group were contaminated with kerosene whereas those only lightly injured were 'clean'. Investigators also noted that some flotsam was heavily contaminated by kerosene. The contaminated bodies and flotsam were all recovered from the Southern area. (Jones' emphasis).

Jones went on to consider what was known about the passengers and cabin crew, as discussed in Chapter 2. Jones considered that it was unlikely that the passengers originating in London had moved seats to any significant extent when re-boarding in Athens after the stopover. He commented that one group of passengers, now identified as the party of Jehovah's Witnesses who joined the

---

[53] https://moretimespace.wordpress.com/2009/02/21/fred-jones-obe-mraes-ceng. Fred Jones was the author of 'Air Crash: The Clues in the Wreckage'. He passed away in 2003 at the age of 82.

[54] Accident Note No. Structures 337: Note on the Loss of BEA Comet G-ARCO over the Mediterranean Sea on 12th October 1967 by F.H. Jones C.Eng., AFRAeS., Royal Aircraft Establishment, March 1968.

flight at Athens, were block-booked in the rear tourist cabin. However, although the part of the cabin occupied by members of the group had been ascertained, it was impossible to determine which individuals sat in specific seats. The body of one member of the group, he commented, had not been recovered.

Jones noted the weather data at the approximate time of the accident, adding that the wind strengths and directions at various heights were specifically relevant to his calculations of the trajectories of falling items.

RARDE had supplied Jones with certain information derived from their examination of the cushions, pathological evidence and their experiments attempting to reproduce the explosion in the cabin. He was advised:

a)   The explosion had occurred just above the floor of the aircraft.
b)   The explosion had occurred under the rear of a tourist type seat.
c)   That seat was occupied at the time of the explosion.
d)   That seat was on the extreme port side of the aircraft.
e)   One body, that of Mr. Afatitis, was injured in a manner to suggest that he had been in a seat one row to the rear, and one seat to the right, of that under which the explosion had occurred.
f)   No other body recovered contained evidence of a comparable nature to suggest close proximity to the explosion[55]

As was his practice, whenever possible, when conducting examinations of wreckage, Jones arranged for the flotsam to be laid out on a full-scale layout of the Comet on the laboratory floor at Farnborough. Jones found that all the flotsam originated in the Comet's fuselage, and he noted that all the materials aft of the front wing spar were contaminated by kerosene, and all those forward were not. Clothing associated with individual passengers, whose seating was known, could also be classified in this way. Jones also concluded, from the examination of the ten wristwatches, that Charlie Oscar had struck the sea at about 0325hrs GMT, 0525 local time, some seven minutes after SFO Thomas's last radio call. Finally, he included the earlier findings from examinations of the Graviner fire extinguisher and the F100 drop tank. His report summarised his analysis and conclusions, which subsequently represented a significant conclusion to the final Accident Report.

> The investigations by the AIB established the times and positions of the aircraft along its flight path… the flotsam and bodies were found nearly twenty miles back along the track from the estimated position of the last message.
>
> Although no airframe wreckage was recovered from the sea sufficient material was found in the form of carpets, furnishings, seat

---

[55] *These points are as summarised in Jones' report. They are somewhat more concise than the more cautious Mason and Tarlton, who noted some other injuries that might have been caused by the bomb and also stated that there were a number of bodies who might have had shrapnel fragments which was not identified in their forcibly-expedited post mortem examinations.*

cushions, passengers, etc., to give guidance as to the likely locations of the major parts of the fuselage in the sea. The natural division of all this material, by state, recovery area and identity, into two groups strongly indicated that the forward fuselage had landed in the sea in the northern area and the rear fuselage, and associated wings containing fuel tanks, in the southern area. Some seat cushions were found to the south between 1 to 1½ miles from the southern area. It is considered that separation of the fuselage into at least two major portions must have occurred before the aircraft struck the sea, to account for the distribution and state of the flotsam and bodies.

The examination of the flotsam suggested that the division of the fuselage, in the fore and aft sense, could have occurred at about the transverse datum position (centre-section front spar). Consideration of the general passenger injury pattern supported this finding. In general, those passengers forward of the transverse datum position had sustained relatively slight or intermediate injuries, whereas those to the rear had sustained intermediate or extreme injuries. It is apparent that such a division could only arise from the passengers experiencing very different circumstances, as in the case of breakage of a fuselage in the air.

Therefore, trajectory calculations were made on the premise that a fuselage separation occurred in the air at the front spar position. The design firm indicated that this would be a likely separation point under an ultimate loading condition.

Plots were first made from a specific point at 29,000 feet altitude, and the resulting scatter of debris and bodies at sea level noted. This distribution was too large to be reconciled with that seen by the search aircraft. Trajectories were then plotted from sea level upwards, from the general positions for items, as suggested by charts and maps from the search aircraft. A very close interception area of plots was found at about 15,000 feet altitude. It was concluded that the aircraft had not broken up at its cruise altitude, but at the lower altitude, to produce the general pattern in the sea of flotsam and bodies, and the damage and injury pattern to bodies. This conclusion was supported by the pathologists' report that there was no evidence of explosive decompression in any of the bodies, although this would have been expected if major disruption of the aircraft had occurred at a higher altitude.

A further indication that a fuselage separation had probably occurred in the air was given by the evidence of the discharged fire bottle. It was concluded from the recovery point of the bottle that it had discharged in the air due to operation of the inertia crash switch, located in the nosewheel bay, in the nose of the fuselage, and that this operation could be associated with inertia loadings brought about during a breakage of the fuselage at the front spar position.

If the aircraft had broken up at about 15,000 feet, then the heavier pieces of wreckage, containing passengers, or the falling bodies of the passengers, would have taken about two minutes to have fallen to the sea. If, therefore, the time of the final impact deduced from the watches (i.e. 0325 GMT) is correct, then break-up of the aircraft would have occurred at about 0323 GMT. This is five minutes after the last recorded message from the aircraft and would allow ample time for the aircraft to have passed its last estimated position on track at 29,000 feet and returned to the position of the break-up at 15,000 feet. No evidence was found by the RAE to give any indication of the flight path of the aircraft during the descent from 29,000 feet to 15,000 feet, or to explain the final break-up.

An attempt was made to locate the likely site of an explosion, which other investigations have shown to have occurred before the aircraft struck the sea. To recapitulate it appears that the explosion occurred under a tourist seat on the left had side of a row of three, that the seat was occupied, that the body of the occupant was not recovered and that the only body recovered with injuries of the type expected from an explosion, (i.e. no.6), was that of the occupant of the middle seat in the row behind. Unfortunately, passenger no. 6 was one of a group with a 'block-seating', so that his precise location in the cabin was not known, although it would have been in line B in one of the rows 3,4,5,6,7. The port side seats in this area would also have been occupied by members of the group, but none of these were injured in a manner to suggest they had been in close proximity to an explosion. However, one of the group was not recovered.

The nature of the damage to the seat, over the explosion, and to body no. 6 in line B, suggests that the effect of the explosion was not uni-directional. It is likely then that a person seated immediately to the rear of the explosion would also be injured by it. Since no such person has been recovered, it is possible that this was the person sitting in Seat 4A (known but not recovered) or was the missing group member, who may have been sitting in either seats 3A or 7A, i.e. behind either of two known but not recovered passengers. It would seem then that the explosion could have occurred under seat 4A, 5A or 8A, and that passenger no.6 was in seat 3B, 4B or 7B.

The aircraft itself was not at fault. The results of the ancillary lines of enquiry supported the view that the cause was the detonation of a bomb, and not to have been anything else. Scarcely six weeks had passed since Charlie Oscar had been lost, but the investigators had made the most of what little they had to work with.

It was now established that she had not been lost in a mid-air collision with another aircraft, been brought down by a disintegrating engine or failure of the airframe. On 20th November, with relatively little fanfare, the Comet fleet was cleared once more to fly at normal cruising altitudes. All that remained was to find out who had planted the bomb, and why.

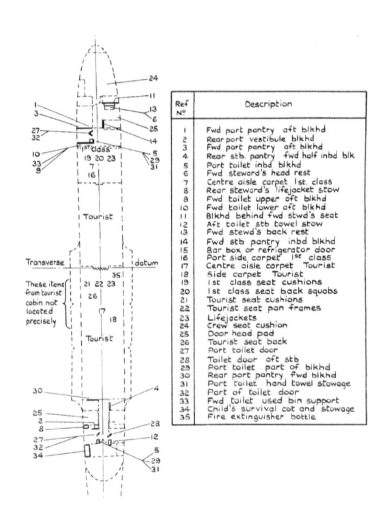

Ref N°	Description
1	Fwd port pantry aft blkhd
2	Rear port vestibule blkhd
3	Fwd port pantry aft blkhd
4	Rear stb. pantry fwd half inbd blk
5	Port toilet inbd blkhd
6	Fwd steward's head rest
7	Centre aisle carpet 1st. class
8	Rear steward's lifejacket stow
9	Fwd toilet upper aft blkhd
10	Fwd toilet lower aft blkhd
11	Blkhd behind fwd stwd's seat
12	Aft toilet stb towel stow
13	Fwd stewd's back rest
14	Fwd stb pantry inbd blkhd
15	Bar box or refrigerator door
16	Port side carpet 1st class
17	Centre aisle carpet Tourist
18	Side carpet Tourist
19	1st class seat cushions
20	1st class seat back squabs
21	Tourist seat cushions
22	Tourist seat pan frames
23	Lifejackets
24	Crew seat cushion
25	Door head pad
26	Tourist seat back
27	Port toilet door
28	Toilet door aft stb
29	Port toilet part of blkhd
30	Rear port pantry fwd blkhd
31	Port toilet hand towel stowage
32	Port of toilet door
33	Fwd toilet used bin support
34	Child's survival cot and stowage
35	Fire extinguisher bottle

A list of the pieces of wreckage recovered from the scene, and their original locations in the aircraft (RAE Report).

116

Above left: Fred Jones, OBE, C.Eng., AFRAeS, who examined the wreckage of G-ARCO at the Royal Aircraft Establishment. It was at least his fourth Comet examination (Lucas Black). Above right: A contemporary publicity photo of passengers enjoying their flight in a BEA Comet 4B (Capt. Maurice Hepworth). Below: Compartments of the Comet 4B fuselage. Note position of the aileron servo unit bay, underneath row 5 seats (Comet 4B Technical Manual, BEA October 1967).

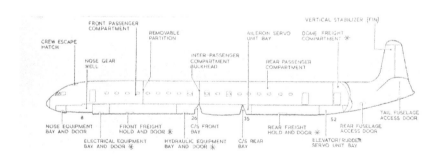

Above: The Tourist Class cabin of a Comet 4B. The bomb was believed to have been located in the footwell of the third or fourth row of seats from the back, against the left-hand cabin wall (Malcolm Hill). Below: G-ARCO on the apron at Heathrow, c. 1962. (JH). In both photographs the arrow indicates the place Fred Jones believed to be the likely site of the explosion.

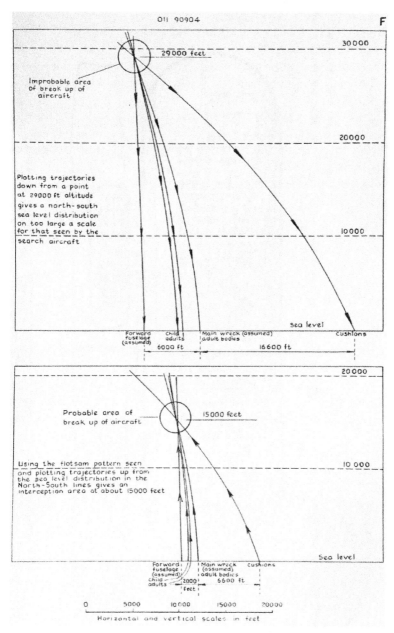

Fred Jones calculated the wreckage pattern that would have resulted from the airframe disintegrating at a number of different altitudes. The spread from the cruising altitude of 29,000 feet would have been much greater than the actual pattern. The best fit was from a disintegration at 15,000 feet (RAE Report).

119

The Bomb Theory

Some 27 seat cushions, recovered from the sea were submitted to RARDE by Eric Newton, where the investigation was conducted by Mr. V.J. Clancey, Principal Scientific Officer, with the assistance of other specialists[56]. They used sophisticated techniques, for that time, such as stereo-scan electron microscope, X-ray diffraction and fluorescence, electron microprobe analysis and micro-chemical analysis.

RARDE had been asked to become involved because of its facilities and experience in explosives technology. It also had specialised experience of forensic work in connection with explosives, and of investigating accidental explosions as well as bombs.

Evidence of an explosion of a high explosive, determined as being of a military or similar type, rather than ordinary gelignite, came primarily from the detailed examination of one particular cushion, identified as having come from Charlie Oscar's tourist cabin. This was supported by slight damage to another cushion, part of a torn shirt and also pathological examination of certain of the bodies, one of which had injuries believed to stem from an explosion.

The details of the evidence[57] were, firstly, superficial damage to the cushion, which consisted of a fan-shaped piece cut out of the cushion and surface-blackening, of a kind typical of an explosion. Straight cuts radiated from a common origin and must have been produced by a number of individual objects moving at very high speed, in the manner of fragments of material from an explosion. There were perforations in the cushion, through which wires were pushed. These defined the trajectories of the fragments that caused the perforations as emanating from the same origin as the cuts. X-rays showed the presence in the cushion of a large number of microscopic particles of metal. Their very small size, from 10 milligrams in weight down to microscopic, was consistent with having been produced in an explosion. The presence and distribution of such tiny particles of metal was also produced in laboratory trials with an explosive in a light metal case.

The examiners then carried out trials firing small particles at a similar cushion, whilst measuring the velocities. The penetration in the suspect cushion was caused by particles travelling at between 5,000 and 10,000 feet per second (3,000

---

[56] These are named in the above RARDE report as: Mr. Alfred Nichol-Smith, Chief Experimental Officer (in charge of metallurgical studies), Dr. George Todd, Principal Scientific Officer (analytical studies), Mr. R.L. Durant, Principal Scientific Officer (X-ray), Mr. J. Markham, Experimental Officer ((Stereo-scan electron microscope), Mr. D.F.T Winter and Mr. K.J. Jarvis (fragment velocity measurements) and Mr. H.J. Yallop and Mr. D.P. Lidstone (explosive trials). All are worthy of mention for their work.

[57] Accident to Comet 4B, G-ARCO – Interim report on examination of a seat cushion. D.F. Runnicles, Principal Superintendent, Explosives Division, RARDE, 1st January 1968, via The National Archives.

to 6,000 miles per hour). Such velocities could only be produced by an explosion. When the team examined the particles recovered from the cushion from Charlie Oscar under an electron microscope, they found many surface features characteristic of explosive effects[58]. They then compared the particles produced in their test explosion and found markings so similar that this was deemed conclusive evidence. Further corroboration came from metallographic examination of the recovered fragments, which showed crystal structure features characteristic of explosive effects. Finally, laboratory trials showed that similar metal fragments could only be produced using a military or similar high explosive. Notably, they could not be produced from the bursting of an aerosol can or other 'innocent' source.

Having determined beyond any doubt that the damage to the cushion had been caused by a high explosive device, sometimes referred to as an 'infernal machine', the examiners then set out to establish the precise location of the device when it exploded. They were assisted by the bespoke shape of the cushions produced for each of the five seats across the Comet's tourist cabin. The geometry of the damage to the cushion, location of fragments and the trajectories indicated a position where some parts of the cushion were screened by the seat structure. Because the two sides of the seat assembly were different, one bordered by the curved fuselage wall and the other by the aisle, and the two sides of the cabin required the designs to be mirrored, the only possible position for that particular cushion was on the port side of the aircraft i.e. under a seat numbered 'A', with the device being sited between the seat support and the cabin wall. The precise location was '...an origin in a limited volume some 12 inches below the seat, roughly in the vertical plane of the rear edge of the cushion and about 3 inches from the line of the port edge of the cushion'. This suggests that the location would therefore be consistent with the device being in the passenger footwell of the seat immediately behind that from which the cushion originated, and where it would have been clearly visible to any occupants in adjacent seats. The electron probe and X-ray analysis of the metal fragments showed that some were steel and some aluminium alloy. These were shown, with one exception, to be quite different from the few small steel fittings and the more widespread alloys used in the aircraft structure and seat. They were also different from the metals used in British detonators, and the team wished to continue with examination which would include comparison with detonators of foreign origin. The sole exception was a fragment of metal with a speck of brown paint; the alloy matched one used in a Comet passenger seat. Significantly, no fragments

---

[58] 'The particles have been produced mainly by spalling and have in the main a cupped shape with rolled edges. On their surfaces they show diagnostic features, such as cracking, the effects of hot gas washing and bombardment by high speed micro-particles. In some cases, they have caused the cushion material to melt and adhere to their surfaces.' -

Mr. V.J. Clancey of RARDE, Fort Halstead, shows the blast-damaged seat cushion at a press conference. His work proved conclusively that the damage was caused by a device consisting of military-grade plastic explosive (TNA).

of alloy used in the flooring were found; this proved that the device was not placed beneath the cabin floor, such as in the baggage hold. This was corroborated by the absence of any fibres from the carpet. Many fibres were recovered from the damaged seat cushion, having been driven in by the force of the explosion. These were subjected to chemical, microscopic and X-ray examination, which showed their origin to have been the fabric covering the seats.

There was also damage, blackening and tears to the bottom surface of the cushion which showed that the explosion took place while the cushion was in its normal position on the seat frame, and that it was weighed down in a way typical of there being a passenger sitting on it at the time.

A second seat cushion had minor damage which appeared consistent with the first. The perforations in the second cushion suggested, though not conclusively, that the seat had been behind a little to the starboard of the explosion. Once again, there was blackening to the under surface, except where it had been masked by the seat webbing.

Veal's minutes note that he held a meeting on 13th November, those present with him being Harper, Gordon-Burge, Head and Newton. The group discussed the position regarding the examination of the seat cushion, with Harper being tasked to attain a positive identification of the cushion. This was subsequently followed back through the aircraft manufacturers, via the companies in the supply chain, to Dunlopillo in Aberdare, South Wales, who had produced the foam material for the damaged item. As an evidential chain it was exemplary. Veal then noted:

> '...The possible effect on the structure of an explosion of the size postulated was examined. It was felt that as an alternative to causing cabin failure, damage causing local collapse of the floor could occur with resultant damage to the aircraft controls which could set up a catastrophic situation. Mr. Harper was given the explosive pressure characteristics and agreed to examine the implications towards cabin and floor structure.'

Part of a white nylon shirt had a few small perforations in the region of the right-side front which could, the investigators thought, have been produced by high velocity particles. However, they could not be certain of this.

The investigators considered the amount of explosive required to cause the precise damage recorded; from previous experience and laboratory trials, they estimated that the damage could have been produced by 'about a pound of high explosive' which had possibly been inside a mild steel tube or similar container.

On the basis of the evidence derived from the seat cushions, Ken Mason was asked to re-evaluate the finding from Case No. 6, Mr. Afatitis. The X-rays taken during the post mortem were examined again, and minute opaque particles were noted, these being very similar to those found in the cushions. Further supporting evidence, not conclusive in itself but considered likely to occur in cases of blast, was found in the presence of isolated cases of amputation of the legs of three passengers, a number of burst abdomens, the lung damage of the passenger initially thought to have drowned, and injury to the buttocks of an elderly female passenger, Miss Parzopoulou[59].

Mason did note, however, that it was impossible to say that these injuries were not compatible with those to be expected in a severe aircraft accident due to a cause other than blast. In particular, he urged caution in ascribing sabotage as a definite cause, considering:

i. Mr. Afatitis was the only case to show such injuries; his wife's body provided no such evidence, though she was one of the last victims to be examined and her use of her maiden name meant that the relationship was not realised until weeks later.

ii. The skin lesions were very superficial. However, the explosives experts consulted considered that was not incompatible with the blast theory.

---

[59] The passengers so described were all amongst the group of Jehovah's Witnesses who boarded at Athens and are believed to have been sitting together in the rear Tourist Class cabin..

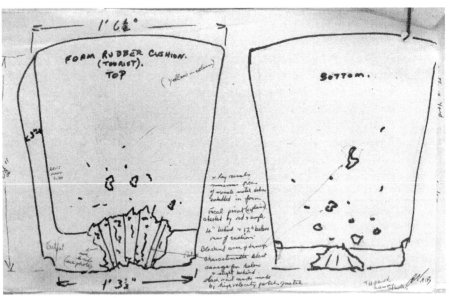

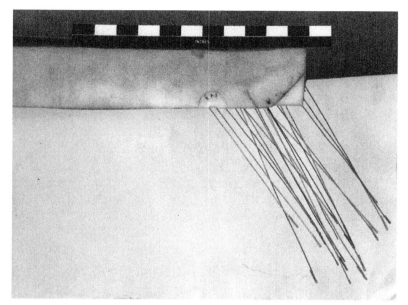

Left side (above) and rear (below) of the cushion from seat 4A or 5A. The wires extend back from the tracks made by very small fragments from the explosive device. They show that the device was on the floor of the cabin, next to the fuselage wall. Opposite page: annotated sketches showing the location of the device in relation to the seat cushion (TNA).

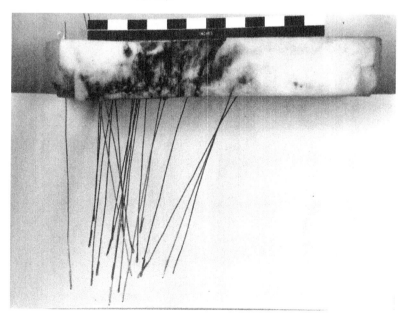

Mason and Tarlton could not state that the injuries sustained by Mr. Afatitis provided prima facie evidence of an explosive device causing the catastrophe. However, they did believe that such medical evidence could corroborate any such conclusion based on engineering evidence. Furthermore, they believed this would be of a device comprising plastic explosive rather than a grenade, and that this had made a difference to their ability to consider the injuries to the bodies to be prima facie evidence. At the time of Charlie Oscar's loss, previous bomb attacks on aircraft[60] had been undertaken with what were considered at the time to be conventional explosives, including the deliberate detonation of hand grenades or packages of dynamite or gelignite by suicidal passengers, and the use of a 'plastic bomb' was unique[61]. In light of the damage to the seat cushions, however, what might have been circumstantial evidence seen in the bodies was now sufficient to corroborate what the experts now collectively believed: an explosive device had been the root cause of the disaster.

---

[60] See Appendix 11– Airliner Bombings prior to CY284.
[61] Some consideration had also been given to a notorious 1943 murder in Rayleigh, Essex, in which a man in a bath chair had been killed by a device placed underneath the conveyance. On that occasion, the explosive had been an anti-tank mine.

Reference...EW/A/0102

LOOSE MINUTE

IDENTIFICATION OF CUSHION

In order to establish as close as possible the identity of the cushion which reveals evidence consistent with explosive damage a sample of the material from it was sent to the material manufacturers i.e. Dunlops Ltd. They have replied that this is a piece of P.J. Super Gold material as supplied to Progress Mercantile Co. Ltd., 246, Brixton Hill, who make up the cushions for B.E.A. (see attached).

Progress Mercantile Co. Ltd., have examined the damaged cushion and another undamaged one salvaged from the Mediterranean at the same time. They identify the cushion as made from P.J. Super Gold material, and made up by them to a specific pattern for B.E.A. Comet 4B tourist seat (see attached).

Both B.E.A. & Hawker Siddeley Aviation, who have also seen the damaged cushion, identify it as a B.E.A. Comet 4B tourist seat. I have also satisfied myself that from size, shape and pattern that it conforms to a B.E.A. Comet 4B tourist seat.

The cushions salvaged from the sea following the crash of B.E.A. Comet G-ARCO were packed in a box under Mr. Head's (A.I.B.) supervision in Greece. The box was flown to the U.K. by B.E.A. and was opened by A.I.B. personnel at the R.A.E., and the cushions laid out in the hangar. From there they were taken to R.A.E. & D.E. Woolwich by myself. From all the evidence there appears to be no doubt that the cushion damaged by explosive was indeed from the B.E.A. Comet 4B G-ARCO which crashed in the Mediterranean on 12th October, 1967.

(E. NEWTON)
Chief Investigating Officer.

C.I.A.
MR HEAD

A.I.B.,
Room 427,
Shell Mex House.
Extn. 107.
1.12.1967.

Minute sheet confirming the provenance of the seat cushion with damage caused by blast from an explosive device. This audit trail links the seat cushion to the Comet 4B (TNA).

'A v. First Class and Thorough Interim Account'

Following the work carried out by the team at RARDE, and the associated investigatory activity, Veal now believed that he had found the probable cause of Charlie Oscar's demise. Given his rise to high rank within the RAF and Civil Service, he was not, it would seem, a man given to rushed conclusions or driven by an urge to broadcast his achievements. As a result, his pronouncements were restricted to facts, and contained caveats that allowed for the possibility of further developments. On Friday November 10th, 1967, the following press release was telephoned to the Press Association for dissemination to the world's media:

> A number of lines of investigation are being followed up by the Accidents Investigation Branch of the Board of Trade, based on the Comet debris recovered from the Mediterranean and on other evidence.

> One of the seat cushions, which is believed to be from the tourist cabin, has been found to have sustained damage which is consistent with that which would be caused by an explosive device within the cabin at floor level. There is other evidence which is consistent with this having occurred, but which it would be premature to suggest confirms such an eventuality. Further experimental work and other investigations will be necessary before any definite conclusion can be reached regarding the relationship of this evidence to the cause of the Comet accident and before any further statement can be made.

Veal's rationale was probably that it was unlikely that any other, and more likely, cause would be established, and so it was in the public interest to make it known that the destruction of the aircraft was deliberate, rather than due to an inherent fault with the Comet.

In a minute to the Board of Trade, via Mr. Riddoch, on 15th November, John Veal considered the matter of a public inquiry, in anticipation of the likely demands for one forthcoming from various quarters:

> The President was given briefing on the implications of the evidence obtained from a cabin cushion on 10th November. There have been no further developments in the investigation which I can report at this stage. Although the possibility of the accident having resulted from a cabin explosion seems at the moment to be the most likely explanation, a number of other possibilities are still being followed up.

> The main purpose of a preliminary report on an aircraft accident is to enable the President to take a decision on whether the accident should be the subject of a public inquiry or whether the inspector's investigation should be completed. The criteria applied are:

128

(a) Whether the preliminary enquiries point to the possibility that serious negligence on the part of anybody, including manufacturer, operators, flying crew, traffic control or otherwise, might have been a contributory cause of the accident;

(b) Whether there was a serious structural failure or failure of equipment or any other notable occurrence which ought not to have occurred without serious negligence;

(c) Whether the procedure of a public inquiry would be more likely than an inspector's investigation, which is held in private, to enable the cause of the accident to be determined;

(d) Whether the accident itself was of a sufficiently serious kind, or attended by other circumstances likely to disturb public confidence either in the safety of travel by air or in the manner in which the functions of the Department or of the operators are being conducted, regard being had to any representations made by interested parties;

(e) Whether such measure of blame may be attributed to an individual as to prejudice his career.

At the moment it is not possible to answer questions (a) and (b) with certainty, although the preliminary indications are that the answer may be 'No'. I think the answers to(c) and (e) must inevitably be 'No'. As regards (d) there may have been some disturbance of public confidence, but it would appear that this has mainly been due to the press treatment of the circumstances. There has in addition, of course, been very considerable concern expressed by Comet pilots due to the absence of any indication of the probable cause of the accident.

In any public inquiry there would, of course, be problems related to bringing witnesses from Athens who were concerned with the handling of the aircraft on the ground during its stop, and those concerned in the search for and retrieval of the victims. These would be practical rather than insuperable difficulties. There have been no representations that there should be a public inquiry, and, in my view, nothing would be gained by it. If the President decides against a public inquiry, the inspector's investigation will be continued, and a report submitted. This, in accordance with current practice, would of course be published.

Jan Riddoch agreed with Veal in rejecting a public inquiry, adding:

I…strongly advise against one. Apart from the reasons he mentions, there may possibly be security matters involved and one cannot rule out the possibility of criminal proceedings…it is virtually impossible to institute criminal proceedings after the conclusion and report of a public inquiry, because the adverse findings of the court may seriously prejudice the possibility of a fair trial; further, the evidence available to sustain a prosecution is likely to become stale in awaiting the conclusion of the inquiry.

The final say was Mallalieu's, as noted by PG Statham, a secretary, on 21st November:

The Minister of State has read the papers about the accident to Comet G-ARCO on 12th October. He agrees that there should be no public inquiry into the accident.

The media has never been slow to speculate on activities behind the scenes, and on 26th November *The Sunday Telegraph* published a short and unattributed article, headed *MI6 in Comet Crash Inquiry*, in which it linked the Prime Minister at the time, Harold Wilson, with the matter:

Mr. Wilson is taking a personal interest in an investigation by British Intelligence into the destruction by a plastic bomb of the BEA Comet between Athens and Cyprus last month.

Following reports from MI6 it is almost certain that 66 people lost their lives because of an attempt to assassinate Gen. Grivas, commander of the Cyprus armed forces. Mr. Wilson is forced to play this down because of the Cyprus crisis.

Despite reports to the contrary, the whole investigation has been kept out of the hands of the British police. Normally Scotland Yard would be called in to discover who planted the bomb, and where.

This is invariably the case when a British plane and a Commonwealth country are involved.

Instead the criminal aspect of the inquiry has been handled entirely by Government intelligence acting in conjunction with the Foreign Office and the Board of Trade.

Gen. Grivas flew from Athens to Cyprus in another Comet on the day of the crash. His bodyguard, Mr. A Solomou[62] was on board the lost aircraft and it is almost certain that those who planted the bomb thought the General was on the same plane.

There is little doubt that the bomb was planted at Athens airport. Political extremists owing allegiance outside Greece may well have been responsible.

If the assassination attempt had succeeded it would have touched off the crisis between Greece and Turkey a month ago.

The Sunday Telegraph article, along with Veal's succinct press release identifying a bomb as the most likely cause, caused ructions in Greece. The same day, the Civil Aviation Administration in Athens put out its own release in rebuttal[63]:

---

[62] There is no evidence that Avraam Solomou was acting as bodyguard for General Grivas.

[63] Source is a telex from the British Embassy in Athens, the text being a translation by the Embassy from the Greek.

Following a BBC broadcast and comments in the domestic and foreign press…we again state that according to detailed proof received by us up to 20th November the above comments by the press and BBC have no relation with the true causes of the accident. We advise who are in a hurry to jump to irresponsible conclusions to wait until the appropriate legal authority submits its official report. This legal authority…is the Board of Trade, Great Britain. They should also wait for the concurring opinion of the appropriate Greek authorities.

The press release by the Greeks caused some consternation in the British Embassy, who telexed Veal the following day:

You will no doubt have seen the column in yesterday's Sunday Telegraph…In our opinion such speculation can only irritate the Greek Civil Aviation Administration by implying criticism of the security arrangements at Ellinikon airport. We should be grateful therefore if you could let us have your comment on the ST column and any further evidence on the "explosive device" mentioned in your own statements.

Veal immediately replied, in an attempt to provide reassurance:

If Sunday Telegraph article is other than complete speculation or kite flying, we are unaware of sources of information. The only information put out by us on explosion aspect is press release you have already have and answer to a parliamentary question on 22 November on Comet salvage in terms "In view of this (impracticability of general salvage and difficulties and improbability of successful salvage of flight recorder) and evidence which indicates detonation of a high explosive in the aircraft cabin my Right Hon Friend[64] has decided that the question of salvage should not be pursued". Letter indicating present position in respect of investigation is on its way. Expect investigation of explosive aspect to be completed shortly confirming occurrence of explosion.

BEA's General Manager (Operations), PCM Shillitoe, wrote to JWG James, his Operations Director, on 1st December, on the subject of Security at Athens and Nicosia:

At your request I endeavoured to discuss with Manager Greece or Woodroffe and with Savva the question of security at Athens and Nicosia in the knowledge that an explosive device placed on the Comet caused the accident to CO.

---

[64] Parliamentary term used when referring to a senior member of the same political party as the speaker.

SUNDAY TELEGRAPH 26 NOVEMBER 1967

M.I.6 in Comet Crash Inquiry

SUNDAY TELEGRAPH REPORTER

MR. WILSON is taking a personal interest in an investigation by British intelligence into the destruction by a plastic bomb of the B.E.A. Comet between Athens and Cyprus last month.

Following reports from M.I.6, it is almost certain that 66 people lost their lives because of an attempt to assassinate Gen. Grivas, commander of the Cyprus armed forces. Mr. Wilson is forced to play this down because of the Cyprus crisis.

Despite reports to the contrary, the whole investigation has been kept out of the hands of the British police. Normally Scotland Yard would be called in to discover who planted the bomb, and where.

This is invariably the case when a British plane and a Commonwealth country are involved.

BODYGUARD ON BOARD

Instead, the criminal aspect of the inquiry has been handled entirely by Government intelligence acting in conjunction with the Foreign Office and the Board of Trade.

Gen. Grivas flew from Athens to Cyprus in another Comet on the day of the crash. His bodyguard, Mr. A. Solemou, was on board the lost aircraft, and it is almost certain that those who planted the bomb thought the General was on the same plane.

There is little doubt that the bomb was planted at Athens airport. Political extremists owing allegiance outside Greece may well have been responsible.

COMPENSATION DELAY

If the assassination attempt had succeeded it would have touched off the crisis between Greece and Turkey a month ago.

Questions of international compensation are involved, but the Government is unwilling to aggravate the tense situation by pressing the matter immediately.

A B.E.A. spokesman said the airline had the relatives' interests very much in mind, but the investigation had been taken completely out of their hands by the Board of Trade.

The Sunday Telegraph article that caused ructions in Greece, and which was played down by Veal (TNA).

Unfortunately, both Antram and Woodroffe were away from Athens on Monday, but they had arranged for the Air Attaché to be at the airport to see me and I also spoke subsequently to the Station Superintendent and the Senior Operations Officer, Eastern Mediterranean.

Air Commodore Forbes-Johnson, the Air Attaché, was unaware that definite confirmation had now been received by us that CO was damaged by an explosive device and that this caused the aircraft to crash. He was expecting information from Group Captain Veale (sic) so that the final conclusion of the investigating party could be passed to the Greek authorities. I asked Forbes-Johnson that, as soon as he got official confirmation from Veale to pass to the Greek authorities he would seek their cooperation with BEA in endeavouring to take every possible precaution to prevent explosive devices of any sort being taken on to our aircraft either willingly or placed on board for sabotage. Forbes-Johnson agreed to do this but would discuss the whole question with Antram on his return to Athens on Wednesday evening.

On the way back from Cyprus on Wednesday afternoon I saw Woodroffe and explained to him what I had told the Air Attaché on the Monday. I also asked Woodroffe to send back to London as soon as possible his recommendations for action which could be taken at Athens in an effort to tighten up security.

I told Savva of Cyprus Airways that we had now conclusive proof that CO's accident was caused by an explosion on board and that Comet aircraft were as (safe) as ever. This was the first he had heard officially that this was the case. I asked him to make this absolutely clear to all Cyprus Airways flying staff on the Viscounts and to all cabin staff on both types of aircraft. In fact, as far as Comet cabin staff are concerned, they were to be extremely vigilant at both Athens and Cyprus to ensure that no unauthorised cases or parcels were present on the aircraft, and when in doubt to consult the Captain.

Because of the previous Falcon activities in the Eastern Mediterranean, Traffic Superintendent Cyprus Airways had got out instructions regarding safety precautions on the ground to take on all Cyprus Airways Viscount services to prevent sabotage. I agreed that these precautions should now be applied to all our Comets except for the case of freight which need not be held for 24 hours. In addition, no last-minute freight or baggage was to be accepted without proper examination and the baggage of passengers who had checked in and failed to respond would be offloaded before aircraft departure.

133

It seems to me now important that the official findings of our Comet accident should be produced as soon as possible so that in particular the Greek authorities, having accepted this, must take proper action to prevent a recurrence.

James forwarded the report to Veal, reminding him:

'We spoke about this at the BALPA cocktail party the other evening…I shall be very grateful if the Greek authorities and Forbes-Johnson can be advised in sufficiently authoritative terms of the cause of the accident, so that the former may be persuaded to institute the necessary checks at the airport to prevent a recurrence.'

Veal's reply to James, sent on 12th December, stated:

I have, of course, been in correspondence with General Skarmaliorakis, the Civil Aviation Administrator in Athens, and with Forbes-Johnson about evidence found during the investigation. I first wrote to the Administrator on 15th November telling him, amongst other things, about the cushion picked up with the cabin debris which showed damage consistent with what could be caused by an explosive device at cabin floor level. I followed this up with a further letter on 28th November in which I said that further investigation of the cushion, the damage to it and the particles it contained, indicated the detonation of a high explosive device within the cabin at floor level. I also told him that the medical evidence provided confirmation of the detonation of an explosive device.

We of course have no evidence that the infernal machine [65] responsible was introduced into the aircraft at Athens. Although some people might regard this as a reasonable assumption, I suppose the Greeks could argue that somebody took it on board in London and left it there when disembarking at Athens. Personally, I do not see that we are likely ever to get any evidence to resolve this aspect. This may indicate that your people will need to be very careful how they handle the matter with the Greek authorities but subject to this I would have thought I had already told General Skarmaliorakis sufficient for you to take some action in respect of preventative measures.

The work of the accident inspectors continued and on 12th December, Veal convened a meeting to bring together the various strands of the investigation, with the usual representatives from RARDE, RAE, Hawker Siddeley and the AIB. Mr. Clancey of RARDE gave a resume of the work of his colleagues, showing photographs of the fragments of metal retrieved from the cushion. The very high speed of the various particles detected, between 2,000 and 5,000 feet per second for the larger fragments and perhaps up to 15,000 feet per second for

---

[65] 'Infernal machine' is an archaic term for an explosive device.

the smallest ones, had helped Mr. Clancey to form the opinion that there was 'a complete certainty of the detonation of a high explosive'.

Mr. Clancey continued, explaining that, although originally it had been thought that the evidence suggested that one ounce of explosive had detonated, it now seemed possible that the device had contained at least four ounces. As stated previously, it was believed that the locus had been at the left-hand end of a left-hand row of seats.

Mr. Clancey's RARDE colleague, Mr. Jarvis, added that the pressures associated with one ounce of explosive would be 200 psi at a distance of one foot from the point of the explosion, reducing to 30 psi at two feet and 13 psi at 3 feet. However, these pressures would be quadrupled if the device had comprised four ounces of explosive. It was clear that the detonation of an explosive device could potentially cause catastrophic damage and the almost-immediate break-up of the fuselage structure.

On 18th December, Veal was finally ready to submit his formal interim report:

> Owing to the non-availability of the main aircraft wreckage the investigation of the accident has been concentrated upon examination of the cabin debris recovered from the Mediterranean, the results of the pathological examination of the bodies of the victims, the general circumstances of the flight and a F.100 drop tank subsequently recovered near Rhodes. In parallel with this the defect and repair history and the previous flight recorder data of G-ARCO have been studied and a detailed engineering investigation of other Comet aircraft has been made. Present conclusions on the matter are that: -
>
> (i) None of the victims of the accident were wearing life jackets and no wreckage, other than cabin debris and a fire extinguisher bottle, was seen in the crash area, with the possible exception of a circular object which may have been a cabin pressure dome.
>
> (ii) Examination of a fire extinguisher bottle, which had been installed in the right wing of the aircraft, shows it to have discharged as a result of action of the inertia switches, and that impact damage was sustained during the discharge process. It appears from investigation of the probable break-up sequence that the discharge of the bottle and the impact damage it sustained were associated with the break-up of the aircraft at a height. There is a clear demarcation between kerosene contaminated and non-contaminated cabin debris and bodies of victims which indicates at least a partial break-up of the cabin at a not inconsiderable height. Owing to the imprecise information on the points at which the various pieces of cabin debris were recovered it is not

135

possible to construct an accurate trajectory plot from which the probable height of the break--up might be determined. However, the work done in this connection and the amount of scatter suggests that the break-up was well below the original cruising altitude and might have been between 10,000 and 20,000 feet.

(iii) The injury pattern of the victims, 80% of whom suffered head and other body injuries and 20% of whom had little external injury, has been investigated against the limited information available on seat positions and taking account of injuries sustained by the victims of other accidents in which a structural break-up has occurred at altitude. The pathologist, in considering whether sabotage might have occurred, had in mind that this would require the presence of large metallic fragments in the bodies. No such fragments were found by X-ray although three pieces of aircraft material were found as a result of visual examination. As a result of evidence obtained from a seat cushion further investigation of the X-ray photographs was made and this is dealt with below together with the implications of the pathological findings.

(iv) One cushion picked up with the cabin debris, which was positively identified as a Comet tourist cabin cushion, showed damage which, as a result of exhaustive investigation and experimental work at the Royal Armament Research and Development Establishment had been caused by detonation of a high explosive device. The primary evidence for this is the gross damage at the rear of the cushion, penetration holes through the cushion and the inclusion in the cushion of a number of ferrous material and aluminium alloy particles. Examination of the particles has been carried out using electron microscopy and other methods which show that the pieces of ferrous and aluminium alloy recovered possess the characteristics of damage due to high explosive detonation and has enabled the origins of the particles to be ascertained. Investigation of the penetration grooves using a probe technique indicates that the origin of the explosion was approximately at cabin floor level and between two rows of seats. There is evidence that the cushion was in the left-hand seat of a left-hand row, i.e. adjacent to the side of the fuselage. Another of the cushions recovered has also been found to have sustained a number of penetrations which indicate that this cushion was

136

in the row behind that in which the other cushion was located. Cushion damage due to blast and carbon deposits within the penetration grooves of both cushions provide supporting evidence of the occurrence of an explosion. It has been calculated that the velocity of the larger particles found was between 2,000 and 5,000 feet per second and up to 15,000 feet per second in respect of the really small ones.

(v)   It was originally suggested that a F.100 fuel drop tank recovered from the sea, which had suffered gross impact damage and bore traces of red paint, might be related to the circumstances of the Comet accident. On visual examination the red paint was seen to be substantially different in colour from the paint on BEA Comets and chemical analysis has established that it is essentially different. The paint appeared under examination to have been in a wet condition when it came in contact with the fuel tank and it appears that its origin was something on which the tank was resting or which had been brushed against the tank. The damage to the tank is consistent with water impact damage and checking through American sources given reason to believe this was one of a pair of tanks dropped from a United States aircraft in July.

(vi)   Examination of the meteorological evidence indicates there was no reason to consider the weather was a factor in the cause of the accident.

Careful consideration was given to the possibility of search for and salvage of the aircraft wreckage and United States Navy experts were consulted on the matter shortly after the occurrence of the accident. From information obtained during recent surveys of the sea bottom it seems clear that the wreckage lies towards the southern edge of an abyssal plain.

Original examination of the problem indicated the area included a spot depth of 1583 fathoms but because of greater uncertainty about the exact position of the wreckage the likely area may well include a spot depth of 1600 fathoms.

This depth coupled with the distance from land and the likely nature of the slopes of the sea-bed, introduces exceptionally difficult problems. Having regard to these problems and experience gained by the United States in deep sea salvage work, it appears that salvage of the wreckage in any worthwhile quantity is quite impracticable.

Consideration has been given to the possibilities of search alone, or search associated with attempted salvage of the flight recorder.

Although search using.; modern sonar sidescan techniques could be used as a means of locating the wreckage, such a search even if successful in locating the wreckage and plotting its distribution would not provide useful evidence in relation to the investigation, having regard to the hydrofoil effect on the wreckage position in descending through the sea depths involved.

Experience of other accidents suggests that much of the wreckage would consist of small pieces which would make any search extremely difficult, lengthy and costly. It seems likely the flight recorder could only be located if it is still contained within the tail of the aircraft. In an accident of this sort the tail may well have been broken into relatively small pieces. Salvage in this case would involve a submersible such as the Reynolds Aluminaut. This might be able to secure the flight recorder with one of its articulating arms but this again would be dependent upon the wreckage not lying below the 9,000 feet limiting depth for the Aluminaut. Even if recovered it could well be found that the flight recorder did not contribute to the determination of the cause of the accident.

Thus, search and salvage would be a lengthy, costly and perhaps hazardous operation with little or no prospect of success. It should be remembered that the Palomares bomb salvage operation to which the Comet problem has been likened was in fact undertaken in water which is only about a quarter of the depth of that in which the Comet wreckage lies. The position of the bomb was known with reasonable accuracy and the salvage site was quite close to the shore. In reaching a decision not to attempt search and salvage the primary reason was impracticability, but in addition the evidence available of the detonation of a high explosive in the aircraft cabin has provided an argument that salvage is unnecessary.

When evidence of an explosion on board had been found from the cabin debris, the evidence available from the pathological examinations of the bodies was reinvestigated in an attempt to discover whether this showed any damage consistent with involvement in an explosion. This was complicated by the fact that only 51 bodies were recovered although 66 persons were killed in the accident and it was impossible to carry out complete pathological examination of all the bodies available. In addition the extent of the pathological examination was limited by the facilities available. This reinvestigation has shown in respect of one of the bodies sufficient medical evidence to provide confirmation of the occurrence of the detonation of an explosive device. In addition this medical confirmation is that the device was of the plastic explosive type and not of a grenade type.

This note is essentially an interim account of the present position of the investigation but it is intended to make clear that detonation of a high explosive device was associated with the loss of the aircraft. A report on the whole matter is being prepared and when complete will be submitted to the President of the Board of Trade in accordance with the Civil Aviation (Investigation of Accidents) Regulations, 1951.

As an adjunct, a note from Veal to Riddoch on 21st December adds:

'RARDE…have now reached a position of certainty that there was detonation of a high explosive device and that this was larger than originally estimated, being probably of the order of 4 ounces[66].' A handwritten addendum to Veal's copy of this note states: Thank you. The President has commented: 'A v. first class and thorough interim account.'

Veal also took the opportunity to inform Riddoch that his final report was dependent on the completion of subsidiary investigations, and that it was unlikely to be available until about the end of March. Veal had noted, in a message to Ken Mason, also on 21st December, that he had prepared the report as a resume of the investigation. He was still awaiting the final RARDE report, which he anticipated would follow by the end of January. He also noted:

'I am being pressed to submit my official report as soon as I can, and I have intimated that I would hope to do this within two or three months. This is, of course, dependent upon my receiving your final report and that of RARDE by the end of January.'

Mason replied on 5th January:

Thank you very much for your (report) of 19th December 1967 and the photostat of the report by Mr. Christopoules. As I told you on the telephone, I am a little worried about what is to happen to this report. In the interests of international cooperation, I do not want to argue with it publicly and I hope that you will be able just to ignore it.

It is apparent from this that Veal was not unaware of the pressure from various parties, not least BEA and the press, to state unequivocally what he considered to be the cause. There were also queries from the Greek and Cypriot authorities who were equally eager to see the matter cleared up. To this end, Veal sent a copy of his interim report to General Skarmaliorakis of the Greek Civil Aviation Administration and awaited his response.

John Veal had included the Attorney General in the limited circulation list for the interim report. The Attorney General, having read this, clearly deemed the matter of importance as, on 3rd January, a message was passed to Veal asking that he might see any further reports, including the final report, when available.

---

[66] 4 ounces is approximately 113 grams.

Meanwhile, back on 19th December, Hugh Gordon-Burge had issued a provisional report of the BEA Air Safety Branch, which he presented to The Chairman and Chief Executive of the airline, as well as their Air Safety Committee. In his covering note, he acknowledged that Veal had made available to the ASB much of the AIB's information on a confidential basis, and explained that, for this reason, his own report must be restricted to those on the circulation list. Inevitably the ASB report mirrored that of Veal, though it did add the following provisional conclusions:

1. The documentation of the aircraft was in order.
2. The pilots were properly licensed.
3. Whilst the aircraft was at cruising level between Rhodes and Cyprus, an explosive device detonated at floor level in some part of the tourist cabin.
4. The explosion within the cabin probably caused damage to the aircraft such as to render it effectively uncontrollable. Thereafter, and in the subsequent enforced descent, the aircraft broke up.

The original draft also included a line stating the first presumed cause: '*The accident probably resulted from the detonation of an explosive device within the cabin.*'

On 1st January 1968, following a telephone conversation with John Veal, Gordon-Burge wrote to the Chief Inspector of Accidents, sending a copy of the ASB's report and provisional findings. The report, he explained to Veal:

'…was prepared in response to the desire of members of the Air Safety Committee to come to a provisional finding based on all that was known and on all that had been done on looking at the Comet generally. It is felt that for the sake of our crews, our passengers and the aircraft we ought now to express our belief that the cause had been found.

The enclosed Finding represents the views of the Committee, as expressed at their meeting on Thursday last, 28th December 1967. Their wish is that their findings should be given the normal circulation of such documents, both within and outside the Corporation. I hope you may be able to see your way to allowing us to do this.'

There can be little doubt that BEA breathed a corporate sigh of relief when it appeared most likely that neither the Comet as an aircraft nor itself as an operator of the aircraft, would be found blameworthy in the tragedy. It was clearly to the airline's benefit that the cause, a malevolent act of mass murder though it was, might have happened in any aircraft and to any operator. The travelling public would have no particular reason to shun BEA or avoid booking a flight on a Comet. Dependent as it was on revenue from passengers, BEA needed to make sure that this information was shared as soon as possible.

Sir Anthony Milward, BEA Chairman, certainly appeared to feel the need to reassure the public when he spoke to a correspondent for The Times newspaper during a visit to the Cardiff Business Club on 8th January. The unnamed reporter appears to have had something of a scoop when their paper broke the news the following day, under the headline *'Comet was sabotaged, BEA says.'* Attributing the information to Sir Anthony, the article continued:

'Scotland Yard detectives have been called in by the airline to investigate. A separate investigation by the Board of Trade accidents inspector is still being carried out. Tonight an official said that no comment could be made.

(Sir Anthony) told me: "Our tests have proved it was sabotage. We made our own inquiry into the crash and a seat cushion showed that an explosive device appeared to have been on board."

He had no positive theory why the aircraft...was sabotaged. "It appears that someone thought the former EOKA leader General Grivas or one of his henchmen might have been on the aircraft, although I have no evidence that this was so", he said.

"Our own inquiries are now at an end and we have handed everything over to Scotland Yard. The official Ministry inquiry is still being carried out. I do not know whether that will agree with our findings."

Sir Anthony revealed that one BEA senior captain who was "highly strung" had refused to fly in Comets until after the result of the inquiry into the crash was known.

But he reassured the public that Comets were reliable aircraft. "I have the utmost trust in them. All restrictions which were placed on the aircraft after the crash have now been lifted and there is no need for anyone to worry", he said.

Meanwhile, the Londoners Diary section of the *Evening Standard* reiterated some of Sir Anthony's assertions the following day in a short piece titled *'Comet Delay'*:

Yesterday's statement by the BEA Chairman Sir Anthony Milward that the Comet crash off Turkey last October was definitely caused by sabotage does not indicate that the Board of Trade is ready to make any announcement about the result of its investigations.

In November they made a cautious statement that "one of the seat cushions thought to be from the tourist cabin is believed to have sustained damage consistent with that which would be caused by an explosive device" but they hedged this with remarks like: "Further experimental work and other investigations will be necessary before any definite conclusions can be reached."

And many months must still elapse before the final report is made public.

The paper then twisted the knife further by reporting that Captain William Baillie had expressed:

'…some dissatisfaction today with the length of time taken over a report such as this. He said: "John Veal told me about two months ago that there was clear evidence that a bomb had exploded under the seat – ballistic and chemical evidence.

"Whether it was put there with the express purpose of blowing the aircraft up or not, we don't know. BEA must have been carrying many passengers into Nicosia with warlike devices in their luggage."

Captain Baillie is inclined to think the bomb was not aimed at General Grivas.

It is fair to say that John Veal was not best pleased with the comments from the BEA men to the press. On 10th January, he sent a somewhat terse letter to Henry Marking, the airline's Chief Executive.

'The Times' of 9th January contained a report of an interview with Sir Anthony Milward in which he spoke about tests carried out by BEA in its investigation of the Comet accident.

As BEA have not provided me with evidence on your 'tests which proved it was sabotage' or your 'inquiry into the crash and a seat cushion which showed that an explosive device appeared to have been on board' I wish in accordance with Regulation 7(1)(b) of the Civil Aviation (Investigation of Accidents) Regulations, 1951, to take statements from those concerned. I should be glad, therefore, if you would let me know the names of the persons responsible for the tests conducted by BEA in respect of the sabotage aspect.

On 11th January, John Veal noted a conversation he had had, probably with Jim Templeton, from the Air Registration Board:

Throughout the investigation there has been close cooperation with the BEA Flight Safety Branch and they have been kept informed of the progress of the investigation and, in particular, of the work which has been done at the RARDE into the explosion aspect. To the best of my knowledge there is no truth in the statement by Sir Anthony Milward about tests which they have carried out into the explosion aspect nor, as far as I know, have BEA been in touch with Scotland Yard. The Special Branch and Box 500[67] have been kept informed by

---

[67] Box 500 is the pseudonym by which MI5 has traditionally been known, the label originating from the Post Office box used as its address. MI5 (Military Intelligence, Section 5) is also known as the Security Service, its role being counter-intelligence and domestic security. MI5 comes under the Home Office. However, Veal and his team refer to staff at 'Defence Intelligence', which might actually have been the 'Defence Intelligence Staff', a branch of the Ministry of Defence, possibly

me of the possible sabotage aspects so that they might make their own inquiries and I understand that the latest interim report which I have provided is being considered by the Assistant Commissioner and that the Director of Public Prosecutions is being consulted whether any further action should be taken.

Veal, however, was in no rush to make public the full details of his investigations. Writing to Marking on 9th January, he opined:

'Any expression of belief (in the cause of the crash) of this sort, or consideration of the need for it is, of course, a matter for you, but I am concerned that it is proposed to associate it with a report which is based to a considerable extent on information which I have released to BEA in confidence. Inclusion in it of a reference to the 'still confidential nature of relevant evidence, which has not been released by the Chief Inspector of Accidents' serves merely to make my position in the matter even more difficult.

I was under the impression from what had been written in the Press following the last statement in the House, and from the cessation of requests for more information, that there was now a general acceptance that the Comet accident resulted from detonation of a high explosive device in the cabin. If you have evidence that there still is public concern about the safety of the aircraft which needs to be allayed perhaps you could let me know so that consideration can be given to some further official statement about the progress of my investigation.'

As soon as he received them, Marking wrote two letters replying to Veal, in which he expressed his regrets for embarrassment caused and staying that had not been the intention. Marking offered to speak to the Air Safety Committee and ensure that they withheld publication of their report until a more suitable time. The second later, sent to Veal the same day, pointed out that Marking could not comment on the remarks attributed to his chairman, so he had referred Veal's letter to him. Details of any subsequent discussion on the matter, with or without coffee, between Marking and Gordon-Burge are not held in the files. On 25th January, Milward, however, did write something of an apology to Veal, though he could not help adding, *'I think, however, that Mallalieu's latest statement in the House has made our point adequately because he does make it clear that there was conclusive evidence of an explosion in the cabin.'*

On 15th January, the Greek Civil Aviation Administrator, Brig. Gen. A. Skarmaliorakis, replied to Veal. His take on events, and the outcome he desired,

---

working in conjunction with MI6, the Secret Intelligence Service, which comes under the Foreign Office. As the existence of MI6 was kept secret at that time, it is likely that access to its staff would have been via MI5.

were significantly different from those of BEA. The text of the letter as delivered to the AIB was:

I hereby wish to thank you so much for having kindly kept me as informed on the progress of the investigation carried out with respect to the accident of BEA's Comet G-ARCO.

Nevertheless, with a view to avoid eventual mistakes which might lead to undesirable misunderstandings between those concerned, I would like to note the following:

As you also believe the complete investigation of an accident like the one in question, in spite of the difficulties encountered, is considered by us of a primary importance for the influenced fields of the air navigation.

Such a necessity not being covered yet from the elements into our hands up to now, calls certainly for a reconsideration of the possibility to raise the wreck from the sea or at least to use a teleoptic or photographic machine which might prove adequate for the investigation of the bottom of the sea.

We are of the opinion that the lack of complete evidence for the rejection or adoption of certain indications of the causes of the accident does not constitute a certainty for formulating any views.

I should not fail to tell you dear Group Captain Veal that, apart from other points of your informative letters, on the accident in question, the following are considered by us as not proving yet convincing indications on the causes of the accident occurred.

a. The detonation of a high explosive device within the cabin of the aircraft at an altitude of 29000 ft.

b. The damages caused to the fuel drop tank of the a/c F.100 due only to the impact on the sea and the fact that the adaptation points thereof on the a/c do not present indications of a forced

c. detachment (this may be ascertained only by a trial dropping of the tank).

d. The impossibility of ascertaining the date of the history of the tank and from which a/c has been dropped.

We would greatly appreciate any action on your part tending to clarify the aforementioned and contributing to the effective investigation of the accident in question, which is of great concern to both of us, to you as competent of the investigation and to us for sentimental and more general reasons.

On the occasion I would like to inform you that, following your invitation, two representatives of our Administration will be made available and leave for London very soon in order to follow the investigation of the accident in question.

BRITISH EUROPEAN AIRWAYS

From the Chairman
Sir Anthony Milward, C.B.E.

Bealine House, Ruislip, Middlesex.

Telephone VIKing 1234   Telegrams BEALINE LONDON

CH/251

25th. January, 1968.

Group Captain J.B. Veal, C.B.E., A.F.C.,
Civil Aviation Department,
Board of Trade,
Shell Mex House,
Strand,
London, W.C.2.

Dear Group Captain Veal,

Thank you for your letter of the 22nd. January.

May I say at once that I do appreciate the necessity of you working in well with the scientists at RARDE and the other people who help you over these accidents, and we would certainly not want to do anything to upset this side of your work.

I am always told how very happy is the relationship between BEA and your Department and my remarks at Cardiff were not intended to spoil them in the least.

I think, however, that Mallalieu's latest statement in the House has made our point adequately because he does make it clear that there was conclusive evidence of an explosion in the cabin.

Yours sincerely,

Anthony Milward

Sir Anthony Milward's technical and somewhat-qualified letter of apology following his comments on the investigation made to a business audience in Cardiff (TNA).

The Greek authorities had as much interest in the actual cause as BEA, but they wished for a significantly different cause to be identified. For the airline, a security incident, involving the detonation of a bomb on a perfectly-serviceable and properly-operated and maintained aircraft would exonerate them completely. It would also allow the benighted Comet to retain its regained reputation as a safe aircraft in which crews and passengers could be absolutely confident. But that cause, much as it got BEA off the hook, would implicate security procedures at Athens airport and the accountable authority would ultimately be Brigadier-General Skarmaliorakis' Civil Aviation Administration. He, therefore, would rather have been informed that the cause was a mid-air collision with a non-Greek aircraft in international airspace.

The two representatives introduced by Skarmaliorakis were Mr. G. Papadimitropolous and Mr. Hazardas. On 20th January, along with Mr. M. Carder of Olympic Airways, who might have been a translator, they met with Messrs. Clancey of RARDE, Forsyth of RAE and Norman Head of the AIB. Clancey produced the cushion and accompanying photographs and explained the details of the evidence. He also showed the visitors x-ray photos of the passenger, Mr. Afatitis, injured by the explosion.

In the course of what was described[68] as 'a considerable discussion', Clancey went into the rationale for the theory that the bomb had been placed on the left-hand side of the aircraft, between the seat and the side of the fuselage[69]. The Greeks were then shown the available wreckage of Charlie Oscar, as well as the F.100 drop tank. Following this, Forsyth explained the wreckage plot and the evidence suggesting the break-up at 15,000 feet. The Greeks were apparently satisfied that the drop-tank had been jettisoned on a different occasion when it was pointed out that there was no drain plug in the tank. After being presented with relevant documentation, the Greek visitors expressed the opinion that they agreed with the findings, though they said they expected some difficulty in persuading some of the people in Athens that the cause had, in fact, been a bomb. They were offered the opportunity of further discussions with their own explosive experts should they so wish.

The picture of exactly how Charlie Oscar and her passengers came to grief was now as clear as it was ever likely to be. But an explanation of how and an explosive device came to be on the aircraft, who put it there and why, were questions beyond the scope of both Mason and Veal's expert teams.

---

[68] Unattributed 'Note for the Record' – Meeting with representatives of the Greek Aviation Administration at RAE on 20.1.68, The National Archives, Avia101/218.

[69] Various descriptions of the locus place the bomb either underneath, just behind or at the side of the seat in question. However, the most compelling description is 11½ inches below and 4½ inches behind the back of the cushion. This is supported by sketches contained in the National Archives files.

'An Impressive, Fascinating and Convincing Report'

On 12th July 1968, John Veal was at last in a position to present his final report into the Charlie Oscar disaster. By way of introduction, he attached a comprehensive covering letter, which reiterated the basic facts of the crash and the thorough investigation. After highlighting the excellent work of those involved, including RARDE and the RAF Institute of Pathology and Tropical Medicine, Veal went further into the police investigation:

> The Greek authorities, because of initial content, particularly in British newspapers, that the occurrence was an attempt on the life of General Grivas and because of the apparently adverse reflection on security at Athens, advanced the view that loss of the aircraft had resulted from a collision, probably with a Turkish fighter. When an F.100 drop tank was recovered from the sea three weeks later they pressed this view with renewed vigour, but investigation showed that the tank had been dropped from a U.S. fighter probably about three months before the Comet accident. The Greek authorities have been kept informed of the progress of the investigation and their representatives were shown the explosion evidence during a visit to London. I understand from our own police that security arrangements at Athens are now very strict and that access of unauthorised persons to the aircraft and apron is now effectively prevented.
>
> Inquiries were initiated through the appropriate channels immediately after the accident against the possibility that there had been sabotage of the aircraft for political reasons, but with negative result. Immediately evidence was forthcoming that an explosive device had in fact been detonated on board, information was passed to the Special Branch. Subsequently arrangements were made through the. Home Office for the criminal aspects to be investigated by Scotland Yard; this was undertaken by Detective Superintendent Browne a copy of whose report is in the envelope at Doc. 2. There is circumstantial evidence which points to the possible involvement of one particular passenger whose body was not among those recovered. A copy of the police report has been sent to the Director of Public Prosecutions by the Commissioner of Police.

Veal finished off by spelling out the two significant future developments, to aid the recovery of flight recorders and, hopefully, to make it more difficult for bombs to be smuggled onto aircraft in the first place.

> My report recommends that (a) development of underwater separation, flotation and location devices which would facilitate recovery of the flight data recorder when an aircraft crashes in the sea

should be actively pursued with a view to separation, flotation and location capability being required for future flight data recorders, and b) the feasibility of developing means of detecting the presence of explosive devices should be further studied with a view to assisting airlines and aerodrome authorities in their security measures. These recommendations are being followed up by the Director of Flight Safety. Developments currently taking place should lead to the achievement of the objective of (a), but it is necessary first to achieve adequate safeguards against inadvertent ejection.

The possibility of detecting explosive devices is already receiving a great deal of attention particularly in the military field in respect of mines, but civil aircraft freight and passengers introduce their own special problems. Although I have no great expectation that there will be any immediate break-through in this field, the feasibility study recommended would at least provide concrete evidence of effort if, unfortunately, we were faced with another event like the Comet; and it has to be remembered that there have been seven known cases of sabotage of civil aircraft by explosive during the last six years, while three of these occurred in 1967. At best, through the co-ordination of scientific effort and by application of advanced technology some advance might be made.

In this connection it is interesting to note that the final conclusion of a paper on accidents due to sabotage which is being prepared by the United States National Transportation Safety Board is, "Since the inflight bomb explosion problem is worldwide in nature, it is suggested that consideration be given to pooling international technical resources to achieve a successful solution to the bomb detection problem." The feasibility study recommended, which will be pursued with the appropriate Research Establishment through our scientific adviser, would make a practical contribution towards this objective.

At the Board of Trade, the new Minister of State, Bill Rodgers, commented: *"An impressive, fascinating and convincing report. I support the recommendations."* The President of the Board of Trade, Anthony Crosland, was equally complimentary:

"The thoroughness of this report reflects exceptional credit on Group Captain Veal and his staff. The recommendations are wholly acceptable. I imagine our thanks have been conveyed to RARDE and other outside bodies who co-operated so helpfully in the Inquiry."

Crosland suggested, as an afterthought, that if no 'thank you' letters had yet been sent, he would be quite prepared to write them himself.

The press, meanwhile, had lost none of its enthusiasm for generating dramatic headlines, no matter how carefully phrased any press releases or similar comments might be. On 21st November 1968, for example, the *Birmingham Post* excitedly revealed, *'Comet death crash – it was a bomb meant for Grivas':*

The British European Airways Comet 4b which crashed into the Mediterranean last October was destroyed by an explosion in the tourist class accommodation, states the report of the Board of Trade Accident Investigation Branch, published today.

And Scotland Yard investigations reveal that it was planted in a plot to kill former EOKA chief, Gen. Grivas, leader of the Cypriot armed forces...

After Board of Trade crash investigators had found the first signs that the aircraft had been damaged by an explosion at the end of January, detectives from Scotland Yard carried out a thorough investigation into the possibility of sabotage.

Superintendent Percy Browne and Det. Sgt. Peter Hill flew to Greece and Cyprus and spent most of February and March on the investigation. They interviewed relatives of passengers and looked into allegations that the explosive device was meant for Gen. Grivas, who was returning from Cyprus to Greece that day. He actually returned on a later flight.

A Scotland Yard spokesman said last night that Supt. Browne's report on the criminal aspects of the crash had been submitted to the Director of Public Prosecutions.

"It had been decided, that on the evidence available, no action should be taken," he said.

The crash investigators base their report that the Comet was destroyed by an explosion of a military-type explosive in a mild steel container on the evidence contained in a foam rubber seat cushion...the Board of Trade report blandly states that "the aircraft broke up in the air following the detonation of a high explosive device within the cabin."

But the report cannot completely answer the vital question – was the explosion accidental or was the aircraft sabotaged?

But at a press conference in London, Mr. V.J. Clancey, the explosives expert (from RARDE) who investigated the evidence, was in little doubt about how the blast was caused. He explained that his laboratory tests into the type of explosive used had proved beyond doubt that it had been a military-type explosive like TNT or RDX which had wrecked the Comet.

High-velocity explosive would not explode without a detonator or a timing device, he said. It was almost unknown for a detonator to go off by accident.

Home-made timing devices were another thing altogether, he said. The could go off at almost any time. But timing devices were not put on board an airliner with powerful high explosives without a purpose. The experts also ruled out the possibility of an accidental explosion of something like an aerosol hairspray in a passenger's handbag...

The Board of Trade investigators recommended in the report that flight recorders should be developed to detach themselves from an aircraft when it submerges after a crash at sea. The box could then float to the surface, and if fitted with a radio location device, recovery would be made far easier.

They also recommended that the Board of Trade should start studies into developing an effective device which would detect explosive devices in an aircraft or in passengers' luggage.

Part Three: Crime and Politics

Call in the Yard

The conclusion by RARDE, accepted by Veal, that the cause of the disaster was a bomb was not exactly a bolt from the blue. From the first day, there had been widespread speculation, in the press and elsewhere, that this was no accident, but a deliberate act of malice. Indeed, it was speculated, as stated above, that it was an assassination attempt on the life of General Georgios Grivas. As a potential offence of mass murder, therefore, the matter was of significant interest to the authorities, including the security services.

Two members of the Defence Intelligence section of the security services, identified as Suckling and Arnott, approached John Veal's team the day after the crash, asking for a list of passengers who joined at Athens, a booking list and also for a check to be made to see if Grivas had been booked as a passenger to Cyprus over the following week.

On 20th October, whilst the security services were doubtless digging around in the shadows, Michael Lester, the Company Secretary of BEA, wrote to Jan Riddoch, with details of a former BEA employee who had left the airline in acrimonious circumstances:

> 'Mr. Georgiou was employed as a loader and the corps of loaders does, of course, include some of the rougher elements of the community. I gather he was not popular and some of the loaders had sons in Cyprus and at least one of them had been killed. I think this gave rise to a certain amount of acrimony against Georgiou and the upshot of it was that he resigned from BEA. The (attached) file deals with Georgiou's subsequent complaint that he was improperly dismissed.

> Georgiou made a number of verbal threats to blow up various bits of BEA property, including an aeroplane and in about the middle of April last year he went so far as to write to me threatening to blow up one of the aeroplanes. He was investigated by the police at the time and appears to have undertaken to behave himself.

> One of the passengers on the Comet was a Mr. S. Georgiou[70] who is down on the passenger list as being an American citizen though I do not know what evidence there is to substantiate this as his body was not recovered. Mr. S. Georgiou was traveling on a 21-day excursion to Nicosia. He flew from New York to London on the 9th October on BA506 arriving on the morning of the 10th. He had a 24 hour stop-over in London and left on BE284 for Athens and Nicosia on the 11th October. When he left London, he had 4 kilos of excess baggage and

---

[70] Sotiris Georgiou was in seat 4A. As stated, his body was never recovered.

we are pursuing enquiries with BOAC to see whether he brought any excess baggage in with him from New York[71].

This passenger was checked in for the Athens / Nicosia flight but as his body was not recovered we do not know for certain that he actually boarded the aircraft and I understand there is some question of the aircraft having left Athens one passenger short – although this is not confirmed[72].

A handwritten 'PS' confirms, *'BOAC say he had no excess baggage New York – London.'*

Veal replied formally to the security services a fortnight later, on 26th October, enclosing a copy of the passenger list and a statement from Mr. Mastin. He added:

> 'It is understood that General Grivas travelled to Cyprus on the service which also departed from Athens later on 12th October.
>
> Since Mr. Tench spoke to you, Mr. Lester, the Secretary of BEA has brought to our attention threats made by a Mr. George Georgiou, a Cypriot who is a former BEA employee…It seems somewhat unlikely that Mr. George Georgiou could be the same person as Mr. S. Georgiou who was stated as having US nationality. However, I should be glad if you would consider whether any follow-up can be made in respect of this particular threat.'

Ronnie Martin, the BEA Manager in Beirut, also felt it would be useful to pass on an account from an unnamed friend of his, who had apparently been booked on Charlie Oscar but, due to a last-minute cancellation had been able to secure a seat on the Olympic Airways flight later on 12th October:

> 'When he got to the airport there was somewhat more commotion than usual, but eventually cleared the usual airport controls and went into the departure lounge. His flight was delayed and on enquiring into the reason was casually brushed off. Eventually a further delay was announced, and, on this occasion, he gathered that a VIP party was travelling. The further delay was bought about by Olympics (sic) bringing another aircraft out of the hangars and loading it with baggage etc. which had already been loaded on the aircraft which was supposed to have operated the service.
>
> My informant was travelling economy and on boarding the aircraft found the 1st Class compartment closed. Whispers had it that General Grivas was aboard and that he should have been on the BEA Comet which left Athens early on the same morning. Even at that time none of the passengers seemed to be aware of the BEA disaster because on flying over the scene of the accident the Olympic stewardess was

---

[71] It is possible that, as Mr. Georgiou was travelling to visit family in Cyprus, he bought additional items whilst in London, thereby avoiding excess baggage charges from New York.
[72] Nor does it appear to be mentioned elsewhere.

heard whispering to someone that that was the approx. point where the BEA Comet had crashed. This was heard by a few passengers and she was questioned – and informed them that an accident had occurred earlier that morning.

PS I understand that Grivas and his party disembarked off the Olympic service at Nicosia.

As with other correspondence, Veal passed this to a Mr. Sidwell, of DI6[73], a branch of the security services, commenting:

'...I think the delay referred to in the letter was occasioned by Olympic Airways changing the aircraft as a precaution in the knowledge that an accident had occurred.'

On 9th November Veal and Head discussed with Sidwell the relevant developments in the investigation, in relation to the sabotage aspects. Sidwell explained that the passenger lists were being followed up through Athens and Nicosia, but so far these had been negative. Sidwell assured the investigators that those concerned were aware of the urgency of the matter. It had, though, been established that George Georgiou was still living in London, so had not been on the aircraft.

Sidwell accepted the possibility that the damage to the cushion might have been caused by high explosive and pointed out that there were a very great number of 'experts' in Cyprus who would be capable of handling such a device. He did, however, find it difficult to believe that anyone would use the small amount of explosive suggested by the RARDE experiments. Sidwell thought it was a reasonable explanation that, in fact, it had been a bigger device and there had been incomplete combustion; in that case the peppering found on the body of Mr. Afatitis, since it showed evidence of high temperature, could have been incompletely burnt particles of explosive.

Sidwell was informed of the possible need for the AIB to put out a press release about the explosion. He did not think that it would prejudice the enquiries being carried out by DI6; in some respects, it might possibly help them.

The same day, Veal and Newton discussed the finding of RARDE with Chief Inspector Bryan, of Scotland Yard's Special Branch. They again mentioned the proposed press release and, after consulting his Commander, Bryan confirmed the police would have no objection, having regard to the elapsed time since the crash and what the two policemen considered to be the 'improbability of any successful criminal proceedings'.

On 17th November, Veal received a letter from one Frank Ellson-Jones, purportedly Technical Adviser to de Havilland, the original manufacturer of the Comet, speculating on the possible mechanism by which a bomb might have

---

[73] Possibly a branch of the Defence Intelligence Service, part of the Ministry of Defence.

been triggered. It appears, on the face of it, entirely plausible and has, in fact been suggested to the author by other credible sources[74].

'When aircraft are operating through such a politically dangerous area the thought that hostile elements will be prepared to sacrifice the aircraft and its entire complement in an attempt on the life of one person cannot be excluded...the question of remotely detonating a bomb at the point on the route where the wreckage would fall into deep water arose...I realised that this would be a relatively easy mater since the construction of a battery-powered transistorised receiver is both simple and cheap. Such a receiver would make an excellent trigger because, if it were crystal controlled to the Nicosia FIR frequency (126.3 MHz), the first signal it would receive on the Athens-Nicosia leg would be at 30 deg E which is the changeover point between the FIRs and, by coincidence, is also in the area of the deepest water under airway RED 19.

The receiver specification would be very simple because there is always plenty of VHF signal around inside an aircraft cabin or baggage hold when the onboard transmitter is operated.'

Veal wrote again to Mr. Suckling at MI5 on 17th November. His letter covered both the threat from Middle Eastern terrorist groups and the thoughts of Mr. Ellson-Jones

I enclose a copy of a letter which I have received from our Civil Air Attaché in the Middle East which appears to refer to the Palestine Liberation Army. I think you already know from Mr. Sidwell that one of the tourist seat cabin seat cushions has been found to have sustained damage consistent with that which would have been caused by an explosive device within the cabin at floor level. An interesting possibility of how such an explosive device might be remotely detonated is suggested in a letter from Mr. Ellson-Jones, a copy of which I also attach.

On 20th December, Veal had sent a copy of his interim report to Chief Inspector Bryan. In addition to the explanation given to other recipients reiterating the most likely cause as being a bomb explosion, Veal added in this letter:

You asked whether it would be possible to provide some interim report against which you could consider whether any police action could or should be taken in the matter and the purpose of this letter is provide this to you.

Shortly after the accident we got in touch with Mr. Suckling of Box 500 and asked him to look into the possible sabotage question. This of course was before we had any evidence whatsoever about the

---

[74] These include colleagues of the author with relevant experience in such matters, as well as Louis Loizou, who had military experience with the Cypriot defence forces.

occurrence of an explosion. I have had no final report from him but when I previously enquired, I was told that nothing had come to light in Athens or Nicosia.

Chief Inspector Bryan spoke to Veal on the telephone on 4th January to acknowledge receipt of the interim report. He told Veal that preliminary consideration had been given to the matter but there was some doubt whether there was any police action that could be taken and sought Veal's views.

Veal replied that he had brought the matter to the attention of Scotland Yard because he felt that he had a responsibility to do so; however, it was not for him to decide what action the police should take. If they felt that nothing could be done, Veal thought that he would have to accept that decision, though he would like to have something in writing should that be the case, as he would need to refer to it when submitting his final report.

Chief Inspector Bryan was subsequently told that the Attorney General was taking an interest in the investigation and had asked for and been given a copy of the interim report. The Attorney General had also been advised that the matter had been referred to the Special Branch.

On 30th January, there having been a discussion involving Whittick, Veal and Riddoch, the latter wrote back setting out the reasons why there should be police inquiries. The Home Office man had raised the question of cost, as the Metropolitan Police was funded equally by the Exchequer and the ratepayers of London.

Riddoch explained that the purpose of an accident investigation is to establish the cause, this having been done, adding that the AIB considered it important from the safety point of view to ascertain the means by which the explosive device was placed on board, so that precautions could be taken to prevent a recurrence. He pointed out that it was not known whether the bomb was put on board in Athens or the UK, but there was no doubt that the act was deliberate. Nor was it known whether the purpose was political or to obtain an insurance pay out. Riddoch stressed:

> Whatever doubts you may have about the responsibility of the Metropolitan Police for investigating crimes on board British aircraft, I hope that there is no doubt whether such a serious crime as the Comet accident, involving the death of 66 people on a British aircraft (many of them British subjects) should be investigated.
>
> You suggested a meeting to clarify the general responsibilities of the Police in investigating crimes on board aircraft. We would be grateful if you would arrange such a meeting. I confess I am in a state of confusion about the jurisdiction and responsibilities of the various authorities.'

On 31st January, Detective Superintendent Percy Browne, of Scotland Yard, telephoned Veal to say he had now taken over the docket on the Comet accident.

The meeting suggested by Whittick took place in his office on 5th February. There were representatives from the Home Office, Riddoch and colleagues from the Board of Trade, Mr. John Macrae of the Foreign Office along with Mr. K. Parker and Assistant Commissioner P.E. Brodie of the Metropolitan Police.

Whittick explained that police forces in Britain were locally funded, each being responsible for policing in its own local area, costs of each being met half by central funds and half by local ratepayers.

A police force could not normally accept the responsibility for investigating an offence that happened outside its own area, though the Metropolitan Police did have certain responsibilities extending to other parts of the UK, so there would need to be some special justification for a British police force to investigate a crime committed outside the UK, though it was pointed out that the incident had occurred in international airspace. The Home Secretary's policing remit did not appear to extend beyond the UK so, Whittick explained, it did not appear to be up to the Home Office to make the case for the Metropolitan Police to investigate the crime.

Riddoch reiterated the points he had made in his letter to Whittick, essentially confining the role of the Board of Trade in criminal investigations to matters concerned with safety. The Board paid the Airports Authority for assistance given by their airport police teams in investigating any such offences, which primarily involved offences against the Air Navigation Order involving the safety of passengers. He noted that the attitude of the Greek authorities, persisting in attributing the loss of Charlie Oscar to a collision with a Turkish aircraft, meant that the established cause, sabotage by bombing, was not being investigated. Riddoch felt that there was no alternative to the Metropolitan Police investigating the crime.

Mr. Parker, whose role was Receiver for the Metropolitan Police District, said that precedents related to serious crimes aboard ships and were not wholly consistent. However, they did indicate that, as a rule, the cost of a police investigation overseas was reimbursed. In one case, involving sabotage, the Ministry of Transport had footed the bill and in other cases, the ship owners had reimbursed the police. Not surprisingly, perhaps, he felt that the burden should not fall upon the Metropolitan ratepayers.

The group agreed amongst themselves that, while the law on jurisdiction was quite clear – a court in the UK could deal with an offender in the UK who had committed an offence on a British ship or aircraft overseas – there was no specific provision in the statutes on actually investigating such crimes. Rather than taking the easy option, perhaps, of letting the matter rest there, they agreed that if the Board of Trade so requested the Commissioner of the Metropolitan Police, that force would investigate the murder of the passengers (and, one assumes, the crew). The Board of Trade would pay for the investigation, subject to Treasury approval, and the Foreign Office would inform the Greek

Government of the proposed investigation. Finally, they noted that the Director of Public Prosecutions had already agreed to bear the costs of any prosecution.

Veal, along with Head and Newton, met with Detective Superintendent Browne and Detective Sergeant Lee[75] on 12th February. They agreed to provide Scotland Yard with information on the passengers, including a passenger list and list of those missing. Also, they would forward correspondence with the American Life Insurance Company concerning one of the passengers, Mr. Michael Thomaides[76]. Reports from RARDE and Institute of Pathology would also be sent on. Browne wrote to his (unnamed) Chief Superintendent on 14th February, outlining his travel plans. He and DS Hill would:

> '...travel by air to Athens on Wednesday 21st February 1968, arriving at approximately 3.30pm, GMT. On our arrival I will inform the British Embassy of our address in Athens.
>
> It is not possible to say what line the enquiry will take or how we will be received by the Greek authorities. If, however, any difficulties arise an official of the British Embassy will be consulted.
>
> I ask that this report be forwarded in triplicate to the Under Secretary of State, Home Office, with a request that a copy be forwarded to Mr. Macrae, Central Department, Foreign Office, for his information.'

It is interesting to note that the involvement of Det. Supt. Percy Browne in the investigation was not exactly a closely-guarded secret. The *Cyprus Mail* had already announced on February 10th:

> 'A top London murder detective has been named to head a probe (into the Comet crash) ...Scotland Yard police headquarters said Detective Superintendent Percy Browne will inquire into the cause of the cabin explosion...Supt. Browne, who normally investigates murders and other major crime, will start his inquiry soon, and will probably go to Greece and Cyprus.'

On 19th February, Riddoch waxed lyrical about the legal aspects in a minute to a colleague, Mr. Gilling, which was copied to Veal amongst others. It articulates the Under-Secretary's thoughts quite clearly:

> Recent discussions with the Home Office and Scotland Yard about police enquiries into the BEA Comet accident have shattered some of my illusions about Scotland Yard. In general, they do not investigate crimes outside the UK unless they are asked to do so and are paid for doing so.... Above all, Scotland Yard are reluctant to undertake enquiries abroad if they do not result in prosecutions in this country.

---

[75] The name of the Detective Sergeant accompanying Detective Superintendent Browne is given variously as DS Peter Hill or DS Lee.

[76] Mr. Thomaides was well-insured because of the value of his business. There was never any suggestion that he was involved in anything improper and he did not feature further in the investigation.

Interpol are efficient and cooperative but won't have any truck with offences which have a political nuance. I gather that Interpol do not charge for specific services but presumably the UK pays some sort of annual subscription. Where help is sought from police forces in other countries, this is given on a knock for knock basis.

We ourselves are concerned with the enforcement of air navigation legislation and we pay for the use of the Airport Constabulary. The Board of Trade are about to take on the prosecution of offences against air navigation legislation from the DPP but whether we pay for the costs of prosecution or not I do not know.

We are also concerned with the investigation of accidents, and the definition of "accident" is being expanded in the Civil Aviation Bill. The new definition could cover a wide spread of offences on board aircraft.

When the Tokyo Convention Act comes into force, and the Tokyo Convention itself, there will be a duty placed on aircraft commanders to report offences and to deliver offenders on landing to the local police or immigration authorities. Under the Convention the State of Reception has to take the offender into custody and make preliminary enquiries and notify the State of Registry. At most aerodromes in the UK presumably it will be the Airport Constabulary to whom offenders are delivered but, if so, I do not know who would be responsible for making enquiries into the offence.

In cases where the Convention is not applicable, I imagine that the same sort of procedure will have to be followed.

Where do we stand in all this as regards responsibility for action and as regards cost?

To enforce the Air Navigation Order is one thing (in doing so we have no monopoly of enforcement – the local police can also make enquiries and institute proceedings). The need for police enquiries following an aircraft accident is rare but with the widening of the definition of "accident" the Home Office or the police may say that we have a wider responsibility for paying for inquiries. The Home Office may also argue that the Tokyo Convention Act is a piece of civil aviation legislation and it falls to us to enforce it. I think we should resist this. We should not get into the police business any more than we can help. It is better to leave the police business to the experts even if we have to pay them on a lump sum basis. The question of cost is bedevilled by the absence of a national police force and by the existence of a large number of police forces, including the Metropolitan Police, each of which draws half its money from the ratepayers and half from the Exchequer.

In my recent letter to Mr. Brodie of Scotland Yard, copied to the Home Office, regarding the Comet enquiries, I mentioned the need for clarifying the responsibilities of different authorities, particularly when the Tokyo Convention Act came into force. I understand the Home Office are preparing instructions to the police forces and, if so, a draft of these would provide a suitable opportunity for clarifying the whole issue. If the initiative comes from the Home Office, so much the better. If, however, they do not produce something soon, I think we shall have to contact them. Would you please follow this up and gather all the loose ends together?

Browne and his bag-carrier, as such junior officers accompanying senior detectives were known, travelled to Athens as planned on 21st February. However, it appears that their arrival in the Greek capital came as something of a surprise to the staff of the British Embassy there. Macrae, having been contacted by his colleagues overseas, had telephoned Brodie's office to pass on the chagrin of the diplomatic service over what was seen as a somewhat unwelcome surprise. Brodie immediately sought to smooth the ruffled feathers, writing to Macrae:

'I am extremely sorry that you have not been made aware of the fact that Detective Superintendent Browne and his colleague had left this country.

Several days ago, when I became aware that the enquiry had reached the stage when Browne was almost ready to go abroad, I was informed that he had been personally to the Foreign Office and had made all the necessary arrangements. Furthermore, a report left here at the end of last week to the Home Office giving full details of what was proposed. An additional copy of this report was made available to the Home Office who were requested to send it on to you. It appears that the individual in the Home Office who should have dealt with this matter was unavoidably not available for a day or two early this week and nobody else had taken any action on the report.

I write this letter not with the intention of trying to shift blame but merely to let you see that this appears to be one of those cases where "the best laid plans of mice and men…" I am only sorry that you appear to have been left in the dark. I can assure you that this was not intentional, and I do hope that you will accept my sincere regret.[77]

---

[77] The Foreign Office seems to have been exceptionally annoyed, no matter how courteously their message to Brodie might appear. Similarly, his reply, couched in niceties, was little short of a grovelling apology, suggesting that the sudden appearance of the two policemen in Athens had given rise to a wave of severe anxiety in the British Embassy. It appeared that the Foreign Office had concerns about what Browne might uncover. Copies of the letters are in Appendix 7.

On 23rd February, Macrae wrote to Tom Bridges, concerning the unannounced arrival of Browne and Hill in Athens:

> As I told you on the telephone…I am very sorry that two members of the Metropolitan Police should have arrived in Athens before we could warn you of their coming and explain some of the background. This is the story.

Macrae explained that Charlie Oscar had been lost following the detonation of the bomb, and that the AIB investigation was to establish the cause, not attribute blame. Further investigation into the cause was better carried out by the Metropolitan Police, he went on, as the police would not be constrained by the limitations of the Board of Trade's remit. Macrae then filled Bridges in with the agreement that the Board of Trade would formally request the Metropolitan Police to make enquiries into the events leading up to the explosion, and therefore to the deaths of the 66 people on board and would pay for the investigation. He added:

> 'We for our part agreed to alert you and ask you to take such action with the Greek authorities as deemed necessary and appropriate.
>
> We expected next to get a letter from the Police setting out the line of their investigation and their proposed plan of action. Instead of which I learnt from you that the two police officers had already arrived in Athens. This is the more regrettable in that it seems quite possible that potentially tricky political questions could arise during the course of the investigation. For example, supposing the police should discover that the explosion was caused by a Greek (or for that matter a Turkish Cypriot) who was hoping to liquidate General Grivas[78] (something that has of course been canvassed in the Press). For this reason, it seems right that the police should keep in close touch with the Embassy about how their investigation is going, even if they make such day to day arrangements as are necessary with their Greek opposite numbers through their own channels. In view of the mix-up which has just happened, I am making sure that clear instructions in this sense are sent to Detective Superintendent Browne.
>
> As to the question of informing the Greek government about the investigation, I think this is entirely a matter for your discretion. As I mentioned on the telephone, it occurred to me that the action you were required to take (by the Foreign Office) provide a suitable starting

---

[78] The Foreign Office was clearly concerned about this line of enquiry. As stated, it had indeed been touted in the press right from the day of the crash, so this might be a matter of the FO wishing to avoid any potentially embarrassing lines of enquiry. However, as it is so specific, is it possible that the FO had been privy to intelligence suggesting that this was, indeed, the root cause, which they needed to keep undercover? Such intelligence might, for example, have been from an SIS (MI6) source or even that the plot involved such a source who needed protection. Note: many EOKA fighters had given information to the security services during the Cyprus Emergency.

point, but much would depend on how those instructions were carried out.

…I am sending a copy of this letter to Tony Tyler in the Commonwealth Office and to Timothy Daunt in Nicosia, as I believe it is possible that the police will wish to visit Cyprus in the course of their investigations. In that case the Commonwealth Office may well wish to inform the Cyprus government about the police investigation and, if you can find out about their plans to visit Cyprus, it would obviously be helpful for Tyler and Daunt to know about (the) plans.

Mr. SS Bampton, of Home Office department F2, wrote on 26ᵗʰ February to PE Brodie, Assistant Commissioner Crime at the Metropolitan Police:

'The Foreign Office are most anxious that your police officers should keep in close touch with the Embassy on this investigation, even if they make such day to day arrangements as are necessary with their Greek opposite numbers through their own channels, as it is possible that potentially tricky political questions could arise during the course of the investigation. I imagine you will already have given instructions to this effect, but I have assured the Foreign Office that I would pass on this instruction to you immediately.'

Brodie then took prompt action to ensure the sentiments of the Foreign Office were passed on to Browne. On 27ᵗʰ February, he sent a carefully-worded missive to the detective, being couched in such a way that it would not because embarrassment should it have inadvertently been viewed by unauthorised eyes, however that might have occurred:

'Bampton from the Home Office has been in to see me today and he tells me that someone from the Embassy in Athens has been in touch with Macrae in the Foreign Office here about your presence in Athens.

It appears that the Embassy staff in Athens are slightly apprehensive about any possible political repercussions should your enquiry develop in a certain direction. For instance, if you should find evidence to suggest that the explosion in the Comet was arranged in order to do harm to someone in politics in Cyprus or Greece then a very delicate situation would arise.

I think I need say no more than to ask you to keep very closely in touch with the Embassy staff and if anything, that savours of politics should arise, I know you would discuss the matter with them and would be most careful not to embarrass the Foreign Office.

Of necessity, this letter has to be in rather vague terms, but I am sure that you will take the point.

I wish you luck in your enquiry and I shall look forward to hearing all about it when you return to this country.'

The Assistant Commissioner forwarded the letter to Macrae, with a covering note stating:

'I enclose a secret and highly-confidential letter to Detective Superintendent Browne who is investigating the BEA Comet aircraft crash. I should be extremely grateful if you could arrange for this letter to be sent out to him in Athens through the Diplomatic Bag. We understand he is staying at the Hotel Stanley, 1 rue Odysseus, Place Kaiskis, Athens.

Macrae forwarded the letter to the Hon. Tom Bridges, with an additional level of cover:

In my recent undated letter to you I said that the police would be sending instructions to (Browne) to keep in touch with the Embassy in case of political developments arising during the course of his investigations.

I enclose, under Flying Seal[79], a letter from (Brodie) to Browne, which I should be grateful if you would pass on. I think the letter should serve its purpose from our point of view. Although the contents of the letter are not particularly startling you should know that Brodie was most apprehensive that the letter should pass through unauthorised hands. He had hoped that it could be sent through the bag already sealed and when I explained that our rules did not permit this I had to assure him that you personally as the addressee of this letter would seal it and see that it was delivered by safe hand to Browne before he would entrust me with the letter!

Bridges replied on 6th March, updating Macrae and giving him a bit of reassurance:

'We were a bit surprised when (Browne) arrived out of the blue but had been expecting a visit before very long as a result of what we had seen in the press and it did not matter much. With the help of the Foreign Ministry I arranged for Browne to meet the Greek Interpol Bureau. This meant a slight delay, but he has since told us that his enquiry has been making good progress and that the Greek authorities are being very helpful. I do not of course know the details, but I gather that the particular line of enquiry he is following does not involve politics.

On 19th April, RG Smith of CA4(1) of the Board of Trade sent a minute to a Capt. Hunt in Veal's department. This noted that the Metropolitan Police would investigate the events leading up to the crash with the Board of Trade meeting the costs in certain circumstances. Smith wanted to know if the police had, as previously agreed, submitted any progress reports, adding wryly, *'Have you*

---

[79] Under Flying Seal denotes a letter with a seal attached, but not closed, so that it may be read by the person entrusted with forwarding it to the addressee.

reached any conclusion so far as to whether there is sufficient progress to justify the public expenditure involved?'

Veal responded four days later:

> ...Superintendent Browne telephoned me about 15 days ago to tell me the current position regarding his enquiries and to ask about further reports by the RARDE.
>
> Superintendent Browne and Sergeant Lee spent some five weeks in Cyprus and Greece pursuing their enquiries and their investigations included approaches to the close relatives of all those killed in the accident.
>
> Superintendent Browne told me that there were four main lines of investigation and that one of them appeared to be promising. He thought at the time that it would take them some four or five weeks to complete what he had to do and to make his report. On this basis we should expect to hear something within the next fortnight but if we do not I will get in touch with Superintendent Browne again. One item which is likely to hold up this final report is the availability of the RARDE report because this contains much important expert evidence.

Tom Bridges contacted John Macrae on 25th June in connection with the continuing Greek interest in criminal proceedings:

> It was reported in the Athens press that further investigation of this subject was being undertaken by the Public Prosecutor in Athens. I am not sure exactly what the significance of this is, but I presume that some of the results of Detective Superintendent Browne's investigations have been made available to the Greek authorities by Scotland Yard and that the former wished to investigate the possibility of a prosecution[80] in the Greek courts. No doubt Scotland Yard know more about this.
>
> I have now received a letter from the investigating authorities in the Athens Magistrates' Courts asking us to supply the Prosecutor of the Court of Misdemeanours here with a copy of the findings of the British authorities about the accident. I have replied to this letter by saying that, to the best of my knowledge, our own enquiries have not yet been completed, but that I have forwarded their request to the appropriate authorities in London.

Bampton wrote to Veal on 16th July, concerning a request from the Greek authorities for a copy of the findings. It appeared that there was some slight

---

[80] Why the Greeks would consider a prosecution when Scotland Yard said there was no evidence is not made clear. It suggests that either Scotland Yard had inferred that there was, in fact, someone worth prosecuting or that the Greek authorities were using this as a 'legal' means of finding out what Scotland Yard knew.

confusion as to whether the findings referred to the Accident Report or the police investigation:

I have discussed this with the Assistant Commissioner of the Metropolitan Police and as you will appreciate from the nature of their report, it will be out of the question to send a copy of it to the Greek authorities, and it would be extremely difficult to prepare an edited edition.

One way of dealing with this, subject to your agreement, would be to let the Greek authorities have a copy of your report on the cause of the crash. At the same time, a covering note could be sent to our Ambassador explaining that if he were pressed for a copy of the police report he should tell them that the enquiry has now been completed, but it was inconclusive and there was insufficient evidence to indicate who might have been responsible. This approach would meet with the agreement of the Metropolitan Police and the Foreign Office and I should welcome your views on it.

Brodie acknowledged the letter to Veal, a copy of which Bampton had thoughtfully sent the Assistant Commissioner, adding:

'You will no doubt remember that when I spoke to you on the telephone I mentioned that Detective Superintendent Browne was still with the Director of Public Prosecutions. Perhaps, therefore, the proposed covering note to our Ambassador saying, "that the Police enquiry was inconclusive and there was insufficient evidence to indicate who might have been responsible" should be delayed until the Director of Public Prosecutions has given his decision.' Bampton acknowledged, 'I take the point that we should say nothing to pre-judge the decision of the Director of Public Prosecutions.'

On 29th July, Brodie wrote to Bampton, confirming:

'A reply has now been received from the Director of Public Prosecutions to the effect that "no action can be taken on the present evidence". In the absence of any further evidence, I do not think that the Director will take any action in the future[81].

Bampton sent a letter to Brodie on 1st August, in connection with the request from the Greek authorities for a copy of the 'findings'. There was still concern over the existence of the police investigations, and Bampton expanded on the earlier advice:

'The best way of dealing with this request would seem to be to give the Greek authorities a copy of the report prepared by the Chief Inspector of Accidents at the Board of Trade and omit all reference to

---

[81] A firm decision to finalise the matter suggested that the suspect was believed (Papapetrou) or known (Solomou) to be dead, and that any accomplices were unlikely to be brought to justice, either because of a lack of evidence or else because the chances of bringing them to trial in the UK were minimal or non-existent, e.g. in the case of Yiorkadjis.

the police investigation. The Board of Trade have no objection to this procedure, and I enclose a pre-print of their report. This will not be published until September, but the Board of Trade would not object if it were passed to the Greek authorities before this on the understanding that it is to be treated as confidential until the report is actually published. I have removed from the report the brief letter of submission to the President of the Board of Trade, as this does refer in passing to the investigation by the Metropolitan Police. Although this letter will be published in the report, it seems unnecessary to draw the attention of the Greek authorities to the police investigation[82] and it would not be obvious that such a letter would be included in a pre-print copy.

If our Ambassador in Athens is questioned about the police investigation, I suggest that he might say that the police inquiry was inconclusive and that there was insufficient evidence to indicate who might have been responsible.'

Macrae wrote to Bridges on 6th August, replying to his letter of 25th June:

Your enquiry has in fact placed us in a bit of difficulty since, unlike the report prepared by the Chief Inspector of Accidents, the contents of the report by the Metropolitan Police Officers are such that it would not do to supply it to the Greek authorities. Much of it is political dealing with the personal histories and allegiances of individuals concerned and the information could well be used (or misused) by the Greek authorities for their own purposes. In any case it is not normal practice for copies of police reports to be made available outside of the Home Office, even to other Government Departments. For your own information the report has been sent to the Director of Public Prosecutions who has confirmed the police's own view that there is insufficient evidence for further proceedings.

Macrae went on to suggest, as had Bampton to Brodie, that the Greek Prosecutor of the Court of Misdemeanours be given a copy of the Accident Report rather than that prepared by the police, along with the by-now standard line that, '...the (police) enquiry was inconclusive...'

By return, Bridges reassured Macrae that the Accident Report was probably what the Prosecutor actually wanted, as no mention of the police report had been made. He added that, should the Greek authorities wanted supplementary information, i.e. relating to the police investigation, there was no reason why they should not apply for it through Interpol. Bridges then proposed an alternative course of action:

---

[82] This contradicts the earlier correspondence, from the time of D/Supt. Browne's visit to Athens, that the Greek authorities were already aware of the police investigation, and that the Foreign Office had facilitated the detective's visit to the Greek Interpol Bureau.

167

The Director of Civil Aviation, Major-General A. Skarmaliorakis, RHAF (retired) has followed this matter with close interest and clearly resented the publication of the press reports last November indicating that the accident had been caused by an explosion on board the aircraft. He seemed to think that this implied some criticism of the Greek security arrangements at Athens airport, and issued a statement to the press implying that premature publication of these findings before the issue of the final report was irregular and unsatisfactory…Skarmaliorakis is a man of some political importance here, having been close to the leaders of the military coup last April, from the beginning. For these various reasons I would prefer him to obtain a copy of the report personally from the Air Attaché, rather than learn about its existence from his staff who are collaborating with the Public Prosecutor in investigating this accident.

Confirmation of the personal delivery to Skarmaliorakis of the report came in a telex on 28th August from Sir M. Stewart of the Athens Embassy, to the Foreign Office, stating that the Director of Civil Aviation, '… *made no comment of substance but was obviously pleased by the letter and glad to have copies before publication.*'

On 14th October 1968, a Mr. G. Angel penned a note concerning the establishment of a precedent that the Metropolitan Police should be tasked with investigating offences on British aircraft while they are overseas:

I am doubtful about the wisdom of attempting to lay down rigid rules to deal with exceptional incidents such as the loss of the Comet aircraft. So much depends on the circumstances: for example, the political issues in Greece were a special reason why we could not be confident in an investigation carried out by the Greek police…They appear to commit the Metropolitan Police to investigating crime on aircraft even in circumstances when it might be more appropriate for the local police where the aircraft lands to investigate. They also imply that the Metropolitan Police will not investigate offences on board aircraft except at the request of the Board of Trade or an airline authority. I would think that if a serious offence such as murder appears to have been committed on a British controlled aircraft…the police should be interested to investigate quite apart from the wishes of the Board of Trade or the airline authority. One accepts that investigation by the Metropolitan Police involves the inhabitants of London in a disproportionate share of the cost, but cases are likely to be so few that it should be acceptable on de minimis grounds[83].'

---

[83] 'de minimis grounds' infers that the issue is likely to arise so infrequently that the question of fairness of burdening the ratepayers of London with additional costs is not worth quibbling over.

Details of the police investigation itself are still, at the time of writing, not available to the public. It is known that Browne and Hill spent around five weeks in Greece and Athens, but the witnesses they spoke to and material evidence they collected are still officially secret. The two officers certainly had their work cut out.

In April 1968 a 14-year-old schoolboy called Roy Tuthill was found murdered in the grounds of Lord Beaverbrook's estate in Givens Grove, Leatherhead, starting one of the Surrey Constabulary's longest police enquiries. Detective Constable Dave O'Connell was seconded to the murder squad assembled at Leatherhead. In an online post many years afterwards, he recalled,

> "Scotland Yard were asked to assist. In those days if a county force called in the Metropolitan Police within twenty-four hours of the murder being discovered the Home Office bore the cost of the enquiry. This was a great incentive for the counties to call in the Metropolitan Police. The Met maintained a murder squad consisting of five Chief Superintendents who rotated as the requests for assistance came in. They were assisted by a Detective Sergeant who became known as the "bag carrier".
>
> The officer appointed to lead this enquiry was Chief Superintendent Percy Brown (sic). The enquiry in my opinion was doomed from the start and ranks as the worst led enquiry I have had any connection with.
>
> To start with detectives from all over the county were told to be at Leatherhead Police Station for briefing at a certain time. The senior officers arrived some two and a half hours later after clearly having enjoyed the benefits of a good lunch. The first words dispensed by Chief Superintendent Brown were, "You will be lucky to detect this one." This was said from behind a cloud of smoke emitting from a huge cigar.
>
> The detectives on the case worked very hard but there was little direction to the enquiry. As luck would have it the local Detective Inspector Philip Doyle was a fine copper who realised that things were not as they should have been. He made up his mind to try as far as he could to ensure that all the evidence that was gathered was properly documented and preserved. As time dragged on, he also took a more active part in directing certain parts of the operation. His dedication was later to prove vital.
>
> Eventually the enquiry wound down with no detection and very little progress."

Lines of Enquiry

In the *Evening News*, a London paper on February 17th 1968, a headline announced a *'Dragnet for Comet Killers – Disaster plotted in London'*, telling its readers,

'A police comb-out of 'Little Cyprus', the Greek Cypriot area of Camden Town, was going on today in a search for the men who plotted the Comet air disaster.

Fresh information has reached Scotland Yard about the Comet…police believe the object of the plan was to assassinate former EOKA leader General Grivas, who was wrongly thought to have been on board.

Det. Supt, Percy Browne, who has been transferred to Scotland Yard from his post as Paddington CID, has discovered that the plot was hatched in a Paddington gaming club.

A number of known Greek extremists are being sought by police.

Inquiries are being intensified in the Camden Town and Paddington areas and several clubs and cafes are being visited.

Three days later, the news was spiced up a bit by the *Daily Sketch*, which revealed,

'Murder squad detectives investigating the sabotage of the BEA Comet last October will fly to Athens tomorrow.

There, Detective Superintendent Percy Browne and a sergeant will interview a number of men in the presence of Greek police…Scotland Yard men have been told that a time bomb was put on the plane in a bid by political extremists to assassinate Colonel (sic) Georgios Grivas.

If that information is correct, the Greek Government could face insurance claims for millions of pounds.

Before Det. Supt. Browne leaves London, he will interview a Greek who fled to Britain as a political refugee after a split with Colonel Grivas.

Other Greeks also living in London have already been interviewed.

An important statement has been taken from a Greek in a London jail.'

The *Daily Sketch* of 26th February was somewhat more detailed, and asserted that the perpetrator had died, stating,

'A man passenger among the 66 who died…had personal insurance for the flight worth many hundreds of thousands of pounds.

This development was revealed while Scotland Yard murder squad detectives are in Athens following leads to establish why the plane was sabotaged.

Greeks in London have claimed to police that the aircraft was blown up to assassinate the former EOKA leader, General Grivas.

Now the huge insurance cover has come to light, Det. Supt. Percy Browne, who leads the investigation has been briefed to establish whether there is any link between the insurance and the explosion...No insurance pay-out is likely until the Yard's investigation has ended.

Apart from personal insurance policies held by individual passengers, BEA stands to pay out more than £1 million in compensation for the loss of lives.

A newspaper report appeared in the Cyprus Mail of 5th September under the by-line of Anthony Chivers asked, *'Did saboteur die in Comet crash?'* It went on:

Scotland Yard know the name of the man who they believe was behind the bomb plot which resulted in the Comet crash off Cyprus last October.

He is alleged to be either a Greek or Greek Cypriot businessman. It is believed that his wife is living in London. But the one question which the Police cannot answer is this: Is the man behind the plot alive or dead?

For the bodies of eleven people were never recovered...and until they are all recovered – which is likely to be never – Scotland Yard would not be able to disentangle the final puzzle of this whole mystery.

Not until then would they be able to establish whether the man whose name they have was actually killed in the crash. Or whether someone else was using his name.

(The mystery) began a few weeks after the crash when Det. Supt. Percy Browne, accompanied by a detective sergeant, went to Greece and Cyprus.

He discovered that one of the passengers whose name was on the passenger list had taken out a large life insurance.

Then, Police believe, he somehow tricked another man into flying in his place, using his passport, his ticket and his seat.

After the plane had taken off, the organiser of the plot would disappear, leaving the people he had named as beneficiaries to claim full settlement.

In an official statement about the case, Scotland Yard said: "A Police investigation into the Comet disaster was carried out and a report was subsequently submitted to the Director of Public Prosecutions. It was decided on the evidence available that no action could be taken.

I learn it is extremely unlikely that the insurance policy in respect of the person known to the police will be paid out.

A spokesman for the Association of Insurance Companies said: "In such a case we should certainly refuse payment. It would have to be proved to our satisfaction that death was accidental and not due to some criminal act.

"It is a cardinal rule of law that no person should benefit from a criminal act and that would certainly apply to any beneficiary who was a party to that act, or who was party to any conspiracy."

Following the publication of the final AIB report, John Edmonds at the British Embassy in Ankara, contacted JMO Snodgrass at the FO's Central Department, advising him that,

'The Turkish press reported the Board of Trade's findings, but not in sensational terms. All newspapers said the bomb was placed in the aircraft to kill General Grivas, but they avoided speculation as to who was responsible.

For what it is worth, the local AP[84] correspondent, who is also the Times stringer, (said) that it had been "well established" that one of the passengers insured himself for £200,000 and then committed 'suicide'; but newspapers had been asked not to publish this because stories of this kind are even worse for airline business than assassination theories.

As this case could still have some political significance here, we should be grateful for any comments you may have, together with a copy of the official accident report.'

Edmonds received his reply from Macrae, who commented,

'...we do know – as the Press was told- that (the police) found insufficient evidence for further proceedings. Of the papers here, only The Sun carried headlines to the effect that the crash was caused by a bomb meant for Grivas, but the evidence does not really substantiate the story. We are therefore unable to comment authoritatively on the question of who was responsible for the accident. On the whole, the insurance theory seems the most likely, although we cannot corroborate the details (in your letter).'

The perpetrators of the atrocity would have needed access to a certain level of specialist knowledge to construct an explosive device sufficient to bring down an aircraft. In particular, the bomb maker would have needed access to the military-grade plastic explosive established by RARDE as the material used. In addition, there would need to be a means of detonation, in the case of Charlie Oscar this being a timer or a radio frequency (RF) detonator. Alternatively, for a suicide bomber, there would need to be a means of setting off the explosive device on demand.

---

[84] Associated Press news agency.

Two aircraft were destroyed by bombs at Nicosia airport in 1956. (Left) The departure of Handley Page Hermes G-ALDW of Skyways, on a charter flight carrying families of service personnel was delayed by two and a half hours. A bomb exploded whilst the aircraft was still on the ground. If the flight had left Nicosia on time, all on board would certainly have lost their lives. (Right) A Cyprus Airways Dakota was also destroyed by a bomb, six weeks after the Hermes. It is believed that EOKA was responsible for both attacks (www.militaryhistories.com) Below: C4 plastic explosive Its malleable nature means that it can be concealed in innocuous-looking items. Estimates of the amount used in the device on Charlie Oscar varied between four and sixteen ounces .

EOKA had used bombs during its struggle against the British forces, so it is reasonable to assume that there were still people with the requisite skills on the island seven years after independence. The organisation had also been willing to use violence against women and children in pursuit of its aims, and indeed to destroy aircraft with civilians on board. On 3rd March 1956, a Handley Page Hermes, G-ALDW, of the charter airline Skyways was due to take 68 members of the British armed forces and their families from Nicosia back to the UK. A bomb, placed in a hat rack, exploded, destroying the aircraft though fortunately without casualties. The occupants were saved because the departure had been delayed by two and a half hours. Just over six weeks later, on 27th April, a bomb destroyed a Cyprus Airways Dakota on the ground, also without casualties.

International terrorism was still in its infancy, especially with aircraft and the travelling public as targets. Suicide bombings, as a political weapon, were also rare at that time in Europe. However, there were emerging threats, especially in the Middle East and, to a lesser extent in Northern Ireland, though the situation in the latter was to escalate dramatically in the following very few years. There had been one potential line of enquiry in this regard, however.

Just before the start of the 'Six Days War' in June 1967 between Israel and its Arab neighbours, there was a threat from Middle Eastern groups to target airlines which flew to Israel. This would have included both BEA and Cyprus Airways. On 15th June 1967, Colin Mastin of SA (I) 3, had written to Captain Woolfe, Chief Pilot of Cyprus Airways, asking, '...*Recent events in your part of the world have obviously affected Cyprus Airways operations; has this caused any problems that we should know about?*

Captain Woolfe then travelled to England with copies of the letter[85] sent to Cyprus Airways and all airline operators operating into Israel. The letters in English and Arabic demanded that all airlines declare in the world press before mid-June that they would cease trading with Israel, and actually do so before mid-July, otherwise action would be taken against those airlines that continued their operations.

All operators involved, and the Lebanese government, took the letters seriously and various security actions were taken in Beirut. Captain Woolfe took matters further and imposed security at all stations that the Cyprus Airways Viscounts operated to. While the aircraft was on the ground at an outstation a steward remained at the cabin door and monitored persons coming on board the aircraft. One of the pilots kept watch under the aircraft and monitored the baggage. Normally the aircraft was not fuelled, catered or cleaned. Mr PCM Shillitoe and Captain AS Johnson of BEA knew about the threat as they subsequently went to Beirut to decide about BEA aircraft night-stopping once more.

---

[85] For a translation of the full text of the letter see Appendix 5.

There is no evidence in any of the CY284 files open to the public that there was an Irish dimension to the bombing of Charlie Oscar. If the IRA had the capability to put a bomb on an aircraft, it would most likely have been either on a troop-carrying flight or on a route to or from Northern Ireland. On 23rd July 1974 a small bomb was found on a BA Trident airliner flying from Belfast to London. It did not explode.

Despite the existence of the 'Falcon Forces' letter, there has never been any suggestion that Charlie Oscar was brought down for terrorist purposes. Had it been, there would certainly have been claims from the group responsible, and others wishing to further their cause by suggesting they had the capability to destroy an airliner in flight. There were no such claims made.

Persons of Interest

It will be recalled that in early April, Detective Superintendent Browne told Veal that there were *'four main lines of enquiry, one of which was promising.'* It is likely, from the information contained in the National Archives files, that at the time these were:

1. Sotiris Georgiou, who was sitting in seat 4A on the London to Athens sector.
2. Andreas Antoniades and his associates, as named by Peter Georgeides.
3. Avraam Solomou, whose behaviour at Ellinikon Airport gave cause for concern, and who was named later as the carrier of the device.
4. Nicos Papapetrou who also had a number of insurance policies, these all being taken out shortly before his trip and covered him for one flight only.

Sotiris Georgiou

The threats to the airline made by former BEA employee George Georgiou raised an immediate suspicion that they were the same person. Sotiris Georgiou had also acquired an additional four kilogrammes of luggage during his day's stopover in London. The fact that he was sitting in one of the two seats considered most likely to have been where the device exploded would have been an immediate reason for suspicion.

The suspicions about Sotiris actually being George Georgiou were allayed when it was established that the latter was still alive and well in London after the crash. The excess baggage accumulated by Sotiris Georgiou was gifts and items purchased for family members that were not readily available in Cyprus. The luggage would have been carried in the hold so would not have included the bomb. There is no indication in the files of a specific motive for Sotiris Georgiou to blow up the aircraft. His body was amongst the missing, which means that he was quite possibly still in the same seat when the bomb exploded. If he was not responsible for the bomb, it would not, therefore, have been under seat 5A, the one in front of Georgiou. The bomb would have been brought on board by the person in seat 3A, immediately behind him, and who has not been identified.

Andreas Antoniades

There was, languishing in Brixton Prison, London, a man who believed he held to key to the mystery. Prisoner no. 41320 Peter Panayiotes Georgeides, originally from Cyprus, had been convicted of armed robbery and was imprisoned for a few years. Perhaps in an effort to gain some points for good behaviour, he wrote to the Chairman of BEA on 9th January 1968:

> Sabotage is certainly the cause of the BEA Comet which crashed in flames off the coast of Cyprus.
>
> The man responsible (one of them) is Andreas Antoniades an ex-EOKA terrorist and expert in the "explosives squad" of General

Georgios Grivas, head of the then EOKA and later supremo of the Cyprus National Guard. If you'd care to send someone to come and see me from your office, I will give them further details on the matter.

Antoniades, or "Keravnos" as he is called, fell out with Grivas and was "sentenced" to death by the General, so Keravnos defected over to the British side SIB and gave away the organisation's secrets, and as a result many EOKA lieutenants got executed or imprisoned.

Antoniades later came to this country so that he could escape the General's own "exterminating-traitor-squad".

Early last year he, Keravnos, had ambitions to assassinate the Archbishop Makarios and Grivas and take over Cyprus.

Before the trouble with the Turks started, the first step was to liquidate Grivas who was in control of the armed forces.

Makarios would follow etc.

I will not continue any further sir, but if you want to clear this dreadful matter, then you only have to come or send someone to see me.

PS. I was present at a meeting (prior to the Comet explosion) when a top-ranking army person came to this country to discuss plans for a take-over.

The letter to Milward was copied by someone in the Home Office, all prisoners' mail being subject to scrutiny. The copy was forwarded to the office of Anthony Crosland from where it made its way via Jan Riddoch to Veal. The covering letter stated that Milward had not been informed that the letter was also being sent to Crosland. A handwritten addendum stated, *'Action already taken in connection with BEA copy'*. The Chief Inspector of Accidents, on 23rd January, forwarded it to Chief Inspector Bryan at Scotland Yard.

In 2007, the BBC news website broke a story that some of Britain's leading heroin smuggling suspects were protected from police investigations because they were working as informers for HM Revenue & Customs and its predecessor units[86]. In one case in 2001, Foreign Office diplomats moved to secure the release of Antoniades, who was described in the article as 'an informer held in Germany on a warrant from the Greek authorities'. The allegations suggested a special form of protection was being given to several people suspected by police of being leading importers of heroin. A former officer of the National Crime Intelligence Service (NCIS) told the BBC:

"Customs told me he had been an informant and that he had been the best informant Customs ever had and what he had given the UK far exceeded the damage he had done, which was absolute rubbish."

---

[86] Informer role protected drugs traffickers. www.news.bbc.co.uk, Sunday 4th March 2007

A2/17.

In replying to this letter, please write on the envelope :—

Number 41320   Name GEORGEIDES. P.

H. M. PRISON,
JEBB AVENUE,
BRIXTON,
LONDON, S.W.2.

Dear sir,   9 . 1 . 68.

Sabotage is certainly the
cause of the BEA comet which
crashed in flames off the coast
of Cyprus.

The man responsible, (one of them)
is Andreas Antoniades an
ex E·OKA terrorist and expert
in the "explosives squad" of General
George Grivas head of the then
E·OKA and later supremo of the
CYPRUS National guard.

If you'd care to send someone
to come and see me from
your office I will give them
further details on the matter

Antoniades or "Keravnos" as he
is called fell out with Grivas
and was "sentenced" to death
by the General, so Keravnos →
                                    P·T·P.

No. 243   (28150—3-10-62)

178

defected over to the British
side S.I.B. and gave away to
organizations secrets, and
as a result many EOKA lieutenants got executed or imprisoned

Antoniades, later came to this
Country so that he could
escape the Generalls own
"exterminating-traitor-squad".

Early last year he, Keravnos,
had ambitions to assassinate
the Archibishop Makarios and
Grivas and take-over Cyprus.

Before the trouble with the
Turks started the first step
was to liquidate Grivas who
was in controll of the armed
forces.
Makarios would follow etc.

I will not continue any further
sir, but if you want to clear
this dreadfull matter, then you
have only to come, or send
someone to see me.

Yours very sincerely [signature]

I was present at a
meeting (prior to the
Comet explosion) when a
top ranking army person
came to this country
to discuss plans for a
take-over.

A copy of the letter sent to the Metropolitan Police by Peter Georgeides, a prisoner at HMP Brixton claiming to have inside knowledge of the plot to destroy Charlie Oscar (TNA).

Antoniades, who was 75 at the time of the article, was by then believed to be living in Dubai, and had never been convicted of any drugs offence. A number of people, some from the Turkish and Greek communities, subsequently launched appeals against drug trafficking convictions based on his information. Antoniades, a Greek Cypriot, came to the UK in the late 1950s after working as an agent for British intelligence, according to the BBC, and was once jailed for four years after a shooting incident in west London. He went on to work as an informer until the 1990s when reports emerged he was involved in drug trafficking. The reason for protecting Antoniades from prosecution was that "…a public trial in Greece would reveal Mr Antoniades' long career as an informant for Customs and Excise and put his life at risk from criminal elements". Antoniades found himself charged with attempted murder and a letter[87] was sent

---

[87] FO 371/144714 Protection for former member of Special Branch of Cyprus, Code RGC file 1642, via Fanoulla Argyrou.

by Antoniades' mother to the Under-Secretary of State at the Foreign Office on 30th July 1959, in which she states,

'My son worked for the Special Branch here in Cyprus during the recent emergency and his life was in constant danger throughout that period and in fact he was shot at many times and was seriously wounded by terrorists and for these reasons the British Government took him under their protection and flew him to England. I therefore feel that your Government is responsible for him and he would not be in this trouble if he had been properly cared for.

In London my son is still in great danger from members of the Cypriot community who would be only too glad to get rid of him and would go to any extreme to do so and I am sure that my son has been framed in some way due to his work against the terrorists in Cyprus.'

It is possible, of course, that Antoniades was, as alleged by Georgeides, involved in a plot to kill Grivas. There is no evidence to substantiate this, just as the suggestion that Antoniades was an informant, as opposed to being part of the Special Branch, is hearsay, although the institutionally circumspect BBC was confident in stating this on its website. There is nothing else about Antoniades himself in the CY284 files, and it would be necessary to establish whether he had any association with Avraam Solomou or Nicos Papapetrou in order to make a clearer link to the destruction of Charlie Oscar.

Given that both Antoniades and Georgeides moved to the UK some time before the Charlie Oscar incident, it is quite possible that their paths might have crossed. Both men were jailed in Britain for similar periods of time following convictions for violent crimes. The information that Antoniades arrived in the UK shortly before power in Cyprus passed to the former EOKA leaders, having been connected to the British authorities, suggests strongly that he would not have been a friend of Grivas, who was ruthless in his treatment of those he considered to be traitors. By the same token, it is equally unlikely that Antoniades would have found many allies elsewhere in the higher echelons of the new Cyprus government. From what little is known of Antoniades, he does not appear likely to have been well enough connected to 'take power in Cyprus.'

It might be the case that Georgeides had fallen out with Antoniades and his letter from prison was simply an opportunity at get at, or get rid of, Antoniades. If so, the ruse presumably failed as there is nothing available to show that Antoniades was ever arrested in connect with the loss of CY284.

Avraam Solomou

Avraam Solomou was first named as a suspect in an Evening Standard newspaper article by John Miller, published on 21st November 1967. The piece, titled *'Comet Bomb: Special Branch Step In'*, states:

The bomb was probably the size of a pencil and hidden in a brief case.

But its base, a military type of explosive, was so powerful that it virtually ripped the airliner apart.

The theory is that it was put in its briefcase under an innocent passenger's seat.

The link seems to have been Cypriot chauffeur Mr. A. Solomou, one of the 66 people who died.

He has been described variously as a henchman of General Grivas, commander of the Cyprus armed forces, or a bodyguard of Mr. Spyros Kyprianou, the Cyprus Foreign Minister.

His presence could have misled saboteurs into thinking General Grivas was to have been aboard.

The Sunday Telegraph article of 26th November also mentioned Solomou, suggesting that he was a body guard of General Grivas. Solomou drew attention to himself at Athens, prior to boarding the flight, due to a ticketing discrepancy which resulted in him forcefully demanding to be allowed onto the flight. Three days before the Sunday Telegraph article appeared, a Miss Roberts from MI5 had phoned Veal's office, having chased up their representative in Cyprus about Solomou:

Mr. Solomou, who is No. 55 on the list (of recovered victims) was chauffeur to the Foreign Minister, Mr. Kyprianou, and a former EOKA fighter during the Cyprus emergency of 1955-59. The Director of the Cyprus Special Branch completely discounts the possibility that this was an attempt against Grivas because he never travels at that time of day. They have no record of any of the Cypriot passengers in their index.

There are two points of significance in this very concise reply to Veal's query concerning Solomou. Firstly, the Cyprus Special Branch came under the Cypriot Interior Ministry. The Interior Minister, Polycarpos Yiorkadjis, is of interest because of what some in Cyprus believed to be his involvement in the Charlie Oscar affair (see chapter 'Dark Deeds and Political Rivalry'). Secondly, the phrase '...*no record of any of the Cypriot passengers in their index*' infers that no Cypriot on the flight was known to them at all. This latter assertion is surprising in the context of their information that Solomou had been an EOKA fighter. It is highly unlikely that they would not keep a file on him as a former fighter and someone with direct access to a Government minister such as Kyprianou. It is, of course, entirely possible, that they actually meant 'no person other than Solomou'.

C.~~I~~.A.

Miss Roberts telephoned from Box 500.
She sent a telegram to their representative
yesterday asking for a reply to her letter, and
received a telegram back.

Mr. Solomou, who is No. 55 on the list,
was chauffeur to the Foreign Minister, Mr. Kiprianou,
and a former EOKA fighter during the Cyprus
emergency of 1955-59. The Director of the Cyprus
Special Branch completely discounts the possibility
that this was an attempt against Grivas because
he never travels at that time of the day. They
have no record of any of the Cypriot passengers
in their index.

23/11/67   A.I.

CODE 18-76

A minute in Veal's files notes information passed via the security services that Grivas '...never travelled at that time of day.' (TNA).

Leonidas Leonidou commented on the loss of Charlie Oscar in a biography of General Grivas. He wrote[88]:

The scientific investigation carried out by British specialists took a number of months and showed that the crash was caused by the detonation on board of a bomb. It is considered most likely that the intention was to kill General Grivas, who is said to have cancelled his seat on this flight at the last minute.

Six years later, a close associate gave to Dhigenis, as Grivas was also known, information that he had subsequently received:

"I can tell you that I have authoritative information that the crash of the Cyprus Airways Comet, on the 12th October 1967, was aimed at you. It was known that you were to travel on that flight from Athens to Nicosia. You were saved because, at the last minute, you postponed the trip. They had placed a time bomb, which had been made by people trusted by the Cyprus Home Office. The postponement of your journey, which they did not expect, and the failure to reset the bomb, caused the aircraft to crash due to the explosion and for the person entrusted with placing the bomb to die, as he was supposed to cancel his departure from Athens if you did not board the aircraft. Are you aware of all this? Why did our newspapers not write about it?"

And the writer adds:

"These shocking details again involve the Minister for the Home Office, Polycarpos Yiorkadjis, because the explosion took place under the seat of Avraam Solomou, the then driver of the Foreign Minister of Cyprus, Spyros Kyprianou, and who was acting under orders from Yiorkadjis. If indeed General Grivas was the target of the attempt, then the timing of this action rather supports the view that this murderous attempt against Dhigenis is part of a wider, complex and sinister plan..."

Eleftherios Papadopoulos, also established this from other sources. Mr. Papadopoulos was imprisoned for his involvement in the coup against Makarios on 15 July 1974. In one of his books covering his testimonies to the Committee of the House of Representatives he wrote that, after he came out of prison, he was informed by two friends that a former official of the Cyprus Government wanted to have a meeting with him. Papadopoulos wrote:

When I was released from prison in 1984, my associate Andreas Paraskevas and late Pantelis Katelaris (doctor), told me of the wish of a former high-ranking government official, who knew a lot about a lot of

---

[88] Leonidou's original source is "Operation Kofinou" by Spyros Papageorgiou, page 43. Papageorgiou himself was considered to be a supporter of General Grivas and wrote a number of biographies about him.

people, to meet with me. Although I did not see what of common interest we had to discuss, I accepted.

He told me: *"I am one step from my grave. I have cancer. I am fighting it, but I know I will not be the winner. I called you to tell you some secrets, which I do not want to take with me (to the grave). Come back tomorrow and bring with your paper and a tape recorder. I will name some people and events. I want you to promise me that you will not publicise all that I will tell you before 2016."*

Indeed, he named some people and events. A lot I already knew from other sources. Nevertheless, all important. Many shocking. He also referred to the crash of the "Comet" near Kastellorizo. He told me:

"The explosives were sent by Polycarpos Yiorkadjis in a box with timing devices". Recipient was an employee of the Cyprus Embassy in Athens, who manufactured the bomb.

It was handed over to A. Solomou, driver of the Minister for Foreign Affairs Sp. Kyprianou, as a package for his Minister. Both of them knew nothing. The bomb was timed following a telephone call from Cyprus. Its target was Dhigenis".

When I told him that all these were extremely serious, however many were not proven, he showed me some pages from his diary. I begged him to allow me to go through its pages. He adamantly refused.

"No" he told me. *"I myself have sins. Unfortunately, I also sinned in some instances with these thugs".*

In the pages he showed me there were names, events, dates, times, dialogues and extracts from official documents. Unfortunately, 11 days later he died. His daughter, whom I begged to allow me to read through her father's diary, she told me that she was ordered to burn it together with four suitcases full of documents. I can only imagine what a rich archive had been lost"[89].

On 12th January, JE Papalexopoulos, a check-in clerk at Ellinikon Airport, probably employed by Olympic Airways had submitted a short report on Avraam Solomou's problem with his ticket when he presented himself for check-in on 12th October:

The late Mr. Solomou presented himself at the check-in counter on 12 Oct 1967 and asked to be processed for flight CY284 of that date. When asked for his ticket, Mr. Solomou stated due to a mix-up at Nicosia airport he was no longer in possession of his return ticket to Nicosia.

As Mr. Solomou did not have his ticket cover, nor did he know the number of his ticket, I explained to him that under the circumstances

---

[89] 'My evidence to the Ad Hoc Committee of the House of Parliament of Cyprus for the "Cyprus File', Volume A' pages 534 to 536, published Nicosia 2010, Eleftherios Papadopoulos.

I could not possibly accept him for this flight. As an alternative I offered to signal Nicosia and ask for details of his ticket and also authority to issue a new ticket against an indemnity form. I also informed the passenger that this, of course, would take some time and therefore he should consider as impossible to fly to Nicosia on that specific flight, i.e. CY284/1210.

Mr. Solomou, nevertheless, was quite determined to fly as he had planned and asked to speak to higher authority. Consequently, I had to turn him over to the duty officer, Mr. Coliandris, who listened to Mr. Solomou very carefully and then repeated to the passenger what I had already told him, i.e. that we could not possibly accept him on CY284/1210.

Being occupied with the closing of the service, I could not follow the rest of their conversation, but after a while Mr. Coliandris asked me to issue a new ticket against indemnity form and then send a signal to Nicosia for the relevant details and authority.

An indemnity form was prepared and duly signed by Mr. Solomou and a new ticket ATH/NIC was issued by me as per the D/O's instructions. As soon as the a/c departed I sent a signal to NICOSIA in accordance with the above.

To the best of my knowledge this signal remains unanswered.

The report was forwarded by PD Antram, BEA's Manager, Greece, to the airline's Air Safety Branch, on 15th January with a covering note outlining his own concerns:

In view of the suggestion that the cause of the accident to Comet GARCO was an explosion of a device carried on board, I believe the following information which has just come to light may be of some significance.

It appears that Mr. Solomou presented himself for carriage without any ticket and was quite adamant that he had to go on this flight.

I have called for statements from the staff who handled this passenger and attach them for your consideration.

You may consider Mr. Solomou's insistence on travelling as suspect. Perhaps he was carrying explosives which he wished to deliver as soon as possible.

Finally, although almost every other passenger on the police list of passengers has their personal address noted, Solomou's is given only as 'c/o the Embassy of the Republic of Cyprus in Athens'.

The account in the book 'Operation Kofinou' by Spyros Papageorgiou, appears to be that the person entrusted with planting the bomb on the aircraft was to cancel his flight if Grivas did not board. This suggests that the actual plan, if Grivas had flown as anticipated, was for the person to board the aircraft as a passenger, conceal the bomb and then fabricate an excuse to leave the flight before it departed. How this would be achieved without rousing suspicion, and indeed without anyone noticing that the bomb had been placed surreptitiously and that the passenger and left without it, is not made clear. Sources have suggested to the author that the bomb planter did not manage to leave the flight and tried unsuccessfully to defuse the bomb. Again, this would not have gone unnoticed by the other passengers and the crew. Finally, if Solomou had intended all along to fly on CY284, he would certainly have ensured that his ticket was in order before turning up at the check-in desk. It is possible that the account has suffered somewhat in the retelling and translation.

In Solomou's defence, it is unlikely that he would have deliberately carried out the bombing as a suicidal venture. He was, by now, a family man with a job working for one of the most powerful men in Cyprus. The account given by George Papadopoulos, given to him by his contact who was in hopeless expectation of death, is similar in many respects to that of Papageorgiou, as related by Leonidou. The difference in detail is simply that, in the latter case, Solomou had no idea that he was carrying the device.

Solomou is described variously as chauffeur or personal assistant of the Foreign Minister of Spyros Kyprianou, this being an established fact, but also as a bodyguard or henchman of Grivas, which is not believed to have been the case. Sources have told the author that it is quite likely that Solomou was a *de facto* bodyguard of Kyprianou and might well have been a plain clothes police officer. Whether or not he would have been a member of the Cyprus Special Branch is impossible to say but, seven years after independence, it is feasible. That would explain why the Cyprus Special Branch did not mention Solomou as being on its records when contacting Veal. Certainly, Solomou had been a fighter with EOKA during the independence struggle so was no stranger to the use of force. However, that in itself certainly does not suggest he would have been prepared to destroy an airliner in more peaceful times, especially one carrying Cypriot cabin staff and passengers.

According to the few notes in the files, Solomou had been in Athens for a holiday. However, when he tried to check in at Ellinikon Airport in the early hours of 12th October, he was clearly determined to get on the flight. If, as asserted by the various sources above, he had been instructed to carry an urgent package for Spyros Kyprianou, and to get it to the Foreign Minister that very morning, it would explain why he was so hell-bent on being allowed to fly. Due to his role, it is certain that he would not have questioned the instruction to carry the package, or what it contained.

Traditionally, official diplomatic mail travels via the 'Diplomatic Bag' process and is immune from search. In most cases, small items were, at the time, carried in briefcases padlocked to the wrist of the courier. If Solomou's bag, containing the device, been so attached to him, he would have suffered very serious injuries which would have immediately been apparent to the pathologists, had his body actually been recovered at all. It appears, therefore, that the bag was not attached directly to Solomou.

There is no information about the size of the bag containing the device which, if it had contained sixteen ounces of explosive, may well have been the size of a baked bean tin. That would have fitted easily into any carry-on bag and it is likely that Solomou, if he was the carrier, had accepted the package and simply carried it in his personal baggage.

According to the files, however, there are two striking reasons why the carrier might not have been Solomou at all.

The seating plan for the ATH-NIC sector has Solomou sitting in seat 16C. However, it is noted that this is speculative, and no basis for the assumed seat allocation is given. The analysis by Fred Jones gives a clear rationale for the device detonating behind seats 4A or 5A, and this is borne out by the prevalence of extreme injuries and missing passengers from this part of the aircraft.

In addition, Solomou's body was in the 'slight injury' category. His injuries were described in the pathology report. These were facial injuries, lacerations on his right side, multiple rib fractures including a fractured sternum, dislocated pelvis and left knee. Internally, he had suffered a severe haemothorax and ruptured heart (the primary cause of death) and diaphragm. He also suffered from severe abdominal injuries. His injuries appeared consistent with a sudden and very violent, deceleration whilst strapped into his seat and possibly hitting his head on the seat in front of him. They were markedly different from those expected had he fallen from height into the sea or been caught in the blast of an exploding bomb.

If Solomou had indeed taken the device on board, deliberately or unwittingly, he had certainly not been sitting next to it when it exploded. His body was recovered amongst the 'Turkish group', which strongly suggested that Solomou had been in the forward part of the cabin when the fuselage broke at the wing spar. This would have been the case, had he been sitting in row 16, as indicated on the seating plan. It is, of course, entirely possible that Solomou was not sitting in row 16 but further back, in seat 3A or 4A. The only plausible hypothesis that would accord with the facts is if Solomou had left his bag in the footwell of his seat and had made his way forward for an unknown reason. He would certainly not have returned to his seat after the explosion and in all likelihood would have strapped himself into an empty seat some distance away from the damage.

Nicos Papapetrou

BEA's Insurance Manager, a Mr. Springbett, had been making enquiries into the insurance cover held by the victims of the crash. In late January, he contacted Veal to pass on information that passenger Nico Papapetrou had taken out three significant policies, shortly before travelling, these being two sums of £10,000 each with The Sun Alliance Group and The General Insurance Company of

Cyprus, along with a policy for £5,000 with the Eagle Star company. Veal forwarded this information to Chief Inspector Bryan, adding:

> It is understood that these insurances were taken out on 1st October in Cyprus. His body was not recovered.
>
> It is understood that Mr. Papapetrou was a shoe salesman earning £80 a month but it is also apparently known that he was a professional gambler. In the twelve months prior to the accident he had made five visits by air from Cyprus to Greece but is believed never to have taken out any insurance except on this last occasion. In the winding up of his affairs after his presumed death in the accident his estate was sworn at less than £2,000. In view of the occurrence in North America of aircraft accidents in which insurance has been found to be an underlying factor it is felt that this aspect should be further investigated.

On 1st September 1968, an article in the *Sunday Times* pointed the finger of suspicion firmly in the direction of Papapetrou. Under the headline, *'Missing link in the Comet crash'* and the by-line of 'John Shirley in Cyprus and John Ball in London', it told its readers:

> 'It is better for me to die. My whole life has been a disaster.'
>
> These are the words of a small-time Greek-Cypriot smuggler working as the manager of a shoe shop in the small town of Larnaca, Cyprus. He is almost certainly the missing link in the mystery explosion that sent a BEA Comet 4B crashing into the Mediterranean off Rhodes last October.
>
> Nicos Papaetrou (sic), faced with gambling debts, two girlfriends in Athens and expensive fees to pay for his daughter's dental course in the Greek capital, was talking to a friend just 48 hours before a 16-ounce bomb – of military origin – blew a hole in the Comet's fuselage.
>
> Papaetrou and 65 others were on the plane. They all died. In the fortnight before the crash, Papaetrou had taken out three insurance covers totalling £23,000. There may be a fourth.
>
> Following in the tracks of a Scotland Yard team, headed by Detective Superintendent Percy Browne, who flew to Rhodes to examine the scant wreckage, we found this new witness whose memory of a conversation points directly to Papaetrou as the cause of the crash.
>
> All documents concerning the flight were collected by the Yard and one by one the victims were crossed off his list. Then Supt. Browne came to 44-year-old Papaetrou and discovered the insurance covers.
>
> It was Papaetrou's fifth journey between the island and the Greek capital that year; he had told his wife, Nina, at their blue-pained, double-fronted rambling bungalow in 28th October Street, Larnaca,

MR SOLOMOU ATH/NICOS CY284/12.10.67 C-ARCO

In accordance with your instructions to submit a short report as far as
the above mentioned passenger was concerned, I have to report the
following :-

1. The late Mr Solomou presented himself at the check-in counter
    on 12 Oct 1967 and asked to be processed for flight CY284 of
    that date. When asked for his ticket, Mr Solomou stated that
    due to a mix-up at NICOSIA A/P he was no longer in possession
    of his return ticket to NICOSIA.

2. As Mr Solomou did not have his ticket cover nor did he know
    the number of his ticket, I explained to him that under the
    circumstances I could not possibly accept him for this flight.
    As alternative I offered to signal NICOSIA and ask for details
    of his ticket and also authority to issue a new ticket against
    an indemnity form. I also informed the passenger that this, of
    course, would take some time and therefore he should consider
    as impossible to fly to NICOSIA on that specific flight, i.e.
    CY 284/1210

3. Mr Solomou, nevertheless, was quite determined to fly as he
    had planned and asked to speak to higher authority. Consequently
    I had to turn him over to the D/O, Mr Coliandris, who listened
    to Mr Solomou very carefully and then repeated to the passenger
    what I had already told him, i.e. that we could not possibly
    accept him on CY 284/1210.

4. Being occupied with the closing of the service, I could not
    follow the rest of their conversation, but after a while
    Mr Coliandris asked me to issue a new ticket against indemnity
    form and then send a signal to NICOSIA for the relevant details
    and authority.

5. An indemnity form was prepared and duly signed by Mr Solomou
    and a new ticket ATH/NIC/ was issued by me as per the D/O's
    instructions. As soon as the a/c departed I sent a signal to
    NICOSIA in accordance with the above.

6. To the best of my knowledge this signal remains unanswered.

*The report from check-in clerk J E Papalexopolou concerning Solomou's behaviour at ATH
when denied a seat on CY284 (TNA).*

189

FROM: D/O Ch. Colliandris   13.1.68

Mr SOLOMOU ATHENS/NICOSIA CY284/1210 G-ARCO

The above named passenger reported at the Airport Check-In desk to
travel to Nicosia on the above flight.
He was in possession of a carton ticket N° 0482/229985 in favour of
Miss Iacovidou Nicosia/Athens only and stated that when he checked in
at Nicosia airport the above wrong ticket was given to him by CAL
Official instead of his own which was a return one Nicosia/Athens/Nicosia
issued by CAL Town Office Nicosia on the 29th or 30th September, prior
to his departure.

He also stated that he was the personal driver of Cyprus Foreign Minister
Mr Kyprianou and he had to be back to Nicosia for duty on that day.
After a long discussion on the incident I realised that the liability
on the loss of the ticket was C.A.L's and gave instructions to our
Check-In staff to issue a ticket against indemnity form forwarding
immediately the attached signal to C A L Nicosia :

"NICAPCY NICTOCY
O/B CY284 MR SOLOMOU TRAVELLING ATH/NIC TKT N° 0602/8798588 ISSUED
AGAINST INDEMNITY FORM AS PAP STATED LOST ORIGINAL TKT NIC/ATH/NIC
ISSUED CAL T/O NIC 29 OR 30 SEP STOP PAP ALSO STATES HIS TKT MIXED DURING
CHECK-IN WORKS AND GIVEN COVER OF TICKET 0482/229985 FAVOUR MISS IACOVIDOU
NIC/ATH STOP ATTN NIC TO CY PSE ADV NUMBER OF ORIGINAL TICKET 30 SUPPORT
FORM OF INDEMNITY. "

*The report from Mr. Coliandris, Duty Officer at Athens for Olympic Airways, evidencing the
conversation he had with Avraam Solomou, resulting in the latter being allowed to travel on
CY284 (TNA).*

190

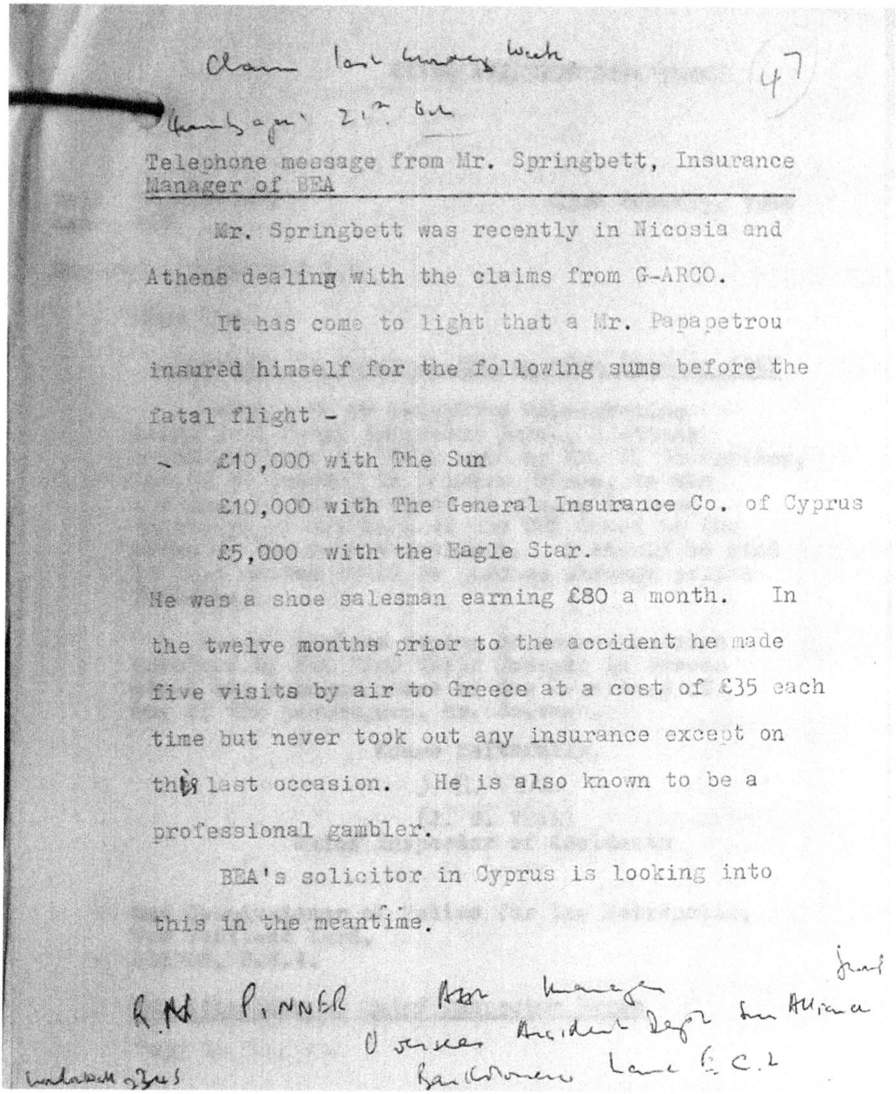

Claim last [illegible] week
[illegible] 21st [illegible]

Telephone message from Mr. Springbett, Insurance Manager of BEA

Mr. Springbett was recently in Nicosia and Athens dealing with the claims from G-ARCO.

It has come to light that a Mr. Papapetrou insured himself for the following sums before the fatal flight -

£10,000 with The Sun

£10,000 with The General Insurance Co. of Cyprus

£5,000 with the Eagle Star.

He was a shoe salesman earning £80 a month. In the twelve months prior to the accident he made five visits by air to Greece at a cost of £35 each time but never took out any insurance except on this last occasion. He is also known to be a professional gambler.

BEA's solicitor in Cyprus is looking into this in the meantime.

R M PINNER [illegible handwriting]

Note to John Veal giving details of the suspicious insurance dealings by Nicos Papapetrou before his flight on CY284 (TNA)

that they were business trips. But they were not for the Nicosia shoe firm of Galides Ltd., for whom he managed the local shop.

As he counted his meagre commission – he earned between £50 and £60 a month – he talked of breaking into the leather industry and manufacturing leather handbags. The journeys to Athens were to look for materials.

The detectives discovered Papaetrou had for years kept only one personal accident policy worth £2,000 with General Insurance Ltd. of Cyprus, which did not cover him for aviation risk.

But on September 30 last year he walked into the Larnaca branch office of the company and took out a personal accident cover for £8,000 – valid only for the month of October and covering a single journey abroad to Greece and England.

Within a few days he took out another policy, this time with the Cyprus branch of Eagle Star for £5,000. Then there was a third policy which he drew up with Sun Assurance Ltd. for £10,000.

A fortnight later the Comet exploded. Already it is understood Eagle Star have paid out to Papaetrou's widow. But the Sun company have been waiting for the official verdict on the crash before making final settlement. And General Insurance are contesting their obligation to pay on what their Nicosia manager termed "certain discrepancies in the claim".

Apparently, the dead man did not notify General Insurance of the two other policies he had taken out. The manager explained, "It is a technical matter. It is nothing to do with the cause of the accident."

But as the Yard probe went deeper, they discovered that Papaetrou, father of two daughters, had connections with a smuggling syndicate. In Athens he had two girlfriends called Helen and Titica. He gambled at casinos in Athens and on Corfu.

He spent most of the money he made through smuggling on the two girlfriends or in the casinos. But as his luck began to sour gambling debts built up and creditors demanded their money back.

Then he was thought to have been unable to pay for the goods he obtained for smuggling to Greece. A few days before his last trip he pleaded with an old friend, a retired shipping agent, who had travelled with him on some early trips, for a £1,000 loan. He only got £500.

But not only was his luck running out on the gambling tables, his marriage was beginning to crumble. However, he was still having to pay for his younger daughter, Christala, aged 19, who was undergoing expensive tuition at an Athens school of dentistry. Finally, he was almost caught red-handed with a consignment of watches worth £940 at Athens airport. Papaetrou's contact man, believed to be a customs official, failed to show up, and a brown leather suitcase stowed in the aircraft was opened. He denied it was part of his luggage and managed to hoodwink the customs investigators. But not only had he lost the consignment but also the smuggling link had been broken and he faced yet another debt.

The family of Nicos Papapetrou have commented that they consider the contents of the *Sunday Times* article to be wholly incorrect.[90]

In the introduction to his book *The Occult*[91], Colin Wilson wrote:

I open a weekend colour supplement and read that for a week before the explosion that destroyed a BEA Comet aircraft on October 12, 1967, Nicos Papapetrou was haunted by premonitions, and dreams of death and mourning, so that an hour before take-off, he tried to book on another flight. That is not past history, but then, Papapetrou was carrying the bomb that accidentally exploded. He was an explosives smuggler and had made six similar trips earlier that year; why did he get premonitions on this one?

The passage about Papapetrou is included by Wilson to support his contention that premonitions are still experienced in the present time, as well as historically. Unfortunately, the original source, which was a weekend newspaper, and the date of original publication cannot be identified. It is possible that the account was made available in parallel to the detailed article in the *Sunday Times*, albeit that piece suggested that Papapetrou had intended to commit suicide, rather than the detonation being inadvertent.

On 11th September 1968, Jan Riddoch at the Foreign Office sought legal advice from the Board of Trade's solicitor on whether portions of the police report dealing with Papapetrou could be released to the Sun Alliance and London Insurance Group. He presumed that the insurance company would help to support or negate their assertion that (i) the death of Papapetrou had not been proved beyond doubt; (ii) that if he had died, then his death was due to suicide and (iii) that he had failed to disclose the existence of other insurance policies. The insurers had a significant interest in that they stood to pay out £10,000 unless they could show grounds why the policy was invalid. In the event, the police refused to make the report available, a situation that remains the same over fifty years later.

---

[90] Elina Rossidou, grand-daughter of Nicos Papapetrou, in correspondence with the author.
[91] The Occult, by Colin Wilson (Hodder & Stoughton, 1971).

Watching the Detectives

The two Metropolitan Police officers had their work cut out. They were to investigate one of the biggest mass murders in modern British history. In later years, terrorist atrocities would become far more frequent but at the time, the Charlie Oscar incident was unprecedented for the British authorities.

The bombing of Pan Am flight 103 on 21st December 1988, resulting in the deaths of 270 people, was on a different scale to CY284, but the two crimes were similar in their nature. The police investigation into the Lockerbie atrocity bore no comparison to the limited resources given to Browne and Hill, involving the resources of the FBI as well as Dumfries and Galloway Constabulary. 15,000 witness statements were taken. The investigation into the downing of Charlie Oscar was to be a much lower key affair.

The police report itself is still withheld from the public, but a cover note in the Metropolitan Police files, which contain fourteen pages of documents, notes that 266 other pages of documents have been removed, under Exemptions[92] S (2) 31, S (2) 38 and S (2) 40. Similarly, in the Home Office file (HO 287/2146), three sections are removed, totalling 255 pages. One of these is identifiable as the Pathology Report which was publicly available in full as AVIA101/255. A second section comprises 183 pages, removed under Exemptions 31 and 40. This was probably the compilation of witness statements. The third section, under the same Exemptions, comprises 29 pages and is annotated 'Report'.

The Schedule to Statements Relating to Deceased Passengers, contained in HO 287/2146[93] albeit redacted to remove the addresses of the passengers, shows that statement numbers 57 to 138 refer to the victims. It would be usual practice for there to be one statement from the next of kin confirming the planned journey and giving relevant background detail such as the purpose for traveling. In some cases, a married couple, such as the Griffiths, or a family group such as the Taskers, is covered by a single statement. Other individuals are covered by more than one statement. All told, this accounts for 82 statements covering the 59 passengers. There would also have been statements for each of the crew, adding a further seven to the total. This would leave at least 49 statements from additional witnesses. However, a total of 183 pages for 138 statements is a paltry number considering the lines of enquiry that the two officers might reasonably have been expected to have recognised. There is the possibility of course that the documentation contains only a selection of the more substantial statements.

---

[92] Exemption 31 covers information relating to law enforcement, 38 to Health and Safety and 41 to 'information provided in confidence'. Exemptions 31 and 41 allow witness statements and the substantive police reports into the incident to be withheld. In this case, from correspondence challenging the withholding of these documents, it is known that Exemption 38 is used to withhold the Pathology Report as it contains images and information deemed to be too disturbing to view. As noted, the full report is available separately.

[93] See Appendix 13.

The additional 49 witness statements should have included the four BEA cabin staff on the London – Athens sector, the six passengers who disembarked, the airport staff at Athens and London Heathrow, the three flight deck crew of Mike Foxtrot, the air traffic controllers at Athens and Nicosia, the investigation teams at RARDE, the AIB and the Royal Aircraft Establishment. These would all be required to validate the documentary, aural and eye-witness evidence of all aspects of Charlie Oscar's last journey.

The 'passengers of interest' would have generated additional statements. Avraam Solomou's behaviour had attracted attention at the airport which was witnessed by both JE Papalexopoulos, the check-in clerk, and Mr. C. Coliandris, the BEA Duty Manager, who authorised Solomou to travel at very short notice.

Even though the information quoted in the books by Leonidas Leonidou and Eleftherios Papadopoulos did not come to light until much later, Solomou was first named in the Evening Standard article on 21st November 1967 as the person carrying the bomb on board. The information is quite specific and although the article was played down, it would be a strange thing for someone to have dreamt up. Also, one identifying feature on Solomou's body noted by the pathologists was the presence of scars from bullet wounds from his time with EOKA. These should have been recorded as of possible significance.

The police team might have reasonably been expected to consider the following enquiries into Solomou's presence on the flight.

- Next-of-kin statement confirming that Solomou was planning to be on the flight, or at least to try to travel from Athens to Nicosia.
- Why was Solomou so determined to get onto the flight?
- If he had been told to be back in Nicosia the following morning, who had passed on that message and from whom had it originated?
- What was he carrying in the way of cabin baggage?
- Was he searched?
- What was his demeanour immediately prior to boarding, once his ticket had been sorted out?
- Where and when had he bought his original ticket?
- Was he travelling for personal purposes or for his work for Spiros Kyprianou.
- If travelling for work, had he visited the Cypriot Embassy in Athens, or had they had any contact with him?
- What were the exact purposes of his trip to Athens?
- Where had he stayed before checking in for CY284?
- Who had he visited?
- Had he been formally allocated seat 16C?
- If not, who provided the information that he was sitting there, and on what basis?

195

- What was known about his involvement in EOKA, and what specialist weapons-handling expertise did he have?
- What were his past and present relationships, if any, with Yiorkadjis and Grivas?

At the very least, statements should have been taken from Mr. Papalexopoulos, Mr. Coliandris, Mrs. Solomou, any other airline or airport staff who had direct contact with him, and finally an appropriate person in Mr. Kyprianou's office. If further details had emerged, it would be reasonable to obtain statements to substantiate or disprove the inference that Solomou's suspicious behaviour was in fact of significant concern. It would have been as important to eliminate Solomou as a suspect as to have shown there were grounds to dig even deeper. However, Avraam Solomou accounts for only two statements in the police file.

Sotiris Georgiou would have been more challenging as he originated in the USA. However, even in 1968 it would not have been beyond the realms of practicality for the FBI to assist with a next-of-kin statement. The lines of enquiry for Mr. Georgiou would have included:

- Purpose of his visit to Cyprus.
- Details of any military service, explosives expertise, or lack thereof.
- Links or otherwise, to George Georgiou, the disgruntled former BEA employee.
- Evidence of his seat allocation in 4A.
- Details of his cabin baggage.
- Evidence of any adverse behavioural indicators: was he unusually nervous, for a passenger?

The minimum requirement for statements for Sotiris Georgiou would have included his next-of-kin, check-in staff at London, cabin staff on the London – Athens sector and, if possible, George Georgiou. Only statement number 83 refers to Georgiou.

Had the investigation team made contact with the Georgiou family, they would ascertain the answers to the points above. The purpose of his trip to Cyprus was simply to visit his parents, his brother Nick and family, as well as to explore the idea of finding a Cypriot future bride. Although, he had been in the US for less than four years, he was home sick and wanted to go back for a three-week visit. He had never served in the military and was never trained in the use of arms or explosives.

There was no link between Sotiris and George Georgiou, the disgruntled former employee of BEA. He did, coincidentally, have a brother named George who at the time of the disaster, was living a few thousand miles west of London, in Clairton Pennsylvania, where he managed a dry-cleaning business. During his stopover in London between his BOAC and BEA flights, Sotiris spent the time with his English in-laws and also shopping.

196

It is, of course, entirely possible that Sotiris may have changed seats while en route to Athens, or when reboarding Charlie Oscar after the stopover there. The BEA cabin staff make no mention of such a change, however.

Sotiris had two suitcases and a smaller carry-on bag. He was taking gifts to his family in Cyprus. The acquisition of further gifts in London accounts for the four kilos of excess baggage he was noted as checking in at London.

According to Sotiris' brother Polyvios[94], the people who knew him throughout his all-too-short life characterized Sotiris as a level-headed, handsome, even-tempered; socially involved, generous young man, who went to evening classes to improve his English. According to his two German employers he was well-disciplined and a hard worker that had dreams about opening his own car repair shop in New York. He was a trained car mechanic and at the time of his death was employed by Great Neck Imports, a firm specializing in Mercedes car models. He had acquired US citizenship in Wilmington, Delaware in 1965, fourteen months after arriving in the US. This rather quick naturalisation was the result of his father regaining his own US citizenship after a ruling by that country's Supreme Court.

Polyvios' mother-in-law and brothers-in-law were the last members of his extended family to see Sotiris alive as he boarded BE284 at Heathrow.

According to the *Sunday Telegraph* team, Nicos Papapetrou came to light when it transpired that he had taken out separate insurance policies with four different companies. In addition to the next-of-kin statement, it would also have been important to establish:

- Where and when did he buy the insurance policies?
- Who had interacted with him in selling the insurance? Was it definitely Papapetrou who had bought the policies?
- Had he expressed suicidal thoughts at any time previously?
- What was he carrying in the way of cabin baggage?
- Was he searched?
- What was his demeanour immediately prior to boarding?
- Where and when had he bought his ticket?
- Was he travelling for personal purposes or for his work for Galides, his employer?
- What were the exact purposes of his trip to Athens?
- Where had he stayed before checking in for CY284?
- Who had he visited?
- Had he been formally allocated seat a seat?

---

[94] Polyvios Georgiou in correspondence with the author, 2018.

- Was he associating with the group of Jehovah's Witnesses before boarding?
- What military or specialist weapons-handling expertise did he have?

This would entail the usual statements from his wife and check-in staff, along with the ticket seller, any surviving witnesses from the Athens departure lounge, his daughter in Athens and the four insurance agents. This would add up to at least seven statements; whilst Papapetrou was the subject of four statements, 135 to 138, it would have been reasonable to expect significantly more.

By way of comparison, a number of other passengers are the subject of several statements. Of note are the McComb family (six statements) and Mrs. Liassides (four). None of these victims rated any kind of a mention in terms of arousing suspicion, which under their apparent circumstances is entirely understandable. Yet they merited more statements than the named suspects.

On the face of it, to carry out a thorough investigation would require a much larger team of police officers than Detective Superintendent Browne and Detective Sergeant Hill. Nowadays, for a mass murder enquiry, the team would have reported to an Assistant Chief Constable in a county force or perhaps a Deputy Assistant Commissioner in the Metropolitan Police.

The cost of the investigation, which so exercised the minds of various parties, would mostly have comprised the time of the two officers, their travel, hotel and subsistence. The wages, in 2018 prices, of the two officers[95] for a two-month period would have amounted to around £20,000. Flights, depending on the number taken, would probably have added £10,000 for a number of round trips. Hotel accommodation would add perhaps £200 per night, and subsistence around £100 per day for the two officers. Taxi fares would probably amount to another £500 per week, if a lot of travelling was entailed. All told, the order of magnitude of the taxpayers' burden would have been £50,000 and £60,000. The cost of the Lockerbie investigation itself is not known, but the trial alone cost $60 million. When three Islamist terrorists plotted to blow up transatlantic airliners in August 2006, the investigation and trial were estimated to total £100 million. The investigation into Charlie Oscar would have been an absolute bargain, had the suspect been identified.

If the investigation was carried out today, Browne, or his equivalent, would manage a large team carrying out enquiries throughout Britain, Greece and Cyprus, digging into the backgrounds of each passenger, sifting through all available documentation, tracking down anybody who had any involvement at all with BE/CY284. Crucially, there would be intensive work going on behind the scenes exploring the potential political scenarios. The immediate assumption that the bomb was intended for General Grivas must have had some foundation for being so strongly held. If there was, indeed, some foundation for the belief, then it would have been in the interests of the Cypriot Government to determine

---

[95] Superintendent £85,000 p.a., Sergeant £40,000

what that was; at the very least, the reader might consider that Grivas himself would be keen to know.

The Metropolitan Police had not seemed particularly eager to take on the investigation in the first place. There was then considerable reticence to involve the Greek authorities, or even let them know that the investigation was going on. No mention at all is made of involving the Cypriot government or its agencies. The Foreign Office sent a clear message to Assistant Commissioner Brodie to tell Browne to raise any political angle to them before proceeding further. The importance of this message was clearly understood by Brodie, who sent a very secretive letter to Browne through the Diplomatic Bag system. If the instruction had been routine, and a matter of not treading on toes, it could have been handled by telephone, or perhaps by a member of the staff at the Athens Embassy having a quiet word with Browne and Hill about diplomatic niceties and protocols.

It seems that the Foreign Office had very great concerns about something being spoiled if Browne was not given the hard word. To this day, 'national security' remains one of the reasons given by the National Archives for not releasing some of the information in the files. Such measures, although likely to attract media criticism, are easier to understand if they are necessary to protect a highly-placed intelligence source, perhaps in a government position. During the Cyprus Emergency, EOKA was riddled with informants, leading to the extreme measures by Grivas, perhaps including what Georgeides had succinctly termed the General's *'exterminating-traitor-squad'*. It is unlikely that Grivas had succeeded in tracking them all down.

Part Four: Analysis and Conclusions

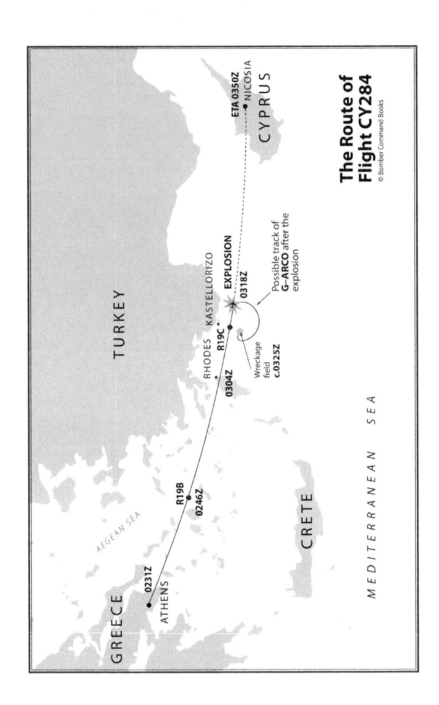

The Route of
Flight CY284

© Bomber Command Books

GREECE

ATHENS
0231Z

AEGEAN SEA

R19B
0246Z

TURKEY

RHODES
0304Z

KASTELLORIZO

R19C
EXPLOSION
0318Z

Possible track of
G-ARCO after the
explosion

Wreckage
field
c.0325Z

CYPRUS

NICOSIA
ETA 0350Z

CRETE

MEDITERRANEAN   SEA

Analysis

No one will ever know what happened on board Charlie Oscar during her final few minutes of flight, and it is unlikely that the true reason and the actual perpetrator will ever come to light. It is possible, though, to reconstruct the likely course of events after SFO Thomas started his greeting to Nicosia.

At that point, the bomb exploded in the passenger cabin. Sited in the passenger footwell of seat 3A or 4A, and partially under the seat in front of it, the device fragmented, forcing microscopic fragments of shrapnel in all directions, and at unimaginably high speeds. The occupant of the seat in whose footwell the bomb had been located, would have been very seriously wounded but, mercifully, would have known little about it. The over-pressure, of the order of several hundred pounds per square inch immediately next to the device, undoubtedly tore a significant hole in the fuselage, forcing the metal skin outward into the airstream. A smaller hole was left in the cabin floor. Initially measuring some thirty inches square, the breach in the pressure cabins wall immediately allowed all the air in the fuselage to escape.

In a split second, the cabin temperature and pressure plummeted, causing a dense fog to form, compounded by dust and debris, though these were almost immediately displaced as the air forced its way out of the fuselage. The intense, though short-lived, rush was enough to carry with it the shattered body of the occupant of the seat, never to be recovered. It is most likely that this was Sotiris Georgiou, known to have been sitting in 4A on the London to Athens sector, strongly indicating that the bomb had been brought on to the aircraft by the person sitting in 3A on the Athens to Nicosia flight.

The force of the blast diminished greatly with every foot from the centre of the explosion, especially as the aircraft seats provided a barrier to the wave of pressure.

Achillea Afatitis, one of the group of Jehovah's Witnesses and who was probably standing in the aisle, four or five feet away, was peppered with shrapnel, but avoided being sucked out of the aircraft as he was blocked by the row of seats between him and the hole in the cabin wall.

The passenger behind whose seat the explosion occurred, and whose identity will never be known for certain, probably sustained serious lacerations to their back and legs, and may also have been lost at that point.

As the pressure within the cabin equalised with that outside, the mist cleared, and the temperature dropped. The emergency oxygen masks dropped and those who were still conscious and capable of doing so, donned them. The others remained mercifully oblivious to the traumatic situation developing around them.

The pilots would have put on their oxygen masks and run through the procedures for sudden loss of pressure. This involved a controlled descent to a

Above: The control cables (centre) for the emergency hydraulic power change-over system on a Comet 4, shown with the side panels removed in the rear freight hold. The other, thicker, cables further up are the control input cables direct from the control columns and rudder pedals. Both rudder and elevator cables pass through this area, leading to a potentially catastrophic loss of control if they were sheared by shrapnel from an explosion. However, there is a duplicate elevator control run on the starboard side. The hydraulic pipes are for the elevator and rudder servodynes. Below: The aileron servodynes sat almost directly underneath the likely location of the bomb. Damage to these controls might have severely affected the handling of the Comet. (Simon Growcott)

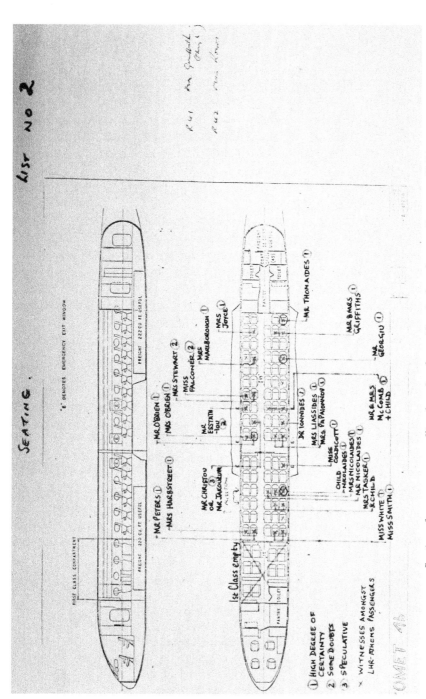

Seating of passengers travelling from London to Nicosia, based on recollections of BEA staff, crew and passengers disembarked at Athens.

205

lower altitude, flying at around 330 knots, with the airbrakes deployed and the throttles closed. In the case of explosive decompression, the Operations Manual advised '...*the stresses in the airframe should be kept at a minimum by holding the air speed within reasonable bounds by avoiding all unnecessary and violent manoeuvres.*'

The next stage in the procedure would come when they had descended to below 13,500 feet, which would be in four to five minutes. From their cruising height of 29,000 feet, this length of time would not present an overwhelming problem for the passengers, as they had access to the drop-down oxygen masks in the cabin. The role of the cabin staff would have been to instruct the passengers to remain in their seats with their seatbelts fastened, whilst they awaited the intentions of the captain. It is unlikely that Capt. Blackwood anticipated ditching at that time, otherwise the passengers would have been instructed to put their lifejackets on.

The closest airport was now Rhodes, some 120 miles back along their track and 60 miles closer than Nicosia. Assuming the airport was open at that time of morning, it would probably have been the obvious choice of diversion airfield and was some 25 minutes flying time away.

Assessing the situation at first hand would have been the task of SFO Palmer. It would have been a scene of devastation, but it is fair to assume that he was trained to cope calmly with what he found. The noise of the engines and the slipstream, no longer mitigated by the cabin wall's soundproofing, would have been pronounced.

The cabin staff, by now doing their best to keep the passengers as calm as was possible in the circumstances, would try to move those nearest to the damage to empty seats away from the hole in the fuselage. There was a need to maintain the overall balance of the aircraft. It would not have been feasible to move all the passengers forward as that would have made the aircraft nose-heavy beyond its design limits, but it is quite likely that those passengers sitting on the left-hand side of the cabin, and behind the site of the explosion, would have been moved away first.

The situation would have merited a 'Mayday' call, but it is possible that the patchy radio coverage, which had necessitated Charlie Oscar's earlier transmission being relayed by Capt. Emmerson in Mike Foxtrot, now let them down completely. No distress call was ever received.

Underneath the cabin floor, it is possible that one or more of the hydraulic pipes had been severed or critical components of the system disabled by the blast. In theory, the Comet's triplicated hydraulic system should have been able to cope with just such an emergency. Equally, it is possible that damage to the aileron servos, which were almost directly underneath seat row 5, affected the ability of the pilots to control the angle of roll of the aircraft. The five minutes or so indicated on the watches allowed Charlie Oscar time to descend to about 15,000 feet.

For whatever reason, the g-forces on the aircraft, resulting from the out-of-control situation it was now in, eventually became too much and Charlie Oscar broke in two, around the forward wing spar. The shock to the airframe caused the fire extinguishers to activate, and one broke free to be found amongst the floating debris. The front portion of the fuselage, from row 11 forward, devoid of wings, descended vertically at high speed whilst the rear part, from row 10 back, retained some slight forward motion, taking it some 2,000 feet to the south.

As stated at the start of this chapter, there is no direct evidence of the above account, but it is based on the emergency procedures outlined in the Comet 4 Flight Manual. An uncontrolled, steepening turn would account for the distance of 25 to 30 nautical miles travelled in the five minutes between the explosion and disintegration, being so much greater than the straight-line distance of 10 nautical miles between the estimated location of the aircraft when the last call was made, and the place at which the wreckage was estimated to have fallen into the sea. It might also explain why the heading of Charlie Oscar when she disintegrated was believed to be south or south-east, rather than the west-north-west that would have taken her to Rhodes.

The account by Nikos Misomikes confirming that he saw no bodies wearing lifejackets, supports the notion that the disaster was not immediately considered catastrophic, and Capt. Blackwood did not consider that it would be necessary to ditch the aircraft. Ditching far out at sea, with sporadic radio contact, in the dark, would in any case be a measure to be used only in extreme circumstances. It is therefore possible that the pilots were attempting to bring Charlie Oscar back under control, up until the point where the fuselage broke.

The movement of passengers to seats away from the hole in the fuselage might also account for five of the passengers originally seated in the rear of the aircraft being recovered in the northern wreckage field, which is where the front section of Charlie Oscar's fuselage came down. The ferrying of bodies recovered by the Kastellorizo sailors to the *Navarinon* would also possibly explain why six victims believed to have been travelling in the front section of Charlie Oscar were stated to have been amongst those found amongst the wreckage of the rear part of the aircraft.

The Metropolitan Police Investigation

The investigation into the criminal aspects of the incident was limited in its scope, resourcing and, apparently, in its enthusiasm, and has remained shrouded in secrecy. It is now more than half a century since Charlie Oscar was blown from the sky. After the initial flurry of activity around the recovery operation, analysis of the sparse wreckage and the pitiful remains of the victims and the prompt and effective accident investigation which showed conclusively that the cause was a bomb, there have been over fifty years of silence. Twenty-three files in the National Archives, comprising some 2,500 pages, provide a comprehensive record of the correspondence relating to almost every aspect of the work carried out by Ken Mason, John Veal, Eric Newton, Fred Jones and their teams.

Three files, relating to the police investigation, remain mostly unavailable to the public, and these have been a source of much speculation. These files remain wholly under lock and key with a release date of 1st January 2067. In 2018 the National Archives secured permission from the Metropolitan Police and the Home Office to disclose part of their contents to the author.

It has long been assumed, by those having an interest in solving the mystery of flight CY284, that the Metropolitan Police files have the potential to reveal further details about the incident. The few newly-released documents in the closed files hold no 'smoking gun'; in fact, they reveal very little that was not already known. Unfortunately, the final 29-page police report, along with the 138 or so witness statements, are amongst the retained information in the files. The justification for continuing to retain these documents is three-fold. First, the Metropolitan Police recognises that the incident was a crime of mass murder, and they might reopen the case 'if new evidence comes to light'. Second, it comprises information given in confidence to the investigating officers and this might disclose the political sympathies fifty years ago of the witnesses, many of whom are most likely deceased now. Finally, some of the information might compromise national security as it might reveal the identity of intelligence sources, if any. After an appeal, the Met eventually decided that it could change its stance, that it would neither confirm nor deny that it held other information on Charlie Oscar, to a confirmation that in fact, it does not. All the remaining information gathered and retained by the Met sits in those three files in the National Archives. The National Archives Freedom of Information team explained to the author why they would not release further documents from the police files[96]

> 'Some of the information you have requested is being withheld under section 23 (1) and 24 (1) in the alternative. Section 23 (1), exempts information held by a public authority from disclosure if it was provided to that public authority by the bodies dealing with security matters, or if that information relates to those bodies, and section 24 (1) exempts information from disclosure if its exemption is required for the purpose of safeguarding national security.
>
> Sections 23 (1) and 24 (1) are being cited in the alternative as it is not appropriate, in the circumstances of the case, to say which of the two exemptions is actually engaged so as not to undermine national security or reveal the extent of any involvement, or not, of the bodies dealing with security matters.

---

[96] The files are MEPO 2/11089, MEPO 2/11090 and HO 287/2146.

Section 31(1) of the FOI Act exempts information if its disclosure would, or would be likely to, prejudice –

a)   the prevention or detection of crime
b)   the apprehension or prosecution of offenders
c)   the administration of justice.

...Section 31(1)(a-c) is engaged for some of the information in MEPO 2/11089 & MEPO 2/11090 because it relates to evidence – in the form of investigation reports and related witness statements – about a crime that remains unsolved. The information is directly relevant to the investigation into the crash of BEA Comet G-Argo (sic) over the Mediterranean Sea that resulted in the death of all passengers and crew, as such the Metropolitan Police Service would desire that the details of the investigation remain confidential for the lifetime of any hypothetical suspect.

In relation to these specific files, it is not possible to identify particular information from investigation reports and witness statement that could be released into the public domain without the risk of compromising any future police actions. Information that appears innocuous may have significance to an experienced investigator that is not immediately obvious to the lay reader; or may assume a new significance in the light of newly discovered evidence or developments in forensic or investigative techniques.

The Metropolitan Police have confirmed that it is extremely difficult when considering any unsolved case as to the 'significant likelihood of future investigation' as it cannot be predicted what information or evidence may come to light in the future that would generate a renewed investigation. Increasingly police services throughout the country are setting up 'cold case' teams to review their case files on unsolved murders. As recently as last year, The National Archives provided case papers to police services in order to assist with enquiries into an unsolved murder from the late 1940s. In considering this exemption we therefore have to acknowledge that there does remain a possibility, however remote, that this case could be investigated at some point in the future and that the information contained in these records could be significant to it.

As a result section 31(1)(a-c) has been applied to all information created by the investigating authorities in these records, as we are unable to identify (and therefore redact) particular information that might be released into the public domain without the risk of compromising any future police actions.

The purpose of this exemption in this instance is to protect details that could be used in a future investigation should a suspect be identified, charged and brought to trial. The closure period is based on an assumption that the suspect(s) would have been at least 16 years old at the material time.

The premature release of this information into the public domain may be detrimental to any future investigation and subsequent prosecution. To release significant information which could potentially jeopardise a future prosecution for murder would not be in the public interest. Therefore it has been determined that the risk of prejudice outweighs the reasoning for disclosure in this specific case and the exemption at section 31(1)(a-c) of the Freedom of Information Act applies to the information...

...Section 38(1)(b) is engaged for a limited amount of information in these records because it contains the identities of police informants. While there is an important public interest in the transparency of police investigations and their investigative methods, in this case, this must be balanced against the risk of placing in the public domain, information that could put at risk the safety of an individual. It has been determined that release of the identities of these individuals would be likely to endanger these individuals and to prejudice their physical safety by exposing them to the risk of physical harm from reprisal attacks, thus section 38(1)(b) is engaged...

...It remains the expert opinion of the Metropolitan Police Service and therefore of TNA that, despite the passage of time, there continues to exist a real possibility of endangerment for these individuals, who could be at risk from retaliation or reprisal action if their names were to be released into the public domain. The public need the reassurance of knowing that FOI access rights are not going to be allowed to be exercised to their detriment. To release information which would be likely to expose individuals to the risk of physical harm or pose a danger to their safety would not be in the public interest. Therefore, it has been determined that the risk of endangering the physical safety of the individuals identified in these records significantly outweighs any reasons for disclosure and the exemption at section 38(1)(b) of the FOI Act applies to this information...

...In your internal review request you mentioned that there are a number of open records related to this case and highlighted a lack of consistency between open and closed information.

I can confirm that I consulted a number of AVIA files in relation to your internal review request and can confirm that they do not contain the same information or investigation reports held within MEPO 2/11089 and MEPO 2/11090. This is because Metropolitan Police records (MEPO records) typically contain papers and reports directly relating to a criminal investigation including witness statements, information relating to possible suspects, forensic evidence and possible lines of enquiry.

The FOI Centre have referred three records, AVIA 101/225, AVIA 101/218 and AVIA 101/220[97] to be reviewed under our Reclosure policy.'

The Cypriot authorities have told sources that they hold no information whatsoever about the incident, this seemingly including the six copies of the AIB report they were sent in 1968. In 2014, the Cyprus Police reviewed the case, pursuant to a Presidential decree, but this apparently revealed no new information.

It is inconceivable in the current age that the criminal investigation into the loss of Charlie Oscar would have been so light-touch. Investigations into similar events, such as Lockerbie in the UK and the two separate losses of Malaysia Airlines Boeing 777s in 2014, were multinational affairs in which the cost, quite rightly, was not a deciding factor. With two officers dedicated to investigating CY284, the investigation plan should have been overwhelming; in fact, it appears to have taken Detective Superintendent Browne some six weeks to conduct an investigation spanning three countries, before concluding to the evident satisfaction the civil servants that there was no evidence upon which to proceed.

The very fact that the Metropolitan Police continues to retain the written evidence, in case new evidence comes to light half a century later, begs the question of why their enquiries were wound down after such a short time. This is inconsistent with contemporaneous investigations into the murder of single individuals, let alone 66 people. Times have indeed changed.

It is clear from the correspondence available that the British Foreign Office was most concerned that no embarrassment be caused to its interests by the police investigation. John Macrae of the FO, in his letter of 13th February 1968 to his colleague John Edmonds in Ankara, felt that the most likely explanation was that the motive was an insurance scam. Whether that can be construed as an innocent comment on the various theories, or an indication of the way they had hoped the investigation would proceed, is open to conjecture. The Foreign Office and, at their behest, Assistant Commissioner Brodie went to considerable lengths get a 'secret' letter to Athens to instruct Browne not to dig too deeply into political lines of enquiry without consulting the FO first. This tends to suggest that there were some serious concerns on the part of the FO about where the investigation might well lead. There is no way of knowing what other documentation might have been excluded from the files, and it is not at all likely that any incriminating material would have been kept on file. However, the

---

[97] AVIA101/218 – Demarcation of Investigation; AVIA101/220 – Diaries and Documentation; AVIA101/225 – Pathology Reports. These files were publicly available at the time of writing, and their information is used throughout this book, under Open Licence V2.0.

continued retention of material on the grounds of national security indicates that there is still sensitivity around certain information or its source.

During the 'Cyprus Emergency' or 'liberation struggle', depending on the viewpoint of the reader, it was, as stated earlier, known that the British Security Services, particularly the Secret Service, MI6, could rely on a flow of information from within EOKA. After the cessation of hostilities, there is rarely an amnesty for informants who have supplied sensitive intelligence to the enemy's security apparatus. If any such sources were inadvertently identified, for example in a criminal investigation, their lives would still be endangered; the seven years since Cypriot independence was unlikely to have led to a 'forgive and forget' attitude on the part of the more ruthless elements.

It has been suggested to the author that Polycarpos Yiorkadjis had been an informant for the British; perhaps his various escapes from British custody during the struggle had been more than simply fortuitous but had provided a cover for a covert debriefing by his handlers. If, indeed, this is the case, such a source, relying on continuing discretion by a foreign power, in the top level of government, would have been an asset worth preserving. The attitude of those tasked with handling him might have been outright repugnance at his involvement in mass murder, tempered by the reality that bringing him to justice would not help those lost.

The Metropolitan Police asserts to this day that it might reopen the criminal investigation if there is new evidence. The hearsay evidence, that Yiorkadjis had orchestrated the plot using Solomou as the carrier, appears to have come to light some time after Detective Superintendent Browne and Detective Sergeant Hill had returned to England, and moved on to their next cases. Whilst hearsay evidence itself is not generally admissible, it would be a good starting point to re-examine that area of the work of Browne and Hill. Nowadays, such a low-key nature of the original enquiries, along with implied direction by the Foreign Office and the paucity of the resources made available, would raise significant questions over the effectiveness of that investigation. The Sixties were an earlier era when power and influence were concentrated within the Establishment. Bodies such as Government departments and police forces were not expected to be transparent and accountable to the extent they are today. It is, surely, far from impossible that a senior police officer would have taken heed of some clear guidance from the Foreign Office to focus on certain areas and not be too concerned about others.

The police and Home Office in Britain have been willing to re-open cold cases and there would be merit in a thorough review of the original case, to identify missed opportunities and examine new leads. The mass murder of 66 people surely makes this worthwhile, notwithstanding the passage of half a century since the crime itself. The Metropolitan Police Service in the 21st century is far removed from the organisation it was in the Sixties, and it is to be hoped that they might be willing to take on this task, should a case be made to them.

The last word? The Birmingham Post of August 30th 1968 was still asserting that the bomb was meant to kill General Grivas (TNA)

Missing link in the Comet crash

By John Shirley in Cyprus
and John Ball in London

"IT IS better for me to die. My whole life has turned into a disaster."

THESE ARE the words of a small-time Greek-Cypriot smuggler working as the manager of a shoe shop in the small town of Larnica, Cyprus. He is almost certainly the missing link in the mystery explosion that sent a BEA Comet 4B crashing into the Mediterranean off Rhodes last October.

Nicos Papaetrou, faced with gambling debts, two girl friends in Athens and expensive fees to pay for his daughter's dental course in the Greek capital, was talking to a friend just 48 hours before a 16oz. bomb—of military origin—blew a hole in the Comet's fuselage.

Papaetrou and 65 others were on the plane. They all died. In the fortnight before the crash Papaetrou had taken out three insurance covers totalling £23,000. There may be a fourth.

Following in the tracks of a Scotland Yard team, headed by Detective-Superintendent Percy Browne, who flew to Rhodes to examine the scant wreckage we found this new witness whose memory of a conversation points directly to Papaetrou as the cause of the crash.

List of victims

All documents concerning the flight were collected by the Yard men and one by one the victims were crossed off his list. Then Supt. Browne came to 44-year-old Papaetrou and discovered the insurance covers.

It was Papaetrou's fifth journey between the island and the Greek capital that year; he had told his wife, Nina, at their blue-painted, double-fronted rambling bungalow in 28th October Street, Larnica that they were business trips. But they were not for the Nicosia shoe firm of Galides Ltd. for whom he managed the local shop.

As he counted his meagre commission—he earned between £50 and £60 a month—he talked of breaking into the leather industry and manufacturing leather handbags. The journeys to Athens were to look for materials.

The detectives discovered Papaetrou had for years kept only one personal accident policy worth £2,000 with General Insurance Ltd. of Cyprus, which did not cover him for aviation risk.

But on September 30 last year, he walked into the Larnica branch office of the company and took out a personal accident cover for £8,000—valid only for the month of October and covering a single journey abroad to Greece and England.

Insurance policies

Within a few days he took out another policy, this time with the Cyprus branch of Eagle Star for £5,000. Then there was a third policy which he drew up with Sun Assurance Ltd. for £10,000.

A fortnight later the Comet exploded. Already it is understood Eagle Star have paid out to Papaetrou's widow. But the Sun company have been waiting for the official verdict on the crash before making final settlement and General Insurance are contesting their obligation to pay on what their Nicosia manager termed "certain discrepancies in the claim."

Apparently the dead man did not notify General Insurance of the two other policies he had taken out. The manager explained, "It is a technical matter. It has nothing to do with the cause of the accident."

But as the Yard probe went deeper they discovered that Papaetrou, father of two daughters, had connections with a smuggling syndicate. In Athens he had two girl friends called Helen and Titica. He gambled at casinos in Athens and on Corfu.

He spent most of the money he made through smuggling on the two girl friends or in the casinos. But as his luck began to sour gambling debts built up and creditors demanded their money back.

Then he was thought to have been unable to pay for the goods he obtained for smuggling to Greece. A few days before his last trip he pleaded with an old friend, a retired shipping agent, who had travelled with him on some early trips, for a £1,000 loan. He only got £500.

Marriage crumbles

But not only was his luck running out on the gambling tables his marriage was beginning to crumble. However, he was still having to pay for his younger daughter, Christala, aged 19, who was undergoing expensive tuition at an Athens school of dentistry.

Finally he was almost caught red handed with a consignment of watches worth £940 at Athens Airport. Papaetrou's contact men, believed to have been a customs official, failed to show up, and a brown leather suitcase stowed in the aircraft was opened. He denied it was part of his luggage and managed to hoodwink the customs investigators. But not only had he lost the consignment but also the smuggling link had been broken and he faced yet another debt.

EXTRACT FROM
'THE SUNDAY TIMES'
DATED 1ᵗ SEPT. 1968.

As if in response to the newspaper report saying Grivas was the target, the following day, 1ˢᵗ September 1968, this article was published in The Sunday Times. Rich in detail, the article dismissed all notions of a political plot and supported the view of the Foreign Office that an insurance motive was more likely. The Papapetrou family does not accept the contents of the article. (TNA).

214

Who Bombed Charlie Oscar?

The accident investigation proved beyond any doubt that a bomb brought down Charlie Oscar. Not only was there positive evidence of this, but every other plausible cause was considered and ruled out.

Terrorism is defined by NATO[98] as *'the unlawful use or threatened use of force or violence against individuals or property in an attempt to coerce or intimidate governments or societies to achieve political, religious or ideological objectives.'* Although there had been a warning letter from the 'Falcon Forces' in June 1967, warning airlines flying to Israel to stop doing so, no group claimed responsibility for the destruction of Charlie Oscar, and nothing in the National Archives files so far released suggests that terrorism was progressed as a motive.

The attempted assassination of General Grivas has proved extremely resilient as a presumed motive for the bombing of Charlie Oscar. Grivas actually did travel from Athens to Nicosia later the same day as the crash of Charlie Oscar. The first-hand account by Louis Loizou and the information quoted by Leonidas Leonidou separately verify that Grivas originally planned to travel on CY284 and only the Cyprus Special Branch, under the auspices of Polycarpos Yiorkadjis, specifically says otherwise. The idea that Grivas was the intended target never truly went away, and indeed was resurrected in a headline in the *Birmingham Post* on 30th August 1968, under the headline, *'Comet death crash – it was a bomb meant for Grivas.'* However, this was countered the following day by an article in *The Sunday Times*, telling its readers, under the headline, *'Missing link in Comet crash'*, that Papapetrou has committed the atrocity for the insurance pay out. One of these must have been 'fake news' in today's parlance. It might be considered that the second article, rich in detail of the troubles of Nicos Papapetrou, had been fed to the paper's journalists by sources with a vested interest in ensuring that history recorded this version of the truth.

It appears that no one has suggested publicly that there was a Turkish dimension to the destruction of CY284 and nowhere in the National Archive's accessible files does that possibility arise. Yet the Turks, more than anyone other than a deadly political rival, might have had a clear interest in the removal from the stage of General Grivas. It is, perhaps, significant that the downing of Charlie Oscar preceded rather than followed an escalation of violence, for which Grivas was held responsible by many people.

Whilst researching this book, it was suggested to the author that the British Secret Service, or the CIA, might have been behind the plot. However, it is not clear what they would have had to gain directly from the death of Grivas, especially considering the extreme measure the destruction of an airliner would represent. With Grivas no longer hiding furtively in the back streets of Limassol

---

[98] NATO Glossary of Terms and Definitions, 2014.

or Nicosia, those organisations would surely have been able to take him out, had they so wanted, without murdering 66 innocent people. There would have been hell to pay had the British Secret Service destroyed a British airliner carrying British passengers and crew. Equally, the Americans would have been unlikely to destroy a civilian aircraft belonging to one of their major allies, deliberately at least, and especially when their stock on the world stage was getting lower due to Vietnam. It is, however, interesting to note that a novel, Cat's Paw[99], is based on exactly the premise discounted here, the bomb being placed by a CIA agent working in collaboration with the British. The book was, according to its author, simply a work of fiction inspired by the intrigue surrounding the loss of Charlie Oscar.

Surrounding the established facts of the destruction of CY284 are other elements that certainly do not diminish the aura of subterfuge. The depth of the Mediterranean varies but is greatest in the vicinity of the Ionian Sea; Charlie Oscar fell in the vicinity of the Strabo Trench. It might have been coincidence but equally could have been by design. If the bomb had been triggered by the initial radio call as Charlie Oscar was about to enter the Nicosia Flight Information Region, its maker would have been reasonably certain that the aircraft would come down in an inaccessible part of the sea. The technology to construct such devices was certainly available at that time. Whilst a timing device could have caused the detonation at the same spot, it would be less precise and subject to the possibility of a delayed departure, as had happened to Hermes G-ALDW in 1956.

Speculation about the motive for the destruction of CY284 centred from the outset on an assassination attempt against General Georgios Grivas. This was reportedly confirmed by MI6 according to The Sunday Telegraph on 26th November 1967 (see p. 132), though the author remembers the theory being mentioned on the BBC News shortly after the crash. Later on 12th October, the reader will recall that Olympic Airways changed the aircraft assigned to their Athens – Nicosia flight. Whilst Veal considered that this might be a precaution, it suggests immediate concern on the part of Olympic Airways that their aircraft, now due to convey the General, might also have been targeted.

Half a century later, many Greek Cypriots remain convinced of this motive. The Cypriot authorities, however, have never accepted the theory. The alternative hypothesis, as noted and examined above, was that Nicos Papapetrou had destroyed the aircraft, with a bomb carried either by himself or by an unwitting stooge. This possible cause gained strength through the police investigation and was clearly more politically palatable to the British Foreign Office than the loss of the aircraft and occupants as collateral damage in an assassination attempt.

---

[99] Cat's Paw by Christopher Malinger (Malinger Publishing, 2017).

In order to identify the person most likely to have brought the bomb on board, it is necessary to specify exactly where the bomb was located, and who was sitting with it. The wording used when describing the location of the device is important. There are several versions of the precise position and a composite estimate, based on the damage to the seat cushion, was that it was between eleven and twelve inches below the rear of the seat cushion, up to four inches behind the rear edge and three inches to the side of the cushion. Therefore, when Jones et al describe the bomb as being under one of the numbered seats, this does not mean it was fully underneath. Rather, it was more or less directly under the back of that seat, slightly off centre and on the floor. This would be where a passenger would place a bag, under the back of the seat ahead of them, but where it would be readily accessible. For example, if the bomb was described in the files as 'under seat 4A', this means that it was probably in the footwell of seat 3A.

Jones based his assumption that the device was under the back of seats 4A or 5A on the basis that the bomb carrier was most probably amongst the missing passengers, and that the passenger with the shrapnel wounds, Achillea Afatitis, was sitting in the seat row behind the explosion, to account for the pattern of his injuries. Furthermore, he assumed that the passengers who had travelled from London and who were continuing to Nicosia from Athens did not change seats, and that the group of Jehovahs' Witnesses all sat in the block of seats in the rear cabin, primarily rows 4 to 7 inclusive. Reasonable though those assumptions might be, they are assumptions, nonetheless. The seating plan in Fred Jones' RAE report shows that Mr. and Mrs. Thiakou, both members of the Jehovah's Witnesses group, were sitting in seats 16D and 16E, across the gangway from Avraam Solomou. This shows that, in fact, at least some of the group were quite happy to find empty seats in other parts of the aircraft.

If Nicos Papapetrou had been carrying the device, he would, by Jones' reckoning, have been sitting in one of the seats that Jones then went on to assume would have been occupied by a Jehovah's Witness, whereas Papapetrou was not a member of that group.

There is very strong circumstantial evidence that Jones was close to the mark in his assessment of where the bomb went off, as there is a concentration of missing passengers along the port side of the cabin, and passengers with extreme injuries towards the rear.

Jones was the only person who assessed where the device was when it detonated, and he was a man with a solid reputation for deriving the causes of aircraft losses using impeccable logic. Therefore, the best guess remains that the device did indeed explode somewhere towards the rear of the cabin. This would also account for a loss of control of the aircraft resulting from damage to the hydraulic system and other controls directly underneath the seats indicated by Jones.

The possibility of an unidentified person at either Heathrow or Ellinikon airport smuggling the bomb on board was considered during the investigation, but the bomb was not positioned such that it would have been well-hidden. From the presumed position, the device would have been clearly visible to the passenger sitting in the seat adjacent to it. If someone had the opportunity to place it, the device might have been better concealed in the life-jacket housing or on the hat rack.

By far the most likely person to have brought the bomb on board was either Nicos Papapetrou or Avraam Solomou, resulting in two possible motives for the destruction of Charlie Oscar. Leonidas Leonidou and Eleftherios Papadopoulos, stated that Avraam Solomou carried the bomb onto the aircraft, albeit without knowing. Solomou was named in connection with the bombing at an early stage, when the investigation was still being carried out. As the journalist did not reveal his source it is impossible to know where this information came from, but it is quite explicit. Whilst the newspaper articles in November 1967 do not allege Solomou carried the bomb on board himself, they emphasise that his presence might have caused the plotters to identify CY284 as the flight on which Grivas was travelling. This should have been of immediate interest to the police investigation, but in fact resulted in only two statements being taken

However, as has been outlined above, the information in the pathologists' report shows that Solomou was not next to the bomb when it exploded, as his injuries showed no sign of blast damage. Also, his body was recovered in the northern debris field, indicating that he had been in the forward section of the aircraft when the fuselage broke apart. A plausible explanation is that Solomou was sitting in the rear of the tourist cabin, along with most of the passengers starting their journey at Athens. Half an hour before landing it is not unreasonable for a passenger to have left his seat to use the aircraft toilet compartment to freshen up, and therefore Solomou could easily have been away from the bomb when it exploded. Along with other passengers in the vicinity of the damage, he would then have had to move further forward as his seat would no longer exist. This would account for his injuries and the fact that he was found with passengers from the front of the aircraft when it hit the sea.

The absence of Nicos Papapetrou's body means that his proximity to the bomb cannot be proved or disproved. Other passengers were also missing from other parts of the cabin and so his disappearance in itself proves nothing. The accounts of his involvement in smuggling, his comments about it being better if he died, and his parlous financial situation are uncorroborated, and their provenance is uncertain; there is only one newspaper article to give any substance to these notions. The Papapetrou family consider the Sunday Times article to be lies. Of course, the fact that Papapetrou took out four insurance policies would arouse suspicion and, assuming it is true, would be a very clear indication that something was not right. But to prove Papapetrou's responsibility beyond reasonable doubt, or even on the balance of probabilities, requires more information about the man and all the circumstances surrounding his final, well-insured, journey.

There were possible precedents for the plots attributed to Papapetrou. On 16th November 1959, a National Airlines Douglas DC-7B airliner carrying 42 passengers and crew disappeared whilst flying over the Gulf of Mexico between Miami and New Orleans. In a case with similarities to Charlie Oscar, scattered debris and ten bodies were recovered. One theory advanced was that the perpetrator tricked another man to travel in his place; there was a bomb in his luggage and the plan was hatched so that the perpetrator's wife could collect on his life insurance. The passenger concerned, William Taylor, had boarded the flight using a ticket issued to a Robert Spears, a convicted criminal. It was believed that the two men had become friends whilst in prison. Despite using Spears' ticket, Taylor had purchased life insurance of his own at Miami airport before departure. His ex-wife applied to collect the insurance after the crash, and the substitution came to light. Spears disappeared after the crash but was arrested in Phoenix, Arizona, in 1969 in Taylor's car. He was never charged in connection with the loss of the aircraft, and there was no evidence ever produced connecting Spears directly with the disaster.

Less than two months later, on 6th January 1960, another National Airlines aircraft was lost, along with the lives of the 34 passengers and crew. Flight 2511, from New York to Miami, was a Douglas DC6, which was a substitute for the Boeing 707 originally scheduled to operate, but which was unserviceable. The aircraft crashed near the town of Bolivia, North Carolina. One part of the aircraft skin was found some 25 miles from the rest of the wreckage. As with CY284, pathological examination indicated that the body of one passenger, Julian Frank, had substantial evidence of the explosion of a dynamite bomb. Frank was under investigation of misappropriating up to one million dollars in charity scams. He had insurance policies totalling $900,000, including insurance cover bought on the day of the flight. The Civil Aeronautics Board (CAB), which carried out the investigation, concluded that the aircraft was brought down by a dynamite explosion in the passenger cabin, beneath the right-hand seat in row 7. This was close to Frank's seat, but as with the AIB report into Charlie Oscar, the CAB did not attribute blame to any named person. The case was referred to the FBI but was never concluded. It remains open to this day.

On May 22nd 1962, a Boeing 707 was operating Continental Airlines flight 11 from Chicago to Kansas City. 42 minutes into the flight, the aircraft disappeared from the ATC radar. An explosion had occurred in the right rear lavatory, leading to the separation of the rearmost 38 feet of the fuselage. The 707 crashed in a field near Unionville, Missouri, with the loss of the 45 souls on board. Thomas Doty, a passenger on the flight, had boarded at the very last minute and had, like Frank, bought additional insurance just before departure. He was covered to the extent of $300,000 and was being investigated on suspicion of armed robbery.

Doty had also bought six sticks of dynamite shortly before the flight. The FBI concluded that Doty had blown himself up in the rear lavatory, having carried the dynamite in his briefcase and then placed it in the used hand towel bin. His widow was refused the insurance pay-out.

The three cases cited were all domestic flights in the United States and the attacks were carried out before airport security was particularly intense. The latter two involved devices consisting of dynamite (the first case had no actual evidence of an explosion as the aircraft, like Charlie Oscar, crashed into the sea and little wreckage was recovered).

The supposed plot by Papapetrou was complex. The newspaper article *Did saboteur die in Comet crash?* which appeared in the *Cyprus Mail* on 5th September 1968 stated that *'...the Police believe he somehow tricked another man into flying in his place, using his ticket, and his seat.'* It would have been quite difficult to carry out this ruse on an international flight but not impossible. Papapetrou would have had to lend the unwitting victim his passport, in which case the man would have to bear a passable resemblance to him. Quite how Papapetrou might have persuaded the other man to undertake the task is not explained, though it is feasible that Papapetrou promised the man a significant amount of money. It is also plausible that the other man was a fellow smuggler, who thought the package in his bag was contraband, and that impersonating another smuggler was part of a cunning plan to fool the authorities. If the man with Papapetrou's documents was an impostor, then there would most likely have been a person similar to Papapetrou reported missing shortly after the crash.

Naturally any plot, whether suicide or murder, would not have succeeded without Papapetrou being able to acquire explosives and build a bomb, or perhaps by such a device from a bomb-maker. Either of these would require very specialised knowledge and suggest he had an even murkier past than that of a smuggler. Had Papapetrou, as suggested in the article cited by Colin Wilson, previously smuggled explosives, he would most likely have known that the only remotely safe way to do so would be to ensure that they did not have a detonator with them. The fact that the explosion occurred means that the device was indeed viable and therefore was inherently unsafe.

To assess whether Papapetrou had the capability to acquire or build a viable explosive device comprising military-grade plastic explosive, more information is needed about his background. If he was carrying the device, and had built it himself, he would necessarily have learned how to do so, either through military training or else with EOKA. The statement by the Cyprus Special Branch that they had no passenger names on file as being of interest makes the latter seem unlikely. Had they considered Papapetrou to be the culprit, and he was not involved in a political plot, they would have had good reason to suspect him, and to say so. It is quite unlikely that a skilled bomb maker would have avoided coming to their attention, especially as the number of EOKA activists with the required expertise would have been relatively small. Little information is available about Nicos Papapetrou, other than that already considered. It would certainly be a more compelling case if he was known to have been an EOKA fighter; his age would have made that possible. He might, equally, have served in the armed forces and still had contacts to help him in his task.

A further question is why Papapetrou would have blown himself up on his return journey, if it was a suicide. If he had made or acquired the device in Cyprus, as would probably have been more likely, it would have been expected that he would have carried out the deed on a flight from Cyprus. Otherwise he would have had to take the bomb on the outbound flight and then carry it around in Athens before activating it on the way home. That lacks credibility, meaning that he would have had to acquire the device, or its constituent parts, in Greece.

The *Sunday Times* article states that one insurance company had paid out on Papapetrou's policy, though the others had been awaiting the conclusion of the police investigation. No official statement was made that the investigation had been finalised, and that insurance fraud was believed to be the motive. The police line was that there was insufficient evidence to proceed against any person. This is, perhaps, understandable as Papapetrou's body was never recovered, so it was not possible to establish whether he had, in fact, travelled on the flight, losing his life in the process. If he had persuaded someone else to take his place, and the insurance policies were eventually honoured, the only way he could have benefited himself would be if his wife had colluded with him. It would have been a selfless, though perverse, act for Papapetrou to disappear leaving his wife, in total innocence, with all the money and it is not clear how he would have built a new life for himself with no apparent means of support. It might, however, have looked extremely suspicious if Mrs. Papapetrou had received the money and promptly left town.

If Papapetrou had detonated the bomb himself, it is highly unlikely that it would be on the cabin floor, partially under the seat, at the time. Therefore, he would need to have set it to explode, then sat and waited for the end to come. If he had given the bomb to an unwitting stooge, the question arises of who that might that have been. It would be useful to establish if an associate, similar enough to withstand the scrutiny of a passport check, had been reported missing in Greece or Cyprus at the time. If the plot had been, as postulated, to allow his family to collect the insurance and for him to meet up with them, this would have meant the entire family leaving Cyprus shortly after the event and starting their new life somewhere else, assuming the policies were eventually paid out.

The Papapetrou family, as stated earlier and confirmed in conference with the author, maintain that the theory that he was responsible is wholly untrue. He spent his time in Athens before the flight staying with his daughter, who clearly recalls that there was nothing unusual about his behaviour, Furthermore, until contacted by the author in the context of this book, the family had never even realised that Nicos Papapetrou was a suspect.

221

It is possible that the theory that Papapetrou was responsible was promulgated by the British authorities to selected journalists in order to put the whole incident to rest. If he was totally innocent, the damage done to his reputation, and that of his family, would have been immense but the dead cannot, under British law, be libelled. If, however, the bomb had in fact been detonated by Papapetrou, or by his unwitting stooge, the story would have ended there.

Suicide-by-bomb was the explanation preferred by the Foreign Office, especially as it would have avoided the diplomatic sensitivities around any remotely political motive for the attack. The *Sunday Times* journalists were apparently very thorough and capable, and put together a plausible explanation of why Papapetrou might have wanted to end his own life in such a way. They appear to have exceptionally well-informed and it is unfortunate that their account cannot be compared with the police report. They appear so well-informed that the reader might speculate on whether they were given information by, or on behalf of, the investigating officers. The reason for doing so might have been to ensure that the insurance scam story was accepted as the truth, and thereby finally lay to rest the Grivas theory.

It would have been a bizarre coincidence and a savage irony if General Grivas, whose life was considered to be potentially at risk from a political rival, had lost his life because he just happened to be travelling on an aircraft destroyed in a bomb attack carried out by another passenger for insurance fraud.

The documents relating to the police investigation, and to the involvement of the British Home Office and Foreign Office in the aftermath of the disaster, contain no information supporting the contention that Grivas was planning to fly on CY284. The only significant reference is the message to John Veal from MI5, relaying the assertion by the Cyprus Special Branch that Grivas never travelled at that time of day. In 2018, the author travelled to Cyprus to launch the first edition of *Bealine Charlie Oscar*. A public meeting and press conference were organised in Limassol by Cypriot journalist and broadcaster Christos Iacovou. This was attended by some seventy journalists, relatives of the victims and other interested parties, including a former member of EOKA who had sheltered Grivas during the conflict. At the end of the conference, the son of Avraam Solomou, who had been eight days old when his father was killed, told the meeting that his father had indeed attended the Cypriot Embassy in Athens shortly before boarding the flight. His family had been told that two envelopes were given to Solomou, addressed to Polycarpos Yiorkadjis and President Makarios. The envelopes had apparently been too small to contain a bomb. Mr. Solomou added, poignantly, that all his life he had borne the burden of being accused of being the son of a mass murderer.

Neophytos Sofocleous, director of Grivas' office, was a close associate and confidante of the general. Mr. Sofocleous told the author, through Christos Iacovou, that he had personally made a booking for General Grivas to travel on flight CY284 from Athens to Nicosia on Thursday 12th October 1967. However,

Yiorkadjis had contacted him shortly before the flight asking for confirmation of Grivas' movements. As Mr. Sofocleous was suspicious of Yiorkadjis' motives, he decided to change Grivas' travel arrangements at the last minute as a precaution. He rang Cyprus Airways to cancel the booking and General Grivas to tell him of the change of plan. Mr. Sofocleous maintains that he was not aware of a direct threat to CY284, so did not alert the airline to the possibility of an attack.

Writer and journalist Nicos Papanastassiou has made separate enquiries at various times and provided further details of what then transpired.

An explosive device, in a 'safe' condition, was transported by courier to the Cypriot Embassy in Athens. It is believed that the courier was Avraam Solomou, who knew nothing about its contents. Solomou was travelling with a colleague, Miss Iacovidou. Solomou was called back to the Embassy on the evening of 11th October and told to take a package under diplomatic cover to Yiorkadjis. Such activities were a routine part of Solomou's duties. The package was to be carried in a cabin bag. The family of Avraam Solomou was told that the cabin bag containing the bomb was given to Solomou at the Cypriot Embassy[100].' It was not stated whether the person handing over the bag was aware of its contents or not. The bomb was a wholly viable improvised explosive device with a timer, which was set shortly before it was packaged up and handed to Solomou. The device was timed to explode over the deepest part of the Mediterranean on the route from Athens to Nicosia. It was expected that there would be no trace of the flight, so no plot could subsequently be proved.

Solomou travelled to Athens Airport in a Cypriot Embassy vehicle and, at the airport, he found that he had inadvertently brought Miss Iacovidou's flight ticket, rather than his own. This resulted in the somewhat heated discussion reported by the check-in staff at Athens airport.

Grivas, meanwhile, had prepared to travel to Athens airport and was in his car awaiting his driver. He was called back to take a telephone call from A, who had become aware of what is described as 'suspicious activity by Yiorkadjis' men'. Grivas told another trusted colleague that he had been required to attend an urgent meeting with Greek military personnel and that he would have to take the Olympic Airways flight later on 12th October. On arrival at Nicosia, Grivas greeted Mr. Sofocleous warmly, telling him, 'Thank you. You saved my life.'

In September 1967 Cyprus was a very volatile environment politically and militarily. General George Grivas, who still ultimately controlled the Cyprus Defence Military High Command, was at odds with the Cypriot president, Archbishop Makarios III. Makarios, meanwhile, was supported by Polycarpos Yiorkadjis, who already controlled the police and Cyprus Special Branch. Certain actions against the Turkish Cypriot population had been directed by

---

[100] Solomou family to Fanoulla Argyrou at open meeting in Limassol, October 2018.

Makarios which Grivas was reluctant to support. Grivas therefore intended to return to Cyprus, and that potentially conflicted with the interests of Yiorkadjis.

Grivas was born in 1897 in Cyprus, attending school at the Pancyprian Gymnasium. In 1919, he left Cyprus, moving to Greece. Taking citizenship of the latter country, he enrolled at the Athens Military Academy. After completing his military studies, including time at the École Militaire in Paris, Grivas joined the Greek Army as a sub-Lieutenant. The Greco-Turkish War was in progress and he was duly posted to the 10th Division of the Greek Army, fighting in what is now Turkey. He participated in the Battle of Sakarya, in 1921. Grivas was decorated for his bravery in the conflict and promoted to Lieutenant. Further promotions followed and, by 1935, Grivas was a Major.

Following the outbreak of the Second World War, Grivas was posted to the Albanian Front, serving as Chief of Staff of the 2nd Division. When Greece was occupied by the Axis powers, he set up and led a small guerrilla organisation, initially called Grivas Military Organisation and later known as Operation X, which comprised officers of the Greek Army. The group, which as well as

Above: Grivas and some of his EOKA fighters in the Troodos Mountains during the campaign for Cypriot self-determination. The photo was on film stock subsequently seized by British troops (Nik van der Bijl).

fighting the occupiers was anti-communist, focussed its operations in parts of the Athens suburbs and expanded to between two and three thousand members.

By 1946 Grivas retired from the Greek Army in the rank of Colonel. In Athens he got acquainted with Archbishop Makarios III who eventually asked him to join forces and prepare for an armed struggle in Cyprus. Following some secret visits to the island in 1954 and clandestine arms shipments, the EOKA uprising began on 1st April 1955 for Enosis of Cyprus with Greece. With Makarios accepting Independence, Grivas left the island in 1959.

The prime suspect for such an attempt on the life of Grivas has been, in the view of many Cypriots, his political rival, Polycarpos Yiorkadjis, the Interior Minister in the Makarios government. In this role, many considered that Yiorkadjis set up a vast information network and became notorious for using the police as his 'personal army'.

Yiorkadjis was born in 1932. During the 'Cyprus Emergency' he was an active member of EOKA, assuming the nom de guerre 'Laertes'. He would rise to become the commander of EOKA operations in Nicosia. Captured by the British on a number of occasions, Yiorkadjis managed to escape on a number of occasions, earning himself the nickname 'Houdini'. This apparent ability to escape from custody whenever he was captured might easily have given rise to the suspicion that Yiorkadjis was an informant for the British forces. As in any conflict, information and intelligence were passed from either side to the other by sympathisers or paid agents. This applied to the Cyprus Emergency; indeed, Peter Georgeides had referred in his letter from prison to the Chairman of BEA on 9th January 1968, that Grivas himself ran an 'exterminating-traitor-squad' (see p.179).

The inference of the Foreign Office input to Detective Superintendent Browne was that they had concerns about what might be revealed if the detective started making in-depth enquiries in the political arena.

According to some sources, Grivas was not the only prominent figure originally booked on CY284 on 12th October 1967. The Cypriot newspaper *Filelefteros* published an article on 1st October 2006, stating that Michalakis Triantafyllides, at that time Attorney General and head of the Supreme Court of Cyprus was to travel on the aircraft from Athens but changed his mind and returned to the island by ship. Glafkos Clerides, then President of the House of Representatives and later to become President of the Republic of Cyprus, was also due to fly on CY284 from London but changed his mind because of some further business in England[101].

---

[101] Polyvios and Renos Georgiou, brothers of passenger Sotiris Georgiou, knew Clerides well and met him many times in the years after the crash. Clerides knew that Sotiris had been killed and discussed the disaster on a number of occasions. At no time does Polyvios recall Clerides saying that he had been booked on the flight. (Polyvios Georgiou in conversation with the author, 2018).

A Cypriot source, who wishes to remain anonymous, told the author in 2018:
"Yiorkadjis did have many reasons to want to get rid of Grivas, as Grivas was often opposing this man's attempt to control the armed forces of Cyprus. The fact that the two other government officials, Triantafyllides and Clerides, booked seats on this flight but cancelled their trips at the very last moment suggests that they knew about the bomb, and they had only booked on the flight to ensure that Grivas would not suspect anything. Also, the bomb was carried as a package by a person cooperating with the Ministry of Foreign Affairs. He was supposed to go to his assigned seat, leave his bag, and then find an excuse to deplane. Some sources state that, once onboard and realising that Grivas was not onboard, he decided to travel in order not to arouse suspicion and cancel the timer of the explosive device, but he failed, killing himself and the others.

Other writers have suggested that the Greek junta was behind it, but at the time they did not have any real motives to do so, as Grivas at the time was not against them, and he was considered by the Greeks more useful for them as a 'tool'. The crazy thing is that while if you read most sources (albeit in Greek) the story is evident, but no-one has actually put it down as a complete plot. The complex relationships between President Makarios, General Grivas, the Greek junta, and Polycarpos Yiorkadjis, remain a sensitive issue among Cypriots to this day. Yiorkadjis did not like the independence that Grivas wanted for the military forces and he probably feared his popularity."

The involvement of Polycarpos Yiorkadjis in the destruction of Charlie Oscar is, by now, almost impossible to prove. However the author received information from a credible source who was a member of the security forces in Cyprus at the time of the incident, and who was aware of this book being prepared. The source, who does not wish to be named, told the author:

'Yiorkadjis asked me to disclose Grivas' movements before the attack on the aircraft, but I refused, as I knew why Yiorkadjis would ask for this. The attack (against Grivas) could not take place in Cyprus. I spoke to Grivas' nephew and advised him not to board the aircraft, as I knew the Press would be aware that Grivas was travelling to Cyprus, so Yiorkadjis would also know. Avraam Solomou (the courier) was just sent by Yiorkadjis as a lamb to the slaughter, as were the other 65 people on the flight. Yiorkadjis and Makarios had no regrets at all over the attack, they didn't bat an eyelid. They even went to the funerals of some of the victims, such as Dr. Ioannides.

Yiorkadjis was acting on the orders of Makarios, as he did most of the time. He had also carried out various other acts for Makarios but the problem is there is no concrete evidence. Yiorkadjis had some incriminating recordings of Makarios, as I suspect other agencies had.

That is why the (Met Police) files are sealed until 2040. Numerous politicians, some at a very high level, and various other people know all about this, but there is no concrete evidence until the files are opened. No one now wants to stir up the past; the Cypriot government is worried about compensation and the British government is worried about political reasons.'

The source also told the author that he had tried to warn Makarios not to go to Macheras as there would be a planned assassination attempt on him. The President paid no heed to this warning.

The suggestion that President Makarios knew of, or even instigated, the bombing of CY284 raises very serious political considerations. It would be bad enough for a serving government minister to organise the destruction of a civilian airliner carrying, amongst others, nationals of his own country. For the Head of State of that country to condone or, worse, direct, such an act exacerbates it further. To deliberately destroy an airliner belonging to the flag carrier of another country, carrying nationals of three other nations, would today be considered tantamount to an act of war. The aftermath of Lockerbie, which saw Libya branded a pariah state, bears testimony to incidents of such gravity. One could understand why the British Foreign Office would see the emergence of evidence of 'a political dimension' to be fraught with danger.

The credibility of Yiorkadjis as the mastermind of the plot is enhanced by his alleged involvement in other assassination attempts against key political figures. In 1968 he was linked to failed assassinations of Greek PM in that he assisted Alekos Panagoulis, a Greek political opponent of the junta, in his attempt to assassinate its leader, Georgios Papadopoulos. Following the attempt, the Greek powers prevailed upon Makarios to ask for Yiorkadjis' resignation. Following his effective removal from his post, Yiorkadjis became one of the President's principal political rivals. On March 8th 1970, President Makarios intended to attend the annual memorial service for an EOKA fighter, Grigoris Afxentiou, which was to take place in the mountains of Marcheras. The president travelled by helicopter and, as he took off from the Archbishopric in Nicosia, shots were fired, damaging the helicopter and wounding the pilot. Despite this, the pilot carried out a successful forced landing. Makarios, helped by passers-by, managed to escape, taking the pilot to Nicosia General Hospital. The assassination attempt had failed.

The President certainly believed that Yiorkadjis had played a part. As he emerged from the wrecked helicopter, Makarios told onlookers, '*Yiorkadjis did this.*'[102] Yiorkadjis, according to some sources, attempted to leave Cyprus and boarded a flight to Beirut. However, his attempted departure was discovered, and he was ordered off the aircraft. There are conflicting and

---

[102] "Under the Threat of Guns". Time Magazine. 30 March 1970.

uncorroborated accounts of the machinations that ensued, but it did not end well for Yiorkadjis. One week after the attempt on Makarios' life, Yiorkadjis was shot dead in a remote location near the village of Mia Milia, outside Nicosia.

Makarios was interviewed in a German newspaper, which was published on 16th April 1970. The article was cited by Greek writers[103] in 2014 and 2016. It was the first time, apparently, that Makarios spoke about the attempt on his life. The interviewer asked Makarios about a group of 'terrorists', known to Makarios and the government. There was no assurance that they were being kept under observation by the police. The journalist wanted to know if the six suspects, arrested after the attempt on Makarios' life, and Yiorkadjis himself, were part of that group.

Makarios replied:

> "Whilst the police investigations are continuing, I do not think I am in a position to reply to your question in detail. I confine only in saying, that there is evidence implicating certain persons in relation to the attempt against my life and that the ex-Minister Yiorkadjis was associated with these persons and that he was implicated in the organisation of the attempt."

Polycarpos Yiorkadjis, the article noted, had proclaimed his innocence the whole time. He had stated in the Athens newspaper "BIMA" that Makarios' advisers were simply engaged in throwing mud at him and that he was, by then, sure that some people wanted to get him out of the way for their own interests.

The article was published the same day six persons were accused for the attempt on Makarios' life. Among the charges was that the six of them, between 1st September 1969 and 8th March 1970, conspired in Nicosia together with the deceased P. Yiorkadjis and with other known persons to the prosecuting authority to bring about a change in government with the use of force or to show use of force and that they conspired together with the deceased P. Yiorkadjis and other persons to murder President Makarios.

More recent is a quote[104] from an article by University Historian Dr. Petros Papapolyviou:

> "...the court case was heard between September and November 1970. The would-be-killers belong to two totally different groups against Archbishop Makarios: A "historical compromise" brought

---

[103] Greek academic (Larissa) Avgoustinos Avgousti quoted an account by authors P. Papademetri and A. Neophytou in a book 'Polycarpos Yiorkadjis, His Last Moments' (2014) Andreas Polycarpou posted the same information an article online, titled 'The historical timeline of Polycarpos Yiorkadjis murder'
:https://www.offsite.com.cy/articles/kyria-themata/topika/83215-poioi-ithela-ton-polykarpo-giorkatzi-nekro-ti-gnorize-kai-poioi (2016).

[104] 'The attempted murder of Makarios' by Dr. Petros Papapolyviou, published 4th June 2018.

together for the attempt devoted friends of Polycarpos Yiorkadjis, who felt pushed aside after his resignation, and men of the hardcore anti-Makarios opposition, who were of the opinion that the president of Cyprus had abandoned his policy in favour of enosis with Greece. For the attempt four persons were found guilty by the Nicosia Assize Court. The Court accepted that "it appears at first sight Polycarpos Yiorkadjis took part in the conspiracy".

Another of the accused, Costas Ioannides… was found innocent due to not enough evidence that would have provided prima facie a case against him…"

The key individuals were men of their time. Grivas was a career soldier, even if his greatest impact had been as an insurgent or freedom fighter, depending on one's point of view. He was not the first such figure to have fought a war of liberation and achieved that aim only to then fall out over the new direction of his country with his fellow politicians. If, as implied, he was involved in the assassination attempts against Makarios and Papadopoulos, Yiorkadjis showed that he was a man capable of extreme violence for political ends. If he saw Grivas as an obstacle to be overcome, killing him would simply have been a tactical option. If he was acting on the orders of Makarios, he would have had little compunction in carrying out his orders.

It is a matter of supreme irony that, having allegedly been involved in the aforementioned two plots, and being implicated, according to the information provided to the author, in the attempt against Grivas, the only person amongst these prominent figures to meet a violent end was Yiorkadjis himself. If, as alleged, Polycarpos Yiorkadjis was responsible for the destruction of Flight CY284, it is yet another tragedy in the tormented history of Cyprus that he caused the deaths of 66 innocent passengers and crew on board Charlie Oscar.

Above: Whilst of poor quality, this is a rare photo of Archbishop Makarios visiting the scene of his attempted assassination. The pilot of the helicopter was seriously injured but survived. Below: The body of Polycarpos Yiorkadjis is carried away after he was murdered at Mia Milia (photo attribution sought).

Above: In happier times… Archbishop Makarios (left) and General Grivas in 1964 (Cyprus Mail). Below left: The studious appearance of Polycarpos Yiorkadjis belied his alleged involvement in attempts to assassinate the leaders of both Greece and Cyprus. He was to meet a violent end himself. Below right: Spyros Kyprianou, Minister of Foreign Affairs, for whom Avraam Solomou was variously chauffeur, personal assistant and likely bodyguard (Ronald Reagan Presidential Library).

Conclusion

It is unlikely that there will be a universal acceptance of the perpetrators and motive for the destruction of Charlie Oscar and her passengers and crew. The population of Cyprus is small, in comparison with many other countries, and close-knit within its communities. Having said that, I believe that the course of events is most likely to be as set out above. Many people in Cyprus have, for the past half century, spoken amongst themselves about what happened on the evening of Wednesday 11th October 1967 and its awful denouement in the early hours of Thursday 12th October.

Of the authorities, the few who emerge from the incident and its aftermath with credit include those involved in the search and recovery operation, and in the subsequent accident investigation. In particular, the Hastings crews found the wreckage very quickly, enabling the recovery of the bodies of most of the victims, along with the seat covers with their vital evidence. The AIB team of John Veal and Eric Newton oversaw an investigation this is, to this day, considered exemplary. It was extraordinarily intricate and left no stone unturned. The work of the pathologists, Ken Mason and Stan Tarlton, is also considered to have been masterful, particularly under the most horrendous of circumstances.

The author's original conclusion was that it was less likely that Nicos Papapetrou had blown up himself, or a stooge, for insurance purposes, than it was that a courier such as Avraam Solomou might unwittingly have brought the bomb on board. The bomb appeared to the investigators to be a relatively sophisticated device, comprising military-grade plastic explosive with a detonator of unknown origin. The fact that it exploded at floor level, partially under a seat, made it more difficult for Papapetrou to detonate manually, and it was less likely that he would have relied on a timer. In October 2018, the Solomou family confirmed that they had been told Avraam Solomou had indeed called at the Cypriot Embassy the night before the flight. A number of separate sources stated that he was given the bomb there, without his knowledge. Avraam Solomou was no murderer, he was as much a victim as everyone else on the aircraft.

Much emphasis was placed throughout the investigation that there was no evidence that General Grivas was due to travel on CY284. For the first time, there is direct evidence that, in fact, Grivas was originally booked on the flight. Indeed, the crew had been told the day before the flight to expect him on board. The ultimate proof is that Neophytos Sofocleous, director of Grivas' office and a trusted confidante of the General, stated for this book that he had personally booked Grivas on to CY284 for 12th October 1967, and that he had cancelled the booking and warned Grivas immediately before the flight, when he became aware of the intense interest of Yiorkadjis in Grivas' travel plans. The credibility of Mr. Sofocleous is beyond doubt; as a 20-year-old EOKA activist in 1956, he was involved in a plot to blow up the residence of the Governor of Cyprus, Field Marshal Sir John Harding.

The involvement of Yiorkadjis in the attempt to kill Grivas has been alleged previously, and is corroborated further by a security officer, who further stated that Yiorkadjis was acting on the orders of Makarios. Yiorkadjis proved himself capable of such a grotesquely violent act against a perceived rival, ultimately in his involvement in the assassination attempt against Makarios three years later. Shortly before his own death in a lonely spot outside Nicosia, Yiorkadjis said *"Anything can happen now. To Makarios, people are like lemons: when they are squeezed dry, he throws them away."* Perhaps, to Makarios in late 1967, Grivas had appeared equally dispensable.

It is unlikely that we will ever know the real reason why the British Foreign Office was so keen for the investigation to avoid concluding that there was a political motive. Cyprus was strategically important in what was the height of the Cold War and Makarios was believed, at the time, to have been getting uncomfortably friendly with the Soviet Union. Implicating the Interior Minister of a sovereign state would have caused a diplomatic furore; if it had transpired that the President himself had been involved there would have been hell to pay. The inference from the documents does point to interference by the British establishment in the police investigation. There was a very clear steer, from the Foreign Office via Assistant Commissioner Brodie to the two detectives to avoid making too much of any links to a political motive. It is, therefore, not surprising that John Macrae of the Foreign Office, wrote to a colleague that '*On the whole, the insurance theory seems the most likely...*' Whether this was wishful thinking, rather than Macrae trying to lay a trail away from anything remotely political, will never be known, but it appears indicative of what the Foreign Office hoped would be the conclusion of the police investigation.

If Yiorkadjis had been an informant for the British Security Services during the Cyprus Emergency a decade earlier, it is highly unlikely that he would subsequently have been let off the hook. As a high-ranking politician, he would have been valuable indeed. The Security Services would also have had a strong hold over him; he would not have wanted his previous role to become common knowledge to any political rival, especially if one really did have an 'Exterminating-Traitor-Squad', as suggested by Peter Georgeides. Under the British Freedom of Information Act there is an absolute exemption on releasing details of such informants, to protect their families and associates even after their own death. It also, of course, protects the reputation of the state.

The Metropolitan Police investigation, by today's standards, was woefully under-resourced and appears, at best, to have been superficial. The apparent allocation of only two detectives to the case suggests that the force saw the investigation as a potential waste of time and money; the comments of the former DC Dave O'Connell observed Detective Chief Superintendent Browne's

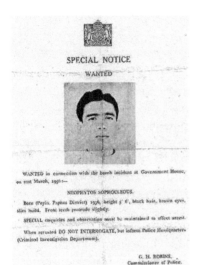
Neophytos Sofocleous was an active member of EOKA who was wanted by the British authorities for attempting to bomb the residence of the Governor. He was trusted by Grivas, becoming director of the General's office. He told the author that he had booked Grivas onto CY284 but then cancelled the reservation at the last minute, warning Grivas not to board the flight (Crown Copyright).

apparently laid-back attitude in the Roy Tuthill murder investigation immediately after Browne's return from the Charlie Oscar case. A significant team of officers appears to have been involved for the murder of a single child; there were three children, two of them British, aboard Charlie Oscar along with everybody else.

In the absence of the full crime files it is not possible to assess how much effort Browne and his colleague put into their investigation. The author has asked all the families in Cyprus he spoke to in connection with this book if they knew of any contact from the detectives; none knew of any such enquiries.

The investigation into the Charlie Oscar atrocity was closed when Assistant Commissioner Brodie told Mr. Bampton of the Home Office: *'A reply has now been received from the Director of Public Prosecutions to the effect that "no action can be taken on the present evidence". In the absence of any further evidence, I do not think that the Director will take any action in the future.'* It is, as discussed earlier, unlikely that the closed files contain any such evidence, though we will need to wait to find out until January 1st 2067. However, there is evidence provided by witnesses, published for the first time in this book, that:

(i) General Grivas was booked to fly on CY284 in the early hours of 12th October 1967.

(ii) His political rival, Polycarpos Yiorkadjis, was actively monitoring Grivas' movements, which included contacting Grivas' office shortly before the flight.

(iii) Yiorkadjis and Makarios were implicated in the destruction of Charlie Oscar, with the intention of killing Grivas.

(iv) Yiorkadjis had the propensity to become involved in complex attempts to kill his rivals. He was later implicated in two other assassination attempts, most strongly against Makarios three years later. The reality of such internecine violence was demonstrated when Yiorkadjis himself was shot dead shortly after the attempt against Makarios.

(v) A viable Improvised Explosive Device (IED) was packaged in a cabin bag and given to Avraam Solomou at the Cypriot Embassy in Athens.

234

Solomou was tasked with taking the bag to Nicosia and told he must fly on CY284. He knew nothing of the package's nature.

The person alleged to have handed the bag to Solomou was named to the author as Dinos Michaelides, who is known to be have been stationed at the Cypriot Embassy in Athens at the time of the bombing. He later rose to high office, serving as Interior Minister under Presidents Kyprianou and Clerides. However, in 1999, Michaelides resigned after allegations of corruption. In 2015, Michaelides and his son were convicted by a court in Athens of facilitating payments to former Greek defence minister Akis Tsohatzopoulos as kickbacks from a deal to supply Greece with Russian-made anti-aircraft missiles. Michaelides and his son were sentenced to fifteen years imprisonment, but Dinos Michaelides was allowed to remain under house arrest until his death in April 2020 [105] . Despite attempts on behalf of the author to contact Michaelides, these were unsuccessful and Michaelides appears to have taken the secret of his true involvement, or innocence, to his grave.

This information was passed on to the appropriate authorities but at the time of writing it is not known what, if any, action was taken. There are still surviving witnesses who could, if asked, provide very useful and credible evidence to a new police investigation. Only this would truly bring closure to what is a devastating incident which is still felt deeply by the relatives and friends of the 66 victims.

---

[105] Cyprus Mail, April 7th 2020, *Former interior minister Dinos Michaelides dies at 83.*

Acknowledgements

The research required for any book dealing with a complex subject is inevitably a daunting task. *Bealine Charlie Oscar* covers some areas in which I have some working knowledge; my working life has been in commercial aviation, policing and, latterly, in police aviation. However, I knew little about the intricacies of air crash investigation, much less about armaments research, and virtually nothing about the political intrigues of Greece and Cyprus in the Fifties and Sixties. Most significantly, I had almost no information about the people at the heart of this book, the passengers and crew who lost their lives in Charlie Oscar. The only exceptions were two of the pilots, Captain Gordon Blackwood and Senior First Officer Dennis Palmer.

As my research extended into Cyprus, both before and after publication of the first edition of this book, two things became clear. Firstly, the bombing of CY284 is remembered in that country to a far greater extent than in the UK and, secondly, it is still capable of attracting controversy and intense emotions. It has never been my intention to stir up old memories needlessly, but I have heard many views expressed that reinforce the sensitivity surrounding the incident. I would like to acknowledge the great courage shown by the people who believe that the truth must be told, and that my book will help them achieve that.

I have had a lifelong interest in the tragedy as Gordon was a neighbour, a close friend of my parents and a colleague of my father. I also remember Dennis Palmer, whom my parents knew as Tony, visiting our home. I had always assumed that the incident was closed and forgotten by everyone except those with distant memories of long-lost friends and relatives. Captain James Booth, a pilot friend and colleague of my own, suggested I post on the *Pprune* forum which immediately produced a response. The site connected me with Michael Thomaides, whose father was on flight CY284, and Fanoulla Argyrou, a London-based Greek Cypriot journalist. Together they have spent many years trying to make progress in establishing who was responsible for the disaster, and it has been a pleasure to join forces with them. Fanoulla's knowledge of where to find the relevant information, and Michael's many contacts in Cyprus, have really made the book possible. Rolandos Constantinides was also helpful in getting me started along the road to unravelling what had happened to CY284.

Much of that information is retained in the National Archives in London, and I am indebted to Fanoulla for her time and patience in helping me access it, and indeed for her return visits to gather small amounts of additional information on my behalf. I am obliged, but nonetheless pleased, to acknowledge access to the 2,500 or so pages of documents, that are available for reading, copying and reproducing in this book under the UK Government's Open Licence V2.0.

Contact with Michael and his family reassured me that I was not re-opening old wounds by publishing this book. On the contrary Michael, and every other family member I have spoken to, still feels the pain of their loss, exacerbated by

236

the absence of closure and the apparent lack of official interest in determining once and for all why, and by whom, their loved ones were killed. I would also like to extend my gratitude to Michael for offering his facilities in support of my visit to Cyprus to promote this book and meet those of the families who were able to join us.

I am grateful to Jill Harper, Gordon's daughter, for sharing information about her father's early life and for trusting me with scarce photographs of Gordon and Joyce. I hope that he, too would have approved of the book. Despite his best efforts, my father could not persuade Gordon to leave the Comet 4B fleet and join him on the Trident aircraft. As Gordon told his family, he would have flown the Comet without pay if BEA had wanted, such was the enjoyment he derived from flying the aircraft. Similarly, Mike Thomas' wife Sally and daughter Alison Whelan kindly supplied information and photos.

Louis Loizou, whose brother, John, was Senior Steward on the flight, provided a wealth of detail about Cyprus Airways' Comet operations, and the story of John and his girlfriend Josephine Coldicott. His recollection of the night of 11th – 12th October 1967 is understandably clear, and I thank him sincerely for being willing to share it in poignant detail. The story of John and Josephine's ill-fated romance is a tragedy in itself.

Many people have assisted me in gathering the information for what has become quite a complex writing project. Individual photographs are attributed to the person supplying them. In particular, I would like to thank the *Cyprus Mail* staff for supplying archive photographs of their newspaper coverage and Crysanthos Crysanthou, journalist of the *Filelefteros* newspaper, for the same facility. Simon Growcott made a special effort for me, gaining access to the freight hold of one of the very few intact Comet 4 aircraft still around, in order to obtain detailed photographs of the controls under the passenger cabin floor, in the vicinity of the device in Charlie Oscar. A picture paints a thousand words, especially when technical matters are concerned.

Roger Aves kindly carried out some research for me on the island of Kastellorizo. That put me in contact with Pantazis Houlis and Nikos Misomikes, who were able to shed some more light on the recovery operation.

The photographs come from many sources and are mostly from the time of the incident. Many were digital images created from old originals or have been scanned from copies of copies. As a result, there are some photographs which lack the quality associated with modern images. However, in most cases their relevance to the book and the scarcity of alternatives outweighs the low resolution of the picture. It is, as so often, a question for the author of 'Is this relatively low-quality image better than nothing at all?' I am very grateful for every one of them. Where possible they are attributed to the source who granted me permission to use them. A number, particularly relating to more generic and contextual material, are unattributed and come from multiple sources on the internet. I apologise for any inadvertent use of such images and invite the original owners to contact me via the publisher.

Technical experts on an historic aircraft like the Comet 4B are hard to find, but I was very fortunate to find three men who could give me advice, guidance and pass a critical eye over many of the relevant details, putting me back on track when my lack of detailed knowledge was in danger of drawing me off-track. They are Graham M. Simons, author of *Comet! The World's First Jet Airliner*, Capt. Simon Searle, formerly of Dan Air, who flew the last commercial flight by the type, and Capt. Bill Innes, a BEA Comet 4B co-pilot at the time of the loss of Charlie Oscar. Bill, in particular, shed significant light on the culture in BEA, and especially on the Comet fleet, when some of those aspects had been misinterpreted by other sources. David Nicholas, who was on duty in the BEA Operations Control Centre at Heathrow on the night of the disaster, has provided a comprehensive overview of how the airline's operations were overseen. This is included as Appendix 10.

Martin Painter's definitive work, *The DH.106 Comet – An Illustrated History*, published by Air Britain in 2002, provided invaluable details on the history of the Comet. I am grateful to Air Britain for allowing me to collate the information on hull losses (see Appendix 8), which I hope will help to dispel the enduring myth that the Comet was a death trap. It most certainly was not.

The labyrinthine world of 1960s Cypriot politics has been explained to me by Fanoulla Argyrou, and I am also grateful to journalists Christos Iacovou and Nicos Papanastassiou for the help they were able to provide. An excellent source of background information on the 'Cyprus Emergency' was the book of the same name, written by military historian Nik Van Der Bijl. I am grateful to Nik for his time during a lengthy phone call discussing the capabilities of EOKA in destroying aircraft, and for permission to use information from his book.

My son, William Hepworth, spent hours photographing documents for me and generally acting as my PA. As always, his enthusiasm and support have been outstanding, as has been the patience of my wife, Mandy, whose threshold of boredom is regularly breached once I start talking about matters such as this one, but who supports me without wavering.

Above all, I could not, and would not, have accomplished the task of producing this book without the support of the family members of other victims of flight CY284. I particularly thank Helen Kyriakos (Rodosthenis Christou and Niki Rodosthenou), Ioannis Ioanniades (Dr. George Ioanniades), George Dimetriou and Andria Soteriou (Katerina Liassides), and Macha Miller and family (the McComb family). Makis Efraim, brother in law of stewardess Thelma Efremi, joined our number and hosted a visit to his splendid fish tavern, To Latsi, in Nicosia. The family of Avraam Solomou has provided useful information, including information that they were given by Cypriot authorities in the aftermath of the incident. Polyvios Georgiou was also very helpful in providing details of his brother, Sotiris.

It is important to stress that I have considered all the information passed to me or unearthed by the research I carried out along with others. Much of it is conflicting and I have used my best endeavours to sort the wheat from the chaff. However, even after half a century the Charlie Oscar incident, which is also referred to in Greece and Cyprus as the Kastellorizo Disaster, is very controversial. My conclusions are not accepted by everyone, but I have made them in good faith and on the basis of interpreting the evidence as objectively as possible.

I hope that, by presenting the evidence in a proportionate and considered way, I can help to bring closure to the families and friends of the victims. I have been thanked for my efforts by those with whom I have been in contact; that makes it all worthwhile. If the information as to the motive and the perpetrators is correct, and I do believe my sources to be credible, I can understand why there has been silence for half a century from the British and Cypriot establishments. It would not surprise me if that silence continues. This is no way excuses the apparent demonisation of Nicos Papapetrou, who appears to have been deliberately made a scapegoat to divert attention from the sinister political machinations that resulted in the downing of CY284. The families have always deserved better.

The search, which spans four nations, goes on for others who lost a friend or relative on that dreadful night half a century ago. I would welcome contact with them, not least to tell them that their loved ones are not forgotten. I can be contacted via my publisher's e-mail address, mtwpublications@gmail.com

Simon Hepworth
Merthyr Tydfil
May 2019

Bibliography

Files held in The National Archives

13 1338 Accident Investigation

AVIA101 208 Report of Explosion in Cabin

AVIA101 209 Submission of Report

AVIA101 210 Chief Investigating Officers Report

AVIA101 211 Comet Engineering Review

AVIA101 212 Feasibility of Salvaging Wreckage

AVIA101 213 Correspondence with Members of the Public

AVIA101 214 Press Cuttings

AVIA101 215 Witness Statements

AVIA101 216 Meteorological Data

AVIA101 217 Technical Information including Photographs

AVIA101 218 Demarcation of Investigation

AVIA101 219 Parliamentary Questions

AVIA101 220 Diaries and Documentation

AVIA101 221 Siting of Wreckage and Provenance of Seat Cushion

AVIA101 222 ATC Transcript

AVIA101 223 Collision Theory

AVIA101 224 Wreckage Plot and Passenger List

AVIA101 225 Pathology Reports

AVIA101 226 Report and Correspondence with Interested Parties

DR 11 51 Loss of G-ARCO

FCO 9 239 combined document

HO 287/2146 Sabotage: Air Accident Reports on Explosion of British European Airways Comet G-ARCO on 12th October 1967

MEPO 2/11089 and 2/11090 Metropolitan Police investigation into an explosion aboard BEA Comet G-ARCO over the Mediterranean Sea on 12th October 1967

Short notes on Police Involvement

Technical Material

Comet 4B Operations Manual - Flying	BEA
Comet 4B Operations Manual - Technical	BEA

Published Articles

Aircraft Accident Pathology	J K Mason	
Civil Accident Report No. EW/A/0102	Accidents Investigation Branch	Board of Trade 1968
Comet G-ARCO: Solving the Riddle	V J Clancey	New Scientist 533-537 1968
Injuries in Fatal Aircraft Accidents	S A Cullen MD	NATO
The medical investigation of the loss of the Comet 4B aircraft 1967	J K Mason & S W Tarlton	The Lancet I 431-434 1969

Published Books

Air Crash – The Clues in the Wreckage	Fred Jones	Robert Hale Ltd., 1985
Aircraft Accident Pathology	J K Mason	Butterworths, 1962
Cat's Paw	Christopher Malinger	Malinger Publishing 2018
Comet! The World's First Jet Airliner	Graham M. Simons	Pen & Sword Aviation 2013
De Havilland Comet 1949-97 (all marks)	Owners' Workshop Manual	Haynes
Fatal Aircraft Accidents - A Pathologist's Notebook	S K Adaval	Knowledge World International 2008
Glafkos Clerides - The Path of a Country	Niyazi Kizilyurek	Rimal Publications (Cyprus) 2008
History of British European Airways	Phil Lo Bao	Browcom Group 1989
History of British European Airways 1946-1974	Charles Woodley	Pen & Sword Aviation 2005
On the Trail of Terror - The Inside Story of the Lockerbie Investigation	David Leppard	Jonathan Cape 1991
Safety is No Accident	William Tench	Collins 1985
The Challenge of BEA	Garry May	Wolfe Publishing 1971
The Cyprus Emergency - The Divided Island 1955-1974	Nik van der Bijl	Pen & Sword Military
The DH.106 Comet - An Illustrated History	Martin Painter	Air Britain
Trust Me I'm the Pilot	Baron de Tourtoulon	Upfront Publishing 2012
TWA 800 - Accident or Incident?	Kevin E Ready and Cap Parlier	Saint Gaudens Press, 2013

DVDs

Flight Plan (DVD)	BEA	1962

Appendix 1 – CY284 Flight Paperwork

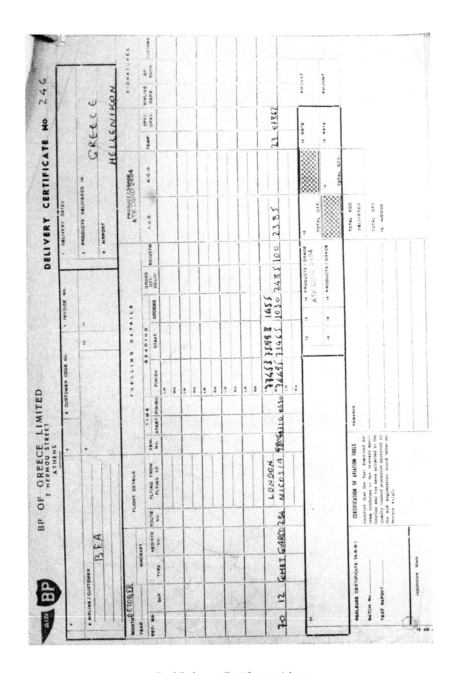

Fuel Delivery Certificate, Athens

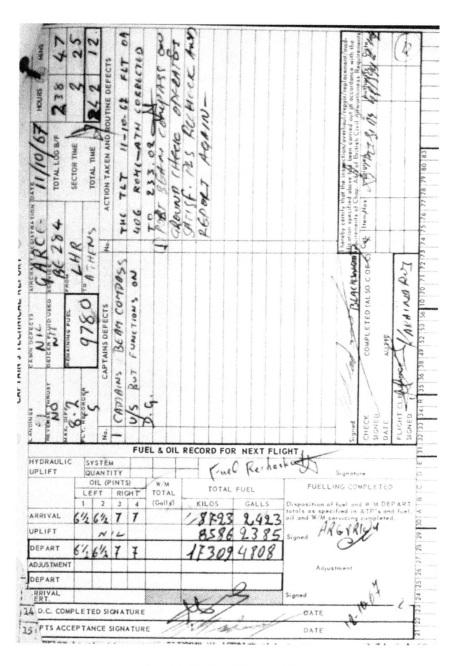

Captain's Technical Record, Athens

PRE DEPARTURE INSPECTION SHEET
Title:(To be carried out immediately before every flight)

Place : ATHENS
Ref.: M-11-18
Issue:6/19.5.66

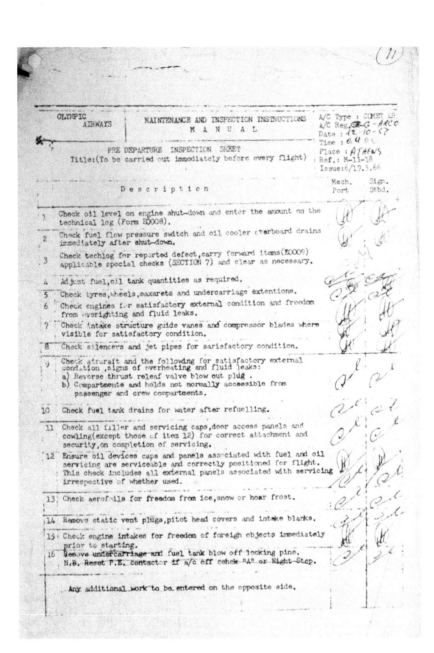

	D e s c r i p t i o n	Mech. Port	Sign. Stbd.
1	Check oil level on engine shut-down and enter the amount on the technical log (Form E0008).		
2	Check fuel flow pressure switch and oil cooler overboard drains immediately after shut-down.		
3	Check techlog for reported defect, carry forward items(E0009) applicable special checks (SECTION 7) and clear as necessary.		
4	Adjust fuel, oil tank quantities as required.		
5	Check tyres, wheels, maxarets and undercarriage extentions.		
6	Check engines for satisfactory external condition and freedom from overighting and fluid leaks.		
7	Check intake structure guide vanes and compressor blades where visible for satisfactory condition.		
8	Check silencers and jet pipes for sarisfactory condition.		
9	Check aircraft and the following for satisfactory external condition, signs of overheating and fluid leaks: a) Reverse thrust releaf valve blow out plug . b) Compartments and holds not normally accessible from passenger and crew compartments.		
10	Check fuel tank drains for water after refuelling.		
11	Check all filler and servicing caps, door access panels and cowling(except those of item 12) for correct attachment and security, on completion of servicing.		
12	Ensure oil devices caps and panels associated with fuel and oil servicing are serviceable and correctly positioned for flight. This check includes all external panels associated with servicing irrespective of whether used.		
13	Check aerofoils for freedom from ice, snow or hoar frost.		
14	Remove static vent plugs, pitot head covers and intake blanks.		
15	Check engine intakes for freedom of foreign objects immediately prior to starting.		
16	Remove undercarriage and fuel tank blow off locking pins. N.B. Reset P.E. contactor if a/c off cehck "A" or Night-Stop.		

Any additional work to be entered on the opposite side.

Pre-Departure Inspection Sheet, Athens.

246

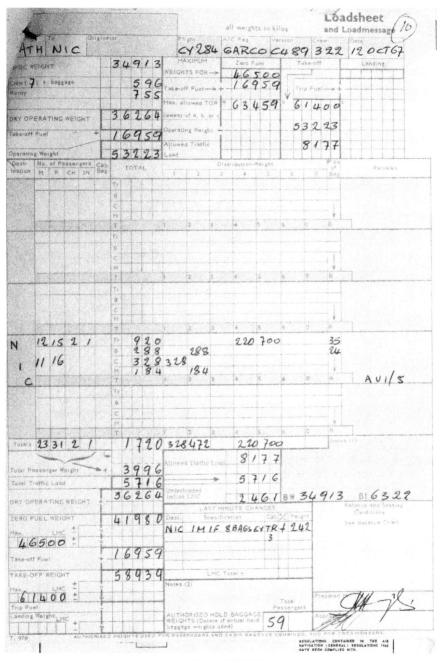

Loadsheet ATH-NIC

247

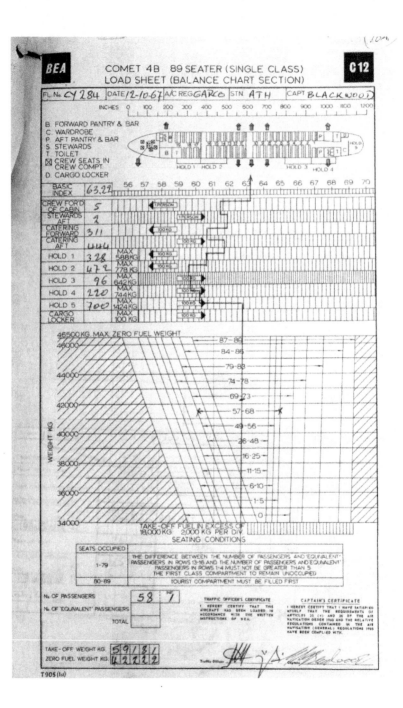

Mass and Balance Sheet, ATH-NIC

T.374(3rd)

PASSENGER MANIFEST

ICAO
ANNEXE 9
APP. 2

OWNER OF OPERATOR BRITISH EUROPEAN AIRWAYS BE 284

MARKS OF
NATIONALITY
AND REGISTRATION CARCO. FLIGHT NO. DATE

POINT OF EMBARKATION LONDON UK
(Place & Country)

POINT OF DISEMBARKATION NICOSIA CYPRUS
(Place & Country)

SURNAME AND INITIALS	FOR OFFICIAL USE ONLY
COLDICOTT ST S	
POWELL	
EFSTATHOU	
GEORGIOU	
TASKER	
TASKER	
LIASSIDES	
NICOLAIDEOS	
NICOLAIDEOS	
NICOLAIDEOS	
FALCONER	
PAPAIOANNOU	
STEWART	
STEWART	
GRIFFITHS	
GRIFFITHS	
TSOLAKARIS	
CHRISTOU	
THOMAIDES	
STONE	
MARLBOROUGH	
MCCOMB	
MCCOMB	
JODOURIS	
JOYCE	
IONNIDES	
DALTON	
MCCOMB	
OBRIAN	
OBRIAN	

Passenger Manifest, LHR-NIC

249

GARCO   CV281/120

ATHENS - GREECE

NICOSIA - CYPRUS

PARTZOPOULOU
RACHOVIDES
KOUTROUBIS
KOUTROUBI
KARAKOSTA
VOUIOTOU
KODOMINAS
KODOMINA
KALOGEROPOULOU
MARKIDI
RIGOS
PALEOLOGOS
PALEOLOGOU
MARKIDES
PAPANIKOLAOU
BOUGIOUKA
THIAKOU
THIAKOS
CHRISTAKI
AFATIDIS
SIFNEOU
ANGEROS
EXARCHEA
RODOSTHENOUS
PAPAPETROU
SHERIS
SOLOMOU.

Passenger Manifest, ATH-NIC

250

GENERAL DECLARATION

(OUTWARD·INWARD)·

Owner or Operator *BRITISH EUROPEAN AIRWAYS·

Marks of Nationality and Registration .... Flight No. .... Date ....

Departure from ATHENS .... Arrival at ....

(Place and Country) Place and Country

FLIGHT ROUTING

("Place" Column always to list origin, every en-route stop and destination)

PLACE	TOTAL NUMBER OF CREW	NUMBER OF PASSENGERS ON THIS STAGE
		Departure Place
		Embarking
		Through on same flight
		Arrival Place
		Disembarking
		Through on same flight

DECLARATION OF HEALTH

Persons on board known to be suffering from illness other than airsickness or the effects of accidents, as well as those cases of illness disembarked during the flight.

Any other conditions on board which may lead to the spread of disease.

Details of each disinsecting or sanitary treatment (place, date, time, method) during the flight. If no disinsecting has been carried out during the flight give details of most recent disinsecting.

Signed if required...................

Other member concerned...............

I declare that all statements and particulars contained in this General Declaration and in any supplementary forms required to be presented with this General Declaration are complete, exact and true to the best of my knowledge and that all through passengers will continue/have continued on this flight.

Signatures......................

*Delete as necessary

Authorised Agent or Pilot in Command *

General Declaration of crew members for immigration and health purposes, ATH-NIC

251

TO: CARGO REVENUE ACCOUNTANT (FQ7) – (direct)
C.C. STATISTICS OFFICER, BEALINE HOUSE (attached to flight documents)

STATION __A T H E N S__   AIRCRAFT __C A R G O__   FLIGHT __CY 284__   DATE __12.10.67__

| OFFLOAD AT :– | Total No. of Bags etc. | Total Weight | | Only insert in this column uplift point and incoming flight details for mails transferred direct from BEA flights. |
		Kgs.	Grms.	
NICOSIA	20	183.	500	EX LOCAL P.O

NOTES

1. Only insert bulk totals for each offload point, except for mail transfer from BEA flights when the total of each applicable AV.7, must be listed separately.
2. Applicable Forms AV.7 (P.2026H) and Transfer Manifests, are to be attached only to Cargo Revenue Accountant's copy of this form.

SIGNATURE

T 540(3rd)

Mail Summary for purpose of revenue accounting, ATH-NIC

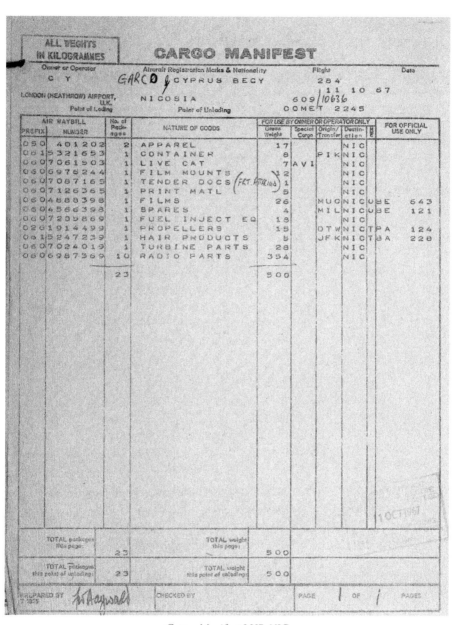

ALL WEIGHTS IN KILOGRAMMES				CARGO MANIFEST					

Owner or Operator: C Y — GARCO CYPRUS BECY
Aircraft Registration Marks & Nationality
Flight: 284
Date: 11 10 67

LONDON (HEATHROW) AIRPORT, U.K. — Point of Loading
NICOSIA — Point of Unloading
609/10636
COMET 2245

AIR WAYBILL PREFIX	NUMBER	No. of Packages	NATURE OF GOODS	Gross Weight	Special Cargo	Origin/Transfer	Destination		FOR OFFICIAL USE ONLY
050	401202	2	APPAREL	17			NIC		
061	5321653	1	CONTAINER	8		PIK	NIC		
060	7061503	1	LIVE CAT	7	AVI		NIC		
060	6975244	1	FILM MOUNTS	12			NIC		
060	7087165	1	TENDER DOCS (FRT. ATTAC.)	1			NIC		
060	7126365	1	PRINT MATL	5			NIC		
060	4888398	1	FILMS	26		MUC	NIC	UBE	543
060	4566398	1	SPARES	4		MIL	NIC	UBE	121
060	7205869	1	FUEL INJECT EQ	18			NIC		
026	1914499	1	PROPELLERS	15		DTW	NIC	TPA	124
061	5247239	1	HAIR PRODUCTS	5		JFK	NIC	TBA	228
060	7024019	1	TURBINE PARTS	28			NIC		
060	6987369	10	RADIO PARTS	354			NIC		
		23		500					

TOTAL packages this page:	23	TOTAL weight this page:	500			
TOTAL packages this point of unloading:	23	TOTAL weight this point of unloading:	500			

PREPARED BY T 1025 — *(signature)*
CHECKED BY
PAGE 1 OF 1 PAGES

Cargo Manifest LHR-NIC

253

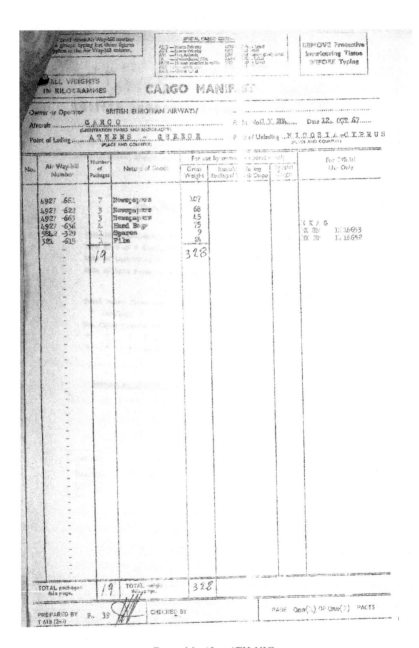

Cargo Manifest ATH-NIC

254

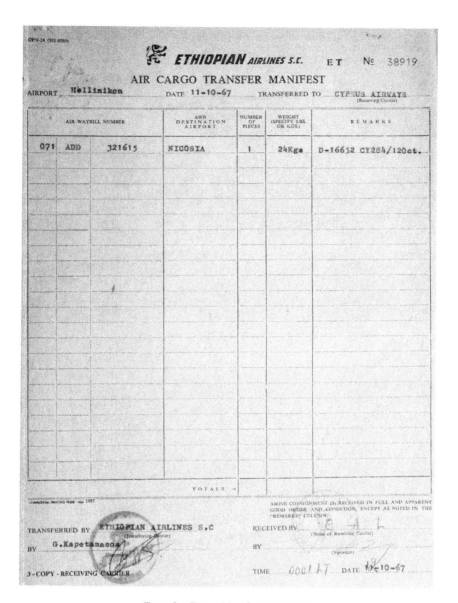

AIR WAYBILL NUMBER			AWB DESTINATION AIRPORT	NUMBER OF PIECES	WEIGHT (SPECIFY LBS. OR KGS.)	REMARKS
071	ADD	321615	NICOSIA	1	24Kgs	D-16652 CY284/120et.

Transfer Cargo Manifest ATH-NIC

255

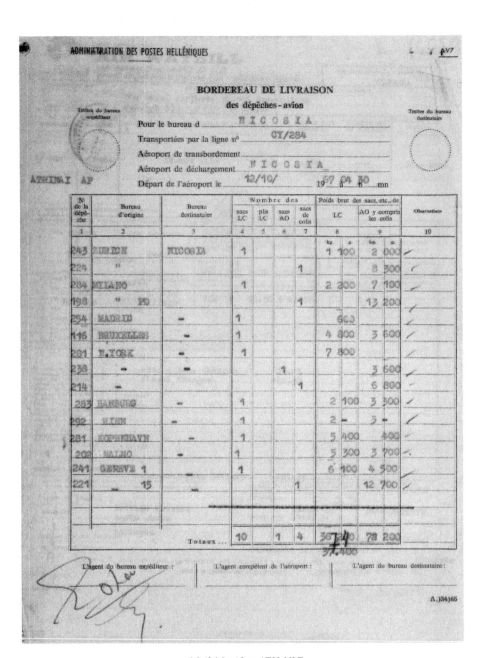

BORDEREAU DE LIVRAISON

des dépêches - avion

Pour le bureau d ___ N I C O S I A ___

Transportées par la ligne n⁰ ___ CY/284 ___

Aéroport de transbordement ___

Aéroport de déchargement ___ N I C O S I A ___

Départ de l'aéroport le ___ 12/10/ ___ 19 67 à 30 ___ mn

N. de la dépêche	Bureau d'origine	Bureau destinataire	Nombre des				Poids brut des sacs, etc., de		Observations
			sacs LC	plis LC	sacs AO	sacs de colis	LC	AO y compris les colis	
1	2	3	4	5	6	7	8	9	10
243	ZURICH	NICOSIA	1				1 700	2 000	✓
224	"				1			8 500	✓
234	MILANO		1				2 300	7 100	✓
198	" PD					1		13 200	✓
254	MADRID	-	1					600	✓
116	BRUXELLES	-	1				4 800	3 600	✓
291	N.YORK	-	1				7 800		✓
238	-	-			1			3 600	✓
214	-				1			6 800	-
283	HAMBURG	-	1				2 100	3 300	✓
202	WIEN	-	1				2 -	3 -	✓
281	KOPENHAVN	-	1				5 400	400	✓
202	MALMO	-	1				5 300	3 700	✓
241	GENEVE 1	-	1				6 100	4 500	✓
221	- 15	-			1			12 700	✓
		Totaux ...	10	1	4		37 240 / 37 400	78 200	

L'agent du bureau expéditeur :   L'agent compétent de l'aéroport :   L'agent du bureau destinataire :

A.)34)65

Mail Manifest ATH-NIC

ETHIOPIAN AIRLINES S.C.

No. 071   № 321615

NOT NEGOTIABLE

AIR WAYBILL

(AIR CONSIGNMENT NOTE)
ISSUED BY ETHIOPIAN AIRLINES S. C. ADDIS ABABA, ETHIOPIA

Number of IATA.

DESTINATION (AIRPORT OF)   NICOSIA

CONSIGNED TO   STREET ADDRESS   CITY AND COUNTRY

The Royal Airforce Cinema Corporation

ALSO NOTIFY   P.O. Box 53   Nicosia

NO. OF PACKAGES	METHOD OF PACKING	NATURE AND QUANTITY OF GOODS	MARKS AND NUMBERS	DIMENTIONS OR VOLUME	GROSS WEIGHT SPECIFY KGS. OR LBS.
1/ One	Pol.	Cinema Film	Addr.	---	24.- Kgs.

DOCUMENTS TO ACCOMPANY AIR WAYBILL   Nil

SHIPPER'S DECLARED VALUE (Specify Currency)

FOR CUSTOMS   FOR CARRIAGE

Nev   Nvd

METHOD OF ROUTING AND CHARGES

Agreed stopping places are those places (other than the places of departure and destination) shown under Air Carriage and/or those places shown in carriers' timetables as scheduled stopping places for the route. SEE CONDITIONS ON REVERSE HEREOF.

SHIPPER MUST INSERT ITEM NUMBER CHARGEABLE TO SELF

AIR CARRIAGE		Chargeable WEIGHT SPECIFY Kgs. or Lbs.	RATE CLASSI-FICATION	RATES	PREPAID		Cur-rency	CHARGEABLE TO CONSIGNEE AMOUNTS IN CURRENCIES AS CHARGED	AMOUNTS IN CURRENCY AT DESTINATION
DEPARTURE (AIRPORT OF)	ADDRESS OF FIRST CARRIER								
1. TO Addis Aba	ABB FIRST CARRIER ET	24K	N	$3.50	$84.00				
2. TO Nicosia	CARRIER Pirav								
3. TO	CARRIER								
4. VALUATION CHARGE FROM TO									
5. VALUATION CHARGE FROM TO									
6. INSURANCE AMOUNT IN WORDS									

If Shipper request insurance in accordance with conditions stated on reverse hereof indicate amount of insurance in words in space under item 6 above (but in no event in excess of the actual value of the goods at destination + 10%). Insurance is payable to shipper unless otherwise designated.

OTHER CHARGES (SPECIFY)

7. ORIGIN		
8.		
9. Sta. & Doc. Charges	$1.05	
10. Fiscal Charges	$0.30	
11. TRANSIT		
12. DESTINATION		
13.		
14.		
15.		
16. C.O.D. FEE		
17. SHIPPER'S C.O.D.		

TOTAL

SHIPPER'S C.O.D., IN WORDS   Paid Ethiopian Dollars $85.35

The Shipper certifies that particulars on the face hereof are correct and agrees to the CONDITIONS ON THE REVERSE HEREOF.

Carrier certifies above described goods were received for carriage SUBJECT TO THE CONDITIONS ON THE REVERSE HEREOF, the goods then being in apparent good order and condition except as noted hereon.

NAME OF SHIPPER   BRITISH EMBASSY   EXECUTED ON 10-20-'67 AT Bole Airport

ADDRESS   Addis Ababa   NAME AND ADDRESS OF ISSUING CARRIER'S AGENT

Ethiopia   M.M. Stifanos

SIGNATURE OF SHIPPER

BY BROKER/AGENT   SIGNATURE OF ISSUING CARRIER OR ITS AGENT   Ethiopia

COPIES 1, 2, AND 3 OF THIS AIR WAYBILL ARE ORIGINALS AND HAVE THE SAME VALIDITY

COPY 5 (INBOUND CLEARANCE)   DUPLICATE AIR WAYBILL NO.

UNITED PRINTERS   No. 071   № 321615

Air Waybill for film from Addis Ababa, ATH-NIC

257

Air Waybill for Caterpillar spares from Brussels, ATH-NIC

NOT NEGOTIABLE

AIR WAYBILL
(AIR CONSIGNMENT NOTE)

Issued by
BRITISH EUROPEAN AIRWAYS CORPORATION
Bealine House, Ruislip, Middlesex

BEA

MEMBER OF INTERNATIONAL
AIR TRANSPORT ASSOCIATION

BOOKED	FLIGHT	DATE

060- 4927 622

DESTINATION (AIRPORT OF)
NICOSIA

CONSIGNED TO
VIVLIOPOLION Z O I

STREET ADDRESS
100, TRICOUPI STR

CITY AND COUNTRY
NICOSIA CYPRUS

ALSO NOTIFY

No. OF PACKAGES	METHOD OF PACKING	NATURE AND QUANTITY OF GOODS	MARKS AND NUMBERS	DIMENSIONS OR VOLUME	GROSS WEIGHT SPECIFY KG. or LB.
THREE (3)	PCLS	NEWSPAPERS VERY URGENT	ADDRS	TOTAL	27,500kgs 23,000kgs 17,750kgs 68,250kgs

DOCUMENTS TO ACCOMPANY AIR WAYBILL.   ONE(1) INVOICE IN DUBLICATE

SHIPPER'S DECLARED VALUE (Specify Currency)		METHOD OF ROUTING AND CHARGES—Agreed stopping places are those places (other than the places of departure and destination) shown under Air Carriage and/or those places shown in carriers timetables as scheduled stopping places for the route. SEE CONDITIONS ON REVERSE HEREOF.	SHIPPER MUST INSERT ITEM NUMBER CHARGEABLE TO SELF.
FOR CUSTOMS	FOR CARRIAGE		
DR.4,125.-	N V DR.4,125.		

AIR CARRIAGE

DEPARTURE (AIRPORT OF) ATHENS	(ADDRESS OF FIRST CARRIER)	CHARGEABLE WEIGHT SPECIFY KG. or LB.	RATE CLASSIFICATION	RATES	LKS RAT80599		CHARGEABLE TO CONSIGNEE AMOUNTS IN CURRENCIES AS CHARGED	AMOUNTS IN CURRENCIES AT DESTINATION
1. TO NICOSIA	FIRST CARRIER CAL	68.5kgs	RED	2,910				
2. TO	CARRIER LESS REBATE 50%			1,455	£4.19.8d- 2			
3. TO	CARRIER							
3a. TO	CARRIER							
4. VALUATION CHARGE FROM		TO						
5. VALUATION CHARGE FROM		TO						
6. INSURANCE AMOUNT IN WORDS			FIGURES					

	7. ORIGIN	AWB CHARGES	3/6d- 7
	8.	T/TERMINAL HANDLING FEES	2/10d- 8
	9.	CUSTOMS CLEARANCE CHARGES	2/5d- 9
	10.	CUSTOMS LABOUR CHARGES	3/8d- 10
	11. TRANSIT		
	12. DESTINATION		
	13.		
	14.		
	15.		
	16. C.O.D. FEE		
	17. SHIPPER'S C.O.D.		

INSURANCE

If shipper requests insurance in accordance with conditions on reverse hereof, indicate amount of insurance in words and figures in space provided above.

SHIPPER'S C.O.D. IN WORDS   £5.12.1d-   TOTALS

471 DRA OR

The Shipper certifies that the particulars on the face hereof are correct and agrees to the CONDITIONS ON REVERSE HEREOF.

Carrier certifies above-described goods were received for carriage SUBJECT TO CONDITIONS ON THE REVERSE HEREOF, the goods then being in apparent good ORDER AND condition except as noted herein.

NAME AND ADDRESS OF SHIPPER	ADELFOTIS THEOLOGON Z O I 189, HIPPOCRATOUS STR ATHENS GREECE	EXECUTED ON 10/10/67 (Date) AT ATHENS
		C A L NICOSIA

SIGNATURE OF SHIPPER

PHONE

BEA. T. OWN. OFFICE ATHENS GREECE L A

BY BROKER/AGENT

Copies 1, 2 and 3 of this Air Waybill are originals and have the same validity.

Original 1 - (For Issuing Carrier) B

ACCOUNT NO. | DC | BC | A | B | F/R OR MIN | PP

Air Waybill for newspapers ATH-NIC

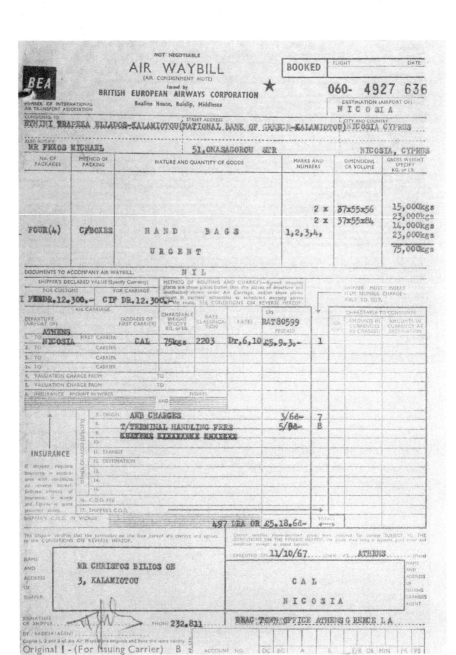

Air Waybill for consignment of handbags, ATH-NIC

260

NOT NEGOTIABLE

AIR WAYBILL
(AIR CONSIGNMENT NOTE)

Issued by
BRITISH EUROPEAN AIRWAYS CORPORATION
Bealine House, Ruislip, Middlesex

MEMBER OF INTERNATIONAL
AIR TRANSPORT ASSOCIATION

BOOKED	FLIGHT	DATE

★

060- 4927 661

DESTINATION (AIRPORT OF)
N I C O S I A

CONSIGNED TO
CH.POULIAS & P.KONIARIS STREET ADDRESS 10 NICOCLES STREET CITY AND COUNTRY
NICOSIA/CYPRUS

ALSO NOTIFY

No. OF PACKAGES	METHOD OF PACKING	NATURE AND QUANTITY OF GOODS	MARKS AND NUMBERS	DIMENSIONS OR VOLUME	GROSS WEIGHT SPECIFY KG. or LB.
7	PCS	SAID TO CONTAIN NEWSPAPERS	ADDR		107

DOCUMENTS TO ACCOMPANY AIR WAYBILL

SHIPPER'S DECLARED VALUE (Specify Currency)

METHOD OF ROUTING AND CHARGES —Agreed stopping places are those places (other than the places of departure and destination) shown under Air Carriage, and/or those places shown in carriers' timetables as scheduled stopping places for the route. SEE CONDITIONS ON REVERSE HEREOF.

SHIPPER MUST INSERT ITEM NUMBER CHARGE-ABLE TO SELF.

FOR CUSTOMS	FOR CARRIAGE
£ 42118.1	

AIR CARRIAGE

			CHARGEABLE WEIGHT SPECIFY KG or LB.	RATE CLASSIFICATION	RATES	CRS		CHARGEABLE TO CONSIGNEE	
DEPARTURE (AIRPORT OF)		(ADDRESS OF FIRST CARRIER)				PREPAID	CUR-RENCY	AMOUNTS IN CURRENCIES AS CHARGED	AMOUNTS IN CURRENCY AT DESTINATION
1. TO	ATH FIRST CARRIER								
2. TO NIC	CARRIER BE	107	MED	0.41	COLLECT	US.$ 21.94			
3. TO	CARRIER								
3a. TO	CARRIER								
4. VALUATION CHARGE FROM	TO								
5. VALUATION CHARGE FROM	TO								
6. INSURANCE AMOUNT IN WORDS	AND FIGURES								

OTHER CHARGES (SPECIFY)				
7. ORIGIN				
8.	AWB FEES	COLLECT	US.$ 0.50	
9.	CUSTOMS CLEAR	COLLECT	US.$ 2.45	
10.				
11. TRANSIT				
12. DESTINATION				
13.				
14.				
15.				
16. C.O.D. FEE				
17. SHIPPER'S C.O.D.				

INSURANCE
If shipper requests insurance in accordance with conditions on reverse hereof, indicate amount of insurance in words and figures in space provided above.

SHIPPER'S C.O.D. IN WORDS

TOTALS

COLLECT

The Shipper certifies that the particulars on the face hereof are correct and agrees to the CONDITIONS ON REVERSE HEREOF.

Carrier certifies that the described goods were received for carriage SUBJECT TO THE CONDITIONS ON THE REVERSE HEREOF, the goods then being in apparent good order and condition except as noted herein.

EXECUTED ON .... (Date) AT .... (Place)
11 OCT 87 ATHENS

NAME AND ADDRESS OF SHIPPER	ATHENS PRESS AGENCY ATHENS/GREECE	SCHENKER & CO ATHENS IATA CODE 27-2-1873	NAME AND ADDRESS OF ISSUING CARRIER'S AGENT

SIGNATURE OF SHIPPER .... PHONE ....
SIGNATURE OF ISSUING CARRIER OR ITS AGENT ....

BY BROKER/AGENT ....
Copies 1, 2 and 3 of this Air Waybill are originals and have the same validity.

Air Waybill for newspapers ATH-NIC

261

AIR WAYBILL

(AIR CONSIGNMENT NOTE)

Issued by

BRITISH EUROPEAN AIRWAYS CORPORATION ★

Bealine House, Ruislip, Middlesex

MEMBER OF INTERNATIONAL
AIR TRANSPORT ASSOCIATION

BOOKED	FLIGHT	DATE

060- 4927 663

DESTINATION (AIRPORT OF)

N I C O S I A

CONSIGNED TO **CH.POULIAS & P. KONIARIS** STREET ADDRESS **IO NICOSIA STREET**   CITY AND COUNTRY

NICOSIA/CYPRUS

ALSO NOTIFY:

No. OF PACKAGES	METHOD OF PACKING	NATURE AND QUANTITY OF GOODS	MARKS AND NUMBERS	DIMENSIONS OR VOLUME	GROSS WEIGHT SPECIFY KG. or LB.
		SAID TO CONTAIN			
THREE (3)					45.- KGS
XXX	PCS	N E W S P A P E R S	ATHN		

DOCUMENTS TO ACCOMPANY AIR WAYBILL

SHIPPER'S DECLARED VALUE (Specify Currency)

FOR CUSTOMS	FOR CARRIAGE
£ 5.0.7	

METHOD OF ROUTING AND CHARGES—Agreed stopping places are those places (other than the places of departure and destination) shown under Air Carriage, and/or those places shown in carriers' timetables as scheduled stopping places for the route. SEE CONDITIONS ON REVERSE HEREOF.

SHIPPER MUST INSERT ITEM NUMBER CHARGE-ABLE TO SELF.

AIR CARRIAGE

		CHARGEABLE WEIGHT SPECIFY KG. or LB.	RATE CLASSIFICATION	RATES	CRS PREPAID		CURRENCY	CHARGEABLE TO CONSIGNEE	
DEPARTURE (AIRPORT OF)	(ADDRESS OF FIRST CARRIER)							AMOUNTS IN CURRENCIES AS CHARGED	AMOUNTS IN CURRENCY AT DESTINATION
1. TO	ATHN FIRST CARRIER						US $	XXXXXX	
2. TO NIC	BE CARRIER	XXXXX	NED 0.41	COLLECT				$18.45	
3. TO	CARRIER								
3a. TO	CARRIER								
4. VALUATION CHARGE FROM		TO							
5. VALUATION CHARGE FROM		TO							
6. INSURANCE AMOUNT IN WORDS			FIGURES AND						
	7. ORIGIN								
	8.	AND FEES		COLLECT			US $	0.50	
	9.								
	10.								

INSURANCE

If shipper requests insurance in accordance with conditions on reverse hereof, indicate amount of insurance in words and figures in space provided above.

SHIPPER'S C.O.D. IN WORDS

	11. TRANSIT		
	12. DESTINATION		
	13.		
	14.		
	15.		
	16. C.O.D. FEE		
	17. SHIPPER'S C.O.D.		
		TOTALS	

The Shipper certifies that the particulars on the face hereof are correct and agrees to the CONDITIONS ON REVERSE HEREOF.

Carrier certifies above-described goods were received for carriage SUBJECT TO THE CONDITIONS ON THE REVERSE HEREOF, the goods then being in apparent good order and condition except as noted hereon.

EXECUTED ON **11 OCT 67** (Date) AT **ATHENS** (Place)

NAME AND ADDRESS OF SHIPPER	BEN NEWSPAPER AGENCY ATHENS/GREECE	SCHENKER & CO ATHENS IATA CODE 27-2-1873	NAME AND ADDRESS OF ISSUING CARRIERS AGENT

SIGNATURE OF SHIPPER............PHONE............

SIGNATURE OF ISSUING CARRIER OR ITS AGENT............

BY BROKER/AGENT............

Copies 1, 2 and 3 of this Air Waybill are originals and have the same validity.

Air Waybill for newspapers ATH-NIC

262

Appendix 2 – CY284 Crew and Passenger List

Title	First name	Surname	Age	Nationality	Boarded	Seat No.	Cabin	Group	Buried
Mr	Achillea	Afaitis	28	Greek	Athens	JW block	Rear	Southern	Rhodes, Greece
Mrs	Reveka	Afaitis	20	Greek	Athens	JW block	Rear	Southern	Rhodes, Greece
Captain	Gordon	Blackwood	45	British	London	Pilot	Forward	Missing	
Police Se	Rodosthenis	Christou	40	Cypriot	London	9D	Forward	Southern	Famagusta, Cyprus
Miss	Josephine Yvonne	Coldicott	24	British	London	11A	Forward	Northern	UK
Miss	Mary Elizabeth	Dalton	22	British	London	Not known	Not known	Missing	
Stewardess	Thelma	Efremi	c.20	Cypriot	Athens	Cabin staff	Rear	Southern	Ayii Omoloyitades, Cyprus
Mr	Costantinos	Efstathiou	34	Cypriot	London	08E	Rear	Northern	Cyprus
Mr	Elias	Evgeros	28	Greek	Athens	JW block	Rear	Northern	Athens, Greece
Miss	Areti	Exarcheas	21	Greek	Athens	JW block	Rear	Northern	Rhodes, Greece
Miss	Jean	Falconer	80	British	London	07E	Rear	Southern	Not stated
Mr	Sotiris	Georgiou		US	London	04A	Rear	Missing	
Mr	Hugh	Griffiths	65	British	LHR	02A/B	Rear	Southern	UK
Mrs	Lily	Griffiths	63	British	London	02A/B	Rear	Northern	UK
Mrs	Anastasia	Harbstreet	25	US	London	15B	Forward	Northern	USA
Steward	Nicos	Hasapopoulos		Cypriot	Athens	Cabin staff	Forward	Missing	
Mrs	Constantinas	Hristaki		Greek	Athens	JW block	Rear	Southern	Rhodes, Greece
Dr	George	Ioannides	48	Cypriot	London	09A	Rear	Southern	Phanoremeni Church, Cyprus
Mr	John	Jakouris		Cypriot	London	8E?	Forward	Southern	Strovoles, Cyprus
Mrs	Margaret Mary	Joyce	56	British	London	02D	Rear	Southern	UK
Mrs	Iphigenia	Kalogeropoulou		Greek	Athens	JW block	Rear	Southern	Rhodes, Greece
Miss	Despina	Karakosta	60	Greek	Athens	JW block	Rear	Southern	Rhodes, Greece
Mr	Charalabos	Kontominas		Greek	Athens	JW block	Rear	Southern	Athens, Greece
Mrs	Stavoulas	Kontominas	54	Greek	Athens	JW block	Rear	Southern	Athens, Greece
Mrs	Eleni	Koutroubinis		Greek	Athens	JW block	Rear	Southern	Not stated
Mr	Georgios	Koutroubinis		Greek	Athens	10B	Rear	Southern	Rhodes, Greece
Mrs	Katarina Eleni	Liassides	52	Cypriot	London			Missing	

Title	First name	Surname	Age	Nationality	Boarded	Seat No.	Cabin	Group	Buried
Senior Steward	Yanakis	Loizou	27	Cypriot	Athens	Cabin staff	Rear	Southern	Ayii Omoloyitades, Cyprus
Miss	Eleni	Markidou	22	Greek	Athens	JW block	Rear	Southern	Rhodes, Greece
Mr	Vasilios	Markidou		Greek	Athens	JW block	Rear	Missing	
Mrs	Lily	Marlborough	54	British	London	04D	Rear	Southern	UK
Mrs	Elaine	McComb	23	British	London	08ABC	Rear	Missing	
Infant	Roydon George	McComb	17 mths	British	London	08ABC	Rear	Northern	Dekelia, Cyprus
Mr	Roydon John	McComb	24	British	London	08ABC	Rear	Northern	Dekelia, Cyprus
Master	Andreas	Nicolaides	4	Cypriot	London	13B	Forward	Missing	
Mrs	Innoula	Nicolaides	23	Cypriot	London	12A/B	Forward	Northern	Limassol, Cyprus
Mr	Loizos	Nicolaides	30	Cypriot	London	12A/B	Forward	Southern	Limassol, Cyprus
Mrs	Maureen	O'Brien	22	British	London	10E	Rear	Northern	UK
Mr	Michael	O'Brien		US	London	10D	Rear	Missing	
Mr	Konstantinos	Paleologos		Greek	Athens	11E?	Forward	Missing	
Mrs	Theognosia	Paleologos		Greek	Athens	11D?	Forward	Missing	
SFO	Dennis	Palmer	35	British	London	Co-pilot	Forward	Missing	
Mrs	Maria Melane	Papaioannou	74	Cypriot	London	10A	Rear	Southern	Cyprus
Mrs	Eirini	Papanicolaou	61	Greek	Athens	JW block	Rear	Southern	Rhodes, Greece
Mr	Nicos	Papapetrou		Cypriot	Athens	Not known	Rear?	Missing	
Miss	Maria	Parzopoulou	60+	Greek	Athens	JW block	Rear	Southern	Rhodes, Greece
Mr	Nicolas	Peters		US	London	15A	Forward	Southern	USA
Stewardess	Penelope	Photiou	c.20	Cypriot	Athens	Cabin staff	Rear	Southern	Athens, Greece
Mr	David	Powell	27	British	London	1E?	Forward	Southern	UK
Mrs	Dorothea	Rachovidou	64	Cypriot	Athens	Not known	Rear?	Southern	Limassol, Cyprus
Mr	Ioannis	Rigou	60	Greek	Athens	JW block	Rear	Northern	Rhodes, Greece
Miss	Elpiniki 'Niki'	Rodosthenous	24	Cypriot	Athens	9E?	Forward	Northern	Limassol, Cyprus
Mr	William Theodore	Sheris		US	Athens	11A?	Forward	Missing	
Miss	Hilary C	Smith	32	British	London	17A	Forward	Northern	UK
Mr	Avraam	Solomou		Cypriot	Athens	16C	Forward	Northern	Tymbou, Cyprus
Mrs	Anna	Stewart	68	British	London	07D	Rear	Northern	UK

Title	First name	Surname	Age	Nationality	Boarded	Seat No.	Cabin	Group	Buried
Mrs	Rosalie	Stone	72	British	London	13D?	Forward	Northern	Not stated
Master	Guy	Tasker	8	British	London	14A/B	Forward	Northern	UK
Mrs	Janet	Tasker	30	British	London	14A/B	Forward	Southern	UK
Mr	Gerasimo	Thiakou	48	Greek	Athens	16D/E	Forward	Northern	Piraeus, Greece
Mrs	Polixeni	Thiakou	22	Greek	Athens	16D/E	Forward	Southern	Piraeus, Greece
Mr	Michael	Thomaides	35	Cypriot	London	01A	Rear	Northern	Famagusta, Cyprus
SFO	Michael	Thomas	33	British	London	Co-pilot	Forward	Missing	
Miss	Arini	Voliotou	25	Greek	Athens	JW block	Rear	Southern	Rhodes, Greece
Mrs	Paraskevis	Vougioukas	31	Greek	Athens	JW block	Rear	Southern	Rhodes, Greece
Miss	Joyce Pamela	White	29	British	London	17B	Forward	Southern	UK

265

SECRET

MINISTRY OF TECHNOLOGY
Royal Aircraft Establishment

Materials Department,

FARNBOROUGH, Hants.
Telex: 85134 *Telegrams: Ballooning Farnborough, Hants.*

Our reference: M.10187/El.69/PJEF   *Telephone: Aldershot* 24461, *ext.* 2824

Your reference:

22nd November 1967

Chief Inspector of Accidents,
Board of Trade,
Accident Investigation Branch,
Shell Mex House,
Strand,
London, W.C.2.

For the attention of Mr. E. Newton

Accident to B.E.A. Comet, G-ARCO, 12th October 1967

In reply to your letter of 27th October, we have now examined the various specimen fragments that you passed to us, and the results are as follows:-

Specimen R.42

This consisted of two pieces of crumpled foil with an adhesive layer between to form a sandwich. The foils were both 0.006" thick, and a microprobe analysis confirmed your report that they were aluminium. We also found traces of iron which suggested that the material was commercial purity aluminium and the microstructure showed it to be in the annealed condition. Mr. R. Harper of H.S.A. Hatfield has given us a sample of acoustic sheet which consists of two aluminium foils (0.006 in. and 0.002 in. thick) laminated with self-adhesive damping tape between, and with a sound proofing compound, 0.08 in. of Aquaplas 100, applied to one side. The specification for this material is DTA 449. A comparison has been made between the adhesive on this sample and your specimen, and we are completely satisfied that it is a piece of acoustic sheet, although there is this anomaly of foil thickness which may be the result of some manufacturing error. Together with this specimen we received a small steel fragment immediately recognisable as the split end off a locking nut, and several fragments of red plastic material, probably the glue used in the sandwich construction of the aircraft partitions.

Specimen R.41

This specimen was 0.45 in. x 0.2 in. x 0.1 in., and although it was badly corroded there remained enough of the original surface to be reasonably sure that 0.1 in. was a genuine dimension of the part. A microsection was made, and the material shown to be a magnesium alloy casting with a Vickers hardness of 64.1 d.p.n. Electron probe microanalysis showed it to be a Mg-Zn-Zr-R.E. (cerium) alloy, and by comparing Zn/Ce ratios with standard test bar materials supplied by Kent Alloys Ltd., we have concluded that its specification is DTD 708, i.e. ZRE1. Figs. 1, 2 and 3 show the microstructure of this specimen. Fig. 1 shows the general corrosion of the casting and Figs. 2 and 3 show that some remelting had taken place. This may be the edge of a broken weld although the microprobe revealed no composition gradients in this region.

/However

However, this is to be expected if the filler rod had been ZRE1. (The melting range of this alloy is given as 545-640°C). The other possibility is that the piece had been partially remelted at some stage during the accident, and the molten zone ablated.

Specimen MX.246

This fragment of material is shown in Fig. 4. It was badly corroded, although signs of the original paint scheme were still visible, and one fractured edge had a 'woody' or laminated appearance; the fragment was approximately 0.116 in. thick. A microsection suggested it to be an aluminium-zinc-magnesium-copper alloy, and this was confirmed by the electron probe analyser. The analysis together with the high hardness, 174-179 d.p.h., showed this to be in all probability the high strength extrusion alloy DTD 363A. Fig. 5 shows the microstructure of the material. Together with this specimen were two pop rivet fragments which we have not examined in any detail.

Structural specimen, light alloy sheet with rivets

This specimen is shown in Figs. 6 and 7. It was found to be an 18g clad aluminium alloy sheet with a rolled edge with the remains of two rivets and indications of two other rivet holes. The pitch of the holes was approximately ⅝ in. The edge of a spot weld could also be distinguished (arrow A Fig. 5 and a microsection confirmed this feature as shown in Fig. 8. A flake aluminium paint was present, and the witness mark of a lap joint as shown by the boundary of the paint was also evident. A microsection (Fig. 9) indicated this to be an artificially aged duralumin alloy which suggested DTD 546. The hardness of 158 d.p.h. confirmed this. The tearing around the sheet was not considered to have occurred at an elevated temperature. The areas of intercrystalline failure that were observed were the result of exploitation of some intercrystalline corrosion cracks occurring at the cut and chamfered edge of the core material. Fig. 10 shows these features.

We understand that Mr. R. Harper of H.S.A. Hatfield has been able to identify this fragment as part of a capping strip from the frame of an engine door.

All of the fragments supplied have been identifiable as aircraft materials, and can be ascribed specification numbers.

for Head of Materials Department

Appendix 4 – The RARDE Report

MINISTRY of DEFENCE

ROYAL ARMAMENT RESEARCH AND DEVELOPMENT ESTABLISHMENT

Please address any reply to
THE DIRECTOR
and quote: FGR 608/012
Your reference: MX 246

Fort Halstead, SEVENOAKS, Kent
Telephone: Sevenoaks 55211, *ext.* 625

Group Captain J.B. Veal, CBE, AFC,
Chief Inspector of Accidents,
Board of Trade,
Civil Aviation Department,
Shell Mex House,
Strand, W.C.2.

1st January, 1968

Accident to Comet 4B, G-ARCO
Interim report on examination of a seat cushion

1. The seat cushion supplied to RARDE on November 1st by the Chief Investigating Officer, Mr. Newton, has been critically examined by the E.2 Branch of the Explosives Division. Detailed metallurgical and chemical examination of the fragments recovered from the cushion has been undertaken by the appropriate specialist Branches of the Establishment. Conclusive evidence has now been obtained to indicate that the seat cushion has been subjected to the effects of a detonation of a high explosive.

The evidence leading to this conclusion is based on :-

1.1 The nature of the physical damage to the cushion which includes blackening of the surfaces, superficial damage and perforations. These characteristics have been reproduced in laboratory trials on simulated cushions using a military high explosive.

1.2 The presence in the cushion of a large number of very small particles of metal, both ferrous and light alloy, from 10 milligrams in weight down to microscopic size. Laboratory trials with an explosive in a light metal case have produced similar effects. Measurements have shown that to obtain comparable penetration, these very small particles must have had a velocity of several thousand feet per second - a velocity which is consistent with a detonation and, as far as we know, could only have been produced by an explosive.

1.3 The micro-structure of the particles of metal as revealed by metallographic techniques and by examination of the surfaces under an electron microscope. The particles have been produced mainly by spalling and have in the main a cupped shape with rolled edges. On their surfaces they show many diagnostic features, such as cracking, the effects of hot gas washing and bombardment by high speed micro-particles. In some cases they have caused the cushion material to melt and adhere to their surfaces. All of these features have been matched with particles produced explosively in the laboratory.

1.4 The presence of fibres attached to some of the metal particles and in the perforations in the seat cushion. These fibres were identified as being derived from the fabric coverings of the cushion. Their position and appearance are consistent with the passage of high velocity metal particles through the fabrics, and indicate that the event occurred whilst the covers were still in position on the cushion.

1.5 Visual indications that the webbing of the seat masked the under surface of the cushion from superficial blackening. This indicates that the explosion occurred whilst the cushion was in a normal position on the seat.

1.6 The presence of straight tears in the under surface of the cushion adjacen' to the lines of webbing. These suggest that the cushion was restrained in pos' tion, for example by being loaded by the weight of a passenger, when the expl occurred.

268

2. Attention has been directed towards ascertaining whether the samples provide any evidence of the nature, quantity and position of the explosive and its container. This work is not yet quite complete, but the following facts have been elicited :-

2.1 The trajectories of the larger particles which perforated the cushion and which produced the major area of damage suggest an origin in a limited volume some 12 inches below the seat, roughly in the vertical plane of the rear edge of the cushion and about 3 inches from the line of the port edge of the cushion.

2.2 The metal particles retained in the cushion have fragmentation and surface characteristics which show they must have been produced from objects in contact with or close to the actual explosive.

2.3 The ferrous particles are of mild steel. A few small steel items have been observed in the seat assembly supplied by the Chief Investigating Officer. These items are, however, quite definitely of a different kind of steel from that of the recovered particles. It seems therefore that the ferrous particles must have been derived from some object not normally part of the Comet structure. It is possible that they originated from a mild steel tube or similar object which may have been a container for the explosive.

2.4 The light alloy fragments, with one exception, do not correspond in composition with any of the alloys used in the fabric of the airplane or the seats. They are of different material from that used in British detonators. They are being subjected to further examination which will include comparison with the materials of detonators of foreign origin.

2.5 One alloy fragment differs from the others in composition and in other respects. On it there is a small adherent area of brown paint. The composition of this alloy matches that of the alloy of which the side support of a Comet seat assembly is made; the paints are also similar. Features observed suggest strongly that the fragment originated by explosive attack and was very close to the centre of explosion.

2.6 No fibres originating from the carpet have been found in the cushion. This would suggest that the explosion took place on or above the floor.

2.7 No alloy particles found in the cushion corresponded in composition with that of the alloy of the flooring. This tends to suggest that the explosion was not below the flooring.

3. Considerations of the geometry of the seat assembly and the distribution of damage and fragments in the cushion suggest that the explosive was on the floor between the seat support and the side of the cabin on the port side close to the rear toe of the delta-shaped support.

4. The remaining 27 seat cushions recovered were sent to RARDE and carefully examined. Only one of them provided any further evidence. In this, X-ray photographs revealed a number of metal particles similar to those in the first cushion. They have not been examined in detail. In this second cushion there were five perforations produced by particles the trajectories of which suggested, but not conclusively, that this cushion may have been behind and a little to the starboard of the explosion. On its under surface there was slight blackening, partially masked by the webbing.

5. Part of a white nylon shirt which was received from the Chief Investigating Officer has a few small perforations in the region of the right side front. These could have been produced by high velocity particles. We are not in a position, however, to say definitely that they were produced by particles from an explosion. A pair of brown trousers and part of a matching waist-coat were also received. These are torn and damaged by water immersion. We have been unable to find any signs of burning or of any definite explosion evidence on them.

/6..

269

6. A full report of the work undertaken by the Establishment in the examination of the seat cushions and recovered fragments will be sent to you by the end of the month.

D.F. Runnicles

(D.F. Runnicles)
Principal Superintendent
Explosives Division.

Copies to :-

Chief Scientist (Army)
D.G. of Arty.
Chief Scientist (Home Office)
H.M. Chief Inspector of Explosives (Home Office)

Appendix 5 – The AIB Report

BOARD OF TRADE
Accidents Investigation Branch
Shell Mex House
Strand
London WC2

April 1968

President of the Board of Trade

Sir,

I have the honour to submit my report on the investigation of the accident to British European Airways Comet G-ARCO which occurred in the Mediterranean, about 100 miles east of Rhodes, on 12th October, 1967.   At the request of the Board of Trade the criminal implications of the case have been the subject of separate investigation by the Commissioner of Police for the Metropolis.

I have the honour to be

Sir,

Your obedient Servant

J. B. VEAL
Chief Inspector of Accidents

SBN 11 510042 3

ACCIDENTS INVESTIGATION BRANCH
Civil Accident Report No. EW/A/0102

Aircraft: de Havilland Comet Series 4B G -ARCO
Engines: Four Rolls Royce Avon 524
Registered Owner: British European Airways Corporation
Operator: BEA on behalf of Cyprus Airways

Crew: Captain G. D. Blackwood)
First Officer M. P. Thomas) Missing, presumed killed
First Officer D. E. Palmer)
Steward N. Hasapopoulos - Missing, presumed killed
Steward Y. Loizou   - Killed
Stewardess T. Efremi   - Killed
Stewardess K. Fotou   - Killed
Passengers: 59 - 48 killed, 11 missing, presumed killed

Place of Accident: About 100 miles east of Rhodes (Approximately latitude
35°55' N longitude 30°01' E)

Date and Time: 12th October 1967 at about 0325 hrs.
All times in this report are GMT

Summary

On a flight from Athens to Cyprus at FL 290 on Upper Airway Red 19 the
aircraft became overdue after making an initial radio contact with Nicosia FIR.
R.A.F. Search and Rescue aircraft took off from Cyprus and located debris from
the aircraft close to R19C, its last reported position. R19C is a reporting point
on the airway, approximately 100 n.m. east of Rhodes.

The R.A.F. aircraft homed ships to the scene of the accident and 51 bodies were
recovered and some floating debris. This debris included two seat cushions
which provided conclusive evidence of the detonation of a high explosive device
within the aircraft cabin. The independent medical evidence fully confirmed this
conclusion.

1. Investigation

1.1 History of the flight

G-ARCO left London (Heathrow) Airport at 2145 hrs. on 11th October 1967, operating British European Airways (BEA) flight BE 284 to Athens. It carried 38 passengers and 2,154 kilogrammes of freight, including 920 kilogrammes for Nicosia. The aircraft arrived at Athens at 0111 hrs. on 12th October and reached its parking area on the apron at about 0115 hrs. Six Athens passengers were disembarked. At Athens the flight became Cyprus Airways flight CY 284 for Nicosia. Four passengers and the Captain remained on board the aircraft whilst it was refuelled and serviced for the flight to Nicosia. The Captain and the two First Officers continued with the aircraft, but the cabin staff was changed, the new staff being those of Cyprus Airways. Twenty-seven passengers joined the aircraft at Athens for the flight to Nicosia.

From the evidence of the BEA and Olympic Airways staff at Athens the aircraft's transit was normal. It was refuelled to a total of approximately 17,000 kgs and only one minor defect, relating to the Captain's beam compass, was recorded in the technical log. This defect was dealt with by the ground crew. The baggage for the passengers joining the aircraft for the flight to Nicosia and the freight was placed in holds 1 and 2; the baggage and freight from London to Nicosia remained in holds 4 and 5.

The aircraft taxied out at 0227 hrs. and was airborne on schedule at 0231 hrs.; it was cleared by Athens control to Nicosia on Upper Airway Red 19 to cruise at flight level (FL)290.   After take-off it climbed to 4,000 feet on the 180° radial of Athens VOR and then turned direct to Sounion which it reported crossing at 0236 hrs. At 0246 hrs. the aircraft reported that it was crossing R19B at FL290 and was estimating Rhodes at 0303 hrs. At 0258 hrs. at an estimated position 36°41'N 27°13'E the aircraft passed a westbound BEA Comet which was flying at FL280. Each aircraft saw the other; the Captain of the westbound aircraft has stated that flight conditions were clear and smooth. G-ARCO passed Rhodes at 0304 hrs. and at 0316 hrs. reported passing R19C at FL290 and that it estimated passing abeam of Myrtou, Cyprus, at 0340 hrs.

This message was not received by Athens direct but was relayed by the westbound aircraft. G-ARCO was then cleared by Athens to change to the Nicosia FIR frequency.

The recording of the R/T communications with Nicosia shows that G-ARCO called them to establish contact; the time of this call was 0318 hrs. + 9 secs. and it is estimated that the aircraft would then have been at a position 35°51'N 30°17'E, approximately 15 n.m. to the east of R19C. Nicosia replied to the aircraft with an instruction to go ahead with its message, but no further transmission was heard. Nicosia continued to try to contact the aircraft but without result and overdue action was therefore taken. At 0440 hrs. R.A.F. Search and Rescue aircraft took off from Akrotiri; at 0625 hrs. wreckage from

G-ARCO was sighted in the vicinity of R19C, the last reported position. The aircraft's estimated track from Athens to the crash position is shown in fig. 1.

1.2 Injuries to persons

Injuries	Crew	Others	Passengers
Fatal[106]	7	Nil	59
Non-fatal	Nil	Nil	Nil
None	Nil		Nil

1.3 Damage to aircraft
The aircraft was destroyed.

1.4 Other damage
No other damage.

1.5 Crew information
Captain Gordon Daniel Blackwood, aged 45 years, qualified as a pilot in the Royal Air Force; he joined British European Airways Corporation in 1946. He held a valid airline transport pilot's licence endorsed in Part I for Comet DH 106 aircraft. His total flying amounted to 14,563 hours, of which 2,637 were on Comets.

First Officer Michael Patrick Thomas, aged 34 years, qualified as a pilot in the R.A.F.; he joined BEA in 1957. He held a valid airline transport pilot's licence endorsed in Part I for Comet 4B aircraft. His total flying amounted to 6,318 hours, including 2,471 on Comets.

First Officer Denis Esmond Palmer, aged 36 years, learned to fly in the Cambridge University Air Squadron and served in No. 612 Squadron, Royal Auxiliary Air Force. He joined BEA in 1955 and held a valid airline transport pilot's licence endorsed in Part I for Comet 4B aircraft. His total flying amounted to 5,537 hours, including 2,550 on Comets.

1.6 Aircraft information
The aircraft was constructed in 1961 and delivered to BEA in April of that year. At the time of the accident it had flown 15,470 hours; its certificate of airworthiness was valid until 11th April 1968. The aircraft had been regularly maintained in accordance with an approved maintenance schedule, the last check 1 having been completed on 14th September 1967; since that date the aircraft

---

[106] Includes 4 crew and 11 passengers missing presumed killed.

had flown 243 hours. The four engines had been completely overhauled between 1965 and 1967 and all were well within their overhaul life.

An overhaul of the aircraft (check 4) was completed in December 1966. During this overhaul a comprehensive inspection was made of the whole aircraft for damage due to corrosion, and repairs were made to all areas where such damage was found. The areas affected were mainly along the belly of the fuselage, and both skinning and stringers were renewed between frames 11-16 and 17-21.

A complete overhaul of the flying controls was also made at this time. The aircraft had flown 2,279 hours since this major overhaul.

1.7 Meteorological information

An appreciation of the weather conditions within a 60 n.m. radius of the crash position made by the Meteorological Office shows that between 0300 hrs. and 0330 hrs. on 12th October 1967 an upper trough with its axis east of the Black Sea to the Nile delta was moving eastwards. There was a north to north-east flow at all levels over Turkey and the eastern Mediterranean west of Cyprus. An anticyclone west of the Black Sea was almost stationary. It is assessed that the following conditions applied:

0 C isotherm: 9,000 feet
Icing: mainly clear; severe in cumulonimbus from 9,000 feet to 25,000 feet.
Cloud: Small probability 2/8 cumulonimbus base 3,000 feet tops 30,000 feet.
Weather: fine. Small probability decreasing with time of isolated thunderstorms.

Winds and temperatures:

Layer	*Mean wind*
Surface - 5,000 feet	$360°/10$ kt.
5,000-10,000 feet	$360°/15$ kt.
10,000-15,000 feet	$360°/22$ kt.
15,000-20,000 feet	$360°/30$ kt.
20,000-25,000 feet	$010°/37$ kt.
25,000-30,000 feet	$010°/45$ kt.

The estimated probable errors are about + 10 degrees and + 5 knots for all layers.

Height	Temperature degrees C
5,000 feet	+07
10,000 feet	-04
20,000 feet	-17
30,000 feet	-46
40,000 feet	-53
45,000 feet	-57 (tropopause)

All heights are pressure altitudes.
Estimated mean sea level pressure at time and place of accident was 1017 millibars (mb).

Clear air turbulence and mountain waves:
It is considered that the conditions were neither especially favourable for the occurrence of clear air turbulence nor for mountain waves near the island of Kastellorizo at the time of the accident. This view is based on the following considerations:
(a)   there is no sign of a stable layer, or a layer with marked vertical wind shear near the flight level (29,000 feet), in the radio-sonde observations from Ankara, Heraklion or Nicosia at 0000 hrs. on 12th October 1967, or in the winds from Nicosia at 0600 hrs.
(b)   the Richardson number deduced from the three radio-sonde ascents for the layer 350-300 mb was in each case substantially greater than unity and values less than this are normally thought to be required for marked turbulence. Even with the higher critical value for Richardson number of three or four postulated by Rakok and Spillane as appropriate in the Colson-Panafsky Index (Quarterly Journal Royal Meteorological Society 91 p. 509), the absence of a stable layer and/ or a layer with marked vertical wind shear makes it unlikely that this index would show the peak claimed to be associated with the occurrence of marked turbulence.
(c)   finally, there is no evidence of strong horizontal shear at 300 mb. Measured winds at 300 mb at 0000 hrs. were - Ankara 040/56 knots, Nicosia 010/45 knots, Heraklion 400 mb 360/39 knots, 250 mb 360/44 knots (300 mb wind corrupt in message).
(d)   as far as mountain waves are concerned the main requirement that there be a wind component of at least 15 knots normal to the Turkish Plateau, say at 6,000 feet, is not satisfied in the Ankara wind sounding and only just in the Nicosia wind: this latter, however, is not really a true measure of the flow across the plateau. The other requirement i.e. a marked temperature inversion is not satisfied in any of the three radio-sonde temperature soundings.

Turbulence

The only other remote possibility is encounter with a thunderstorm top but even this would be unlikely to produce more turbulence than that indicated on the relevant significant weather chart, i.e. severe between 8,000 feet and 25,000 feet. Apart from this assessment there is the evidence of the Captain of the west-bound Comet flying at flight level 280, which passed G-ARCO just to the west of Rhodes, who reported that conditions in the area were clear and smooth.

1.8 Aids to navigation

In the area of the accident the Rhodes NDB and VOR were serviceable and operating. It is a normal practice in BEA to use the Rhodes VOR for track guidance from Rhodes to Nicosia and to establish position over R19C by checking against the outline of the Turkish coast with the aircraft's weather radar on 'mapping'.

1.9 Communications

The communications between the aircraft and ground stations were unremarkable except perhaps for the message at 0316 hrs. which Athens did not receive direct but by relay from another aircraft; this was not however an abnormal occurrence. The substance of all the radio communications was routine information.

1.10 Aerodrome and ground facilities

Not relevant to this accident.

1.11 Flight recorder

A Plessey/Davall flight recorder was fitted but was not recovered. The recorded information from earlier flights with G-ARCO was processed and studied but no significant data were found.

1.12 Wreckage

According to the evidence from the crews of the aircraft and ships, the surface wreckage was confined within a kerosene slick shaped roughly like an ellipse approximately 3 n.m. long and   n.m. wide which, when first sighted at 0625 hrs., was orientated approximately north and south. Debris from the aircraft and bodies were distributed in two main groups, one towards the north and the other towards the south of the area.

To the north, flotsam and bodies were recovered by Turkish ships. The flotsam included part of the forward toilet of the aircraft, lifejackets, some personal belongings and a Graviner fire extinguisher bottle from the starboard centre section and was free of contamination by kerosene. To the south, flotsam and bodies were recovered by German, Greek and United States ships and an R.A.F. rescue launch. The flotsam was mainly cabin furnishings, seat cushions, carpets and parts of the galley; it also included some handbags and other personal belongings, life-jackets and three life cots of the type provided for small children. Some of the life-jackets had inflated, some were encased but not inflated and some had remained in their containers. In general, the flotsam recovered in the southern area was heavily contaminated by kerosene. All the wreckage recovered was brought back to the United Kingdom for detailed investigation and laboratory examination.

The position of the surface debris, after it had been drifting for approximately four hours, determined by the R.A.F. aircraft from radio bearings from Rhodes and visual bearings on prominent features of the Turkish coast was close to the airway reporting position R190.

Later that day, at 1130 hrs., the German ship Astrid fixed the position of two areas containing debris by radar bearings and distance from the Turkish coastline as 35°55'N 29°52E and 35°58'N 29°49.5'E.

By this time the area was orientated approximately 313°-153° and had increased to 3.75 n.m. in length.

From the observations of the position of the surface debris and having regard to the probable surface drift it has been estimated that the approximate position at which the aircraft fell into the sea is 35°55'N 30°01'E.

Examination of debris recovered from the sea

Life-jackets: The impression was gained by some observers in the R.A.F. search and rescue aircraft that some of the victims of the accident were wearing life-jackets. A similar statement was subsequently made by the Captain of one of the ships taking part in the search. Subsequent investigation showed his statement to have been based on a misconception due to the juxtaposition of bodies and life-jackets. Many of the life-jackets recovered from the sea were out of their containers and unfolded and some were inflated; in some cases the tapes were heavily knotted. These knots were haphazard and of far greater complexity than would be expected had they been tied manually and in no case had the tapes been cut. It was concluded that there was no evidence that any life-jacket had been donned in the air.

278

Fire extinguisher: This was a Graviner triple head automatic extinguisher type 71A; it had been installed in the aircraft on 20th June 1967, at position no. 6 in the centre section near the starboard wing root. The extinguisher could be operated by the pilot to discharge into one of three areas as required, viz. the starboard wing leading edge, No. 3 engine, and No. 4 engine. Alternatively, the bottle could be operated by the aircraft's crash inertia switch; in this case all three heads are fired.

Examination of the bottle by the manufacturer and subsequently by the Royal Aircraft Establishment showed that all three fuses and powder charges had fired, and all three charge plugs had ejected normally, indicating operation by the inertia switch. All three indicator plungers had ejected but the piston rods had been sheared at their retaining groves. At ports B and C, the indicator piston rods remained extended and were severely bent, whilst at port A the piston rod was retracted, and the indicator end was visible at the point of fracture of the plunger.

With this extinguisher the pistons remain extended while the discharge of the bottle is in progress and then return to seal off the bottle to prevent entry of the discharge from another bottle. Therefore, extension of the pistons at ports B and C could mean. impact with the water had occurred during the discharge. However, a more likely alternative is that the inertia switch was operated by inertia loading during downward detachment of the forward fuselage from the aircraft in flight.

Seat cushions: Initial examination of the seat cushions showed one to have sustained damage of a type which might be expected from involvement in an explosion. The cushions were therefore sent to the Royal Armament Research and Development Establishment for laboratory examination. Exhaustive investigation and tests by the RARDE provided conclusive evidence that two of these cushions, which were among those recovered from the southern end of the wreckage area and which had come from the tourist cabin of the aircraft, had been damaged by an explosive device detonated within the cabin. (see 1.15).

Passenger wrist watches: 10 wrist watches, recovered from the bodies of passengers, were sent to Farnborough for examination. The watches had stopped because of damaged hands and dials, displaced pinions and/or ingress of water. In all cases it was possible, by

detailed examination, to determine the time indicated on each watch when it stopped. The times indicated were as follows:
4-24-30. 5-25-30. 5-25. 4-25. 5-20. 10-12-30. 5-25. 10-5-10. 6-29. 5-22-30.
It was concluded that the time of impact of the wearers of the watches with the sea, and hence, the approximate time the aircraft struck the sea, was about 0325.
During the examination, it was found that two of the watches were dry, inside, but that the other eight contained traces of kerosene.

Examination of fuel drop tank: On 30th October some three weeks after the accident an aircraft fuel drop tank was picked up from the sea north-west of Rhodes. Because of damage it had sustained and some red paint markings, it was thought by the Greek authorities that it might have a connection with the Comet accident, perhaps providing evidence of a collision. The tank was therefore returned to the United Kingdom for detailed examination. This showed that the damage to the tank was consistent with what would be caused by impact with the sea. The attachment lugs showed that the tank had been dropped through normal release and that it had not been wrenched off the aircraft to which it had been attached. The red paint on the crumpled nose of the tank appeared visually to be of a different colour from that which is used in the BEA colour scheme. This, together with indications that the paint had been wet when applied, measurement of the physical characteristics and chemical analysis show clearly that the smear of red paint on the drop-tank differs significantly in composition from the BEA Comet paint and that the smear is not the result of violent impact with a red painted object.
The origin of the tank, which was identified as coming from an F.100 aircraft, was investigated by the United States authorities. This revealed that the tank was one of a batch which had been supplied to the United States Air Force and that the tank was probably one which had been dropped from a United States F.100 about three months before the accident.

Trajectory calculations: The Royal Aircraft Establishment assisted in the wreckage examination by undertaking an analysis of the evidence provided by the flotsam distribution on the surface of the sea and making consequent trajectory calculations.
Although no airframe wreckage was recovered from the sea, sufficient material was found in the form of carpets, furnishings, seat cushions, passengers, etc., to give guidance as to the likely locations of the major parts of the fuselage in the sea. The natural division of

all this material by state, recovery area, and identity, into two groups, indicated that the forward fuselage had fallen into the sea in the northern area and the rear fuselage and the wings containing fuel tanks in the southern area. Some seat cushions were found to the south between 1 to 1½ miles from the southern area. It is considered that separation of the fuselage, into at least two major portions, must have occurred before the aircraft struck the sea, to account for the distribution and state of the flotsam and bodies.

The examination of the flotsam suggested that the division of the fuselage, in the fore and aft sense, could have occurred at about the transverse datum position (centre-section front spar). The design firm indicated that this would be a likely separation point under an ultimate loading condition. Trajectory calculations were accordingly made on the premise that a fuselage separation occurred in the air at the front spar position. Fig. 2 shows the results of the calculations. Plots were first made from a specific point at 29,000 feet altitude, and the resulting scatter of flotsam and bodies, at sea level, noted. This distribution was too large to be reconciled with that seen by the search aircraft. Trajectories were then plotted from sea level upwards, from the general positions for items, as suggested by charts and maps from the search aircraft. A very close interception area of plots was found at about 15,000 feet altitude but this figure must be regarded only as an approximation and treated with caution owing to the imprecise information of the relative position of the flotsam and bodies at sea level. It was concluded that the aircraft had not broken up at its cruise altitude, but at the lower altitude, to produce the general pattern in the sea of flotsam and bodies, and the damage and injury pattern to bodies. A similar conclusion was reached by the pathologists, basing their argument purely on the medical evidence.

1.13 Fire
There is no evidence from the wreckage or the bodies of the victims which were recovered that there was any fire. The operation of No. 6 fire extinguisher, as explained in 1.12, was probably due to the high inertia loading associated with the break-up of the aircraft in flight.

1.14 Survival
The accident was not survivable.

1.15 Tests and research
Post-accident inspection of the Comet fleet. Following the accident, a comprehensive engineering review and detailed inspection of the entire fleet of BEA Comets was undertaken by BEA in which the Air Registration Board, Rolls Royce Ltd. and Hawker Siddeley Aviation

Ltd. participated. Particular emphasis was laid during these inspections on search for evidence of corrosion of the pressure fuselage; a complete strip down of several aircraft at BEA and another at Hawker Siddeley Aviation Ltd. enabled a thorough assessment to be made. These inspections revealed that although mild corrosion was evident in a number of places none was of a serious nature and there was nothing which could be considered detrimental to the structural integrity of the pressure cabin.

The Avon engines were inspected and although some defects were discovered none was of a type likely to lead to catastrophic failure.

In addition, a complete and detailed inspection and review of all reported defects and failures affecting G-ARCO since delivery to BEA was carried out. This review did not bring to light any abnormal or outstanding defects or failures and the aircraft's service life is considered to have been average with the remainder of the fleet.

Investigation of explosion aspect. Three small pieces of metal recovered from bodies during the pathological examination, which were identified as specimens of Comet aircraft material in subsequent metallurgical analysis at the Royal Aircraft Establishment, were referred in the first instance to the Royal Armament Research and Development Establishment (RARDE) (E2 Home Office Branch) for examination for possible evidence of explosives. This proved negative, no evidence of explosives being found on the specimens.

Damage to one of the 28 cushions recovered from the sea was recognised as being similar to that which had been seen in cushions used to muffle explosions in cases of safe-breaking which were under investigation in the RARDE laboratories and consequently the cushions were sent to the RARDE for examination. It was confirmed by the RARDE that the damaged cushion, which had been identified both visually and chemically as a seat cushion from the tourist cabin, showed marked external characteristics and damage postulating its possible involvement in an explosion. The laboratory investigations were, therefore, concentrated upon this cushion, the primary aim being to establish whether it had, in fact, been involved in an explosion.

It was found that in addition to the superficial characteristics there were very many small particles of metal and fibres embedded in the cushion and about twenty holes perforating it from the lower to the upper surface. The appropriate specialist branches of the Establishment carried out intensive physical and chemical examination of the cushion, the metal fragments and the fibres, together with a comprehensive experimental study of the effects of explosions on similar cushions. To confirm their findings the laboratories carried out practical simulation trials exploding high explosive charges in a mock-up of an aircraft cabin with complete seat assemblies.

As a result, the following conclusive evidence was obtained indicating that this seat cushion (whilst it was in its normal position on a seat) had been subjected to the effects from a detonation of a high explosive.

(a)   The physical damage to the cushion included blackening of the surfaces, superficial damage and perforations (fig. 3). Microscopic examination, X-ray and electron diffraction and fluorescence confirmed that the blackening was substantially due to amorphous carbon and identical to that produced by a high explosive. All these characteristics were reproduced in laboratory trials on similar cushions using a military high explosive. There was no evidence of fire.

(b)   Several hundred very small particles of metal, from 10 milligrams in weight down to those of microscopic size were found embedded in the cushion. Laboratory trials were undertaken projecting small particles at measured velocities and determining their degree of penetration of similar cushions. The results proved that these very small particles must have entered the cushion with velocities of several thousand feet per second. Larger particles would pass through the cushion. The perforations observed in the cushion could have been produced by such larger particles. Similar effects were produced in laboratory trials firing charges of high explosive in a light metal case near a cushion. No process, other than an explosive one, is known which could produce such small fragments of metal with such high velocities.

(c)   The embedded particles had entered the lower surface of the cushion making holes from their points of entry to the points at which they had come to rest. The inside surfaces of many of these holes were blackened.   The particles were frequently found to have fused the plastic where they had come to rest. When they were removed small pieces of fused plastic were found adhering to the metal, proving that they were hot when they entered the cushion. Exactly the same effects were produced in laboratory explosion trials.

(d)   The microstructure of particles of metal extracted from the cushion was investigated by metallographic techniques. Some of the particles were ferrous and some were of light alloy.   They showed characteristics which are found in explosively produced fragments. These include recrystallisation at micro-promontories, due

283

to flash heating, Neumann bands and parallel banding associated with rapid stressing by explosive shock.

(e)   The surfaces of the particles of metal were examined under an electron microscope and their features compared with those of metal particles produced explosively in the laboratory. It was found that many particles had been produced by a spalling action which is characteristic of the effects of a detonation shock. Most of the particles were cup shaped with rolled edges, which is a diagnostic feature. All their surfaces showed many other diagnostic features such as the effects of hot gas washing, bombardment by high speed micro-particles and cracking patterns attributable to very high speed deformation.   All of these features have been matched in the particles produced in the laboratory.

(f)   Cotton and other fibres were found to be attached to some of the metal particles and in the perforations in the cushion. These fibres were found by microscopic examination to be similar to those in several fabrics which normally cover the lower surface of the cushion. Their position and appearance were found to be consistent with the passage of high velocity metal particles through the fabrics and indicate that the event occurred while the covers were still in position on the cushion.

(g)   It was shown in laboratory trials that blackening of the surface of the foamed plastic takes place even when the cushion is enveloped in its normal inner and outer fabric covers. The gases from the explosion, which produce the blackening, are forced through the pores of the fabrics causing blackening of the underlying plastic even where the fabrics are not torn. Hence the presence of the blackening is not contrary to the thesis that the covers were still in position on the cushion when the event occurred.

(h)   The blackening of the lower surface of the cushion shows a pattern indicating that the webbing of the seat masked certain areas. Trials showed that such masking is produced by the rubber webbing. This indicates that the explosion occurred while the cushion was in a normal position on the seat.

(i)   There are straight tears in the lower surface of the cushion adjacent to the edges of the lines of webbing suggesting that the cushion was restrained in position, for example by the weight of a passenger when the explosion occurred. In trials similar tears were produced when the cushion was restrained by a weight but not when it was unrestrained.

In the exhaustive tests undertaken at RARDE attention was directed towards ascertaining whether the samples provided any evidence of the position, quantity and nature of the explosive and its container. The following information is pertinent to this aspect.

(a)   The trajectories of the larger particles which perforated the cushion and those which produced the major area of damage were explored by the use of wire probes (fig. 4). This suggests an origin of limited volume some 12 inches below the seat roughly in the vertical plane to the rear edge of the cushion and about 3 inches from the line of the port edge of the cushion. The trajectories delineated by the entry paths of the small particles embedded in the cushion confirm this position.

(b)   The light alloy fragments were analysed by electron micro-probe and mass-spectrographic techniques. One fragment was identified by its composition and the presence of a small area of paint adhering to its surface as originating in the side supporting framework of the seat. Its shape and surface features suggested strongly that it was produced by explosive attack and that it was very near the centre of the explosion.   All the other fragments differed markedly in composition from the alloys used in the construction of the aircraft and seats. These facts and the absence of any fragments of alloy from the flooring suggest that the explosion did not take place below the floor but took place on or above the floor and near to the side support of a seat.

(c)   The above conclusion is strengthened by the fact that no fibres originating from the carpet were found in the cushion.

(d)   The parts of the lower surface of the cushion where damage occurred, and particles entered are restricted to a clearly delineated area. Other parts of the surface were apparently masked and protected by the various components which form the structure of the seat assembly. The seat assembly itself is asymmetric in respect of the delta shaped supports at the two ends. The support at the inner, or gangway, ends stands in a vertical plane. That at the outer, or cabin wall, end is tilted under the seat. Consideration of the geometry involved, and the trajectories indicate that the explosive was on the floor between the seat support and the port side of the cabin, close to the rear toe of the delta-shaped support.

(e)   Similar considerations also define roughly the possible projection area of an explosive charge in the postulated position. Assuming that the charge was approximately cylindrical, the weight of a charge with the required projection area would be 12-16 ounces.

(f)   The ferrous particles retained in the cushion were found by metallographic examination and micro-chemical analysis to be of mild steel which had been cold worked. They are definitely different from the several steels of which a few small items in the seat assembly are made. They closely resemble the material of common types of steel tubing or boxes. The fragmentation and surface characteristics of these particles show that they must have been produced from an object or objects in contact with or close to the actual explosive. It seems, therefore, that they were derived from some object which was not part of the Comet structure or furnishings and it is possible that they originated from a container for the explosive, consisting of a mild steel tube or similar object.

(g)   Laboratory trials were carried out with explosives cased in thin walled tubes of mild steel using similar cushions as targets. It was found that particles of steel of the kind found in the cushion were produced by explosives with the characteristic high velocity of detonation of a military explosive such as RDX or TNT or by the comparatively rare type of industrial explosive, such as blasting gelatine. They could not be produced by the common industrial explosives, such as the gelignites, which have a lower velocity of detonation.

(h)   The surfaces of the cushion were examined using sophisticated and very sensitive techniques for the presence of traces of the explosive or the products of its explosion. The results were inconclusive except in respect of the carbon deposits previously referred to. Effective detonation of a high explosive does not often leave identifiable traces. The chances of finding any would have been greatly reduced by the immersion in sea-water to which the cushion had been subjected. Small amounts of lead and zinc were found on the surfaces. The lead could have come from the dressings on one fabric component of the seat cover but the presence of the two metals cannot be satisfactorily explained. Most conventional explosives produce carbon deposits under some conditions. Consequently, the particular explosive could not be identified.

(i)   Careful search was made for any fragments which might have been derived from the ancillary parts of an explosive device. Normally timing and igniting or detonating equipment is required. Nothing was found which could be identified definitely as such. The light alloy fragments found in the cushion, which were not derived from any part of the aircraft or seats, differed in composition from the metals used in British and known foreign types of detonator. Their characteristics showed that they were from some object close to the explosion. It is possible that they were derived from an unknown foreign detonator or from a component of unknown kind and function in an explosive device.

In order to verify these conclusions, RARDE carried out practical trials. An assembly was built of light alloy sheeting to simulate part of the cabin of the Comet. A new complete seat assembly was placed in position. An explosive charge of the military explosive PE4, encased in a thin walled mild steel tube and fitted with a detonator, was placed in position, adjacent to the rear toe of the delta support, between the support and the side of the cabin. Targets were arranged to assess damage to adjacent seats, and to persons sitting in them. The results showed conclusively that a charge of about 16 ounces of the explosive detonated in the position indicated would produce effects and damage similar in all details to that observed in the cushion from the Comet.

The effects produced on the targets showed that a person sitting on the attacked seat might be expected to receive severe lacerations to the rear upper part of the buttocks and a small amount of peppering by particles passing through the seat cushion. Peppering of the calves and lower back of the legs and ankles by other particles would be expected but it is less likely that major fractures or lacerations of these parts would occur. Other persons in direct line of sight of the device would be expected to be peppered by flying fragments but the number and position of such people would be very restricted because of the close array of high-backed seats.

The explosion produced a hole in the adjacent side of the simulated cabin of some 3-6 square feet with further tearing of the alloy sheet and considerable outward petalling of the torn edges of the skin. The greater part of this damage was above floor level, but some was below floor level. A comparatively small hole with some tearing was produced in the floor itself. The skin of the far side of the simulated cabin was peppered where there was a clear line of sight between it and the explosion, but otherwise suffered little damage.

The remaining 27 seat cushions recovered from the Mediterranean were also carefully examined but only one provided any further evidence (fig. 5). In this, X-ray photographs revealed a number of metal particles similar to those in the first cushion. There were five perforations produced by particles, the trajectories of which suggested that this cushion may have been behind and a little to the right of the explosion. There was slight blackening of the lower surface of this cushion which was partially masked by webbing. In the laboratory trial similar effects were produced on a cushion placed in the position indicated relative to the site of the explosion.

Part of a torn white terylene/cotton shirt was also examined. This shirt was certified by the pathologists as coming from the unique body described in 1.17.   In it were found a few small perforations in the region of the right-side front.   Similar perforations were produced in trials with similar materials placed a few feet from the explosion. It is not possible however to conclude definitely that these perforations were not produced by some other means.

Subsequently, RARDE received from the pathologist a piece of skin and fatty tissue preserved in saline/formaldehyde solution.

In this was found a particle of light alloy of microscopic size. Although it was corroded by the action of the preservation solution, its surface, when examined under the electron microscope, showed characteristics closely resembling those of the particles from the cushion, indicating that it had originated from an explosion.

1.16 Consideration of salvage

The feasibility of salvage of the Comet wreckage was examined with Ministry of Defence and United States Navy salvage experts as soon as the preliminary investigation of the accident was under way. Cabin debris and bodies were found on the surface of the water in an elliptically shaped area about 3 miles (N/S) by 11 miles (E/W) approximately 3 hours after the accident occurred. Taking account of surface drift, it was estimated that the centre of the debris area at the time of impact was 35°55'N and 30°01'E, although the accuracy of this position is probably not better than +2 miles. No effective marking of the position could be made with the available equipment owing to the extreme depth of the sea.

As there was no precise knowledge of the position of the aircraft wreckage, it was necessary to assume that it was lying somewhere within the debris area and that there might have been further dispersal during its descent from the surface to the sea bed due to hydrofoil effect. Thus, an initial search area some 7 miles by 5½ miles with further extension to 11 miles by 9½ miles was postulated, centred on a position 35°55'N and 30 011E, which might be subject to further reconsideration against more precise knowledge of sub-surface currents.

The sea bed in this initial area according to reliable information from Naval sources contains a spot depth of 1,583 fathoms towards the northern end. Other spot depths are 1,122 fathoms at the southern end, 1,452 fathoms on the eastern side and 1,371 and 1,290 fathoms on the western. Any salvage operation, in addition to the extreme depths, would thus have some very considerable slopes to contend with, and although the bottom is believed to be mainly silt and gravel there is a strong possibility of rocky outcrops.

After careful examination the conclusion was reached that although it would be possible to mount a search operation using Ocean Bottom Scanning Sonar, prospects of successful search were low having regard to:

(a)   lack of precise information on the exact location of the wreckage,

(b)   problems of identification of contact, and

(c)   the probability that much of the wreckage consisted of relatively small pieces.

Having regard to the apparent circumstances of the accident it appeared highly probable that search for, and location of, the wreckage, if this were successful, would make no contribution towards determination of the cause of the accident unless it enabled salvage to be undertaken.

The United States Navy experience in the salvage of the Palomares H-bomb was available as background information against which to assess the feasibility of any attempt at salvage of the Comet wreckage at a depth more than three times greater.

Consideration was given to the use of deep submergence vehicles, such as the Aluminaut, and all other means but after careful study it was concluded that salvage of the main wreckage or of the flight recorder was impracticable. Fortunately, at the time this decision was reached, evidence was beginning to be forthcoming of detonation of a high explosive within the cabin as an explanation of the accident.

1.17 Medical aspects

Of the 51 bodies recovered from the sea, 19 were in the northern part of the wreckage area and were landed at Antalya in Turkey being subsequently airlifted by Royal Air Force aircraft to Rhodes. The 32 bodies recovered from the southern part of the wreckage area were taken direct to Rhodes by a Greek warship. In accordance with standing arrangements pathologists from the Royal, Air Force Institute of Pathology were included in the United Kingdom investigating team. They undertook post-mortem examination of the bodies of 47 of the victims of the accident in Rhodes Hospital under very difficult conditions and under great pressure to complete their work quickly due to lack of refrigerating facilities. The four other bodies recovered from the sea were removed by relatives or other interested parties before any examination was possible.

The medical investigation was directed mainly towards discovering evidence bearing on the sequence of the accident and, of prime importance, its cause. There were two main groups as judged by the

289

injuries sustained. The first (extreme injury) consisted of 21 persons who had sustained massive head injury combined with other severe injury; the second main group (slightly injured) consisted of 12 persons who showed very little external evidence of violence. Between these two extremes lay a third, less well defined, group of persons showing moderate injury (14 cases). Approximately 32 per cent of the bodies were fully dressed and a further 32 per cent retained few or no clothes.

Detailed consideration has been given to the possibility of some relationship between the degree of injury, the amount of clothing retained, probable aircraft seating position, and the salvage group (i.e. northern or southern). It was apparent that:

(a)   the clothing/injury pattern is random;

(b)   no relationship could be established between the salvage group and the probable aircraft seating position, and

(c)   no aircraft seating position/clothing relationship was discernible

but, as regards injury/seating relationship, it appears, as far as the bodies subjected to post mortem examination are concerned, that:

(d)   none of those believed to have been seated in the forward tourist compartment suffered extreme injury and

(e)   all those believed to have been seated in the rear tourist cabin sustained more than slight external injury.

It must be borne in mind, however, that there is no evidence on seating other than the recollections of the London/Athens cabin crew and the BEA Athens traffic officer and that there could have been subsequent changes. The evidence on the absence of clothing must also be regarded with caution since some outer clothing might have been removed by the passengers themselves and some clothing is believed to have been detached during the rescue operation. Previous experiments have shown that falling into water from a height of 1,200 feet may lead to loss of clothing but that this is not invariably so, and the converse cannot be inferred; nor can the effect of explosion blast be excluded. However, the combination of retention of clothing and absence of external injury in a few bodies was regarded as significant by the pathologists and explicable on the basis of some passengers having been retained in a fairly stable part of the aircraft until comparatively low level.

During the post mortem examinations, the possibility that the accident might possibly have resulted from detonation of an explosive was kept in mind. Three small pieces of metal recovered from bodies were the subject of metallurgical examination at the Royal Aircraft Establishment and all were identified as specimens of Comet aircraft

290

material. Their inclusion in the bodies was consistent with fragments which could have been picked up during the accident and did not provide any evidence of having resulted from an explosion. The pathologists did however unearth medical evidence which, while it was recognised as being significant could not be interpreted at the time. This evidence, both general and related specifically to one body was later to provide confirmation of the evidence of detonation of a high explosive device provided by the RARDE investigation, viz.

(a)   one of the slightly injured bodies showed froth at the flares; the histological appearances found in the subsequent pathological examination in Rhodes were consistent with blast. In respect of three of the other severely injured passengers, the nature of their injuries was such that, although it is not possible to say with certainty that they were not due to multiple impacts within the aircraft during descent or at water impact, it would be impossible to contradict an assertion that they were due to blast;

(b)   one male body showed unique features in that

(i)   the upper body was 'peppered' with minute dark specks and the skin colour suggested the possibility of scorching; none of the other passengers showed skin lesions other than those due to immersion in kerosene;

(ii)   the trachea appeared to be burnt;

(iii)   the shirt showed minute holes comparable to the 'pepper' spots on the thorax;

(iv)   there was a curious ante or cum mortem flailing injury of the right forearm.

Histologically, superficial burning in the trachea is confirmed. The lesions in the skin are remarkable and show small punctate wounds with very definite evidence of burning. Because of these unique features, an X-ray of the thorax had been obtained with some difficulty and a subsequent comparison of minute radio opaque fragments seen in the X-ray, and originally mis-interpreted as artefact, with those found in the seat cushions and identified as resulting from detonation of a high explosive, indicated that a common origin was probable. This was subsequently confirmed when a metal fragment was recovered from one of the pathologists' specimens and was identified by the RARDE as similar to the light alloy fragments found in the cushion (see 1.13).

2. Analysis and Conclusions

2.1 Analysis

Against the initial knowledge of the circumstances of the accident it was clear that there had been some form of structural break-up at altitude since the wreckage was scattered over a wide area some 3 miles by XX miles. The absence of the main wreckage and the unlikelihood of effective salvage due to the extreme depth of the water into which the aircraft crashed indicated the need to consider a number of possibilities including

(a) the weather;
(b) the previous history of the aircraft and information available from the previous cassette of the flight recorder;
(c) general information on the aircraft type and the possibility of structural weakness or in-service damage;
(d) control failure causing some out-of-control condition;
(e) the possibility of a collision;
(f) the possibility of accidental or intentional explosion.

As shown earlier in the report an investigation of the meteorological factors showed the improbability of clear air turbulence or turbulence due to thunderstorm activity. It seemed clear that any turbulence which could have existed would not have formed any basis for structural failure at cruising altitude, nor any ready explanation leading to an out-of-control condition and subsequent structural break-up.

Engineering investigation of the aircraft type was commenced very soon after the occurrence of the accident since it was necessary to follow all possible lines of investigation, having regard to the absence of the aircraft wreckage and because there had clearly been some form of structural break-up. This investigation had only been partially completed with negative results at the time that evidence commenced to be forthcoming of the occurrence of detonation of an explosive device within the aircraft. Although some defects were found these were not abnormal, having regard to the type of engineering investigation being undertaken, and nothing was apparent which could explain the catastrophic nature of the accident. The Comet 4 is fundamentally different both in respect of airworthiness requirements and constructional standards from the Comet 1 so that there was no reason to believe that there could be any read-across from the experience of the accidents with the earlier type. The detailed engineering investigation confirmed that this was so.

The maintenance history of G-ARCO and likewise the flight recorder information available from previous flights were found on detailed investigation to contain nothing indicative of any situation which could lead to a failure. The major repairs previously made to the fuselage to eradicate corrosion deterioration appeared from the records to have been properly carried out. With the type of construction involved it seems probable that any defect in the repair scheme, had this occurred, would have shown up in a fail-safe manner.

The possibility of an out-of-control condition other than one due to extreme turbulence or some form of structural failure was examined and discarded. The alternative hydraulic systems available had been proved to be an adequate safeguard against hydraulic failure. Although in respect of the elevators the servodynes have a common final output, there is no record of a failure in this area which could lead to an out-of-control situation, and the power of the system is such that it should be possible for the live servodyne to overcome any malfunction of the second servodyne.

In any case it appears from the termination of radio transmissions and the wreckage area that the aircraft was in level flight at the time at which it was overtaken by catastrophe. It is not conceivable with the type of control system in the Comet 4 that in the circumstances of level flight an out-of-control situation of the sort which appears to have happened in this case could occur through any control failure. Nor could freezing of the elevator controls, which has been known to occur, introduce the possibility, during cruising flight in non-turbulent conditions, of a loss of control situation.

The possibility of collision as an explanation of the accident was immediately pursued but no evidence was found of any other aircraft which could have been in the area at the time being missing; nor was any wreckage of any other aircraft picked up in the immediate area. The medical evidence derived from an examination of 47 bodies excluded a collision in the region of the passenger compartment. On 30th October a drop tank from an F.100 was recovered from the sea near the island of Rhodes and it was suggested that damage to it and red paint on it might be consistent with collision with the BEA Comet.

Tests carried out (see 1.12) show conclusively that there was no similarity between the paint on the drop tank and the standard BEA red, the probability that the damage had been caused by water impact and that the tank was one of a pair dropped from a United States aircraft some months before the accident to G-ARCO.

The wreckage recovered from the sea in the impact area was collected at Rhodes and flown back to the United Kingdom for inspection. The superficial damage to one seat cushion suggested that it might have been involved in an explosion. Consequently, this cushion and the others recovered were sent to the Royal Armament Research and Development Establishment for laboratory examination; the results of this and of experimental work required by this aspect of the investigation is summarised in paragraph 1.15. The evidence derived from the damage to this cushion and the particles enclosed within it and from a second cushion disclosed that these cushions had been subjected to the effects of the detonation of a high explosive, the origin of the explosion being at floor level, within the cabin on the port side between a seat support and the cabin wall.

The cushions were positively identified by visual inspection and chemical analysis as being Comet aircraft tourist cabin seat cushions. When evidence of detonation of a high explosive had been found, the pathological findings were re-appraised in the light of the new information. Only 51 bodies had been recovered from 66 persons on board at the time of the accident and it had been impossible to carry out a complete pathological examination of all the bodies recovered. In addition, the extent of the pathological examination had been limited by the facilities available. Despite this, reconsideration of the medical aspects (see 1.17) provided confirmation of the RARDE findings that a high explosive device had been detonated within the cabin.

The lack of radio warning of disaster and the evidence that none of the victims recovered from the sea was wearing a life-jacket is consistent with there having been no warning of the catastrophe. Owing to the imprecise information on the points at which the various pieces of the cabin debris were recovered and the limitations imposed by the nature of the small amount of material recovered, it *was* not possible, as can be seen from paragraph 1.12, to determine with accuracy the height of break-up of the aircraft cabin. Lack of information on the point of impact of structural components has made it impossible to establish any sequence of break-up of the aircraft; nor, having regard to the depth of water in the area and the effect of hydrofoil action on the scattering of wreckage, would it have been possible to make any reliable deduction about this if the relative location of the parts of the aircraft on the sea bed could have been determined. Nevertheless, it has been possible to reach the conclusion from the distribution of the cabin debris and from the clear demarcation between kerosene contaminated and non-contaminated cabin debris and bodies of victims that the aircraft probably broke up at a height of about 15,000 feet. A generally similar conclusion was arrived at independently by the medical investigators, having regard to experience drawn from other accidents in which there has been a structural break-up at height,

The RARDE work suggests that the explosive charge used was equivalent to about 16 oz. of plastic explosive No. 4 and it is pertinent to consider what effect this would have had on the aircraft. Estimates of blast damage are that over-pressures capable of damaging the cabin structure are restricted to a relatively small radius from the explosion.   If the dynamic over-pressure capable of damaging the structure is taken as 9-10 psi damage from a charge of the size envisaged would not occur at distances greater than some 10 feet assuming that reflections and obstructions were absent. In an aircraft the seating provides very effective screening to an explosion on or near the floor. Hence damage by blast would be expected to occur only quite near to the explosion, and this *was* borne out by experiment at the RARDE. An explosion of the order suggested by the experimental evidence in this case would be expected to open up a hole in the adjacent side of the aircraft of some 3-6 square feet with further tearing and considerable outward petalling of the skin. The greater part of this damage would be above floor level although a smaller part would be expected below floor level. If, as is believed, the explosive was at floor level the hole produced in the floor would be very much smaller. In the absence of flight recorder data for the accident flight any conclusions about the resultant manoeuvres of the aircraft are necessarily conjectural. However, it seems probable that the structural damage resulting from the explosion within the cabin did not result in the immediate destruction of the aircraft but created an out-of-control condition. The evidence of the time of the last radio communication, the time indicated by the watches recovered from the victims, and the position of the wreckage and its distribution taken together with the medical evidence suggests that after the explosion the aircraft descended, possibly in the general direction of Rhodes, from about 29,000 feet to a lower altitude, perhaps around 15,000 feet, with the fuselage substantially complete, then broke up into at least two major portions which fell into the sea at about 0325 hrs. nearly seven minutes after the aircraft made its last call to Nicosia.

2.2 Conclusions

(a) Findings

    (i)   The aircraft was airworthy and its documentation was in order.

    (ii)   The flight crew was properly licensed.

    (iii) A high explosive device detonated within the cabin while the aircraft was cruising at FL 290.

    (iv) The explosion severely damaged the aircraft causing an out-of-control condition followed by structural break-up at a lower altitude.

(b) *Cause*

The aircraft broke up in the air following detonation of a high explosive device within the cabin.

3. Recommendations

It is recommended that

    (a)   development of underwater separation, flotation and location devices which would facilitate recovery of the flight data recorder *when* an aircraft crashes in the sea should be actively pursued with a view to separation, flotation and location capability being required for future flight data recorders, and

    (b)   the feasibility of developing means of detecting the presence of explosive devices should be further studied with a view to assisting airlines and aerodrome authorities in their security measures.

Appendix 6– The BALPA Report

ACCIDENT TO COMET IVB G-ARCO

12TH OCTOBER, 1967

TECHNICAL APPRECIATION

Captain E. Pritchard

Preamble

This appreciation of the crash and technical information is based on information available on 30th October, 1967.

G-ARCO, a Comet IVB, was owned and operated by BEA, though at the time of the accident was operating a service on behalf of Cyprus Airways, the CY 284, Athens to Nicosia. Since the aircraft was operating under an Air Operators Certificate held by BEA, it is therefore a BEA accident, and further it is a British Investigation carried out under the Board of Trade since the accident took place over international waters.

The aircraft departed Athens at 0225Z on 12th October, 1967; flight plan filed for cruising level 290; total fuel aboard 17,392 kgs.; passengers 57 + 2 infants; crew 7; total on board 66 persons, all killed.

The aircraft all up weight was well below maximum permitted, the flight plan submitted was standard and cruising level clearance by ATC was, as requested, 290. The en route weather was forecast as fine, with isolated thunderstorms, but none were reported within or near the airway UB 19, no clear air turbulence was forecast over the route.

Crew : Captain G.D. Blackwood   )
        S.F.O. D.E. Palmer   )   BEA Flight Branch
        S.S.O. N.P. Thomas   )

        Mr. J. Loizou   Senior Steward)
        Mr. N. Hasapopoulos   Steward   )   Cyprus Airways
        Miss Yappy Photou   Stewardess   )   Staff
        Miss Melva Trudi   Stewardess   )

The Accident

G-ARCO called Athens when crossing the FIR boundary at Red 19C. This message was relayed by one of BEA Comets G-APYF Commander, Captain Emerson. G-APYF was operating a reciprocal service to 'CY', that is the CY 285 Nicosia - Athens, and had in fact passed 'CO' some ten to fifteen minutes earlier. Athens Control requested 'CO' to change to Nicosia.

/At 0318.09

297

At 0318.09 G-ARCO called Nicosia stating "Nicky Bealine Golf Alpha Romeo Charlie Oscar". This tape-recording has been played back several times and it is believed that 'AR' of Oscar was just clipped off. The voice was not that of Captain Blackwood but it was precise and rapid, without any note of urgency.

Nicosia replied with a go ahead message, but no reply was received; numerous further calls were made without reply. There was no sign of any transmission from the aircraft during the following two minutes.

The time of impact with the sea is not known precisely, but watches recovered from the bodies were stopped at times varying between 0520 and 0525 local (0320 and 0325 GMT).

The precise geographical position of impact will not be known, but the RAF's datum point of 35° 55' N and 30° 01' E is likely to be the nearest that will be obtained.

Wreckage was sighted by the RAF Search and Rescue Hastings at 0625Z, three hours after the accident. The wreckage covered an area of 3 miles N - S by 1¼ miles E - W, outlined by an oil slick. The line of main wreckage and bodies extended N - S within this area.

At 0845Z (two hours twenty minutes later) the oil slick had extended to an area 5 x 3 miles, lighter wreckage had drifted further south, but the bodies remained disposed much as before.

In view of this, it is considered that the disposition of the bodies had been much the same following impact, that is to say along a line N - S 2 to 3 miles long, with a greater concentration towards the southern end.

Wreckage

The following list comprises of the items of cargo and aircraft furnishing that have been recovered.

1. Jump seat cushion

2. Captain and a First Officer's hat.

3. Two large pieces of first class cabin carpet.

4. Seat cushions, life-jackets, carpeting, seat
                                    coverings.

5. Galley bulkheads.

6. Rear toilet door.

/7. Dead

7. Dead cat in air carrier box. *not recovered, only seen*

8. Barograph packed for freighting.

9. Piece of electrical equipment packed for freighting.

10. Three babies' life cots.

11. Fire extinguisher plus some piping attached.

12. Baggage.

Bodies

Bodies were recovered from the sea, by a Greek warship and cargo vessels, and also a Turkish warship. The cargo vessels transferred the bodies they had recovered to the Greek warship which put into Rhodes. The total landed at Rhodes was 32. The Turkish vessel landed 19 bodies at the Turkish port of Antalya, these were subsequently flown by the RAF to Rhodes. The total recovered was 51, the only crew members recovered being the two Cypriot Stewardesses.

An RAF pathological team was flown into Rhodes to examine the bodies, their full report is awaited, but the following is known :-

1. Bodies were severely injured though intact.

2. Some bodies in contact with kerosene.

3. Bodies not wearing life jackets.

4. Some bodies stripped of clothing or retained the tighter fitting under garments and wristwatches found on a few.

5. Small particles of metal found in one or two bodies.

6. One seat frame included in the remains also had a small piece of metal forced into it.

7. Bodies examined do not support, fire, smoke or explosion, nor explosive decompression.

/General

General

The following items are known and are included as background information :-

1. A Russian ship, believed to be a radar ship, was seen to the North of the area, but steamed away from the area.

2. The RAF have made checks on the radar and radio facilities at the times preceding and following the accident.

3. A supposedly continuous radar watch seems to have failed on this occasion, the last aircraft seen by radar was at 0258Z. No R/T calls from the aircraft appear to have been made on any frequencies monitored.

4. All the wreckage to date is from the Comet.

5. No photographs taken by the search aircraft, and none apparently by the ships.

Theoretical Analysis from the Wreckage Recovered

This analysis must not be regarded as final, since it is based on very meagre information yielded by what wreckage has been recovered and the bodies that were examined.

1. The disaster was almost instantaneous. The grounds for this are :-

    (a) the sole R/T call to Nicosia.

    (b) the wreckage found almost at UR 19C, this implies a rapid descent.

2. The aircraft fuselage broke into two sections prior to hitting the sea, and in doing so spilled out some of the passengers ?

    The grounds for this are:-

    (a) some bodies were stripped of clothing, others not. The Elba investigation revealed that when dummy bodies were dropped on land from 29,000 feet clothing remained on. Similar tests were carried out dropping dummies from 1,200 feet into 10 feet of water; the clothes were stripped off. Therefore,

/were

300

were those bodies that were stripped of
clothing spilled out prior to impact, and
those that remained clothed still in the
aircraft hull on impact.

3. If the aircraft did break, did the section aft
    of the trailing edge come down as a separate
    piece ?

    The grounds for this are :-

    (a) dead cat was still in an intact container.

    (b) the barograph and electrical equipment
         were relatively undamaged.

    These items were shipped ex-London in hold 5 (tail
    hold). This implies that the impact on this part
    of the aircraft was less severe by a considerable
    margin than the other part of the fuselage.

4. If the aircraft broke in two prior to impact - why ?
    There is no evidence of an explosion by means of an
    infernal machine, or by a concentration of explosive
    vapours or explosive decompression.

    The grounds for stating this are the pathological
    report to date. No evidence of fire, smoke,
    explosion or explosive decompression on the bodies.
    The most likely cause of the break, if it took
    place, would be due to the aircraft, during the
    descent, exceeding the designed structural load.
    It must have broken at a comparatively low altitude
    since the pathological report does not indicate
    bursting of the fuselage at altitude.

5. The aircraft had electrical power, certainly power
    from the batteries at time of impact. Though
    this is included under the heading of theoretical
    analysis, this can be proved by the recovered
    Graviner fire bottle.

    The bottle recovered was the No.6 bottle, located
    on the starboard side against the spar and wing
    root. The evidence obtained from this bottle is
    that it had activated since there was fluid in
    the short length of pipe that was still attached
    to the bottle. All three heads of this triple-
    headed bottle had been fired, and the only possible

                                            /way of

way of firing this is by the 3 g switches in the
nose operating, and activating the bottle by an
electrical circuit. Therefore, it is reasonable
to assume that the nose struck the water, activated
the g switches, which in turn fired the bottle. To
do this the electrical circuit must be intact,
therefore this section of the fuselage was complete
on impact but immediately broke up, thereby releasing
the Graviner bottle from its attachments.

6. The nose section broke off almost immediately after
impact.

The grounds for this are :-

(a) recovery of the two pilots' hats.

(b) the jump seat cushion.

This would suggest that subsequent break up after
impact followed the lines of the Elba accident.
The nose section broke away.

7. The only seating plan that is available is not
complete and takes no account of the joining
passengers at Athens. The plan that is available
was drawn up by the cabin staff operating the London-
Athens sector and passengers disembarked at Athens.
An attempt has been made to relate the known
position of these passengers with those recovered
and identified, together with their injuries and
clothing state. This reveals no one area of consistency either in injuries or clothing state.
The bodies recovered range from those sitting in
the first and last rows of tourist seats. There
were no First Class passengers aboard.

8. <u>Thunderstorms and Clear Air Turbulence</u>

Neither were forecast over the route, and no
thunderstorms or clear air turbulence were
encountered by Captain Emmerson flying the same
route at almost the same time.

This is therefore the only known information at this
time, and the only two items that have any degree of
certainty are the reconstruction of events leading to the
fire bottle discharge and the fact that there was no
weather en route to cause the aircraft to break up in flight.

/The other

The other theories that have been advanced are based on
reasonable assumption. The question of the metal found in
the bodies or body and the seat frame may reveal little,
since the largest piece is approximately one inch square.
At the time of writing, none of the metal is believed to
have originated from either the turbine or compressor, but
rather from the aircraft skin and/or interior furnishings.

Theories Advanced by Individual Pilots

This technical appreciation would not be complete
without the inclusion of theories put forward by Comet
pilots in BEA, both to me and the Management. These
theories are examined in close detail, together with
the background for advancing them by the Comet pilots.
An attempt is made to examine these theories and tie
them to the facts as are known to date, this is in no
way an attempt to belittle these ideas, but to ascertain
their validity to this accident.

Jamming or Stiffening of Flying Controls In-flight
or During Pre-departure Checks by Flight Crew

There have been presented to me three cases of the
above malfunctioning, one by Captain Blevins, G-APMC,
on 5th March, 1965 is very detailed; one case on 4th May,
1960 by Captain Dorehill, G-APMC; and one case of jammed
controls on pre-departure check. All three cases were
investigated by BEA and the findings at the time accepted.

In brief, the case of Captain Blevins, G-APMC on
5th March, 1965. The aircraft operated the Beirut -
Nicosia - Ankara sector. After take-off from Nicosia,
the First Officer, who was flying the aircraft, complained
of stiffening controls. It was subsequently found by
Captain Blevins that as airspeed increased, the controls
became progressively stiffer. The airspeed was reduced
and the aircraft returned to Nicosia. The controls were
thoroughly checked and a test flight completed. The
symptoms did not re-occur.

The case on 4th May, 1960, Captain Dorehill, G-APMC.
The controls on all three systems stiffened during the
Munich - Athens sector. Control was achieved by heavy
pressure, a descent was started, but as altitude decreased
controls became free and acted normally. The service was
completed to Athens. This was investigated by BEA and
Hawker-Siddeley and the conclusion arrived at and accepted
was ice building up on the elevator cables where they
passed through seals into the pressure hull. The materials
for these were changed. BOAC had three similar incidents in
aircraft that had been cruising in low temperatures for
about 2 hours.

/The third

303

The third case appeared during the pre-departure check. Captain Graham, 20th August, 1961, aircraft G-ARJM. The yellow system was pressurised, the elevator and aileron were found to be jammed. Heavy control forces were used to free the system but this took some time. Investigation suggested inadvertent engagement of the autopilot.

There have, in the past, been quite a few cases of jammed control on various types of aircraft throughout the world, but in all cases the aircraft have flown for a considerable period of time, as indeed the two Comet cases quoted. It is recognised that if the controls jammed in the full deflection or part deflection this would cause an accident, but in the case of the Comet control system, there is no evidence since the Comet has entered BEA service of servodyne failure.

Assuming that controls did jam on 'CO', there was no mention of this by Captain Blackwood to Athens on his FIR boundary report. His initial call to Nicosia has all the marks of a routine transmission. The aircraft was known to be flying at 0318 GMT, the watches recovered are stopped between 0320 and 0325Z giving a time span of as little as two minutes or as long as seven minutes. The span of two minutes indicates an almost vertical descent at close on 15,000 f.p.m., the span of seven minutes indicates that the aircraft flew for that time at least some 50 miles along its track. The wreckage was, for all practical purposes, found at the position of UR 19C. Jamming of the controls in the normal cruise configuration therefore does not appear likely. However, it does not rule out the possibility that full deflection was applied for some reason, the answer must by necessity lie in the wreck.

Hold or Main Door Failure

There has been a recent case where the Captain, in consultation with the Station Engineer, flew the aircraft back to London unpressurised owing to the state of the forward freight bay door. In brief, the door was heavily cracked around the flanges with evidence of drilling to prevent extension of these cracks. On investigation at London by Engineering, it was ascertained that this door had in fact been repaired internally but this information was not available at the time to either the Captain or the Outstation Engineer.

Applying this type of failure to 'CO' is not supportable since this type of failure would have caused a very rapid decompression and the pathological report does not support this type of failure.

/ Corrosion

304

Corrosion

All aircraft commence to corrode from the day they are made, the Comet is no exception. Work on re-skinning the areas of corrosion in the Comet has been in hand for some time. In the case of 'CC', it was practically complete. Again failure of the pressure hull due to this is not supported by pathological evidence. Significant corrosion in unpressurised areas has not been revealed by detailed examination of other BEA Comets.

Turbine Failure

There is only one known case of this causing major structural damage resulting in a crash. This was on a Mexican Airlines Comet. Information is scant, but as a result, work has been carried out to strengthen the area surrounding the turbine. Again pathological evidence does not show that the hull was broken at altitude for any reason.

Cracks in Compressor Casings

Two BEA Comets were found to have cracks running from the bleed valve and extending into the compressor casing. As a result, all Comet aircraft were checked prior to flight. These cracks would not cause a catastrophic failure, and indeed BOAC, when operating Comets, found a compressor casing heavily cracked.

General Comment

Since the accident, BEA Engineering have been carrying out special checks, apart from the check for compressor cracks, prior to every flight. All four high-pressure oil filters are inspected for metal every 20 flying hours; inspection of lower freight doors every Check A. Apart from this routine engineering work, three teams, Hawker-Siddeley, ARB and BEA Engineering are carrying out detailed examination of the Comet. This was done at the time of the first BOAC Comet accident, and whilst every possible area was examined, BOAC were to lose yet another Comet at Elba.

Whilst many theories can be advanced and a number of them rejected on the grounds of what little concrete information is available, the probable real solution lies within the wreck. If it is practical and possible to retrieve this wreckage then every effort should be made, because I feel that in the absence of concrete evidence any explanation offered may be supposition based on theory and not fact.

2nd November, 1967.
8 TEC 6/2/17.

Appendix 7 – Correspondence between Police and Foreign Office

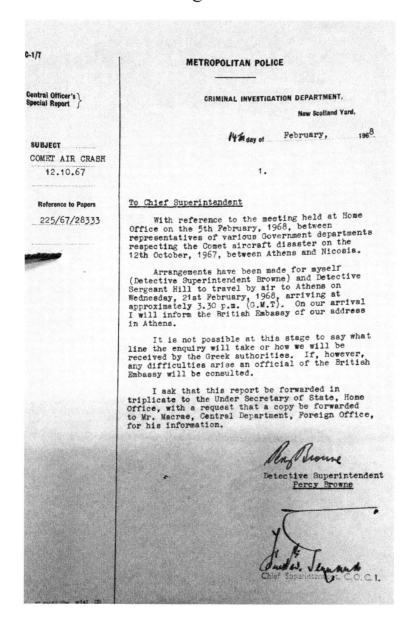

C-1/7

METROPOLITAN POLICE

Central Officer's }
Special Report }

CRIMINAL INVESTIGATION DEPARTMENT,

New Scotland Yard,

14th day of February, 1968.

SUBJECT
COMET AIR CRASH
12.10.67

1.

Reference to Papers
225/67/28333

To Chief Superintendent

With reference to the meeting held at Home Office on the 5th February, 1968, between representatives of various Government departments respecting the Comet aircraft disaster on the 12th October, 1967, between Athens and Nicosia.

Arrangements have been made for myself (Detective Superintendent Browne) and Detective Sergeant Hill to travel by air to Athens on Wednesday, 21st February, 1968, arriving at approximately 3.30 p.m. (G.M.T). On our arrival I will inform the British Embassy of our address in Athens.

It is not possible at this stage to say what line the enquiry will take or how we will be received by the Greek authorities. If, however, any difficulties arise an official of the British Embassy will be consulted.

I ask that this report be forwarded in triplicate to the Under Secretary of State, Home Office, with a request that a copy be forwarded to Mr. Macrae, Central Department, Foreign Office, for his information.

Detective Superintendent
Percy Browne

Chief Superintendent, C.O.C.1.

(CE 21/11)

FOREIGN OFFICE,

LONDON, S.W.1.

CE 21/11

As I told you on the telephone when we spoke yesterday, I am very sorry that two members of the Metropolitan police should have arrived in Athens before we could warn you of their coming and explain some of the background. This is the story.

2. The Board of Trade's investigation following the loss of a B.E.A. Comet while on a flight between Athens and Nicosia led to the conclusion that the disappearance of the Comet was caused by an explosion on board the aircraft. The Board of Trade's responsibility is to find out the cause of an aircraft accident and not to impute blame. In the present case they felt the need for further investigation into how the crash occurred. They considered that such a further investigation could appropriately be carried out by the Metropolitan police. At the same time they recognised that the interests of the police, if they undertook the investigation, would not be limited by the Board of Trade's responsibility as discussed above.

3. Unfortunately there is no simple or general mechanism for invoking a police investigation into accidents of this type. Difficult questions over the responsibility of the police, payment for the investigation, and jurisdiction arise. But at an interdepartmental meeting on 5 February, it was agreed that the Board of Trade would formally request the Metropolitan police "to make enquiries into the events leading up to the explosion which resulted in the loss of the B.E.A. Comet in international waters in the Eastern Mediterranean on 12 October, 1967, and to the death of 66 people (some of them British)" and would pay for the investigation. We for our part agreed to alert you and ask you to take such action with the Greek authorities as seemed necessary and appropriate.

4. We expected next to get a letter from the Police setting out the lines of their investigation and their proposed plan of action. Instead of which I learnt from you that two police officers had already arrived in Athens. This is the more regrettable in that it seems quite possible that potentially prickly political questions could arise during the course of the investigation. For example, supposing the police should discover that the explosion was caused by a Greek (or for that matter a Turkish Cypriot) who was hoping to liquidate General Grivas (something that has of course been canvassed in the Press). For this reason it seems right that the police should keep in close touch with the Embassy about how their investigation is going, even if they make such day to day arrangements as are necessary with their Greek opposite numbers through their own channels. In view of the mix-up which has just happened, I am making sure that clear instructions in this sense are sent to Detective Superintendent Brown.

5. As to the question of informing the Greek Government about the investigation, I think this is entirely a matter for your discretion. As I mentioned on the telephone, it occurred to me that the action you were required to take in para. 1 of Foreign Office telegram No. 1414 of 8 November might provide a suitable starting point, but much would obviously depend on how these instructions were carried out.

The Hon. T. E. Bridges,
ATHENS.

6. I understand that the police will be asking you for help with interpreting facilities. I am sure this does not mean that they want to press into service your own already hard-pressed staff, but rather wish for assistance in finding a reliable and trustworthy Greek/English speaker (I do not see that payment will be a problem), but I expect that Detective Superintendent Brown will already have explained this to you.

7. I am sending a copy of this letter to Tony Tyler in the Commonwealth Office and to Timothy Daunt in Nicosia, as I believe it is possible that the police will wish to visit Cyprus during the course of their investigations. In that case the Commonwealth Office may well wish to inform the Cyprus Government about the police investigation and, if you can find out about their plans to visit Cyprus, it would obviously be helpful for Tyler and Daunt to know about any plans the police may have for visiting Cyprus.

(J. M. O. Macrae)
Central Department

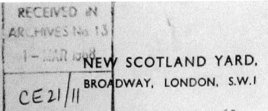

RECEIVED IN
ARCHIVES No 13
1 - MAR 1968

CE 21/11

NEW SCOTLAND YARD,
BROADWAY, LONDON, S.W.I

P. E. Brodie, O.B.E.   27th February, 1968

Dear Macrae,

I enclose a secret and highly-confidential
letter to Detective Superintendent Browne who
is investigating the B.E.A. Comet aircraft
crash.

I should be extremely grateful if you
could arrange for this letter to be sent out
to him in Athens through the Diplomatic Bag.
We understand that he is staying at the
Hotel Stanley, 1 rue Odysseus, Place Kaiskis,
Athens.

Yours sincerely,

P.E.Brodie

Assistant Commissioner Crime

J. E. C. Macrae, Esq.,
Foreign Office,
Whitehall,
S.W.1.

310

ASSISTANT
COMMISSIONER

...die, O.B.E.

Dear Browne,

Bampton from the Home Office has been to see me today and he tells me that someone from the Embassy in Athens has been in touch with Macrae in the Foreign Office here about your presence in Athens.

It appears that the Embassy staff in Athens are slightly apprehensive about any possible political repercussions should your enquiry develop in a certain direction. For instance, if you find evidence to suggest that the explosion in the Comet was arranged in order to do harm to someone in politics in Cyprus or Greece then a very delicate situation would arise.

I think I need say no more than to ask you to keep very closely in touch with the Embassy staff and if anything that savours of politics should arise, I know you would discuss the matter with them and would be most careful not to embarrass the Foreign Office.

Of necessity, this letter has to be in rather vague terms but I am sure that you will take the point.

I wish you luck in your enquiry and I shall look forward to hearing all about it when you return to this country.

Yours sincerely,

/E Brodie.

Assistant Commissioner Crime

Det. Supt. P. Browne,
Hotel Stanley,
1 rue Odysseus,
Place Kaiskis,
Athens.

Appendix 8 – Death of a Comet

The press reports published from the time the news broke, acknowledged the relevance of the aircraft type. The manufacturers, de Havilland[107], and the operators had worked hard to restore the reputation of the Comet after its traumatic introduction fifteen years earlier.

The de Havilland DH.106 Comet was the pioneer jet airliner, designed at the end of the Second World War when jet propulsion was in its infancy. Whilst the powerplant had been designed for military aircraft, its use in civil aircraft had not initially been a priority. In 1943, with the threat of German invasion receding, however, the British government had established a committee under Lord Brabazon to consider the nation's post-war needs in terms of airliners. The committee identified a range of aircraft types to meet the foreseen needs. At this time, the government was still optimistic that it would have an empire to service, with long, thin, routes reaching down through Africa, across Asia to Australia, and across the Atlantic to Canada. It also foresaw that America would perhaps prove as stalwart a trading partner as it had a military ally. The North Atlantic route would require, in particular, a small mail plane which would need to be fast. The specification called for a pressurised aircraft, capable of carrying a one-ton payload at 400 mph.

Having been responsible for creating the Tiger Moth biplane, the first aircraft to be flown by countless thousands of airmen worldwide, de Havilland had excelled itself in the war as an innovative and effective designer and manufacturer of high-performance aircraft. The company's most famous product was the iconic Mosquito, a twin-engined aircraft made predominantly of plywood and powered by the Rolls-Royce Merlin. Less-well known was the Hornet fighter, which pioneered the use of metal-to-wood and metal-to-metal bonding. de Havilland had also designed and built the Vampire fighter, powered by the company's own Goblin engine, and which first flew in September 1943[108]. As luck would have it, Sir Geoffrey de Havilland happened to be a member of the Brabazon Committee and decided to submit a proposal for the Transatlantic mail plane. The specification he proposed was for a turbojet-powered aircraft, designated by his company the Type 106. A contract for development and

---

[107] De Havilland was a mainstay of the British aircraft industry, having been founded in 1920. In 1959, de Havilland was bought by Hawker Siddeley, and fully-absorbed into the expanded Hawker Siddeley Aviation in 1963.

[108] The second British jet aircraft to enter production, after the Gloster Meteor, the Vampire entered service with the RAF in 1946 and was the first jet aircraft to cross the Atlantic. A total of 3,268 Vampires were built, the aircraft eventually retiring from active service, with the Rhodesian Air Force, in 1979. In British post-war aviation terms, it was a stunning success.

Comet 1 G-ALYX 'Yoke X-Ray' at London Heathrow Airport in 1953.

production was awarded to de Havilland in February 1946. The design proposal included the company's own engines as well as airframe; this made the programme even more complicated as there was no powerplant at that time capable of providing the thrust and fuel consumption that would be required if the aircraft was to perform as specified. Just to add further spice to the proposal, the Type 106 was to cruise at forty thousand feet, an altitude almost unheard-of for airliners in the forties.

Having given the matter some further thought, de Havilland finally settled on a long-range airliner with 24 seats. This was attractive to the British Overseas Airways Corporation (BOAC) which, in December 1945, signed a contract for ten of the revolutionary aircraft. In September 1946, as so often happened when British state airlines ordered British-designed airliners off the drawing board, BOAC changed its mind about what exactly it wanted, and amended its requirement from 24 to 36 seats.

The specified engines were originally the de Havilland Goblins, of Vampire fame. Rolls-Royce, however, proposed to offer a new and much-improved turbojet, the Avon. This was a different design from the Goblin and was still awaiting certification. With its customary talent for innovation, de Havilland had developed the Goblin into the Ghost, and this was pencilled in as the powerplant of choice, at least until the Avon became available, which would be in 1950.

The manufacturer recognised that considerable testing of the new aircraft, by now christened the *Comet*, would be necessary. In particular, pressurisation of the fuselage was expected to exert considerable wear and tear on the metal

314

airframe. In order to reduce the risk of fatigue cracks emanating from rivets, the Comet made extensive use of a bonding process using a new adhesive, Redux. The pressure differential required for a cruising altitude of 36,000 feet was 8.25 psi, so testing of the fuselage at 2.75 psi above that was carried out. To make detection of cracks more straightforward, this was conducted in a water tank. The test overpressure for windows was 4.75 psi, with one window being subjected to a massive 100 psi, 12½ times the expected pressure. The window withstood this stern test.

The Comet 1 finally made her first flight on 7th July 1949 and entered service with BOAC when G-ALYP, Yoke Peter[109], inaugurated jet services on 2nd May 1952 between London and Johannesburg.

To passengers who were used to travelling the world in piston-engined aircraft, the Comet was a revelation. It was about 50% faster than most other airliners, had a faster rate of climb and, of course, flew 'above the weather'. Although by today's standards they were incredibly noisy, the cabin layout ensured that most passengers sat forward of the four engine tailpipes. Inside the aircraft, the environment was blissful compared with what the public had endured previously. The Comet was immediately successful, and orders started to arrive at de Havilland, with Air France and fellow countrymen UAT taking three each, along with sales of two aircraft to Canadian Pacific Airlines. The manufacturer was also developing the Comet 2, with upgraded engines, which had attracted several customers. A larger, longer-range version, the Comet 3, was also planned, with orders received from three American airlines, Pan Am, Capital and National. This was especially significant, signalling that, in the short term at least, Britain now led the world in designing, producing and operating jet airliners.

If it all seemed too good to be true, it was. On 26th October 1952 G-ALYZ, operating a BOAC flight, failed to take off from Rome's Ciampino airport and ran off the end of the runway. There were, fortunately, only two minor injuries to passengers, though 'Yoke Zebra' was written off. Worse was to come when, on March 3rd, 1953, CF-CUN, a new aircraft being delivered to Canadian Pacific Airlines, similarly failed to become airborne at Karachi, and ran into a drainage ditch with the deaths of all five crew and six passengers. The airline promptly got cold feet and cancelled the second of its two Comets on order.

The two accidents were strikingly similar, and investigation determined that they were caused by over-rotation of the aircraft as it gathered speed, leading to a critical loss of lift and thrust. Design modifications to the wing resolved the problem, as well as pilot awareness of the problem.

---

[109] The RAF radio alphabet was still in use at this time, with the modern phonetic alphabet not introduced until 1956. G-ALYP was pronounced George Able Love Yoke Peter. G-ARCO would have been pronounced George Able Roger Charlie Oboe had the phonetic alphabet not been updated.

Two months later, on 2nd May, G-ALYV, another BOAC Comet, took off from Calcutta into a severe thunderstorm, crashing six minutes later. All six crew and 37 passengers lost their lives. Witnesses reported seeing the aircraft, minus its wings, plummeting to the ground on fire. The investigation concluded that structural failure of an elevator and the wings had resulted from severe turbulence, exacerbated by the pilot possibly over-stressing the airframe whilst trying to pull out of a dive using the powered controls. Further refinements were made to the design and operation of the Comet, including weather radar, artificial feel to the control system and reduced speed limits in turbulence.

An unrelated accident occurred to a French Comet on 25th June 1953, when F-BGSC, belonging to Union Aeromaritime de Transport (UAT) overran the runway on landing at Dakar, Senegal. The flight had originated in Paris, the pilot carrying out a normal approach and landing. The aircraft then struck a pothole in the runway surface which caused the landing gear on one side to break off. The Comet slid on its belly past the end of the runway, coming to rest some 120 feet beyond. There were no casualties amongst the seven crew and 22 passengers, but the aircraft was written off, having been in service for seven weeks. Even the harshest critic of the benighted Comet could not ascribe blame to the aircraft on this occasion.

Despite the best efforts of all concerned, matters went from bad to worse the following year, with Rome's Ciampino airport coincidentally featuring again. Yoke Peter, the aircraft which had inaugurated jet airliner services less than two years earlier, was on the final leg of a BOAC flight from Singapore to London. Twenty minutes after take-off, the aircraft crashed into the Mediterranean near the island of Elba. All six crew and 29 passengers perished after Yoke Peter apparently disintegrated in mid-air. This time, there were no witnesses and little wreckage in the area, so there was very little to provide any kind of starting point for the investigators. There was speculation, as ever under such circumstances, with the likely causes including sabotage, clear air turbulence or an explosion in an empty fuel tank. In the absence of facts, de Havilland made a number of modifications to mitigate any cause they felt credible whilst BOAC voluntarily grounded its remaining Comet fleet. Meanwhile the Royal Navy conducted an underwater search and recovery operation, which ultimately yielded most of the airframe, engines and control systems. Despite much dedicated and detailed work, no conclusive evidence was found, and no definite cause determined. On 23rd March 1953, the Comets took to the air once more.

On 8th April, just over a fortnight later, 'Yoke Yoke', a BOAC aircraft chartered to South African Airways for the London to Johannesburg route had left Ciampino en route to its next stop at Cairo. Lightly loaded, with fourteen passengers and seven crew, the aircraft crashed, again into the Mediterranean, this time near Naples. There were no survivors.

Enough was enough for the authorities. The Comet's Certificate of Airworthiness was revoked, production was suspended, and the BOAC fleet taken out of service permanently. There followed an intensive and prolonged investigation, led by the Royal Aircraft Establishment (RAE) at Farnborough, which considered both recent BOAC crashes. The investigators considered fatigue as a possible cause of the two disasters. They took the unusual step of procuring a surviving complete airframe from BOAC and testing it to destruction in a water tank. Suspicion was beginning to grow about the design if the Comet's windows, which were square. In fact, the failure of the test fuselage occurred from a fatigue crack from a rivet hole in the Automatic Direction Finder window on top of the fuselage. However, in 1956 further wreckage from Yoke Peter was trawled up and examined; it was found that a fatigue failure of the pressure fuselage had occurred in the vicinity of the three front windows. The investigation concluded that a fatigue failure of the pressure fuselage could be expected anywhere between 1,000 and 9,000 pressurisation cycles. Yoke Peter had made 900 pressurised cycles and Yoke Yoke, 1,290.

The Comet was thereafter stigmatised as a result of its disastrous safety record and the cause of all its misfortune was usually assumed to be mid-air disintegration due to metal fatigue, despite the fact that this had been the primary cause of only two of the six losses of the Comet 1. However, those two disasters had uncovered a fundamental vulnerability in the aircraft, which was now withdrawn from service, and orders for the upgraded Comet 2s were cancelled.

The tragedies befalling the Comet 1 resulted in de Havilland going back to the drawing board. They remained convinced that the basic concept was fine, and that the future of the type lay in a larger and stronger version of the same design. Apart from the few remaining Comet 2 aircraft in production, which were put into service with the RAF[110], the type was now in abeyance while an all-new version came into being. This initially appeared as the Comet 3, which incorporated oval windows, amongst other refinements. A single aircraft of the variant was produced, which carried out the requisite development flying and route proving. Further development of the Comet 3, in particular increased fuel capacity, led to the Comet 4, which was the variant settled on by de Havilland. BOAC ordered 19 Comet 4s in March 1955 and the type, powered by the Rolls-Royce Avon engine which had finally made it into the Comet 2, took to the air on 27th April 1958.

The Comet 4 allowed BOAC, on 4th October 1958, to inaugurate regular transatlantic jet services, the first airline to do so. Unfortunately, from a commercial perspective, the hiatus due to the redesign had allowed the US aerospace industry time to catch up, with the Boeing 707 entering the world stage at the end of the same month, followed in September 1959 by the Douglas DC-

---

[110] 13 Comet 2s served with the RAF who were understandably delighted to be gifted a fleet of modern transport aircraft. The variant had a flawless service history, with no losses, and the last example was retired in January 1975.

8. The American product was larger, faster and had a longer range giving it a significant competitive advantage on the prestige transatlantic routes.

In 1959, de Havilland introduced a new version of the Comet 4 with a stretched fuselage and higher capacity, up to 99 passengers, at the expense of fuel capacity. The Comet 4B first flew on 27th June 1959 and was immediately attractive to BEA as it was specifically designed for shorter routes and greater loads, in line with the airline's European routes. BEA ordered an initial seven aircraft, with subsequent re-orders with commercial operations commencing on 1st April 1960. Ultimately, the airline operated eighteen of the type between 1959, when the first example, G-APMA, was delivered and 1972, when the last Comet 4B[111] was withdrawn from BEA service. That also happened to be G-APMA. Olympic Airways, the Greek national carrier, joined in with orders for two of the type, though in fact it operated thirteen 4Bs at one time or another, in a pooling arrangement that included operations and maintenance. The 4Bs operated by BEA and Olympic were identical and could be flown by pilots of either airline. An examination of Charlie Oscar's maintenance records shows that the majority of the planned servicing was carried out in Athens[112]

The final significant development of the Comet as an airliner[113] was the 4C, which comprised the fuselage of the 4B and the wings and greater fuel capacity of the 4. The 4C first flew on 31st October 1959; eventually 23 were produced.

As with other types, the Comet 4 variants also sustained a series of losses in service[114]. The first three to be destroyed all belonged to Aerolineas Argentinas. The airline took delivery of the type in March 1959 and on 27th August that year, LV-AHP crash-landed at Asuncion, Paraguay, with two fatalities, a crew member and a passenger. LV-AHO, the first Comet 4 to be delivered to the airline, had been in service for eleven months when, on a training flight with six crew on 20th February 1960, she landed very heavily. The undercarriage was forced up through the wings, resulting in a belly landing and fire, fortunately without fatalities.

LV-AHR was operating Aerolineas Argentinas flight 322 from Buenos Aires to New York, via Sao Paolo and Port of Spain on 23rd November 1961. Departing from Sao Paolo at night, the aircraft left the ground but, having reached a height

---

[111] Coincidentally, this was also G-APMA. There is no known record of the total flight cycles and hours accrued by 'Mike Alpha', but other Comet 4Bs delivered in the first batch typically completed around 33,000 hours and 19,000 flights so this is a reasonable estimate. Source: The DH.106 Comet – An Illustrated History by Martin Painter (Air Britain, 2002).

[112] AVIA101 211 Comet Engineering Review – TNA.

[113] The Comet was the basis for the Nimrod maritime reconnaissance / anti-submarine aircraft. Two Nimrod prototypes were converted from unsold Comet 4Cs; the 49 production aircraft were built as new airframes.

[114] 866 Boeing 707s were produced, of which 172 were lost (19.9%). The corresponding figures for the DC-8 were 556 produced of which 83 were lost (14.9%). 26 Comets were lost of the 114 built, 22.8%, not significantly higher overall than the Boeing 707.

BEA's long-serving Comet 4B, G-APMA, on final approach, showing the impressive array of flaps used on the aircraft. G-APMA was the first and the last Comet to serve with BEA.

of some 300 feet, lost power and crashed into trees, bursting into flames as the fuel tanks exploded. All twelve crew and 40 passengers died in the resulting conflagration. The investigation by the Brazilian Air Ministry showed that the co-pilot was sitting in the left-hand seat, that occupied by the pilot-in-command. This indicated that he was being instructed by the captain, who was sitting in the right-hand seat. The investigation noted[115]: *'It was presumed that the co-pilot was under flight instruction. If such was the case, the instructor, who was pilot-in-command, may have failed to brief or supervise the co-pilot properly.'*

Following the conclusion of the investigation, the Argentine government stated, *Argentina has determined, in the light of information it has gathered, that the cause of the accident was: "Failure to operate under IFR during a take-off by night in weather conditions requiring IFR operation and failure to follow the climb procedure for this type of aircraft; a contributory cause was the lack of vigilance by the pilot-in-command during the operations."*

The likely cause was the incorrect use of the elevator travel limiting unit after take-off; the accident accordingly being put down to pilot error.

The following month, at 2143 hrs GMT on 21st December 1961, BEA lost Comet 4B G-ARJM, 'Juliet Mike', on take-off from Esenboga airport, Ankara. The aircraft was flying, as in the case of Charlie Oscar, on behalf of Cyprus

---

[115] Official Report into the Accident of Aerolineas Argentinas Comet IV, LV-AHR, at Campinas Airport, Sao Paulo, Brazil, 23rd November 1961; Brazilian Air Ministry, via Wikipedia.

Airways as flight CY226. The service had originated at London Heathrow and was operated as a BEA service to Istanbul, via Rome and Athens. The Cyprus Airways legs were flown, again as with CY284, with three BEA flight crew and four Cyprus Airways cabin staff. On board were 27 passengers. All went as normal as far as Ankara.

During the 46-minute stopover, there was light snow, resulting in a small amount settling on the wing; however, it was determined that the snow had bearing on the accident. Juliet Mike taxied out to the main runway, which at the start of the take-off run offered just over 9,000 feet. Her take-off weight, at 53,465 kg, was more than a tonne less than the maximum permissible under the conditions. The take-off run, rotation and 'unstick' themselves were quite normal, according to the accident investigation report. However, a couple of seconds after leaving the ground, Juliet Mike rapidly assumed an excessively steep climbing angle. One witness put the angle achieved as '...about twice the normal.' Another put the angle at 45 to 50 degrees. Witnesses also described seeing the aircraft drop a wing and hearing variations in engine noise during the climb. At about 450 feet, Juliet Mike stalled, left wing down, and then sank to the ground in a relatively flat attitude. The crash site was about one mile from the airport's control tower.

Juliet Mike was destroyed by the impact and fire; all seven crew and twenty of the passengers were killed[116]. The investigation found that a small screw in the captain's 'artificial horizon' (attitude indicator) had worked loose, preventing the pointer from moving past a certain point. The pointer remained stuck indicating a nose-up attitude less than the pilot would have expected in a normal climb. Whilst it was the co-pilot who was flying the aircraft, it is believed that the captain was giving advice and guidance. It is likely that he instructed the co-pilot to keep raising the nose, believing that the aircraft was not responding when, in fact, the aircraft was already in a much more pronounced attitude, resulting eight to ten seconds later in a stall.[117]

Comet 4C SU-AMW of United Arab Airlines, crashed at Mt. Khao Yai, Thailand, on 19th July 1962. The aircraft was flying from Hong Kong to Bangkok, an intermediate stop on the scheduled service to Cairo. The pilot reported his position as 90 miles from the Bangkok VOR radio beacon and was given permission to begin his descent. SU-AMW, with her eight crew and eighteen passengers, then flew into the side of Mt. Khao Yai, 52 miles from Bangkok. The accident report concluded:

'The principal cause of the accident was the pilot's action in commencing descent at 1530 hours when the aircraft was 137 miles and not 90 miles from the Bangkok VOR as reported to Bangkok Control, and the aircraft, therefore, collided with a mountain at a point 52 miles distant. It is probable that the pilot-in-command did not actually pass over the point he reported to the Flight Control Units, but only

---

[116] The survivors included four of seven Americans on board, and an Israeli diplomat.
[117] Details are from the accident report by Turkish Ministry of Communications.

estimated he had passed three points which resulted in grave errors of time and distance in his computations. It is also probable that the pilot-in-command had been too self-confident so that his actions were not according to the fundamental principles of air navigation.'

The Saudi royal family had purchased a Comet 4C, SA-R-7, for private use, and this was the next of the type to fall, on 20th March 1963. The aircraft, with nine crew and nine occupants, was flying from Geneva to Nice when it descended into a mountain in the Italian Alps. It was a night flight, and the culmination of a series of training trips for American flight crew, working for Saudi Arabian Airlines. It was considered possible that fatigue had played a part. There were no survivors.

Another 4C of United Arab Airlines came to grief on 27th July 1963. SU-ALD was operating flight 869 from Hong Kong to Cairo via Bangkok, Bombay and Bahrain, with eight crew and 55 passengers, including a delegation of 24 Boy Scouts and adults travelling to the World Scout Jamboree. As the aircraft approached Bombay, the pilot was instructed to carry out a VOR approach to Runway 09 and advised that he might encounter severe turbulence if they went more than six or seven miles from the airport. The pilot then asked to carry out a left-hand turn rather than right-hand due to the weather. The aircraft was not heard from again; three bodies and a dinghy were recovered but no substantive wreckage. The investigation concluded that the pilot had lost control in severe turbulence and crashed into the Arabian Sea near Madh Island.

On 22nd March 1964, G-APDH, a BOAC aircraft leased to Malaysian Airways suffered an undercarriage collapse during a firm landing at Singapore-Paya Lebar airport. There had been nothing untoward with the approach or landing; however, it transpired that there was a fatigue fracture on the starboard main undercarriage leg. The aircraft was written off, though fortunately without loss to the eight crew and sixty passengers. That was the last hull loss before Charlie Oscar.

Although not resulting in a hull loss, there was a further incident involving a Comet 4C, XA-NAT of Mexicana, on 30th October 1966. Whilst descending through 24,000 ft into Mexico City at the end of a flight from Chicago, there was a violent bump as the number 4 engine failed and the turbine section disintegrated. This failure caused extremely hot turbine blades to penetrate the cabin, resulting in numerous small fires, which were extinguished. The cabin lost its pressure and the drop-down oxygen masks were deployed. The turbine blades had severed the hydraulic system, meaning that the landing gear could not be lowered. After holding until daylight, and in order to consume fuel, a bely landing was successfully carried out. The cause was established as the failure of the centre bearing supporting the number 4 engine. Despite major structural damage, the Comet was repaired, returned to service and continued to fly for Mexicana until withdrawn from service on December 1st, 1970. In a notable postscript, XA-NAT suffered a collapse of her starboard main landing gear on landing at Mexico City on her final passenger flight[118]. Of the fourteen losses, only two were therefore due to catastrophic decompression of the fuselage following a fatigue failure. A number of other causes with common factors emerged. These included over-rotation or other problems resulting from the powered flying controls, something that was remedied with the introduction of artificial 'feel', pilot awareness and training. Controlled flight into terrain had also resulted in two major disasters, an unfortunate hole in the runway surface in one and, in the case of Juliet Mike at Ankara, a slightly-protruding instrument screw. For the investigators into the loss of Charlie Oscar, there were plenty of lines of enquiry.

Comet Hull Losses

No.	Date	Type	Registration	S/N	Operator	Fatalities	Location	Cause
1.	26 Oct 52	Comet 1	G-ALYZ	6012	B.O.A.C.	0/8 + 0/35	Rome	Aircraft
2.	03 Mar 53	Comet 1A	CF-CUN	6014	Canadian Pacific	5/5 + 6/6	Karachi	Aircraft
3.	02 May 53	Comet 1	G-ALYV	6008	B.O.A.C.	6/6 + 37/37	Calcutta	Aircraft
4.	25 Jun 53	Comet 1A	F-BGSC	6019	UAT	0/7 + 0/10	Dakar, Senegal	Pilot
5.	10 Jan 54	Comet 1	G-ALYP	6003	B.O.A.C.	6/6 + 29/29	Elba, Italy	Aircraft
6.	08 Apr 54	Comet 1	G-ALYY	6011	South African Airways	7/7 + 14/14	Stromboli, Italy	Aircraft
7.	27 Aug 59	Comet 4	LV-AHP	6411	Aerolineas Argentinas	1/6 + 1/44	Asuncion, Paraguay	Pilot
8.	20 Feb 60	Comet 4	LV-AHO	6410	Aerolineas Argentinas	0/6 + 0/0	Buenos Aires	Pilot
9.	23 Nov 61	Comet 4	LV-AHR	6430	Aerolineas Argentinas	12/12 + 40/40	Sao Paulo, Brazil	Pilot
10.	21 Dec 61	Comet 4B	G-ARJM	6456	British European Airways	7/7 + 20/27	Ankara	Aircraft
11.	19 Jul 62	Comet 4C	SU-AMW	6464	United Arab Airlines	8/8 + 18/18	Mt Kao Yai, Thailand	Pilot
12.	20 Mar 63	Comet 4C	SA-R-7	6461	Saudi Arabian Government	9/9 + 9/9	Cuneo, Italy	Pilot
13.	27 Jul 63	Comet 4C	SU-ALD	6441	United Arab Airlines	8/8 + 55/55	Madh, India	Pilot
14.	22 Mar 64	Comet 4	G-APDH	6409	Malaysian Airlines System	0/8 + 0/60	Singapore	Aircraft
15.	12 Oct 67	Comet 4B	G-ARCO	6449	British European Airways	7/7 + 59/59	100nm E of Rhodes	Bomb
16.	14 Jan 70	Comet 4C	SU-ANI	6475	United Arab Airlines	0/9 + 0/5	Addis Ababa,	Pilot
17.	09 Feb 70	Comet 4C	SU-ALE	6444	United Arab Airlines	0/9 + 0/14	Munich	Pilot
18.	03 Jul 70	Comet 4	G-APDN	6415	Dan-Air Services	7/7 + 105/105	Sierra Montseny, Spain	ATC / Aircraft
19.	07 Oct 70	Comet 4	G-APDL	6413	Dan-Air Services	0/4 + 0/5	Newcastle,	Pilot
20.	02 Jan 71	Comet 4C	SU-ALC	6439	United Arab Airlines	8/8 + 8/8	Tripoli, Libya	Pilot

[118] Details from The DH.106 Comet – An Illustrated History by Martin Painter (Air Britain 2002).

Appendix 9 – Letter from 'Falcon Forces' to Airlines Serving Israel

IN THE NAME OF THE MERCIFUL FORGIVING GOD

WARNING ISSUED BY THE 'FALCON FORCES' TO ALL AIRLINES DEALING WITH THE ENEMY

AF AIR FRANCE	OA AUSTRIAN AIRLINES
AZ ALITALIA	SK SCANDINAVIAN AIRLINES
BA BOAC	SN SABENA
BE BEA	TC TURKISH AIRLINES
CY CYPRUS AIRWAYS	TW TWA
KL KLM	SR SWISSAIR
OA OLYMPIC AIRWAYS	UT UNION DU TRANSPORT AERIEN

The GHQ 'Falcon Forces' reminds airlines of the expiration of its twofold warning:

1. Signify by both officially and via the media of the world press not later than 2400hrs on 15 June 1967 that they will comply with this warning.
2. Liquidate their interests and to irrevocably discontinue all their operations with the enemy by 2400hrs on 15 July 1967.

Forewarned is forearmed.

Henceforth the war of liberation shall have no geographic boundaries.

Appendix 10 – Notes on BEA Operations in 1967

BEA Operations Control at the time of the loss of Comet 4B G-ARCO

by David Nicholas

Introduction

By 1967 BEA was in its 21st year as the UK Government's "chosen Instrument" providing domestic and European air services under the current policy of nationalisation. Other than in the initial years post World War 2 it was government policy for BEA to operate indigenously produced aircraft, and the DH106 Comet 4B was introduced on 1ˢᵗ April 1960 as the first pure-jet type. BEA operated 14 Comet 4B's in its own livery, with a further four ordered and operated by Olympic Airways of Greece. The latter aircraft were painted in Olympic livery and flown by their crews, although the fleet were pooled with those of BEA (who undertook both heavy and line maintenance) and sometimes appeared with BEA "red square" stickers adjacent to the entrance doors. BEA operated the Comet for just ten years, transferring them to their BEA Airtours subsidiary, based at Gatwick, during 1970. The Comets ceased operations with Airtours in October 1973, many of them passing to Independent operators such as Dan Air.

BEA

For those who do not remember the period during which BEA (and its long-haul partner BOAC) a few recollections might be helpful. Firstly, as nationalised industries, both airlines existed to fly the British flag abroad, operating British manufactured aircraft (unless an overwhelming commercial disadvantage could be demonstrated by trying to compete against US built jet airliners on long-haul routes) and providing employment both in UK and abroad. In comparison with the successor airline, the privately-owned British Airways, BEA and BOAC had high staff levels, top heavy management structures, time-honoured restrictive working practices and were protected against leaner and fitter independent competition by government licencing policy which provided an effective monopoly on most routes. The fact that both BEA and BOAC had financial interests in other flag carriers, engaged in pooling agreements to distribute joint revenue and also had a handling monopoly at major UK airports further protected them from the winds of economic change that reached its conclusion in Deregulation of air services.

That said, both BEA and BOAC had well-trained and highly experienced crews and an in-house training school (the College of Air Training at Hamble) which set a very high bar to ensure the maintenance of high standards among new pilots who entered the parent airlines as the wartime generation retired. A high proportion of the pilots in BEA wore medal ribbons attesting to military service in World War 2 (DFCs were commonly seen in the corridors around the BEA Crew Centre in the Queen's Building at London Airport, as well as the insignia of the Queen's Commendation for Valuable Service in the Air).

The Captains in particular retained the status and dignity (in some cases to excess) of their rank and experience, and the Hamble pilots tended to reflect a similar self-regard and confidence. This did not always make them popular with their colleagues, cabin crews, engineers and traffic staff.

At this time, the uniformed staff wore uniforms directly inspired by their military forebears, and had not yet been "downgraded" to reflect American influence as happened from the mid-1970's. The airline was organised into the Traffic Department (responsible for passenger, mail and cargo handling) and Flight Operations, which ensured that properly qualified and trained crews were available to operate each scheduled flight. Engineering arranged base and line maintenance to ensure that a serviceable aircraft was in the right place at the right time to meet the schedule, which itself was a product of the Commercial Department which planned routes and schedules and made them available for sale to passengers and cargo shippers. Other peripheral (but essential) services provided catering, aircraft cleaning, flight documents, ground transportation etc., and all of this undertaken entirely manually, without a computer or Visual Display Unit in sight – they had yet to be invented.

SECURITY

It is perhaps wise to explain that airport security (and indeed "the threat") such as we know it today was to all intents and purposes non-existent. Airport fences were little more than chicken wire on 6-foot poles, there were no surveillance cameras, and photo-ID cards were still some years in the future. Access to the BEA Operations Control Centre was through a couple of fire-doors, each unlocked and unguarded, as was the crew room. The perimeter doors of Queen's Building had glass doors, adjacent to which were signs "Entrance to offices and for crew".

If you walked around the building reasonably dressed (as people did in those days) you would be most unlikely to be challenged at any time in the corridors. The public did on occasions come into Queen's Building but usually left again as once they entered an office or specialised area, they would become conspicuous and invite a polite "Can I help you?".

By walking through the crew centre it was quite possible to get onto the apron area and indeed into parked aircraft (they weren't guarded either). On a night shift break in 1966 I did just that and entered a parked Trident 1C and sat in the cockpit for ten minutes before returning to my shift. I had no malevolent purpose, just an enthusiastic fascination and would have introduced myself to anyone in the aircraft and asked permission to look around; however, there was nobody to ask and the apron deserted. It was far from the last time that I went airside just to look at the aircraft......

In general (and in most countries) the public were responsible and obeyed instructions and prohibitions, and the system worked well enough. This did not really change until after the simultaneous hijacking of three airliners on 9th September 1970 and their landing at a desert airstrip at the behest of the Palestinian Liberation Organisation. This, and a number of other hijackings in that period led to the introduction of passenger searches and the veritable industry that aviation security has evolved into since.

THE PASSENGER EXPERIENCE

Travel, particularly by air, was exclusive and comparatively (with the present day) expensive in the 1960s. It was part of the experience to dress properly and behave responsibly. As a contrast to the passenger experience of today, following a passenger from check-in to the aircraft door occurs as the pre-departure preparations for the flight happen behind the scenes.

Arriving at the check-in desk in the Europa Building (later Terminal 2) the passenger would place his baggage on the big red Avery scale, and the weight in Kilograms (a mysterious term in the British public's world of pounds and ounces) would be indicated by the sweeping hand. Handing his or her ticket to the check-in clerk was all that was needed – no ID check was carried out. The clerk would remove the Flight Coupon ("Good for passage between the points outlined by the heavy line") and enter the baggage weight onto the coupon by hand. It would then be placed on a continuous conveyor belt above the desk and delivered to Coupon Control at the end of the row of desks. There the passenger weight (standard weights were used for Male, Female, Child and Infant) and actual bag weight would be manually entered on a check in list for each flight. Seat assignment was not introduced until the early 70s so free seating was the order of the day – the sooner a passenger boarded the aircraft the better the choice of seats. A card boarding pass, with the flight number and gate written by hand, would be handed to the passenger.

At flight closure (about 45 mins before departure) Coupon Control would send the list (manifest) by means of pneumatic tube to Load Control in Queen's Building next door. There the passenger numbers, baggage details and weights would be entered onto the Load Sheet along with the basic weight of the aircraft, crew and catering, and any cargo and mail on board. Subtracting this weight (the Zero-Fuel Weight or ZFW) from the Maximum allowable Take-off Weight (MTOW) would produce an Open Weight value which the crew could – if required – use for fuel. Once the fuel required was determined and advised to Load Control the Load Sheet could be completed, and the fuelling started. (NB the process was actually a little more complex in practice, but the above explanation covers the basic process).

Having left check-in, our passenger would walk up the central staircase and through passport control (something that the UK discontinued much later but which was very much in operation in the 1960's). From there, the departure lounge was the next stop. Apart from a Duty-Free shop, bar, cafeteria and a branch of WH Smiths there were no retail opportunities airside, and the many windows allowed daylight in and a view of the airport beyond.

Flight departure boarding announcements were made by Tannoy, as were broadcasts when flights were closing at the gate. Flight departures were displayed on Solari Displays – where metal flaps would cycle through from A-Z and 1-9 every few minutes and settle as a line of letters and numbers containing flight information. The clatter of Solari boards (still found today in some European railways stations) is one of the sounds which is redolent of airport terminals at that time.

Once seated on board, our passenger would not have to disembark until reaching his destination, even on a multi-sector flight. Passengers who missed their flight were left behind...and their baggage remained onboard unless retrieval was possible without delaying the flight. No passenger/baggage reconciliation (now mandatory) was carried out, and at no time were passengers or their baggage searched.

OPERATIONS CONTROL

The Ops Control Centre, under the supervision of the Duty Operations Superintendent (DOS) was the communications, command and control centre of the airline. There, on a 24-hour, 365-day basis, the operations staff and those responsible for maintenance control ("Maintrol") worked more or less collaboratively to deliver the daily flying programme across the network and recover the operation after disruption in this era which was just on the very edge of the introduction of automatic landing. Weather (fog was a much bigger problem owing to greater atmospheric pollution), snow, ice, strikes, and political events affected parts of the network on most days, and both crew and aircraft would be out of position frequently as a result. This daily challenge was directed by Fleet Controllers, who with their assistants worked with Maintrol to cover the flying programme of a fleet while ensuring that each aircraft was in the right place overnight for maintenance checks, or back at LHR for base maintenance, or overnighting at an outstation to be in position to operate the first inbound service the next day. News of aircraft movements (arrivals, departures, delays and load messages) poured in by Telex message to the Printer Room alongside the OCC, and would be sorted and distributed by a Filter Clerk who would provide the message to the relevant Fleet Assistant and at the same time update the flight information boards used to inform the Flight Enquiry Clerks whom the public called to request expected arrival times of inbound flights. While something similar happens today (at least in an airline's OCC) it should be remembered that in the 1960's everything was done by means of hand written data and the manual maintaining of flight movement information on a fleet of around 300 aircraft across Europe.

THE NIGHT OF THE LOSS OF CHARLIE OSCAR

It was a normal night in every respect (to the best of my recollection). The outbound flight to Athens and Nicosia had departed before we started work and the reciprocal flight (operated by another aircraft) was preparing to leave Nicosia.

The first message that we received was by telephone to the DOS, probably (I cannot confirm this, but it seems most likely) from Cyprus Airways in Nicosia, who as well as being partially owned by BEA were the Ground Handling Agents appointed by BEA. The message was that the aircraft had lost contact with Nicosia Area Control Centre (ACC) immediately following its first call after crossing the boundary into Cypriot airspace. From recollection the aircraft had transmitted on the Nicosia ATC VHF frequency "Nicky, Bealine Golf Alpha Romeo Charlie Osc…" and had not made any further transmission when asked to "Go ahead….". Although the ATC controller had not detected the truncation of "Oscar", this became apparent when the tape recording was replayed and was assumed to be the moment when disaster overtook the aircraft.

Nicosia ATC advised that the aircraft had not entered radar cover and that they had initiated the Alert Phase (ALERFA). They then rang off with the promise to keep us advised.

A further call after the ETA of the flight had elapsed indicated that no radar or radio contact had been made since the initial message, and the DOS announced the OCC staff that he was initiating the company's Accident Procedure as the aircraft had now passed its fuel endurance without contact.

Subdued, the staff worked on – mechanically continuing the normal procedures required to prepare the company's operations for the new day, while a sense of numbness remained below the surface. Although the shift staff were of varying ages, from close-to-retirement to (like me) teenagers, and of both sexes, nobody wept, nobody lost their composure and the normal procedure of cancelling the inbound flight and publishing across the company the reason as "Operational" was put in motion. The Comet Fleet assistant rearranged the fleet operating pattern for the day to ensure that subsequent services assigned to 'CO were covered by other aircraft, and Crew Control were advised that the aircraft crew was, pending confirmation, to be assumed to be lost (with the future ramifications for the crew rosters for the Comet fleet).

Behind the scenes (I know not by whom as it didn't cross my mind at that moment) someone – probably the Comet Fleet Manager – was preparing to advise the next of kin of the crew that their loved ones were missing, while a similar process took place in the Cabin Crew Centre. The ripples were starting to spread even before the fate of the aircraft was known for certain……….

329

LATER THAT DAY

I ended my duty at 0730, and as the early shift arrived most of the staff were unaware of the night's events and received the news with grim acceptance. The discovery by search aircraft of a fuel slick, floating wreckage and bodies in the sea in the early hours of daylight confirmed the worst fears and raised uncomfortable recollections of the earlier Comet 1 disasters (to which it was later found to have no relevance once the evidence of an explosion was found). In contrast to recent years, the 1960s were a period when fatal accidents were much more frequent than now. Many of the staff had experienced the Vanguard (G-APEE) crash at LHR in 1964, and the earlier BEA Comet accident (G-ARJM) at Ankara in 1961. Other British aircraft had crashed in that decade, often flying into high ground in the years before terrain avoidance systems were introduced. Older staff had experienced the war only 20-odd years previously and had in many cases directly experienced the loss of friends and colleagues in action. The entire culture was considerably different, nobody was offered any counselling and certainly would not be sent home in the aftermath of an accident. The important thing was to protect the integrity of the company's operation regardless of the challenges that occurred. A considerable esprit de corps had evolved over those years.......

FOOTNOTE

The crew of the northbound Comet, which had passed 'CO close to the location where it was lost, were reported to have exchanged greetings with their colleagues by flashing their landing lights as they passed by 2000ft above.
The accident occurred on 12th October 1967 at 05.25 local time (Cyprus).

David Nicholas
3rd November 2017

Appendix 11 – Airliner Bombings Prior to CY284

Date	Airline / Flight	Circumstances	Fatal
10-Oct-33	United Airlines	A Boeing 247 was destroyed by a bomb, with nitroglycerine as the probable explosive agent. A Chicago gangland murder was suspected, but the case remains unsolved.	7
09-Sep-49	Canadian Pacific Air Lines	Joseph-Albert Guay packed a bomb made of dynamite in the baggage carried by his wife. The explosion occurred after take-off, leading to the death of all 19 passengers and 4 crew on the Douglas DC-3.	23
11-Apr-55	Air India	A Lockheed L-749A Constellation carrying delegates to the Bandung Conference was bombed in an unsuccessful attempt to assassinate Chinese Premier Zhou Enlai.	16
01-Nov-55	United Airlines Flight 629	Jack Gilbert Graham packed a bomb containing dynamite in a suitcase carried by his mother. The explosion and crash killed all 39 passengers and 5 crew members.	44
16-Nov-59	National Airlines Flight 967	A Douglas DC-7B aircraft disappeared from radar over the Gulf of Mexico; 10 bodies and scattered debris were recovered but the main wreckage was never found. One theory is that a convicted criminal tricked another man into boarding in his place with luggage containing a bomb, so that his wife could collect on his life insurance. No probable cause for the crash was found.	42
06-Jan-60	National Airlines Flight 2511	A Douglas DC-6 flying from New York to Miami exploded and crashed in North Carolina, killing all on board. Passenger Julian Frank, who was under investigation for running a charity fraud and was heavily insured, is suspected of detonating a dynamite bomb.	34
10-May-61	Air France Flight 406	A Lockheed L-1649 Starliner flying from Chad to France suffered an explosion and loss of tail control systems and crashed in Algeria, killing all on board. The explosion was believed to have been caused by a nitrocellulose-based bomb, possibly targeting officials of the Central African Republic.	78
22-May-62	Continental Airlines Flight 11	A Boeing 707 exploded near Centerville, Iowa, United States. A passenger, Thomas G. Doty, had brought a bomb on board the aircraft after purchasing a life insurance policy.	45
22-Nov-66	Aden Airways	A DC-3 registered VR-AAN crashed at Wadi Rabtah while en route to Aden, Yemen. Investigations determined that a bomb had been placed to kill Amir Mohammed bin Said, Prime Minister of Wahidi (now part of Yemen), by his son Ali who wanted to succeed him as Amir.	30

Appendix 12 - 'Herewith the Letters...'

The crash had generated widespread public interest and concern and, inevitably, a vast array of correspondence from the public found its way to the investigation team. Most was well-intentioned, some extremely constructive and insightful. Other suggestions as to the cause were bizarre. All were courteously acknowledged and either actioned or answered in a way appropriate to their contribution to the progress of the investigation. The following letters are amongst the reams preserved in the National Archives and so form part of the public record. For the most part, there was a straightforward explanation for technical or mechanical phenomena that were outside the normal experience of the writer.

Mr. BF Taylor, Amersham, Buckinghamshire, wrote on 13th October 1967:

I recently flew to Athens in a Comet similar to that which crashed yesterday and wonder if the following point may be of value. My seat was in the forward section of the aircraft, and I noticed that heavy frosting was taking place on the stainless steel or chromium bolt which protruded into the cabin just below the window next to which I was sitting. I was surprised at this as it indicated direct contact with the outside air temperature. Similar frosting was taking place on the other side of the cabin but not apparently under the windows behind the seat in which I was sitting. I have flying experience.

Group Capt. Veal duly arranged for an explanation to be sent to Mr. Taylor:

I suspect that the heavy frosting you noticed on a bolt protruding into the cabin during your flight to Athens resulted from contact with the outer skin of the aircraft so that severe local cooling was taking place due to conduction. Normally, as you will know, the metal parts in direct contact with the outer skin are covered with thermal insulation but there are occasional points at which this is impossible or ineffective.

However, against the possibility that there is some other explanation in this case I am having the matter followed up. I am grateful to you for writing to me about it.

Slightly more bemusement and lack of familiarity with the design of the Comet inspired Mr. AH Wilkinson of Cardiff to write to his MP, the Rt. Hon. James Callaghan, on 16th October. Mr. Callaghan, who happened to be the Chancellor of the Exchequer at the time, duly forwarded the letter to the investigation team.

My wife and I had two weeks holiday in Cyprus and returned on Saturday September 30th by BEA Comet...I sat next to the window at my wife's behest and from Nicosia to Athens I sat looking immediately over the Starboard wing and throughout the journey I observed that, of the two automatic apertures of the engine exhausts in the wing, whereas that furthest from me was in first class operational condition, that nearest the cabin was of lighter calibre, not closing efficiently but rather fluttering instead of sealing down and appeared to be a replacement of inferior quality, calibre and operating efficiency.

I wondered then, without comment to cause nervousness, whether the continual passage of air and/or exhaust gases at 500 mph might not prove detrimental to the wing structure, particularly near the junction with the cabin.

It seemed to me, casually observing at the Terminals, that whereas engine welfare was a priority, structural or fuselage defects were totally disregarded. This seems now more evident since last week's disaster.

John Veal took the opportunity to pass Mr. Wilkinson's letter to Hugh Gordon-Burge at BEA, commenting:

'...it appears that he may be referring to the bleed valve, but I should be glad if you could have the matter looked into and let me have your comments.'

Hugh Gordon-Burge took the time to explain in some detail the cause of Mr. Wilkinson's concerns:

'The automatic apertures to which he refers are in fact the Bleed Valve Duct Vent Doors. The bleed valves themselves bleed air, (not exhaust gases) from the compressor throughout a pre-determined range of engine r.p.m. When they are open large quantities of hot air are vented to atmosphere. This escaping air will keep the vent doors open. It is not unusual for the doors to "flutter" and should they do so, it in no way means any loss of operational efficiency. The purpose of these doors is to prevent foreign objects, snow, ice etc., falling into the compressor when the aircraft is stationary, and they perform no useful function the aircraft is in flight.

All duct vent doors are similar and made to the same specification. There is no possibility that a replacement of inferior quality could be made. As far as the last paragraph of Mr. Wilkinson's letter is concerned he can be assured that the bleeding of hot air from the compressors has no detrimental effect on the wing structure.

Veal expounded this view further in a note to Mr. JH Riddoch, Under Secretary at Aviation Safety and General Division of the Board of Trade, explaining:

'It appears likely that the apertures referred to by Mr. Wilkinson in his letter to Mr. Callaghan are those on the top surface of the wing which are designed to open and close automatically to bleed off compressor air when there is so much available from the compressor that the engine cannot use it. It is not an indication of trouble that one should have fluttering in the way he described, but nevertheless the matter is being brought to BEA's attention.

I presume you are considering the form of reply that should be sent to Mr. Wilkinson. I would have thought it would be sufficient merely to say that the matter has been drawn to the attention of the Accidents Investigation Branch who are looking into the matter with BEA.

An abridged form of this explanation was eventually passed back to Mr. Wilkinson by NW Granger, Private Secretary to the Rt. Hon. Anthony Crosland MP, President of the Board of Trade. The correspondence to Mr. Wilkinson's observation, which had itself been offered in good faith, had thereby tied up staff at BEA, the investigation team, the Board of Trade and the office of the Chancellor of the Exchequer, but at least it was answered with the courtesy and formality that was a trade mark of the British Civil Service in the Sixties. It is to be wondered whether the attention given to Mr. Wilkinson's letter, which drew the attention of the higher echelons of the establishment to a query for which there was a mundane and easily-obtained answer, was due to its inherent value or the fact that it had been sent to one of the most powerful politicians in the land.

Mr. Wilkinson's letter was afforded the honour of its own file as it made its way around the upper levels of Government, BEA and the AIB (TNA).

The weariness of the investigation team's administrative assistance began to show as some more creative suggestions and theories began to arrive in their office, either directly or via the great and the good. Mr. Livingstone of Salisbury (17th October) suggested:

'I think I have a solution as to how you can recover the wreckage of the Comet that crashed last week. It is as follows:

Find the exact location of the wreck. Which can be done with a Royal Navy Destroyer by using Asdic method of finding submarines. Having found the wreck (presuming this is possible) lower three or four heavy lifting magnets to the presumed wreck and lift. The magnets could be lowered by using cable laying ships with very strong cables attached to the magnets.

335

By recovering the wreckage, you would possibly recover the Black Box which holds the mystery as to why the Comet crashed.

To my mind this will work, but whether it works in practice lays in the hands of your experts. And I sincerely hope it does.

He received a detailed reply for his troubles:

'...Leaving aside the question of practicability, I am afraid that magnetic means of recovering aircraft wrecks is inappropriate since very little magnetic material is included in the aircraft's structure. This for the most part consists of aluminium and magnesium alloy. Regarding the flight data recorder, or 'Black Box' as you call it, any data which it contains is recorded magnetically on stainless steel wire. Any strong magnetic field would unfortunately have the effect of wiping the wire clean of its recorded data. I am most grateful to you for the interest you have shown in this matter. Other methods of search and salvage are being actively considered but the very great depth at which the wreckage is believed to lie, some 9,500 feet, may introduce problems which are insuperable with present equipment.'

Mr. RW Moncrieff of Chichester (24th October) expressed his concern about an incident he had experienced whilst travelling from London to Istanbul in 1966:

'The BEA aircraft that we (all the passengers) got into perhaps about 1pm. We sat in it for about an hour and were then told to leave and went back into the waiting halls. The Captain had found something wrong (to do with some pressure, I think) with the aircraft and was unwilling to fly it. An hour later another aeroplane arrived and we all got in. I flew in it safely to Athens...It seemed odd at the time that the captain at London should have been offered an aeroplane that had something wrong with it.

Veal replied,

'...With the complexities of modern aircraft, I am sure you will appreciate that in spite of the careful servicing and maintenance which they receive, technical faults occur from time to time...it is likely that the captain was not knowingly offered an aeroplane which had something wrong with it but that some technical fault was discovered during the pre-flight check.'

More help had been on hand, potentially, in the form of a Mr. McA[119] of Crewkerne (14th October), who wrote to BEA:

'I wonder if might endeavour, with your kind permission, to use my knowledge of astrology in order to throw some light upon the mystery attached to this very sad incident.

---

[119] The author has withheld the identities of the writers of some of the more bizarre letters to the team, as there is no wish to cause embarrassment to any person.

Astrology if used sensibly and seriously can at times be of use in such matters. The science was employed during the last war at times with effect. Whether those responsible at BEA have any faith in the art or not, I would suggest no harm can come from any attempt you may allow me to try...

For my study I would require the following details if you can and are willing to provide them: -

The time, place and day and year of the launching of that particular aircraft which was involved in this disaster.

The same for the moment of the crash including the longitude and latitude of the spot. The time in that country or the corresponding GMT.

It would also be of help if it is possible to have details of any one person who was on board the aircraft, i.e.

Time of birth (as near as possible)

Place of birth

Day, month and year of birth.

...Needless to say, I am offering my services without reward and only ardently hope that I may be of use.

Captain John James, Flight Operations Director, thanked Mr. McArthur and assured him that his letter had been passed to the Air Safety Branch, who might be in touch. More plausible causes were suggested by a number of correspondents who were concerned that one or more pressurised containers, be they aerosols, camping gas or divers' oxygen cylinders, might have exploded. Helpfully, it was recommended that such items might be confined to pressurised sections of the aircraft in future.

More unusual physical phenomena were also touted as being responsible. A lady from Acton, West London, thought that, as three Comets had crashed over the Mediterranean, albeit thirteen years apart, the common cause might well be a magnetised air belt of atmospheric pressure, which if the plane once enters, is rendered helpless due to the magnetism in the air.' She concluded; *'Perhaps if you changed your routes it would be good.'*

More mysterious was Mr. W of Lewisham, who wrote to Capt. Baillie at BEA:

'I can supply the missing clue to the Comet Charlie Oscar crash. It is something that has actually happened to me and could happen to an aircraft. We have a lead on this. If you could arrange it, I could demonstrate it on a mock up.'

Unfortunately, the archives contain no record of whether the opportunity Mr. W sought was ever forthcoming, and therefore history does not relate the clue he felt he could offer.

A Miss E of Palmerston, Co. Dublin (20th October), thought there might be an extra-terrestrial element:

...Lately, in one of our Dublin newspapers, there was an article about a UFO which was seen over Canada by several people. One lady in particular stated that it hovered over her car for a few moments, and whilst there, all circuits in the car failed and it was not until the object moved away that the car would move.

I believe that this was what happened to the aeroplane, hence the pilot could not radio to base, some of the passengers put on their lifejackets in freight (sic), and the plane, after a few moments crashed.

I thank you for listening to my theory.

John Veal's reply was concise:

...I would not wish to speculate on the existence of unidentified flying objects and properties they might have. You may wish to know, however, that no evidence has been forthcoming to substantiate early reports that any of the passengers were wearing life jackets.

I am grateful to you for taking the trouble to write to let us have your theory.

Mr. N of Dorking, Surrey, not only offered a similar solution to the disaster, but also came up with what he probably thought was a compelling explanation for the phenomena described by Miss E of Palmerston, when he wrote:

I would suggest (the crash) was due to an electrical phenomenon as follows:

The aircraft flew into a large, loosely-knit cloud of positive and negative ions, with the result that all electrical circuits were instantaneously disrupted; the resultant sudden concentration of positive and negative ions would cause an explosion similar to a thunder bolt. If the black box is worked by electricity, and if it is ever recovered, it will probably be found with all the wires inside completely fused.

The origin of the "cloud" lay in the large amount of ironmongery floating about in space; ironmongery which collects to itself layers of positive and then negative and so on ions, until it becomes positively charged, at which point it releases the "cloud" which is then attracted to the earth by the earth's magnetism. Still held loosely by its own inherent magnetism, but which remains invisible until compressed by the denser atmosphere at say 8,000 feet; it then begins to rotate around a vertical axis like a dog chasing its tail, but at a very high velocity. At the same time the ions begin to spark, and gradually destroy each other, sometimes reaching the ground before this destruction is complete. From 8,000 feet down, it is known popularly as a UFO.

There is an authenticated case, I believe, in Texas USA where a UFO completely dislocated the ignition mechanism and lighting circuit of a motor-car, shown recently on ITV.

The hissing noise said to emanate from a UFO could be the noise of the sparking taking place in its compressed form by people who have observed these things.

Mrs. S of Guernsey (27th October) was also of the opinion that a flying object from space had caused the loss of Charlie Oscar:

'I apologise for writing to you about what may be a stupid suggestion, but it occurred to me that it could have been possible, even if improbable, for the BEA Comet which disappeared over the Mediterranean earlier this month to have been in collision with a meteorite. I have not heard in the press of such an improbable crash being considered.' For her troubles, Mrs. S at least received the courtesy of an acknowledgement and was told that her letter was being passed to the, doubtless grateful, John Veal. Perhaps not coincidentally, an identical letter was also sent to Mr. Holmes of Canterbury who wrote on 21st October, 'I would like to suggest a possible answer to the Comet disaster last week. The last fragments of a large artificial satellite descending from its orbit and striking the aircraft which would cause severe damage and leading to the aircraft breaking up. I hope this idea may be useful to you and not waste your time.'

As an alternative, Mr. H of Welwyn Garden City (16th October) suggested:

'I must point out it is pretty poignant for me insomuch that no-one knows what went wrong because you have lost the little box and yet I am pretty certain I have a good idea for just this sort of thing happening.

...Mine is simple for passing on indelibly the unknown, and yet acceptable as possibly happening, the dozen or so things that are more likely to make a plane disappear in a second or two. The plane can leave a message of what has happened either by means of pilot operated or automatically operated apparatus and this message will float, or land lightly somewhere near the crash and be 'homed on' infallibly, and there is no limit to the number of that one vital series of messages (sic).

I cannot say much more because I now have to write several more letters on other inventions all dealing with safety factors in Modern traffic from stopping cars when the brake system fails to a much more intelligent signalling device for pedestrian crossings or an assessor of traffic speed and indicator to such oncoming traffic.'

The standard response was once again sent to Mr. H. On the 13th and 14th October, the team was gifted the insight of Mr. B of Oakwood Hospital in

Maidstone. In a two-letter epistle, Mr. B outlined a range of theories. These included metal fatigue:

It was said in the press that this plane has 6 million flying hours logged to it. How many more miles (one could say up to 20 million or more) before it crashed due to metal fatigue of either such a thing as a bolt or skin bursting, or possibly an electrical failure, human factors (the pilot may have dozed off just after making the last radio call and fallen over the controls putting them out of action before anyone else could move him and take over...I know a pilot who has flown over 4,000 miles an hour but this is a special case...no Concordes have flown yet but assuming they do eventually go into regular service how many pilots flying them at speeds over 1,000 miles an hour might not doze off, if only on one or two occasions to cause a crash'.

By now, the admin team had already had their fill of the more imaginative solutions and theories. On 17th October, one member of staff, identified only as 'Audrey', wrote a covering note with some of the mail she was forwarding to John Veal:

'Herewith the letters re the accident which you are going to pass on to the Inspector of Accidents (poor man). We had a letter this morning from a woman who saw it in a dream at 0320 and she wonders if this might help – a bright light with fragments sent out in all directions- a box of 'safety' matches completely full but every match spent and a voice saying "In the beginning was the Word, the Word was with God, the Word was God". Any help? I have written thanking her for her troubling to write but it didn't seem worth sending on to the Inspector of Accidents!

A number of correspondents had proffered solutions that would, they thought, enable the flight data recorder to be recovered in future disasters over water. These included the suggestion, sent on 27th October, to 'incorporate some small explosive charge, fused on the principle of the depth charge, so that when the tailplane reaches a certain depth, the charge could blow out a part of the tail and the flight recorder be ejected on similar lines to a fighter pilot's ejector seat, except that instead of a parachute, a small self-inflating buoy could bring it up to the surface.' In fact, the question of recovery of flight data recorders was highlighted as a significant matter and we will return to it later on.

There was one letter, though, that stood head and shoulders above the rest as a thoughtful insight to the whole tragedy. Mr. Aubrey Cooke, of Walton-on-Thames wrote to John Veal on 26th October. The letter is worth reproducing in full:

Dear Sir,

As a student of aircraft accidents and also as an aircrew member, I would like to make the following observations on the loss of this aircraft. In my opinion the first probable cause of the accident was sabotage, a bomb being placed on board the aircraft around 2 a.m. GMT, Oct 12/67. The likelihood of this could be ascertained by local police enquiries or better still by planting one of your own investigators as a BEA employee on the ramp at Athens on the midnight to check the following:

Who had any contact with this aircraft whilst it was on the ground at Athens during the time it was in transit? As it would be around 2 a.m. GMT there would be very few people on duty, the aircraft cleaners, the baggage handlers, the catering people, the refuelling and aircraft maintenance man. All these should be questioned. Were they all normally on duty at this time, was any substitute at short notice for a regular man, has any of them been off duty since this time, or rather, has not reported for duty since this time? Has any suddenly changed his normal way of living, i.e. now driving around in a brand-new car?

The cargo manifest for the load boarded at Athens to be investigated, item by item, particular cargo originating at Athens and delivered to the airport immediately before the load sheet was closed?

Was there a last-minute consignment delivered by taxi accepted? If so, what was it, and in what hold was it placed.

Have any of the consignees of the items or the cargo manifest, not yet claimed for their goods?

Were any of the aircrew asked to carry a parcel to Nicosia?

What precious cargo or diplomatic mail was loaded at Athens?

The answer to these questions ought to be made available to you without delay to verify the sabotage possibility.

If sabotage is disproved, the next most likely possibility is an explosion or catastrophic fire of the oxygen / oil combination. I do not know the Comet's oxygen or hydraulic system but would ask if there was a history of hydraulic and/or oxygen leaks on this particular aircraft. Did the oxygen system require topping up more frequently than normal, was there a deferred snag[120] on the oxygen system in the Technical log? Had the aircraft mechanic changed an oxygen bottle during transit at Athens?

---

[120] A 'Deferred snag' is an identified fault which would not render the aircraft immediately unsafe or unairworthy, and which would be noted in the aircraft technical record so that it could be rectified at a more convenient time. No such defect would be one that would be considered at all likely to lead to the loss of the aircraft, however.

The third possible cause is an explosion due to a fuel leak and/or turbine breaking up which could have started on take-off out of Athens and not culminated till over an hour later. A u/s[121] fire detector system on that particular system giving no warning. Were there any deferred engine or fuel system snags in the Tech. log? Do the Instrument Reading sheets over the past few flights show any progressive drop in fuel pressure or high or low EGT[122] particularly on the inboard engines since the last hangar check. Were any of the engines approaching overhaul time, running on an extension[123] or recently installed?

No doubt by now you already have the answers to these routine questions.

It was reported that some of the bodies picked up had their lifejackets on, inflated. If correct, it appears that a ditching was pre-meditated. Have any of the bodies of the crew been recovered and if so, were they wearing theirs? If they also had their oxygen mask on it would indicate smoke in the cockpit or loss of pressurisation.

In submitting these observations to you, I am not asking for answers, these will be forthcoming in due course at the enquiry which I would very much like to attend. It would therefore be much appreciated if you could let me know when, where and at what time it is to take place.

Yours truly,

Aubrey Cooke.

John Veal replied to Mr. Cooke on the 31st thanking him for his letter and continuing:

'The matters which you mention in your letter are being investigated as part of the inquiry now being undertaken but I am most grateful to you for drawing my attention to these specific questions.

In spite of the early information that some of the bodies recovered were wearing lifejackets, there is no evidence from the lifejackets themselves that they had been worn. From examination of the evidence it is easy to see how the first erroneous impressions, which were given so much publicity, were created. None of the bodies of the crew has so far been recovered.

In accordance with the Regulations, the Inspector's investigation of the accident which I ordered is taking place in private and a report will

---

[121] Unserviceable.

[122] Exhaust Gas Temperature.

[123] Aircraft and engines must be maintained on a rigorously-enforced timetable, measured in flying hours. In certain circumstances, the period can be extended but the hours extended are 'paid back' in the next period before servicing.

be submitted to, and published by, the Board of Trade if no public inquiry is held. A decision on the latter is one which the President will take when my preliminary report has been submitted to him.

Finally, may I say again how grateful I am to you for your constructive letter.

Yours faithfully,

JB Veal
Chief Inspector of Accidents.

Group Capt. Veal then forwarded Mr. Cooke's letter to Norman Head and Eric Newton, with a loose minute attached:

Please see the attached copy of a letter from Mr. Aubrey Cooke and the attached copy of my reply. This seems to be a most helpful letter and I should be glad if you would make sure the points made are covered in the investigation.

It was simply a matter for the team of sorting the wheat from the chaff...

Appendix 13 – Passenger Statements Index

Title	First name	Surname	Statement No.	Reason for Travel
Mr	Achillea	Afatitis	62	Visiting relatives in Cyprus
Mrs	Reveka	Afatitis	62	Visiting relatives in Cyprus
Sergeant	Rodosthenis	Christou	79	Returning home after holiday in England.
Miss	Josephine	Coldicott	86-88	Holiday in Cyprus.
Miss	Mary	Dalton	89	Holiday in Cyprus.
Mr	Costantinos	Efstathiou	90	Attending brother's wedding in Cyprus.
Mr	Elias	Evgeros	85	Holiday in Cyprus.
Miss	Areti	Exarcheas	65	Attending JW conference.
Miss	Jean	Falconer	92	Holiday in Cyprus.
Mr	Sotiris	Georgiou	83	Holiday in Cyprus.
Mr	Hugh	Griffiths	93, 94	Holiday in Cyprus.
Mrs	Lily	Griffiths	93, 94	Holiday in Cyprus.
Mrs	Anastasia	Harbstreet	125-127	Visiting relatives in Cyprus.
Mrs	Constantinas	Hristaki	64	Attending JW conference.
Dr	George	Ioannides	82	Taken a child to England for treatment.
Mr	John	Jakouris	81	Taking son to school in England.
Mrs	Margaret	Joyce	95	Visiting daughter in Cyprus.
Mrs	Iphigenia	Kalogeropoulou	66	Attending JW conference.
Miss	Despina	Karakosta	57	Attending JW conference.
Mr	Charalabos	Kontominas	63	Attending JW conference.
Mrs	Stavoulas	Kontominas	63	Attending JW conference.
Mrs	Eleni	Koutroubinis	61	Attending JW conference.
Mr	Georgios	Koutroubinis	61	Attending JW conference.
Mrs	Katarina	Liassides	96-99	Visiting her brother in Cyprus.
Miss	Eleni	Markidou	60	Attending JW conference.
Mr	Vasilios	Markidou	60	Attending JW conference.
Mrs	Lily	Marlborough	100-102	Visiting her daughter in Cyprus.
Mrs	Elaine	McComb	103-108	Returning to Cyprus.
Infant	Roydon	McComb	103-108	Returning to Cyprus.
Mr	Roydon	McComb	103-108	Returning to Cyprus.
Child	Andreas	Nicolaides	72	Returning from visit to England for treatment.
Mrs	Innoula	Nicolaides	72	Returning from visit to England for treatment for son.
Mr	Loizos	Nicolaides	72	Returning from visit to England for treatment for son.
Mrs	Maureen	O'Brien	109,110	Returning to Cyprus.
Mr	Michael	O'Brien	109,110	Returning to Cyprus.
Mr	Konstantinos	Paleologos	71	Attending Jehovah's Witness conference.
Mrs	Theognosia	Paleologos	71	Attending JW conference.

344

Mrs	Maria	Papaionnou	74, 111	Returning from visit to relatives in England.
Mrs	Eirini	Papanicolaou	58	Attending JW conference.
Mr	Nicos	Papapetrou	135-138	Visiting daughter in Athens.
Miss	Maria	Parzopoulou	68	Attending JW conference.
Mr	Nicolas	Peters	125-127	Visiting relatives in Cyprus.
Mr	David	Powell	112, 113	Visiting friends in Cyprus.
Mrs	Dorothea	Rachovidou	80	Visiting daughter in Athens.
Mr	Ioannis	Rigou	59	Attending JW conference.
Miss	Elpiniki	Rodosthenous	84	Returning home from holiday in England.
Mr	William	Sheris	122-124	Business trip.
Miss	Hilary C	Smith	114-116	Holiday in Cyprus.
Mr	Avraam	Solomou	128, 129	Returning from holiday in Athens.
Mrs	Anna	Stewart	117, 118	Holiday in Cyprus.
Mrs	Rosalie	Stone	73	Returning home after holiday in England.
Child	Guy	Tasker	119	Visiting father in Cyprus.
Mrs	Janet	Tasker	119	Visiting husband in Cyprus.
Mr	Gerasimo	Thiakou	70	Attending JW conference.
Mrs	Polixeni	Thiakou	70	Attending JW conference.
Mr	Michael	Thomaides	75, 76	Returning home after business trip to Greece (sic).
Miss	Arini	Voliotou	67	Attending JW conference.
Mrs	Paraskevis	Vougioukas	69	Attending JW conference.
Miss	Joyce Pamela	White	120, 121	Holiday in Cyprus.

Index

347

About the Author

Simon Hepworth has spent his working life in aviation and policing. His father served in the Royal Navy's Fleet Air Arm and then joined British European Airways in 1961.

After gaining a degree in International Transport Management, Simon worked as a Technical Sales Engineer for British Aerospace, before moving into the airline industry, operating charter flights to the Mediterranean. After developing his career in general aviation, including holding an Air Operator's Certificate for a commercial balloon rides company, he changed his career direction and joined the police service.

His policing experience included general duties, investigating a wide range of crimes, then setting up a policing team at a major regional airport in the UK. A spell in intelligence followed, after which he moved into police air support. He left the policing ranks in 2018.

In his spare time, Simon has written and published a number of books, primarily covering RAF Bomber Command and the strategic bombing offensive against Germany in 1939-45.

Printed in Great Britain
by Amazon